Explosions in November

The first 33 years of
Huddersfield Contemporary
Music Festival

Richard Steinitz

Published by University of Huddersfield Press
in association with Huddersfield Contemporary
Music Festival

University of Huddersfield Press
The University of Huddersfield
Queensgate
Huddersfield HD1 3DH
Email enquiries university.press@hud.ac.uk

First published 2011

A CIP catalogue record for this book is available
from the British Library.
ISBN 978-1-86218-099-4

Designed and printed by
Jeremy Mills Publishing Limited
113 Lidget Street
Lindley
Huddersfield HD3 3JR
www.jeremymillspublishing.co.uk

University of
HUDDERSFIELD

hcmf//
huddersfield
contemporary
music festival
In partnership with
The University of Huddersfield

COVER IMAGE:
Sandglasses by Justė Janulytė
and Luca Scarzella given its
UK premiere at the 2010
Huddersfield Contemporary
Music Festival.
PHOTO: PAUL GREENWOOD

To all who have shared in the journey

Contents

Preface

This book tells the story of how a modest long weekend of new music, in what the media continued to describe as an unlikely location, became one of the most important and highly regarded festivals in the world. From tentative beginnings, and far beyond my own expectations, Huddersfield Contemporary Music Festival grew into a major international showcase, at which over 330 of the world's finest new music ensembles have performed and most of its leading living composers appeared in person. For twenty-three years I was the festival's first artistic director. Having retired in 2001, I thought it important to document what we had done, and that the result would be published to celebrate the festival's twentieth-fifth anniversary in 2003. That it finally appears for the thirty-third is due to other obligations and more pressing projects, but also because of the sheer scale of the task. Perhaps, however, it is no less appropriate to mark the passing of a third of a century than a quarter; and the closing pages look ahead to the thirty-fourth festival which, as I write, will shortly begin.

Early on, I decided to organise the book both chronologically and thematically. I hope that this twin approach will not confuse the reader. An advantage has been to write more indulgently about individual composers – their characters, music, aspirations and foibles – in a chapter devoted to them; about the hundreds of international performers in another; and to focus specifically on such genres as opera and music theatre, venues and their history, unconventional formats, installations, education, marketing, partnerships and so on. A disadvantage is the frequent cross-referencing. But readers are welcome to turn to other references or not as they wish; and, to assist orientation, the text is liberally sprinkled with dates.

I have tried to write a readable, entertaining and informative narrative, and to position the festival interestingly within its wider social, cultural and political context. A thread running through the book charts the astonishing growth of the festival's host institution, now the University of Huddersfield, which I joined in 1961 – half a century ago. Although intended to be objective, I realise that my account has also become deeply personal, with assessments that are often forthright and perhaps controversial. So I must stress that the opinions expressed are my own, and not those either of the festival, or of the University of Huddersfield and its predecessor, Huddersfield Polytechnic.

I am all the more grateful, therefore, for the sustained support and encouragement of key university personnel, as well as Graham McKenzie, the festival's current artistic director, and his team, during the book's lengthy gestation, and am proud and delighted that it is being published by the relatively new University of Huddersfield Press. The production brief has enabled the book to be designed in large format, and printed in full colour with numerous illustrations. They will conjure cherished memories for those who were present at the events and may intrigue readers who were not. Tracing, obtaining and selecting photographs has been an adventure in itself, especially choosing between literally thousands of digital images taken during the last decade. I would like to record my thanks to the photographers who have allowed their work to be reproduced, in particular Mark Bokowiec, John Bonner, Asadour Gazelian, Keith Glossop, Selwyn Green, Paul Greenwood, Paul Herrmann and Brian Slater. Thanks also to Sophie Hannah, IOU theatre, Colin Rose, Anthony Sargent, Peters Edition Ltd London, Schott Music and West Yorkshire Archive Service for permission to reproduce poetry, documents, photographs and musical scores.

To friends and colleagues who have read drafts of the text I owe a special debt of gratitude. They include Michael Clarke, Lisa Colton, Paul Driver, Heidi Johnson, Mick Peake, Keith Potter, Colin Rose, Michael Russ, Bill Vince, Julia Winterson and Graham McKenzie. All have offered invaluable comments, corrections and additions, and, on occasion, rescued me from embarrassing errors. Many of them have attended the festival for many years, and some have known it from the beginning. Despite this, and having myself been at the centre for over two decades and close to the festival subsequently, it has proved surprisingly difficult to establish every detail with unerring precision. I believe that the final text is accurate and fair, but accept full responsibility for any errors that remain.

Working with the personnel of Jeremy Mills Publishing has been a privilege and a pleasure. In particular I am grateful to Hazel Goodes, publication manager and to Paul Buckley, the designer, for their excellent work, as well as to Abi Bliss for her vigilant copy-editing and index. Within the university I have particularly appreciated the unwavering commitment and encouragement of John Lancaster, Director of Computing and Library Services, and of his successor, Sue White. For three decades the festival has attracted wide-ranging reviews from the press – at times critical, frequently glowing, mostly shrewd and perceptive. From some I have quoted at length, grateful to be reminded of details I had forgotten, and what it felt like to be at some remarkable performances, in language more elegant than I could muster.

Although not involved in the book's production, I wish also to express gratitude to the general managers, administrators and other festival officers who have ensured the smooth running of an exceptionally complex operation. Their dedication has been matched by that of the audience, including a large core of regular supporters, whose enthusiasm and loyalty, year after year, has made every effort worthwhile. It is to them that the book is dedicated. But it will also, I believe, interest anyone involved in, or simply curious, about the developing art of music, the composers who create it, the performing arts in general, and the social and cultural history of the last fifty years.

Richard Steinitz

THEATRE ROYAL HUDDERSFIELD

PROPRIETORS

JACK GLADWIN
CHARLES MACDONA

THEATRE ROYAL

1 *Background*

How it began

The idea of a contemporary music festival emerged early in 1977, at a time when the young regional arts associations were seeding new initiatives. Richard Phillips, music officer of Yorkshire Arts Association, had been on a sabbatical tour of European music festivals – mostly, it transpired, those with adjacent vineyards. To justify this not unpleasant excursion, he announced on his return that Yorkshire needed two new festivals: one devoted to early, the other to contemporary music. The medieval city of York was the obvious choice for an early music festival. But where to locate the other: Leeds, Sheffield, Bradford, Huddersfield? A small committee met to consider their merits. It consisted of Wilfrid Mellers, professor of music at York University and chair of the arts association's music panel; Brian Pearson, Director of Leisure Services in Kirklees (the metropolitan borough containing Huddersfield, Dewsbury and eleven smaller towns[1]); Richard Phillips and myself. Despite the appeal of the cities, they lacked a suitable infrastructure or enabler. I noted apprehensively that discussion appeared to be heading one way. But why me, why now, and why in Yorkshire?

The cultural landscape

In 1961, when I joined the School of Music at Huddersfield College of Technology as a junior lecturer, the north of England seemed in many respects like an artistic wasteland. Huddersfield's Theatre Royal was being demolished as I arrived. Soon the Lyceum in Sheffield, with its fine but flaking Frank Matcham interior, went dark and Sadlers

Wells Opera ceased to visit. Cinemas were closing. The first of the new regional theatres (the Bolton Octagon) was still to be built. There was no West Yorkshire Playhouse, no Opera North, no Yorkshire Sculpture Park, no arts complex at Dean Clough, few smaller performing arts companies. Discussions were earthy – as in the old Yorkshire saying: 'Where there's muck, there's brass' – humour homely, the only bookshop WH Smith's.

No doubt this negative assessment was coloured by the culture shock of moving to the North at a time when travel was tedious and there was little mobility of population. In fact, Yorkshire had many musical strengths, not least its proud amateur choral tradition and some of the world's finest brass bands. Numerous chapel choirs bred talented singers. Music society audiences had not yet grown old and grey. As in other Yorkshire towns and cities, an orchestral series played to full houses in Huddersfield's elegant Victorian town hall, where you could hear the Hallé alongside international orchestras like the Czech Philharmonic, Leipzig Gewandhaus and all five London orchestras. When season tickets went on sale, patrons would queue all night for the best seats. Among ordinary people there was a widespread interest in music as a social pursuit; indeed, some would say that it was an indigenous musicality that enabled Huddersfield Contemporary Music Festival to take root.

I had been attracted to Huddersfield not only by the first music school to be established in a college of technology, but also by the town's exemplary music education service, rightly linked with Leicestershire as one of two national models. The wizened and benign music adviser, Wyndham Williams, had built up a large team of peripatetic instrumental teachers and youth orchestras. Instrumental tuition was offered to primary and secondary school pupils entirely free (as in Venezuela's now famous El Sistema). It was to extend this provision into a conservatoire-style sixth-form training for gifted instrumentalists that the School of Music was created, and, at the time I arrived, Williams was its head. Here musically talented pupils from secondary modern schools could take O and A-levels, study music in depth and continue instrumental lessons with outstanding teachers such as Lawrence Turner, ex-leader of the Hallé. Most went on to pursue musical careers. A few went straight into professional orchestras without further training – like Barry Haskey, who moved from the School of Music directly into the Royal Liverpool Philharmonic Orchestra, and later became associate leader of the BBC Welsh Symphony Orchestra.

But there was little new music. Yorkshire was far removed from the innovative vigour of the South. Huddersfield was primarily a manufacturing town, most of whose citizens lived relatively workaday lives, did not own cars, travelled rarely and devised their own amateur entertainment. Many had been no further than to Blackpool or Scarborough for their annual holiday, and of Modernism and all its works they had little idea. There was no motorway connecting London and the North, and when I ventured to London to see the first UK production of Kurt Weill's *Rise and Fall of the City of Mahagonny* the train journey took five hours. Marooned in what often seemed like a cultural desert, the radio was a lifeline. This was the period when William Glock, controller of music at the BBC, injected new energy into the nation's musical life, promoting the most dazzling and controversial of the European avant-garde in stimulating juxtapositions with the past. To attend one of his Thursday Invitation Concerts in London's Maida Vale Studios was unforgettable. During term-time it was impossible, but through the BBC's Third Programme broadcasts one was stimulated daily, and could remain in touch.

The artistic energy of the postwar years was predominantly metrocentric. There was, of course, the Edinburgh Festival founded by Rudolf Bing in 1947 with the support of the British Council. Ten years later, when John Pritchard became musical director of the Royal Liverpool Philharmonic Orchestra,

he introduced his famous Musica Viva series, copied from Munich, in which performances of new works were preceded by spoken introductions with live music examples, and shorter pieces might be played twice. It was in a broadcast from Liverpool that I first heard Stockhausen's *Gruppen* – its UK premiere. When Pritchard left, the series ceased. Northern cities had fine art galleries, energetic amateur societies and strong social traditions. But these citadels of nineteenth-century industrialism remained drab, even those unscathed by the war. Incomes were low, eating out rare, the buildings black and forbidding.

In 1966 I received an Italian government scholarship to study composition with Goffredo Petrassi at the Accademia di Santa Cecilia in Rome. To walk daily in the 'eternal city' was endlessly inspiring and its concerts were a joy. You could hear baroque oratorios in the churches, Webern and Berio at the conservatoire, Wagner, Strauss and Prokofiev at the opera, Frank Martin, Castiglioni and Nono at the Auditorio. Italian radio presented a compelling weekly series in the RAI concert hall, where I heard live for the first time Mahler's sixth symphony, Schoenberg's *Gurre-Lieder,* Henze's *Novae de Infinito Laudes,* works by Ghedini, Malipiero and Maderna, Petrassi's neo-classic *Psalm 90* and several of his *Concerti per Orchestra.* I returned with a stack of reel-to-reel tapes recorded from RAI's eclectic all-day music broadcasts which, like the BBC under Glock, devoted hours of prime-time to the vast riches of twentieth-century music, including its most recent novelties.

Back in Yorkshire, the sense of isolation had decreased. One evening I went with two colleagues to Leeds Grammar School to hear Aloys Kontarsky play Stockhausen's *Klavierstücke I–XI,* soon after his historic premiere of the complete cycle in Darmstadt. After the interval, Kontarsky performed the long *Klavierstück X* entirely from memory, his wrists bandaged to negotiate the glissando clusters – and with astonishing accuracy as far as we could tell from following the score. It was this monumental recital that convinced me that Stockhausen was a major composer.

York was the first of the postwar universities to establish a music department, and Wilfrid Mellers, appointed professor in 1964, himself a composer and writer, chose three young composers as his colleagues – Peter Aston, David Blake and Robert Sherlaw Johnson – in sharp contrast to most university music departments which were dominated by musicologists. By 1970 Huddersfield School of Music had grown substantially, become part of a new polytechnic, and created the first honours degree in music outside the university sector. Influenced by Glock's revolution, we devised a curriculum combining in equal parts composition, performance, and music history biased towards the twentieth century.[2] From the moment they arrived and throughout their first year, students were immersed in twentieth-century music from Impressionism and *Le Sacre du Printemps* to the Berio *Sinfonia,* which was then just three years old and, in its first recording under Bernstein, utterly mind-blowing. The intention was to saturate students

in a contemporary vitality, largely unfamiliar to them but overwhelmingly powerful. Many had musical appetites and perceptions transformed by this extended encounter with the art of their own time.

In 1970, the year Huddersfield established its degree, there was a development of wider import. Jack Phipps and a small staff were appointed to organise the touring of opera, ballet and drama by the Arts Council of Great Britain – itself a creation of the postwar era. During the lingering austerity of the 1950s and early 1960s such a possibility had seemed unimaginable. So I was astonished one day to pick up a leaflet announcing performances by the National Theatre, Royal Shakespeare Company and dance companies in Leeds and Manchester. The 'DALTA' tours, as they were called, revealed a voracious appetite among the regional public. The acronym derived from the formerly independent Dramatic and Lyrical Theatre Association, now assimilated into the Arts Council. A year later the Arts Council's Contemporary Music Network (CMN) was created, steered with energy and vision by Annette Morreau. In 1975 touring was elevated to become a separate department of the Arts Council (although CMN remained within the music department). Soon after this Richard Phillips set up a Northern Contemporary Music Circuit, shortly to become a Regional Contemporary Music Circuit. It was organised in collaboration with other music officers but continued for only a few years.

Arts Council funds for the touring of small and large-scale theatre, dance, opera and art exhibitions transformed the cultural map of Britain. The subsequent establishment of major regional companies and producing theatres did nothing to diminish their value. Work could now tour multi-directionally; the benefits of co-production were greater, and audiences for the visual and performing arts increased across the country. It was a sad day in 1994 when the Arts Council, which had already ceded responsibility for Northern Ireland, was further broken into three independent councils for England, Scotland and Wales, and touring across borders became more difficult. The government's austerity measures of 2010, whose impact on Arts Council England was announced in October that year, could have a more serious impact. By 2014 the council budget will be reduced by nearly 30%, and the funds available

One of Bob Linney's leaflet designs for the Contemporary Music Network.

to its regular clients will fall by approximately 15%. For touring and other programmes, the budget is to be cut by 64%. A golden age of regional access to top quality performing arts and exhibitions could be coming to an end.

Why me?

I had learnt the nuts and bolts of concert promotion as an undergraduate in Cambridge, both as secretary of the University Musical Club and as a conductor. In 1959 I invited Jonathan Harvey to compose what was, in effect, his first commission (although no money changed hands), for the University String Players, which I conducted and in which he played the cello. Ten years earlier we had both been choristers at St Michael's College, Tenbury, deep in the Worcester countryside, where, six days a week, we sang full choral services morning and evening, from sixteenth-century polyphony to sumptuous double-choir Victorian canticles, at matins often to an otherwise empty church. The experience had a deep effect on both our psyches. Later, with Huddersfield colleagues, I took student ensembles to perform in neighbouring cities, and for fifteen years I was conductor-impresario of one of Yorkshire's historic choirs, the Glee and Madrigal Society, devoting energy to its revival and to such large undertakings as the Monteverdi *Vespers* (its first northern performances since those by Walter Goehr) and UK premieres of works by Henze and Lukas Foss. For want of anyone else, I took on the role of publicist, and was hardly surprised when, departing in September 1972 for a year's study in America, I was pursued by a letter from the chief clerk of Sheffield threatening legal action for fly-posting in the city. True, I had driven over with posters and paste to announce a forthcoming School of Music concert in the cathedral. I wrote back, a trifle smugly, to say that I could not remove the offending items because I had left the country.

A year later, back in Huddersfield and marginally more law-abiding, I co-ordinated the School of Music's concert programme, and persuaded Annette Morreau to include Huddersfield in the Contemporary Music Network. By the 1977–78 season Huddersfield was receiving six CMN tours, some now promoted by Kirklees Leisure Services. Richard Phillips had asked me to join Yorkshire Arts Association's music panel and we had become

MUSIC & MUSICIANS by Ernest Bradbury

PERHAPS nowhere is the ever-increasing interest in music since the war reflected more clearly than in current activity in our universities. Or, indeed, in all seats of learning.

Tomorrow, for example, the second Contemporary Music Festival promoted by Huddersfield Polytechnic will open with three concerts on its first day. Morning, Noon and Night! The first of two dozen events in what promises to be an exhausting week, ending next Wednesday.

Those of us who attended the more extreme offerings at the first Festival last year recall that members of the staff themselves expressed outrage over some of the aural batterings they endured. But it is not all like that, not even this year. The exhaustion perhaps springs from the compression: before the week was up there were faint murmurings of "Enough is enough!"

But the Festival is right, in a changing and, musically speaking, too frequently lazy world. There is always the need, in the words of Charles Ives, for people to "stretch their ears." Except that Huddersfield is not alone. Syllabuses on my desk, lately arrived, show an almost time-consuming round of activities from the universities of Leeds, Hull, York — all of them deserving of attention and only too often mainly concentrated, for some reason, on Wednesday nights. There must be something specially appealing about Wednesdays. But how to give them a fraction of the news space they might well deserve?

Gone for ever are the leisurely days when a former music critic of this newspaper could fill in his winter diary, year by year, almost from memory, with most engagements around December being performances of "Messiah." In my earliest days I could almost do it myself. Certainly the days are gone when a London critic could end his work at Covent Garden in June for three months holiday in Scotland and resume his duties again with the Three Choirs Festival . . .
A   ·   · · ·sities have ···· · ··

Veteran Yorkshire Post *columnist, Ernest Bradbury, laments the loss of the music critic's summer holiday (24 November 1979).*

kindred spirits in that both our car boots were full of leaflets which we would personally distribute. I must have seemed an obvious person to realise his vision of a new music festival for Yorkshire. Richard evidently wanted me to organise it; Brian Pearson hoped that it would happen in Huddersfield, and the twentieth-century emphasis of the polytechnic music department was an ideal context. But I didn't want the job. I was recently married, soon to be a father and composing in my limited spare time. Nor had I any idea how to plan and present a festival. A deep presentiment told me that this was something I should not do. Anxieties about the time commitment and its impact on family life were tempered, however, by my keen interest in new music. And Richard was pressing. Talking it over in our garden, he airily promised an unspecified sum of money with which to engage artists. Reluctantly, I agreed.

Local relationships

It proved to be a meagre £1,400, but this was nearly half the first budget of approximately £3,000. Eighteen months before the festival took place, I wrote to the rector of the polytechnic, Kenneth Durrands, a distant and difficult man, who had come to the institution

Budgets for the 1978 and 1979 festivals.

Contemporary Music Festival 1979, and Fourth YAA Young Composers' Competition

Financial Summary

Income:	1979	1978	Expenditure:	1979		1978
Admission receipts: £563.30 less VAT	£490.60	373	Artists: Fees	£3610	)	
			Travel	623.30	)	1746
Programmes:			Accommodation	514.79		143
Sales	58.50	48	Advertising	994.39		464
Advertising	271	118				
Yorkshire Arts Ass.	3230	1635	Programmes	559		355
Kirklees M.C.	1476.88	565	Reception	116		-
Huddersfield Poly	554	200	Stewards	70		32
Visiting Arts	100	-	Piano tunings	77.50		-
RVW Trust	205	95	Amplification	61.60		26
PRS	250	-	Hall charges (technician)	48.90		-
MU	300	-	Administration Expenses	120		75
A. Guinness	50	-	From 1978	35		-
Tourist Boards	300	-	Competition Prizes & Bursaries	392		195
BBC	-	30	Adjudication	63.50		25
Air Anglia	unspecified					
American State Department	unspecified					
	£7285.98	3064		£7285.98		3064

Not charged:

Normal charges for use of halls
Postage & stationary
Piano removal
Design & art work
Administration fees.

R J Steinitz.

from the engineering giant Vickers Armstrong and had little interest in the arts. I explained that, besides concerts, there would be lectures, seminars, workshops and masterclasses, and that there would be no cost to the polytechnic other than the provision of venues. For any accommodation used the participants would pay, supported by bursaries which we would seek from Yorkshire Arts Association and the Society for the Promotion of New Music (SPNM). The first festival would coincide with enrolment week in September 1978, and would, we envisaged, last seven days and include contemporary dance. In the event, it was deferred until October when term was properly underway. It lasted five days and there was no dance – virtually none, in fact, until 1984, mainly because there was no suitable venue in which to present it. But it did include film, and the second contained music theatre of a sort.

The rector summoned me and gave the proposal his blessing. I promised to keep him informed, asked him to host occasional receptions, sent him the press reports, and invited him annually to a concert. He tolerated these strange experiences with a good grace, and presided at the receptions – until 1984. That year was dominated by music theatre. I should have steered Durrands towards the Fires of London, due to perform Peter Maxwell Davies's engaging *Le Jongleur de Notre Dame* with young instrumentalists from Huddersfield Technical College; or to our own music department orchestra playing Nigel Osborne's *Sinfonia*. Unwisely, I had revealed that the French cultural attaché would be attending a decidedly bizarre concert by the percussion group Trio Le Cercle, whose travel from Paris the French were supporting, and which would take place in the depressingly drab Great Hall. Durrands decided that he should join the French attaché, and invited Councillor John Mernagh to accompany him – a polytechnic governor supportive of the arts, but also blusteringly forthright about his likes and dislikes.

I waited nervously as preparations overran and impatient members of an already sparse audience got up and left. Eventually the three percussionists appeared, vied with each other, beat their bodies, produced smoke, tore paper, fired pistols and occasionally played an instrument. Between each piece were uncomfortable *longueurs* while the stage was reset. The programme began dispiritingly, with

Globokar's *Tribadaboum extensif sur rythme fantôme,* demonstrating 'that Dada is alive but senile and incontinent', as David Cairns pithily remarked in *The Sunday Times.*[3] When it reached *Con Voce* (Mauricio Kagel's protest at the Soviet suppression of Czechoslovakia, during which the players mime in silence), I knew that I had lost all credibility. Kagel's *Dressur* (played on a veritable carpentry shop of specially constructed wooden instruments) made a more engaging finale; but its metaphor of the relationship between circus trainers and their animals stretched my guests' comprehension too far. Afterwards Durrands and Mernagh were withering, and at subsequent encounters Mernagh taunted me derisorily.[4] It was he, however, who in 1986 helped secure £1 million from the soon-to-be-abolished West Yorkshire Metropolitan County Council for Huddersfield's future theatre, and who later persuaded Yorkshire business entrepreneur Lawrence Batley to make up the shortfall.

Mernagh was first chair of Kirklees Theatre Trust which, when the Lawrence Batley Theatre opened in 1994, approved the festival's annual use of the building free of charge.

Such were the hazards of promoting the more *outré* side of contemporary music before the festival had established its reputation. The rector remained sceptical and came to no further events. In the early years I was advised not to inform any of the local authority (i.e. civic) councillors about what the festival was doing. But there were exceptions, notably Councillor Denis Ripley who headed the council's education committee, and became first chairman of the festival board. When Stockhausen was due to visit in 1988, Denis persuaded the mayor, John Holt, that it would be appropropriate to host a civic reception in the town hall. Mayor Holt agreed, but apparently, during an *en passant* encounter with Durands, proposed that the polytechnic should

Trio Le Cercle.
PHOTO: KEITH GLOSSOP

Karlheinz Stockhausen and Suzanne Stephens with the mayor of Kirklees, John Holt, in 1988.

pay the bill. The rector, who had already had an acrimonious financial dispute with the local authority and would not have the cudos of hosting Stockhausen, felt insulted. Soon afterwards, polytechnics were granted corporate status, and Durrands began to question whether the provision of resources brought the institution comparable benefits. Some difficult years followed until, with the polytechnic now a university, John Tarrant became its vice-chancellor in 1995. At an early meeting he expressed his support for the festival, re-affirmed the institutional relationship, and he and his wife took a lively interest in festival events. There was still the matter of whether the university received sufficient credit for its association, which we probably failed to address whilst wooing a new commercial sponsor, the Halifax Building Society, which required sole headline status.

In fact, the festival has flourished through a plurality of partnerships, in which national

organisations like the BBC, and more recently the British Council and Royal Philharmonic Society, have been at the forefront. It was only with the arrival of Graham McKenzie as artistic director in 2006 and Bob Cryan as vice-chancellor in 2007 that the long relationship between the festival and its host institution was effectively re-addressed. In 2008 the University of Huddersfield became the festival's headline sponsor, and the partnership was prominently acknowledged on all publicity and print.

Within the music department, Arthur Jacobs, its head from 1979 to 1984, and his successor George Pratt were unswervingly supportive, motivating students and staff to attend and ensuring that the experience was central to the department's courses. That the first festival did not take place until two years after Richard Phillips's proposal was due in part to my reluctance, but also because it was too late for Yorkshire Arts to allocate funds for 1977–78. The secretarial and administrative help I had suggested to Durrands never materialised. But Kirklees Leisure Services proved a valuable partner. For the first few festivals Brian Pearson's department assisted with marketing, managed the tickets (sold mainly on the door) and administered the accounts. The early festivals were advertised as a joint promotion between Huddersfield Polytechnic, Kirklees Leisure Services and Yorkshire Arts Association. I made artistic decisions and put them into effect, but it was a genuine collaboration. Kirklees allowed free use of its venues – of considerable value when, during Stockhausen's visit, we occupied Huddersfield Town Hall for ten days. The council's cash allocation was necessarily modest, but its officers invariably helpful. As for Yorkshire Arts, Richard and six successive music officers during my twenty-three years as artistic director were all enthusiastic allies. When in 1980 the formal participation of the regional arts association was ruled unconstitutional, the change was more procedural than real and the festival continued to benefit from their ideas, advocacy and friendship.

St Paul's Hall, converted into a concert venue in 1981.
ILLUSTRATION: SELINA THORP

2 *The first festivals*

1978–1980

How to begin? Essentially I thought, given the tiny budget, with the Contemporary Music Network, as it offered outstanding concerts for a token fee, including ensembles from abroad, for which the Arts Council made all the arrangements. In 1978 a Network concert opened the festival; another brought it to a close. An early decision was to invite George Crumb, in whose music I had

become interested in America. It had recently gained a following in Britain, not least through Christopher Bruce's choreography of several pieces toured with live music by Ballet Rambert. But the composer had never visited professionally. Around Crumb I assembled regional artists (the pianist Keith Swallow, Leeds-based Aulos Ensemble and Yorkshire-born composer John Casken), plus the cellist Rohan de Saram, pianist Douglas Young and his ensemble Dreamtiger.

UNIVERSITY of PENNSYLVANIA

Department of Music
201 S. 34TH STREET   D8
PHILADELPHIA, PA. 19174

April 29, 1977

Dear Mr. Steinitz:—

Many thanks for your letter.

I would be delighted to participate in your projected Cont. Music Festival (Sept. 1978), assuming of course all the many details can be worked out!

Since "Music for a Summer Evening" I have composed 2 works:

1) "Dream Sequence" for Vln., Vc., Piano, 1 perc., and offstage crystal goblets (2 players). Dur. about 16 min.

2) "Star-Child" for Soprano, Antiphonal Children's choirs, and a somewhat expanded orchestra. I'm not sure yet about duration, but I would guess somewhat longer than 20 min.

UNIVERSITY of PENNSYLVANIA

Department of Music
201 S. 34TH STREET   D8
PHILADELPHIA, PA. 19174

— 2 —

Of course, an orchestra work might well be outside the scope of your plans (and in any case, I think Boulez plans to do it in London next season). But you might want to consider "Dream Sequence" as a possible premiere. And I might perhaps have something else new by Sept. 78!

I have not spent any time in England since the mid-fifties, and would therefore all the more look forward to a future visit. Please let me know when your plans become more concrete!

Most cordially,

George Crumb

UNIVERSITY of PENNSYLVANIA
DEPARTMENT OF MUSIC
201 S. 34TH ST.   D8
PHILADELPHIA, PA. 19174

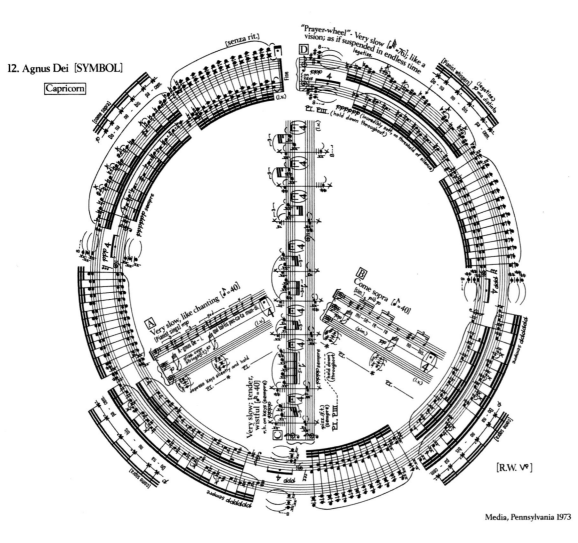

Media, Pennsylvania 1973

Of St Paul's Church on the polytechnic campus, Queen Street Methodist Mission (now the Lawrence Batley Theatre) and Bates Mill, none were yet performance venues. So a minuscule audience heard the first concert, given by the Philip Jones Brass Ensemble and pianist Roger Woodward, in the vastness of Huddersfield Town Hall. Incongruously for a new music festival, it began with Liszt, but ended appropriately with Xenakis's spectacular *Eonta*. To open on Friday, 13 October was evidently foolhardy. As dawn broke, dense fog enveloped the whole of northern Europe and persisted for four days. The Gaudeamus Quartet, due to perform Crumb's *Black Angels* the following day, and then a second concert of Dutch music, sat in Schiphol airport unable to fly from there or anywhere else. It was a cruel blow. After waiting twenty-four hours I picked up the phone. But by then it was Saturday morning and artists' agencies were closed. None of the quartets I could contact were free to perform that evening, let alone play Crumb. Somebody suggested Alan Hacker, clarinettist with the Fires of London and founder of Matrix, who lived in York and whom I knew well. Early that afternoon he agreed to come, assisted by two students. I hurried away to introduce a talk by George Crumb, who was shy and reticent. With no time to prepare, I was little help. Alan arrived and the following morning the Lindsay String Quartet drove over from Sheffield. Between them, and with an impromptu performance of the Kodály Cello Sonata from Rohan de Saram, gaps were filled. But my thematic programming was ruined.

On Sunday evening things improved. Earlier I had worked late into the night helping a bemused town hall technician redirect its infuriatingly inaccessible lanterns, so that Dreamtiger could perform *Voice of the Whale* bathed in oceanic blue, as Crumb requests. After this, they played the European premiere of *Dream Sequence,* spot-lit and spaced out across the platform, whilst from off-stage floated a somnolent E-flat chord, sustained for twenty-five minutes by a group of students rotating wet fingers around the rims of four crystal glasses which I had brought from home. The effect was beautiful. Tired but satisfied, I carelessly left the glasses backstage and never saw them again.

On Monday lunchtime a young pianist, Philip Mead, who had just won the Gaudeamus International Competition for Interpreters of Contemporary Music, played Crumb's *Makrokosmos II (Twelve Fantasy-Pieces after the Zodiac)*, preceded by pieces from Bartók's *Mikrokosmos*. The concert had not been publicised, Philip having proposed it since the leaflet went to press. But his performance from *Makrokosmos II* from memory was riveting. In fact, the music had acquired for him a personal significance, and its final 'Agnus Dei' – with its

staves drawn like a prayer wheel enclosing the peace symbol – an extra poignancy. Two days after Philip had given the UK premiere, his father suddenly died. *Makrokosmos II* was the last music he heard his son perform.

Throughout the day, Keith Swallow and the Aulos Ensemble workshopped compositions submitted for the Young Composers' Competition, an earlier initiative of Yorkshire Arts Association which the Festival now adopted. The ensemble pieces presented no problem. But although a fine musician and sight-reader, Keith was no contemporary specialist, and he was already disconcerted by our choices for his workshop. When the four judges (John Casken, Duncan Druce, Philip Wilby and myself) agreed that, despite its difficulty, *Dillug-Kefitsah* by an unknown 28-year-old called James Dillon deserved to win, and insisted that it be performed, Keith protested.[1] Years later James asserted that, to persuade Keith to perform it, I had diverted some of the prize money to augment his fee. I have no recollection of doing so, but it sounds consistent with the parsimonious housekeeping of those early years.

It was much easier for a conducted ensemble to prepare several new works. Keith had six to learn, although only one to perform in public, so to complete his recital programme I accepted suggestions from his repertoire of music by Ravel, Casella and Liszt (again). In any case, I had not yet decided that the festival should be exclusively contemporary. Part of me would have liked to mix new and early music (in which I had specialised at Cambridge under Thurston Dart), following the model of Glock's invitation concerts. But, with the foundation of the York Early Music Festival a year earlier, lines had been drawn. These were two momentous years for the arts in Yorkshire: the Early Music Festival and Yorkshire Sculpture Park founded in 1977; Huddersfield Contemporary Music Festival and English National Opera North (as it was first called) opening their doors one year later. Both the Contemporary Music Festival and Opera North were actually constituted in 1977, but as the first festival commenced on 13 October 1978, and the opera company unveiled its first production on 15 November, the festival is arguably the senior.

The final concert was given by the Warsaw Music Workshop on its Network tour – at last,

11

despite some rustic strains, proclaiming a progressive agenda. Bizarrely subversive, it attracted a relatively large audience, including music students lured by the promise of forty folk instruments. As the music department's Recital Hall filled up we added chair after chair, oblivious of licensing and safety restrictions (if they existed), until performers and audience were virtually rubbing shoulders. The Poles' iconoclasm was entertaining, and their final procession through the audience, playing hurdy-gurdies and bagpipes accompanied by pre-recorded natural sounds (birds, animals, wind and water), receded to an eruption of applause and animated discussion. Most loved it; some were perplexed. The next morning one of my department colleagues angrily vented his scorn. In this closing concert the festival had properly sprung to life.[2]

During the next two years I had only a vague idea of how the festival should develop. Fully employed by the polytechnic, modestly active as a composer and conductor, and occupied with my young family, there was no time to investigate good practice elsewhere. Nor were there funds to do so. The budget had improved but barely covered the cost of artists and basic advertising. I took no fee, could afford only a few hours of typing assistance, and spent virtually nothing on technical support.
There was too little money to invite the more prominent composers. So the second festival featured contemporary virtuosi: bass clarinettist Harry Sparnaay, cellist Rohan de Saram, James Wood (then more percussionist than composer) and two composer-performers: the trombonist Vinko Globokar and pianist Frederic Rzewski. It was a surprisingly successful recipe. The high point was the UK premiere of Rzewski's huge polystylistic *The People United Will Never Be Defeated!* – thirty-six variations on the protest song by Sergio Ortega which had been adopted as a political anthem by the Chilean left.
The agony of the Pinochet coup still resonated in my family, since my wife's sister and Chilean brother-in-law had been forced to flee with their children and find temporary refuge in England. 'Postmodern' before the term gained currency, dramatic and unexpectedly moving, *The People United* was the first work at the festival to make a strong political and aesthetic statement. Writing in *Classical Music* in January 1986, Keith Potter listed it as one of the ten most significant compositions of the previous ten years: 'extraordinary and compelling' and

'proof that popular and avant-garde materials and methods can be successfully combined to produce political music that is both serious and enjoyable'.[3]

The 1979 festival lasted seven days. It included the British premiere of Crumb's *Makrokosmos III* and an engaging programme from Gemini directed by Peter Wiegold, who also delivered the young composers' workshops and an improvisation day for school children. The low ticket prices of the previous year were maintained: £1.20 (60p concession) for evening concerts, 60p (30p) for all others, or a £6.50 (£3.25) 'season ticket' to hear everything – equivalent to paying around £28 (£15) in 2011. Audiences were generally larger and the programmes more enterprising, earning from Stephen Walsh in *The Observer* the comment that the festival was 'no milksop provincial affair, but a proper display of modern music, including several of its battier manifestations'.[4] Among the latter, he probably had in mind a composer-led collective from Yugoslavia called Acezantez, whose programme involved some simple music theatre. It also contained twice as many pieces as I had agreed, most of them instantly forgettable, no doubt to satisfy their communist masters. Despite the visual dimension, the event grew increasingly tedious, until the singer-dancer Veronika Durbesíc fell backwards off the stage in Venn Street Arts Centre, awakening the audience to gasps of alarm. Unhurt, she jumped back and carried on.

This second festival had also been hit by misfortune. During the summer of 1979, Huddersfield Town Hall was suddenly closed after the discovery of dry rot. This caused the loss of an orchestral concert which would have been shared with the Kirklees series – not any old concert, as there had been the possibility of Boulez conducting the BBC Symphony Orchestra in a revised version of *Éclat/Multiples*. Had Boulez been present, I would have featured more of his music and the festival would have been much enhanced. Instead, most events took place in less than ideal halls, and, as one reviewer observed, the festival 'retreated even further inside the boundaries of the polytechnic'.[5]

A year later the town hall was beautifully restored. But other indicators were unpropitious. Richard Phillips had left Yorkshire Arts and its financial contribution

Melvyn Poore who performed at the third festival.

provoking delight. But, overall, the third festival lacked coherence, and audiences remained small. Afterwards a paltry cheque from the Italian Institute for Cultural Affairs was returned by the bank. It had 'bounced'. Press reports were favourable, but I knew we had to do better.

Developing purpose: the early 1980s

Fortunately, I could learn away from the limelight. There being little opportunity for grand ambition or serious disaster, I began to consider variety and balance, aiming to juxtapose the unfamiliar with contemporary classics, aware that few who knew of these pieces or possessed recordings had experienced them live. It was five years before the festival could afford a sinfonietta-sized ensemble of around fourteen players: ie. one each of the four woodwind instruments, three brass and five strings, plus piano and percussion, as defined by the core instrumentation of the London Sinfonietta.[6]

looked uncertain. Despite support from the Ralph Vaughan Williams Trust and Visiting Arts Unit of the British Council, the leapfrog game of securing funds before confirming artists was frustrating. Late in the day, after sufficient had been promised, I turned to my interest in Italian music. Luigi Dallapiccola – much revered by British composers – had died four years earlier, so I invited my ex-teacher, Goffredo Petrassi; but he was non-committal, and eventually did not come. The Garbarino Ensemble from Milan gave the UK premiere of Petrassi's urbane and stylish *Grand Septuor,* but in the dreary Great Hall it lacked lustre. An obscure duo from Rome, whom I should never have engaged, performed a strange assortment of music for piano and percussion. Much stronger were the British ensembles and soloists, notably Melvyn Poore's solo tuba recital and Howard Riley's late-night improvisation. The latter followed a 'Forum on Improvisation', to which Riley, Poore, Barry Guy, Jane Manning, Frederic Rzewski and Trevor Wishart contributed. It concluded an afternoon during which Frederic had directed volunteers in his *Thirteen Instrumental Studies* – starting materials and frameworks for free improvisation. Trevor Wishart's lecture on 'Sound Transformation and Aural Music-theatre' was a stimulating and thought-

The Network tours which coincided with the second and third festivals featured only pianists – or rather 'prepared' piano and electronics in 1979 (John Tilbury and Denis Smalley), and a two-piano duo in 1980 (Frederic Rzewski and Ursula Oppens). But in 1981 the Network delivered the Dutch ensemble Hoketus, while the Regional Contemporary Music Circuit toured a specially assembled Gavin Bryars and John White Ensemble of nine players. On its own account the festival engaged smaller groups such as Dreamtiger, Capricorn and Gemini, and the regionally based Aulos, Lumina, Northern New Music Players and Music Party – all, except Gemini, now defunct. Most of their programmes contained works by several different composers, in interesting enough conjunctions but without the thematic coherence of later years. And there were compromises: as in 1979 when I agreed to accept Mozart's Clarinet Quintet to complete a programme given by the Fitzwilliam Quartet and Alan Hacker, whom I had engaged to premiere a clarinet quintet by David Blake – which, in the event, was not finished in time, so not performed.

It was near impossible to agree an entirely contemporary programme with any British string quartet, other than the Ardittis – the only UK-based quartet specialising in new music. Intensive touring schedules allowed little time for others to learn new material. Thus, in 1984, the Medici presented Maxwell Davies's only existing quartet along with Alan Bush's *Dialectic* of 1935, Shostakovich's Eighth Quartet and Britten's Third (then, however, less than ten years old). In 1985 the Fairfield Quartet performed Elizabeth Maconchy's recent *Quartetto Corto* alongside Webern and Janáček, both from the early twentieth century – although, as a Live Music Now collaboration exclusively for sixth formers at Huddersfield New College, it was an appropriate choice. In 1982, with similar audience-building intent, I persuaded a somewhat reluctant Huddersfield Music Society to share a concert, resulting in Schnittke's short *Canon in memory of Igor Stravinsky* being sandwiched between piano quintets by Shostakovich and Schumann, and preceded by Tchaikovsky. This was a compromise too far.

By now the festival had a stronger sense of mission, and had sufficiently proved itself to earn increased support from music trusts, the regional Yorkshire Arts Association, and directly from the Arts Council of Great Britain. The 1981 turnover of c.£18,000 was more than double that of the previous year, and six times that of 1978. For practical reasons and to avoid clashes, the festival moved to the end of November and now lasted a week. A better designed leaflet promised the presence of Harrison Birtwistle and John Casken (at that time fellow in composition at the polytechnic), plus Sandor Balassa and Attila Bozay from Hungary, while accompanying the CMN tours were Louis Andriessen (founder of Hoketus), Michael Nyman, Frederic Rzewski, Gavin Bryars and John White.

Most significant for the future was the transformation of St Paul's Church into a handsome concert hall – described more fully in Chapter 10 (page 172). Here, in November 1981, Alan Hacker and The Music Party gave the first performance of Birtwistle's Clarinet Quintet, a personal gift from the composer to Alan. Their inclusion of the Mozart Clarinet Quintet again, although this time on period instruments, caused me unease. But the rarefied beauty of both pieces in the atmospheric acoustic of the new venue was an intoxicating marriage. Among six other works by Birtwistle was the world premiere of *Pulse*

Sampler, performed by Melinda Maxwell and John Harrod. That the festival had two Birtwistle world premieres (neither of which it had commissioned) was reason enough for Harry himself to attend. He was not noted for loquacity and at that time I barely knew him. Beside the billiard tables in the staff bar (temporarily enrolled as the festival club) we engaged in a somewhat halting public conversation while festivalgoers ate their lunch. Nonetheless, it elicited intriguing nuggets about *The Mask of Orpheus*, which he had just completed. He still had to work at IRCAM on its electronic interludes, and the opera was not performed until 1986 by English National Opera – its only fully-staged production to date.

Louis Andriessen.
PHOTO: SELWYN GREEN

November 1981 Monday St Paul's booked for Philip Wood to tune organ

	ST. PAUL'S HALL	Rehearsals for G. Weir + S. Cummings throughout day	(NB Full Orch in Rec Hall)	
WED 18th		+ previous afternoon/evening (17th) 2.30 – 4.30 (4.30 to 7.00 Tune recital)	7.30	± This colour = lights
Philip Wood organ tune before 10.00 THU 19th preferably earlier	SP Rehearsal a.m. lights 8.00	1.00 CONTRASTS S.P. (£1.20)	YAA Workshop (Free) S.P. Weir Recital S.P. (£1.50)	Pos Gavin Bryars, unload? 10.00 (Club or Music?)
FRI 26th 9.30 8.30	S.P. Set up (Free) 11.15 Recital Hall Bryars/White introduction 2 Pianos Stereo cassette	1.50 Eng Exp Music S.P. 2 Pianos (£1.00)	Lontano rehearse S.P. BBC access St Paul's from noon Saturday El Cimarrón S.P. (£2) 7.30	S.P. Capricorn set up? 9.30 Recital Hall + Belinda Maxwell Tape (80p) 10.00
SAT 21st 8.00	+ early rehearsal 11.15 Capricorn S.P. 1.00 Buffet Lunch (Club) followed by Forum with Harrison Birtwistle Members only (£1.50)	Music Party rehearse S.P. aw. Percussion moved to Recital Hall from S.P. 4.15 Recital Hall +Tape Balassa / Bozay / Varga	Music Party S.P. 7.30 (£2)	S.P. Alex Brillie rehearse (Club) 12.00 a.m.
SUN 22nd BBC balance 10 a.m. access from 9 a.m. 8.30	11.30 Brillie/Bozay SP (£1) 10.00–1.00 Lontano Workshop Recital Hall Mapin's Reception room rehearsal + Projection Tape	(Club) 1.00 Buffet Lunch Members only 2.30 – 5.30 Lontano Workshop Recital Hall 3.00 CASKEN Playing Reception Room	NNMP rehearse S.P. NNMP S.P. return percussion to St Pauls Lontano rehearse R.H. 7.30	(Club) (+ Music?) (£1.20) 10.00
MON 23rd 8.30	Lontano Rehearse S.P. Horatus Set up T.Hall	1.00 (– 2.30) S.P. Lontano (£1.20) BBC balance a.m.	Reception Room Cabaret rehearse 2.30 – 4.30 Horatus Workshop Tom Hall 2 Pianos (Free) Tom Hall	4.30 7.30 Tom Hall Horatus (£2)	4.30 Reception Room Cabaret (£3) 10.00 + Bar + Buffet
TUES 24th 8.30	BBC set up + T.H. Healy Earthone rehearse	(£1) delayed & rearr. Healy Earthone + Keith Swallow recital Tape T.H.	Lindsay rehearse + ch. Choir SP 3.00 (Free) BBC NSO 6.00 Rehearsal T.H.	7.30 Lindsay £2 S.P. Colne Valley + BBC NSO Rehearse T H	(Club) (+ Music?)
WED 25th 8.30	Polyphony set up in St Paul's — all day	BBC NSO rehearse T.H. + electronics + projection	7.30 BBC NSO + T.H Colne Valley + Earthone Balcony £5, £4, £3 + £2.50 Gallery £2.50/£1.50 Area £2	12.00 Polyphony St Pauls 9.30 (£1)

Music Shop in 1921 20th to 24th.

The opening day of the festival featured the St Paul's organ, something rarely repeated.[7] In an afternoon workshop, Gillian Weir played pieces submitted for the Yorkshire Arts Young Composers' Competition – won in this category by Christopher Fox, then a postgraduate student at York. In the evening she gave a full-length recital. The inclusion of Ligeti's *Volumina,* during which quantities of keys are depressed simultaneously with both forearms, alarmed my colleague Keith Jarvis, who had devised the instrument's tonal design. But, with its Huddersfield builders, Philip and David Wood, in attendance, there were no problems. The original intention had been to programme Ligeti's two organ études, but the fluctuating wind pressure required for *Harmonies* could not be achieved.

This was one of only four festivals to include any of my own compositions. *Quartet in memoriam* had been composed following the death from leukaemia of my half-brother, at a time when I was also preparing an edition of the *Funeral Sentences* attributed to Thomas Morley, but subsequently overshadowed by Purcell's settings of the same texts. Because the final bars of the Morley are quoted at the end of the quartet, I took the opportunity of its first performance to follow it seamlessly with the complete *Funeral Sentences,* sung *a cappella* by the Polytechnic Chamber Choir standing in the chancel. In *The Musical Times* Martin Dreyer observed that the composition was, in effect, 'a two-movement theme-and-variations in reverse, which travels back through drama and meditation to its source', noting that 'it was played with spellbinding commitment by the Lindsay String Quartet'.[8] In the *Yorkshire Post* Robert Cockroft remarked that 'the gradual dovetailing into the Morley quotation followed by the beautifully sung Sentences was as moving and effective in performance as it was imaginative in conception'.[9] *Quartet in memoriam* was a joint winner of the Clements Memorial Prize for Chamber Music that year. Three years later, in August 1984, the Lindsay Quartet and BBC Singers performed both pieces, also in sequence, on Radio 3.

The 1981 festival included for the first time an orchestral concert, given by the BBC Northern Symphony Orchestra and co-promoted with the town's subscription series. The programme contained Lutosławski's *Musique funèbre*, Balassa's *Cantata Y* (its UK premiere), Colne Valley Male Voice Choir singing the rarely-heard Psalm 18 by Liszt (who appeared to be stalking my early festivals in his role as an innovator), and Prokofiev's Fifth Symphony. It was a curious but effective juxtaposition.

Creative magnetism: Xenakis

Nevertheless, the arrival of Iannis Xenakis in November 1982 signified a 'coming of age'. For the first time I devoted a day entirely to one composer, with eleven pieces spread across two concerts. The first marked the festival debut of the Arditti String Quartet. The second, proposed by Xenakis himself, featured the flamboyant harpsichordist Elisabeth Chojnacka and percussionist Sylvio Gualda, plus two acousmatic pieces on tape. Like the Ardittis, their combination of accuracy, virtuosity and conviction was mesmerising. It confirmed that in the hands of brilliant and dedicated interpreters even the most intractable and perplexing scores can sound utterly convincing. Bernard Jacobson's 'forum' with Xenakis illuminated his thinking and taught me always to seek the presence of the composer – as apologist, demystifier, human being. The daring originality of the music itself set up an extraordinary tension. I feared that the concert advertised for the Saturday evening, given by little-known harpsichord and percussion soloists interspersed with electronic music, would attract only a few. But St Paul's was packed. People came from all over the country: not only regular concertgoers, but others merely culturally aware and curious. Evidently the mathematician, architect, composer, computing innovator, and resistance fighter – upon whom a death sentence pronounced by the Greek government remained unrescinded – held for many a magnetic fascination.

Iannis Xenakis.

The visit of Xenakis reinforced my conviction that music is about ideas, that intelligent people are drawn even to difficult work that embodies concepts which interest them. Improved marketing helped. For the first time the festival leaflet bore an image of the composer, if a little crude before the advent of computer graphics. The concert in St Paul's was visually engaging and effectively lit by a drama student. On its polished wooden floor, Gualda's array of percussion sported enormous earthenware flowerpots borrowed from a local garden centre. Diagonally opposite, Chojnacka's harpsichord glittered regally. Dressed to impress, she confronted her instrument like a lion tamer, throwing successive sheets of music onto the floor until it was surrounded by paper. The theatricality heightened the internal drama of the music. Afterwards I heard somebody say to his neighbour, 'I haven't been so struck by a concert since hearing Klemperer conduct the *Eroica* twenty years ago!' It was an astonishing comparison. Writing in *The Observer*, Andrew Clements confessed that 'I went up to Huddersfield as at least an agnostic, if not a downright non-believer, where Xenakis's music was concerned; I came back utterly converted… Most performances in London that I have heard regarded finding the right notes as the sole objective; as these marvellous interpreters demonstrated, that should only be the beginning'.[10]

The principle of engaging the best advocates, ideally those preferred by the composer, was one to which I subsequently always tried to adhere. Its value was demonstrated never more forcibly than in 1987, when the combined Asko and Nieuw Ensembles gave the UK premiere of Brian Ferneyhough's complete *Carceri d'Invenzione*, assimilated and refined over two years and following three performances in Holland. Herein lay another ideal, to present complex music so honed by repetition that performances would be dazzlingly accurate and exude panache. It was a reason for asking foreign ensembles to include Huddersfield in their schedules. For the Ensemble Modern based in Frankfurt, Lachenmann's *Mouvement (-vor der Erstarrung)* of 1982/84, which they have now performed over a hundred times, is as much standard repertoire as a Beethoven symphony to a classical orchestra. The London Sinfonietta performed *Mouvement* and *'...zwei Gefühle...', Musik mit Leonardo* for the BBC, the first ensemble works by Lachenmann it had attempted, only in 2005. *Mouvement* was repeated in its own QEH season in 2006 along with *Concertini,* and *Schreiben* and *Ausklang* performed in the Southbank Centre's 'Lachenmann Weekend' in 2010. Nearly a quarter of a century after Huddersfield first featured his music, London had caught up. But any other British ensemble or orchestra performing a piece by Lachenmann is likely to programme it only once. For some of the players, it may be a first encounter with techniques and notation far removed from their experience.

Besides Xenakis and Henri Dutilleux, the 1982 festival featured Nicholas Maw and David Bedford. The fluid lyricism of Maw's *Life Studies,* performed by the strings of the London Sinfonietta on a Contemporary Music Network tour, sounded splendidly sonorous in St Paul's, between Britten's early *Prelude and Fugue* and Shostakovich's Fourteenth Symphony. Composed twelve years earlier in 1969, the Shostakovich was not yet well known; and, with Felicity Palmer and Willard White the outstanding soloists, its bleak contemplation of mortality made a profound impression. For *Life Studies* the players stood (except cellists and bass) in a semicircle within the chancel. For the Shostakovich they sat, but also in the chancel, so that we needed only a few feet of platform extension for the conductor and soloists. This allowed six extra rows of seats to be placed in front of the fixed tiers, plus additional chairs

in the aisles from end to end. If my memory is correct, all were occupied. It must have been one of the largest audiences ever in St Paul's, and their hushed attentiveness was palpable.

I would have liked to replicate this seating arrangement on other occasions. But the festival was short-staffed, and there were nearly always more urgent things to do. It occasionally happened, although from 1986 the annual influx of international ensembles led to flight cases cluttering the aisles, and batteries of percussion around the performance area.

Organisation

The first four festivals I organised and publicised mostly by myself, calling on students to steward, light concerts, and help move instruments. Ron Morton from Leisure Services sold tickets. Sound projection was handled by the electronic music studio manager, Mark Bromwich (who later adopted his family name of Bokowiec), and its director, Phil Ellis, who also appeared as a composer. Another ally was Chris Meredith, a lecturer in drama, for whose students working backstage was useful experience. I shudder to recall what some of them did, particularly one heavily built music student who climbed a precariously tall scaffolding tower to reposition the highest lanterns in St Paul's – a procedure now utterly forbidden. Then he crawled under the loose platforms to tie their legs together so that Tom Yang could dance Maxwell Davies's *Vesalii Icones* without the stage shifting under him. For three years a drama student named Nigel Dickinson lit events. At first St Paul's had no theatrical lanterns, so Nigel hired them and attached them to the pillars. He went on to co-found the aptly named Proper Job Theatre Company.

From 1981 a music student was paid to type letters. Others in the School of Art designed posters (see pages 26 and 28). That October, at a societies' fair in the town hall, I manned a festival desk draped in blown-up pages of Birtwistle's Clarinet Quintet. A recent Keele graduate named Philip Wood came by, and, intrigued, offered to help. He proved so useful that Kirklees Leisure Services offered him a permanent job, and in this capacity Philip joined the newly created festival 'steering group' as its first company secretary. In reality the steering

The polytechnic's first electroacoustic music studio which opened in 1979.
PHOTOS: MARK BOKOWIEC

group was a 'board' – but probably given this advisory title because of my suspicion of formal management. Constantly busy, I feared the potential interference and additional work it might involve. During an earlier festival, Dominic Gill (reviewing for the *Financial Times*) had asked me whether I was answerable to an organising committee. 'No,' I said. 'Then never have one. It will be fatal!' In fact the board, as it was eventually called, was consistently helpful – a constructive forum to which all members usefully contributed. If my own proposals were occasionally questioned, the board never seriously objected to any of them.[11]

Keen on jazz, Philip compiled sample cassettes to extend my inadequate knowledge, and on a memorable occasion we went to Leeds to hear the Art Ensemble of Chicago. I wish I could have booked these wonderful, multitalented musicians, but their European tours were increasingly rare and it was not to be. A welcome development was the appointment of Helen Hale in 1982 as the festival's first administrator, although only part-time. Helen had taught at a school in York but wanted to move into arts administration. Her arrival enhanced the whole operation, although, as the festival continued to grow, my own workload hardly decreased. In 1985 Kate Wright joined as an assistant and one year later succeeded Helen as administrator. They were paid by the hour. Only in 1988 was a half-time salaried post of administrator established.

Artistic policy

At the start, the last thing on my mind was a statement of policy. Perhaps I should have had a strategy. Yet there was an appealing play-ethic in bringing together what took one's fancy.

Mission statements and business plans were mercifully a decade away.

As the festival became more purposeful, I realised that it should not only entertain, enrich and inform – but also proselytise. It needed to address different constituencies: aficionados and the uninitiated, music specialists and those of a more general culture, adults and the young, local audiences and international. Besides concerts, I looked for stimulating and interactive activities to fill each day, and sought maximum variety and minimal repetition. To remain fresh, I decided that each festival should have a different emphasis from its predecessors. A contemporary showcase that confines itself to a single aesthetic, to likeminded composers and a regular cast of performers, risks at best being chummy, at worst predictability. Most of all, I thought that the same composers should not be programmed year after year.

That Huddersfield soon acquired a reputation for 'unflinching modernism' was only half the story. In reality the festival was much wider – embracing minimalism and music theatre, Grisey and Górecki, Morricone and Murray Schafer, Rihm and Reich, British composers from Bedford and Benjamin to Tavener and Turnage, and Americana of every complexion. Any exploration of the new implies curiosity. As the festival moved from the 1980s into the 1990s its programmes became broader and the surrounding activities more heterogeneous. By interweaving contrasting strands, we hoped that people drawn to one particular event would sample others and find them rewarding. Much of the festival's success arose from its openness, from not getting typecast – a characteristic I admired in Pierre Audi's Almeida Festival in London. The critics applauded it too. In *The Irish Times,* Michael Dervan, a regular visitor, whilst lamenting that 'the world of new music is beset with factions, ideologies and unholy allegiances', hailed Huddersfield as 'a major non-aligned power in a fractured musical world'.[12]

But the resolve to be neither partisan nor parochial emerged gradually. The first festivals exuded a certain cosiness: in part due to my limited contacts, in part to the lack of time and money to extend them. So the first two festivals contained three duo recitals by Douglas Young and Rohan de Saram, whose shamefully unrigorous content had Sciarrino and Xenakis rubbing shoulders with Debussy, Delius, de Falla and Schumann. During the first thirteen years Lontano, Dreamtiger and Music Projects/London dominated the roster of British ensembles. Lontano's visits were spaced out. But Music Projects performed at no fewer than five festivals between 1985 and 1990.

As funding increased the festival spread its wings. From the mid-1980s, work from abroad became a priority, which the parochialism and timidity of much UK promotion made both necessary and easy to achieve. By 2010 some 331 different ensembles (including choirs) had performed in Huddersfield, nearly half of them from abroad. To my principle of constant novelty there were soon exceptions. Performers like the Arditti Quartet, Asko, Recherche, the London Sinfonietta and New London Chamber Choir – later Psappha, ELISION, musikFabrik, Music Theatre Wales and the Nieuw Ensemble – proved too essential not to re-engage. Other quartets brought different repertoire: the Balanescu and Smith quartets; the Kronos, with its characteristic trawl of non-Western music and a UK premiere of Górecki's Second Quartet; the Brindisi, with quartets by Imogen Holst, David and Colin Matthews; whilst, in recent years, the Quatuor Diotima has taken up repertoire identified with the Ardittis alongside composers of the new millennium. The London Sinfonietta became a regular visitor only from 1992, but with a run of five annual visits between 1996 and 2000[13] (see also Chapter 5).

I welcomed suggestions. But, as any promoter of new work discovers, the flow of unsolicited proposals quickly becomes a flood. At first I tried to consider each and write a reasoned reply, but it soon became impossibly onerous. Self-promotion I found distasteful – especially from pushy composers. The advocacy of

intermediaries was more persuasive, whether from members of the board, performers, audience, critics, fellow promoters or other composers, When Michael Finnissy wrote to recommend the Belgian ensemble Champ d'Action, and Richard Ayres to enthuse about Luc Ferrari, I was touched that they had taken the time and acted on both suggestions. The burden of letters meriting a reply eventually influenced my decision to retire, and I was hardly surprised to hear that one of my successors, inheriting a drawer of unread proposals, chose not to open it. A month after informing the board, I attended a dinner at the Donaueschingen Musiktage and found myself sitting next to the fearsome-looking Helmut Flammer. Herr Flammer had written to me ten years before, enclosing scores which he hoped the festival would perform. Other than that, I knew only one thing about him. There had been a minor 'scandal' after a BBCSO recording of his piano concerto, when Timothy Hugh, the orchestra's principal cellist, flung down a cheap instrument acquired for the occasion, and stamped it to smithereens in protest at what the string section of the orchestra had been required to do. It was hardly a recommendation for music I already thought uningratiating. When Herr Flammer realised who I was, he launched into an inquisitional tirade from which I was not supposed to escape without promising to perform his work. Never more pleased to have announced my retirement, I explained my impotence with barely disguised glee. Disgusted by this outcome, he turned his back on me and conversed with his neighbour in impenetrable German for the rest of the meal.

It was important to programme appropriately for the capacity of different venues: the smallest accommodating 150 or less, the largest around a thousand. Orchestral concerts were mainly scheduled at weekends when there were a greater number of visitors. From 1987, the structure of the festival changed, to embrace two themed weekends, both targeted at a wider national and international public. During the intervening week I tended to group events of more local interest, which, after the opening of the Lawrence Batley Theatre, included opera, dance, animation, jazz and various multimedia hybrids, bringing the festival a substantial new audience. Student visitors from further away could apply for bursaries, as well as accommodation with local families for a nominal payment. Benefiting from the low-priced season tickets, they were able to attend several days for a very modest outlay.

A checklist of ideal ingredients

With the creation of the steering group in 1982 it was time to articulate aims. After agreeing a constitution and membership, this embryonic 'board' turned its attention to policy: the inclusion of jazz and film, the possibility of a fringe, the role of the visual arts; the involvement of the polytechnic, collaboration with local organisations, avoidance of clashes and attempts to make the occasion more 'festive', so that townspeople would feel that it belonged to them. For the group's next meeting in January 1983 I promised to compile a 'Checklist of ideal ingredients: a guide to artistic policy'. It read as follows:

Artists
Use the most outstanding available performers, both established and of recent achievement, but also reserve space for artists with regional connections, emerging young or experimental performers and the best student-based groups.

Media
From solo performers, through ensembles to orchestra/choir (even opera?), balance the conventional [concert] formula with mixed media, electronic and experimental music, music theatre, jazz, cabaret etc.

Music
Ensure a blend of world and British premieres and acknowledged 'classics' of the last thirty years and twentieth century in general. Give second, or further, performances to recent works of proven merit. Spotlight some under-performed areas of twentieth-century music.

Composers
Represent the maximum possible number of living composers, British and foreign. Featured composers should balance world leaders plus younger composers of a variety of styles and attitudes.

General
Minimum repetition of the previous year(s). Aim for a unique content (ie. not only what can be heard elsewhere in Britain). Aim (through different events, perhaps) at a wide audience, both national and regional, specialist and general. Ensure that the programme merits visits by critics (on days convenient to them!) and, if possible, broadcasts by the BBC. Sprinkle with supporting workshops, lectures, films, exhibitions, community & environmental events and related arts. Seek a variety

of venues in Huddersfield, the Polytechnic and Education Authority (eg. Town Hall and Reception Room, Art Gallery, Venn Street, clubs, Parish Church, industrial premises, St Paul's Hall, Great Hall, Recital Hall, exhibition area and lecture theatres in [the] Polytechnic, schools and Banney Royd Teachers' Centre).

There is no indication in the minutes that my memorandum was discussed. But a broadening took place. In 1983 and 1984 related visual arts exhibitions were mounted in Huddersfield Art Gallery by its director Robert Hall, and between 1985 and 1987 the festival itself initiated three visual arts collaborations. The most substantial was an exhibition of sound sculpture occupying all five galleries (see pages 31–32), which had been assembled for the Arnolfini Gallery in Bristol and whose curator, Jolyon Laycock, co-operated in its transfer to Huddersfield. Neither Robert nor the festival had the resources to originate on this scale; and, in the early 1990s, when the opening of a theatre loomed, what we would present in this new venue, and how to fund it, took priority.

No events took place in industrial premises – except for Dean Clough in Halifax – until Graham McKenzie began to use Bates Mill in 2006. Nor were nightclubs used before 1990, when I discovered that the Flicks nightclub in Northumberland Street could provide an evocative ambience for *The Sinking of the Titanic* by Gavin Bryars (see pages 188 and 203). Club gigs remained rare until Graham took a bolder approach, combining installations, video, experimental technology and amplified live performance tailored to each venue.

My checklist omitted any concept of excellence, although the brochure repeatedly asserted that the festival presented 'the finest'. What that meant was not easily defined, although, in assessing student compositions with colleagues, we had agreed criteria that could be applied regardless of style. The music created at any one time inevitably encompasses the second-rate. It was important to explore the highways and byways, and to nurture talent. But as a showcase attempting to woo a sceptical public, the festival needed the best. This equally applied to educational and outreach projects. Most of all it applied to performance. Composers could be of any school or persuasion; they could be as perverse and eccentric as they wished. There

With Elliott Carter.
PHOTO: RICHARD STEINITZ

was only one (admittedly subjective) imperative: that any piece should be good of its type – and, for mercy's sake, not dull!

1983: Carter and Henze

It would have been unthinkable, of course, not to revisit music of the stature of Xenakis. In the following year two other major composers were featured, to whose music the festival would return. They were Hans Werner Henze, and Elliott Carter on the eve of his seventy-fifth birthday. Of the seven works by Carter, the most recent was *Triple Duo*, given a dazzling performance by the Fires of London six months after its premiere. Carter's lithe and muscular counterpoint complemented the luminous quietude, mutating into bracing wind-blown dances, of Maxwell Davies's *Image, Reflection, Shadow,* with its glittering cimbalom part played by the ensemble's percussionist, Gregg Knowles, who had learnt the instrument for the piece. The Ardittis returned to perform Carter's Second and Third Quartets, and a new quartet by James Dillon. Although this was the sixth festival, the Dillon was only its second commission – funded by a new budget set up by Yorkshire Arts Association. The first had been *Sun Paints Rainbows on the Vast Waves,* composed in 1982 by David Bedford for the Polytechnic Symphonic Band and funded by the Hinrichsen Foundation.

Most of the eight works by Henze were small-scale. But a concert given by the Koenig Ensemble and New London Chamber Choir featured two substantial pieces: Henze's recent *Miracle of the Rose,* and his sensuously beautiful *Cantata della fiaba estrema,* composed twenty years earlier. 'Gaspingly decadent love songs,' Paul Griffiths described the latter in *The Times,* remarking on the contrast between 'the wiry intellectual gymnastics of Carter,' and the 'luxury and loveliness' of Henze.[14] The *Cantata* required a soprano soloist who could cope with its extremely high register. Finding British artists unavailable, I discovered a young American coloratura soprano, Elizabeth Parcells, whose knife-edge precision and purity of tone amounted to 'a sensational debut', as Paul Griffiths reported. In September Henze had sent a message via his agent, saying that he was too busy to come. Alarmed, I wrote what I hoped would be a persuasive letter. Henze relented, and, during a short visit, conducted *Miracle of the Rose* with our former student, Roger Heaton, an accomplished clarinet soloist. Afterwards there came an invitation to visit Henze's own summer festival in Montepulciano. In this lovely renaissance hill town and its surroundings, my wife and I spent a rewarding week. One concert included Mark-Anthony Turnage's *Lament for a Hanging Man.* It was the first piece of his I had heard since *Entranced* for piano won a category of the Young Composers' Competition in 1982, and its passion and theatricality were unforgettable. (Richard Barrett was also shortlisted that year in two competition categories, but neither entry won.) The sense of community in Montepulciano was all-encompassing, and I noted enviously the employment of a music animateur to run educational projects throughout the year. Huddersfield could not afford such a post; indeed, it could not afford an education organiser even part-time. Despite this, I had already planned far more community involvement in the 1984 festival.

The visit of James Wood's New London Chamber Choir in 1983 was the first of many. Being amateurs, albeit exceptionally accomplished, the choir's out-of-town concerts had to take place at weekends. Having sung Henze with finesse on the Saturday, the following afternoon they excelled in a technically challenging *a cappella* concert, containing the UK premiere of Ligeti's difficult *Drei Phantasien* and the world premiere of

Cantos Populares by his pupil Roberto Sierra. The choir's assurance in the Ligeti contrasted with the lacklustre debut of the Parisian-based L'Itineraire (belying its reputation), whose electronics malfunctioned, and whose uningratiating choice of music was relieved only by the bright rays of *Treize Couleurs du soleil couchant* by Tristan Murail.

What it cost

Turnover in 1983 had reached £25,367. The seven evening concerts together cost just under £10,000. This was virtually the same as a quotation from the London Sinfonietta for repeating its Carter birthday concert performed in London one month before, and to pay that much for a single concert was out of the question. The highest single ticket price was still only £3 for an evening concert, and £1.50 for students – who for only £12 could attend all thirty-five concerts, receive a programme book and enjoy festival club membership. Some chose a 'weekend pass' for £6, but many music department students purchased the full package and, with the help of bursaries, so did others from further away. We sought and expected a young audience, and low admission charges had been agreed with Yorkshire Arts Association. The £4,450 earned from tickets, programmes and advertising represented slightly less than a fifth of total income. The rest came from music trusts, public bodies and, on this occasion, the festival's first commercial sponsor: Huddersfield-based Holset Engineering. A total of £17,414 was spent on artists, workshops and discussions, and £1,895 on publicity. The festival administrator was paid £1,750. Two prizes of £200 were awarded to winners of the Young Composers' Competition, chosen by Robert Saxton and Simon Bainbridge. One went, with no prompting from me, to my pupil Nicholas Redfern, whose *The Dreams of Fallen Gods, Sad Vales & Streams* employed the lowest pitched instruments possessed by the Vega Wind Quintet in a darkly evocative score.

Awareness of the festival was advanced in the USA by Stephen Montague, in a comprehensive review written for *Musical America*.[15] Stephen had participated as lecturer and pianist, but joined the audience for the rest of the festival. His comparison of the London orchestras' Great British Music Festival, 'the season's biggest yawn', with Huddersfield's 'sparkling

IOU's The Sleep of Reason, premiered at the 1983 festival.
PHOTO: IOU

variety...wall to wall concerts, capacity crowds, and contagious enthusiasm' was gratifying. The article did not lack criticism, but I was pleased to read praise for an event overlooked by other writers. This was the 'fantastic... surreal... wonderful... disturbing, imaginative, amusing' *The Sleep of Reason*, created by the visual theatre company IOU. I had been intrigued by their work since first seeing it at the ICA in London. Although one of the most original small companies in Europe, IOU's administrative base turned out to be in Yorkshire, indeed just up the road in the Colne Valley.[16] I invited the company to make a piece for the festival, but the question was where, as most of its creations were site-specific and out-of-doors. We settled on the then unused Milton church hall, in which they could spend several days preparing. Although musically slender, *The Sleep of Reason* explored a zany, whimsical and enchanting dream-world. There were three late-evening performances. But either the hour or the hybrid art form failed to attract any UK reviews, whereas a 7.30pm performance in St Paul's by the relatively mainstream Northern Music Theatre received seven.

Music theatre

Across the globe, the new genre of music theatre had overturned staid concert routines, whose formalities were being startlingly exploded. Works like Maxwell Davies's *Eight Songs for a Mad King* (1969) made viscerally realistic what might earlier have been interiorised. In its marriage of disparate elements, music theatre crossed barriers, enriching the language and subverting norms. The first festival had included some mild examples by George Crumb. I was keen to go further, and Davies's fiftieth birthday in 1984 provided an appropriate occasion.

Max (to use the name he preferred) agreed to participate, as did Mauricio Kagel, and I set about representing their *oeuvre*. Besides an

orchestral portrait (described in Chapter 3), Max was represented by the Fires of London and dancer Tom Yang performing *Vesalii Icones,* based on the superimposition of anatomical drawings by Andreas Vesalius (1514–1564) on the fourteen Stations of the Cross, whose shocking conclusion has the resurrected figure emerging from the tomb as Antichrist, represented by the dancer wholly naked. The intensity of *Vesalii Icones* was relieved by the comparatively jovial *Le Jongleur de Notre Dame,* also played by the Fires, but with its Overture and Recessional performed by wind players from Huddersfield Technical College. Max's commitment to music education was exemplified in a performance of his *Songs for Hoy,* sung, played and danced by the pupils of five junior and two high schools – the starting point for a joyful concert of home-grown music theatre described in Chapter 12 (page 212). Kagel was represented in the concert by Trio Le Cercle (already mentioned), and by two of his films, a lecture by the composer, and *Kontra-Danse* and *Kantrimiusik* staged by Northern Music Theatre, directed by his pupil, David Sawer.

Kagel's Kantrimiusik *staged by Northern Music Theatre.*
PHOTO: KEITH GLOSSOP

Vic Hoyland's Dumb
Show *staged by Northern
Music Theatre.*
PHOTO: KEITH GLOSSOP

I have already described the rector of the polytechnic's reaction to Trio Le Cercle (see pages 5–6). It was as well he did not witness MW2, a music theatre troupe from Cracow, whose Dadaistic realisations of works by Bogusław Schaeffer were alarmingly anarchic. Founded in 1962 as the first Polish ensemble to specialise in graphic scores, music theatre and 'happenings', MW2 was influenced by the experimental theatre of Jerzy Grotowski and other Poles, for whom physical and visual theatre enabled them to circumvent state censorship of text. Schaeffer was regarded as one of the most original figures to emerge in Poland after the political thaw of 1956. So I was intrigued, but also nervous – more so after receiving a list of props itemising a rope with which to bind and drag a grand piano across the stage, and a 'ritual flame' to be ignited at the end of *Heraklitiana*. The ceilings in St Paul's were liberally endowed with smoke sensors, so it was hardly reassuring, after the performers arrived, to be told by their leader, Adam Kaczynski, that, during a performance in Stockholm, the fire brigade had burst into the hall with hoses at the ready, 'much improving the effect'.

The rehearsal followed an evening concert by Electric Phoenix, and it was well past midnight before the stage was set to rehearse *Heraklitiana*. At the designated moment Mark Bromwich fired an electrical charge to ignite the flame, and Adam, dressed in Greek tunic and laurel wreath, made oblations whilst I watched the smoke curling upwards. How long before it reached the sensors? Not wanting to find out, I suggested we extinguish the flame; but how to do so we had not considered. I recalled seeing a potential 'snuffer' in the vestry, a frying pan among the props, and went to collect it. To my horror, through the window there were unmistakeable blue flashing lights. With a rush of adrenalin I hurried out to find three fire engines purring quietly to themselves in the car park. Of firemen and hoses there was no sign. 'What's happened?' I asked the driver of the nearest. 'Oh, a student's burnt the toast in the bed-sits,' he explained, pointing at the central services tower. Weak with relief, I rejoined the rehearsal where Adam and his colleagues were now running round the building and attempting to climb the pillars. Sanity was hanging by a thread, but I was beyond caring. At last they finished. I tidied up, locked the building and drove home to bed.

In a lunchtime recital, dressed in a dazzling white suit, Philip Mead played Stockhausen's *Lucifer's Dream*, launching, in its final section, a succession of paper rockets – much to the audience's delight. For the Young Composers' Competition we invited ideas involving music theatre, and the chosen four composers devised works for Gemini, whose concert also included my colleague Margaret Lucy Wilkins's melodrama *Struwwelpeter*. The Polytechnic Brass Band excelled in an ambitious programme, containing Birtwistle's *Grimethorpe Aria*, Maxwell Davies's *The Pole Star*, Tippett's *Festal Brass with Blues* and Vinko Globokar's *La Tromba è Mobile*. To perform the Globokar the players strode back and forth, fanned out, wheeled, split and regrouped, directed by my colleague Barrie Webb (see the photo on page 8).

The following evening's performance went without a hitch. The audience appeared to enjoy the anarchy, although Julia Winterson remembers that she was 'terrified and sneaked out at the first opportunity'. Only Gerald Larner, writing with inside knowledge in *The Guardian*, bemoaned the absence of the fire brigade. Two days earlier, the BBC Symphony Orchestra had performed its Maxwell Davies portrait, beginning with *St Thomas Wake* – a deeply unsettling piece of 'instrumental theatre' whose polarities develop entirely through musical means, although enhanced by the visual separation of dance band and symphony orchestra. This was the festival's first own-promoted orchestral concert, and added a weighty new dimension. How it came about is explained in the next chapter.

MW2 from Poland perform Bogusław Schaeffer's Quartet for four actors.

BBC symphony orchestra

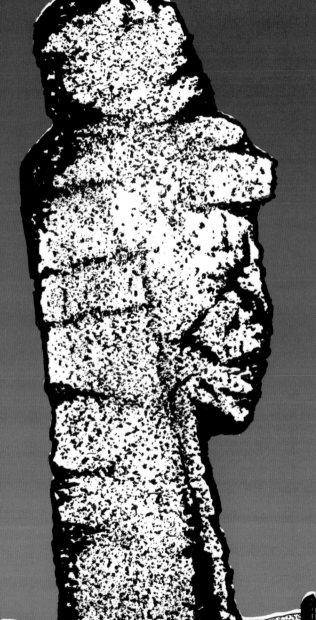

conductor..
elgar howarth
soprano..
elizabeth parcells

peter

maxwell

davies..

st. thomas wake
stone litany
worldes blis

Huddersfield Town Hall Saturday 10th November at 7.30pm

Invitation Concert given by
Huddersfield Contemporary Music Festival
in association with the BBC

*Huddersfield Contemporary Music Festival is promoted in
association with Kirklees Leisure Services and Huddersfield
Polytechnic*

3 *Expansion*

The BBC Symphony Orchestra

At first funds were insufficient to engage an orchestra, but, through buying into the town's subscription series, shared concerts ended the 1981 and 1983 festivals. Both were given by the BBC Northern Symphony Orchestra (or BBC Philharmonic as it became in 1983). The second contained Elliott Carter's First Symphony – a work which gives little hint of his mature style – while the accompanying Piano Concerto by Gershwin, and *Orchestral Suite from Billy the Kid* by Copland, were frankly populist. I had hoped that the concert would feature *Suntreader* by Carl Ruggles, but the conductor, José Serebrier, declined to include it. He had also replaced the advertised *Symphonic Dances from West Side Story* by Bernstein with the blander Copland, so that, despite the concert's usefulness in bringing the festival painlessly to a larger audience, it signalled a disappointing loss of integrity.

Meanwhile, in London, the BBC Symphony Orchestra was presenting its 'College Concerts', given before non-paying audiences in conservatoires and colleges as well as the Maida Vale Studios. In this bold series, the standard of European Modernism raised by Sir William Glock was carried forward by an intrepid team of producers – notably Stephen Plaistow, a friend from my Cambridge days. If the BBC could do this in London, why not in Huddersfield? I wrote to Robert Ponsonby, Glock's successor as controller of music, proposing a similar format, for which the festival would pay out-of-town expenses, and, as in London, the concert would be broadcast and the audience admitted free. To mark the fiftieth birthday of Maxwell Davies in 1984, I suggested a concert performance of his ballet score *Salome*. Commissioned by the Flemming Flindt Circus Company in Copenhagen, the ballet has still not been staged in Britain, nor the complete score performed in concert.

Ponsonby wrote back saying 'no'. But there followed a more encouraging phone call from the orchestra's producer, Anthony Sargent. It was not the idea of a collaboration that was unacceptable, but the piece. Sargent suggested that I reconsider and write again. I did so, this time proposing *Stone Litany* and *Worldes Blis,* preceded by *St Thomas Wake*, with its striking theatrical confrontation between symphony orchestra and dance band, and, to my delight, Ponsonby agreed. Making the detailed arrangements led to a friendship with Sargent that continued when he moved to the South Bank Centre as artistic projects director, and during his eleven years as head of arts in Birmingham and subsequent appointment in 2000 as general director of the Sage in Gateshead. For fifteen years, beginning in 1990, Tony was also a member of the festival board.

I had been present when Max himself conducted the disastrous first performance of *Worldes Blis* at a BBC Promenade concert in 1969, unhelpfully sandwiched between the Elgar Cello Concerto and Walton's *Belshazzar's Feast*. On that occasion the slow, cumulative growth of its thirty-five-minute time span, little relieved by colouristic orchestration, had bewildered the Prom audience, many of whom walked out noisily, leaving an atmosphere of uncomprehending hostility. Shaken by the experience, Max withdrew the score; but he had regained faith in the work, and it had received at least one further performance in London – without, perhaps, throwing off its dour reputation. In a more sympathetic context

I thought it might succeed. Nevertheless, the stunning vindication of *Worldes Blis* in Huddersfield few would have dared predict. It probably gained from being preceded by two other strongly differentiated examples of his orchestral output; indeed, in a pre-concert discussion, Max revealed that this was the first orchestral concert entirely devoted to his music.

To accommodate the large quantity of percussion and extra players in *St Thomas Wake,* the band was placed high up near the organ, with the percussion spread across the front of the stage, while the rest of the orchestra occupied the main area floor. The audience sat in the balcony looking down on three sides. As Elgar Howarth guided the long trajectory of dark, smouldering polyphony in *Worldes Blis* towards its cataclysmic climax, it was like witnessing a volcano erupt from the rim of the crater. In the *Financial Times,* David Murray observed that the music's 'tremendous success was made with an audience who knew they were honouring a difficult but important composer, that the piece would require preternaturally patient attention'.[1] In *The Times,* Paul Griffiths claimed that 'very little composed for orchestra since Mahler's death disturbs and elates on this scale'.[2] It 'was a concert in a thousand,' wrote Martin Dreyer in *The Musical Times*.[3] Listening to a recording of the broadcast a quarter of a century later, the claims do not seem excessive. Elgar Howarth's direction and the orchestra's playing were exceptional. Elizabeth Parcells, who had sung Henze so sensationally in 1983, performed *Stone Litany* with great poise and musicianship. She performed twice more at the festival, but told me that singing contemporary music was so nerve-wracking that she would not pursue it as a career.

Composer-conductors: a Berio portrait

In rehabilitating a masterpiece the festival had found a new role. This was reinforced the following year when Stephen Plaistow offered a revival of Luciano Berio's hour-long *Coro,* performed by the BBCSO and Singers, and conducted by the composer. In this great choral and instrumental tapestry, fragments from Pablo Neruda's *Residencia en la Tierra* are interleaved with folk texts. But due to its length and density, *Coro* had also failed to make the impression it deserved when premiered in London eight years

before. As part of the festival's celebration of Berio's sixtieth birthday, this second collaboration with the BBCSO attracted an

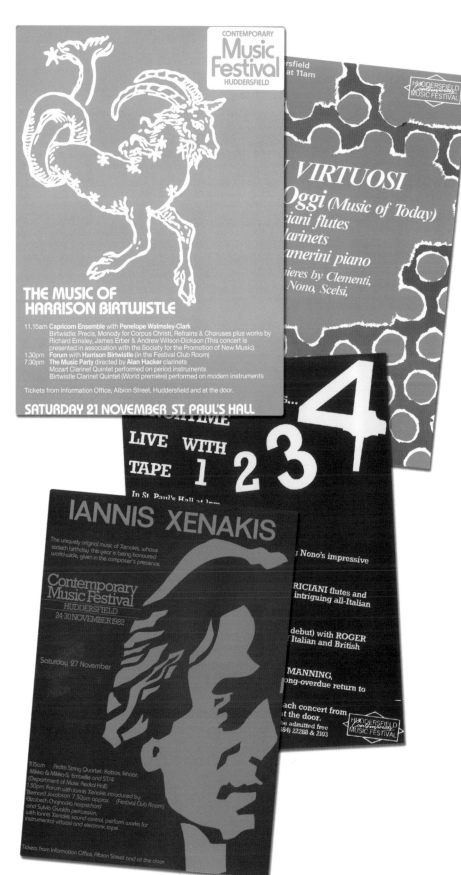

A4 concert posters designed by students in the School of Art.

Antonella Agati in Berio's Visage.

audience three times that of the previous year, most of whom found the epic humanitarian sweep of *Coro* utterly absorbing. Berio himself was delighted, and he and the BBC continued to perform the piece around the world. We had proved that people in the North could hear large-scale contemporary works in world-class performances without having to travel to London.

Composers were more inclined to come when actively involved. Berio liked to conduct his own music and, because he was engaged by the BBC, the cost to the festival was very little. A similar formula later brought Lutosławski, Boulez and Tan Dun, and might also have brought Penderecki – but the only work of his that I wanted to present was *Seven Gates of Jerusalem,* and its three choruses, full orchestra and separate brass ensemble required a much larger venue. It still awaits a British premiere.

I met Berio over dinner, with his agent Andrew Rosner, to plan other performances. *Coro* would be preceded by *Folk Songs* and *"points on the curve to find…"*, and on the previous evening Berio would attend a portrait concert in St Paul's. His suggested artists I accepted, regretting only that the American trumpeter he requested to play the new *Sequenza X* proved insecure in its extreme high register, and Berio had declined my proposal of the British trumpeter John Wallace, whom he did not know. In every other respect this was a remarkable concert. The first part ended with a classic of early electroacoustic music, *Visage,* in which the voice of Berio's first wife, Cathy Berberian, is subsumed in an acousmatic drama of astonishing emotional power. It was Berio's idea to accompany the tape playback with a 'dance-mime' by Antonella Agati, whose disturbing interpretation ended in a devastating portrayal of psychological annihilation.

Circles, which ended the concert, could not have been more different, with its rain-drenched, wind-blown texts by e.e. cummings, and exuberant scoring for soprano, harp and a circle of instruments surrounding each of two percussionists. I had attended the British premiere of this ground-breaking work at a BBC invitation concert in Maida Vale in 1961, when some of the instruments had to be brought from France. Twenty-four years later it was still a challenge to assemble them. Tim Williams, a student in the music department

(now a professional percussionist and artistic director of Psappha), drove to Liverpool to collect a van load, noting ruefully during the performance that some remained unplayed. A thrilling dimension is the improvisational latitude of a score whose semi-graphic notation had become famous, and which Berio suggested should 'be listened to as theatre and viewed as music'.[4] Dazzling both visually and aurally, the piece was radiantly sung by Elizabeth Laurence, the tiny stars on her dress twinkling in the spotlights. St Paul's was so full that we had hastily to set extra rows of chairs filling the aisles from end to end. Too busy to reserve one, I just managed to secure a side seat near the vestry behind a pillar. An overflow of students perched on the steps both sides of the central seats. As this obstructed access to the emergency exits, it had to be firmly prevented in subsequent years.

At our meeting I asked Berio to tell me about *Accordo,* a work composed for four municipal wind bands to play out of doors. I knew only that it had been performed in Assisi, where the bands had occupied four corners of a large piazza; but the score contained no instructions and left crucial aspects unclear. Why were there gaps where nothing was notated? These were 'windows', Berio explained, in which each band

plays excerpts from its repertoire. The idea
sounded fun, particularly for young players.
So I invited the Kirklees Youth Wind Band and
Huddersfield Technical College Wind Band to
take part, as well as the Polytechnic Symphonic
Band and Royal Northern College of Music
Wind Orchestra. As the performance would
be in November, it had to be accommodated
in Huddersfield Town Hall, where, at the first
joint rehearsal, there were mutinous murmurs
from the RNCM contingent who had somehow
to position themselves among the seats in
the balcony.

The performance, however, was a joy.
Its Ivesian conjunction of English folksong,
big band jazz, marches, pop songs and Verdian
operatic excerpts created a glorious cacophony.
With the area cleared of seats, street performers
entertained a promenading audience, among
whom were many children. Barrie Webb began
the piece with a starting pistol and, at the end,
instead of the doves released in Assisi, white
'peace' balloons floated down from the town
hall ceiling. Berio had left Huddersfield the day
before, but not before helpfully attending a
rehearsal. Most of the critics had left as well,
but for *Yorkshire Post* readers Robert Cockroft
described the scene:

The contemporary music festival ended last night in
a carnival atmosphere of joyous bedlam provoked
by one of the oddest works the Town Hall is ever
likely to experience. Richard Steinitz described his
decision to mount Berio's *Accordo* as 'one of my
more scatter-brained notions.' It turned out, in fact,
to be one of his richest inspirations in a festival that
has by no means been short of them... Promenaders
promenaded, jugglers juggled, clowns cycled among
the audience, stilt-walkers stilt-walked and the legion
of enthusiastic young players set about creating
mayhem as the chief conductor (there were four)
began the work by firing a starting pistol. To describe
Accordo in conventional terms is to catch an elephant
in a butterfly net. The volume was indescribable, the
confusion complete (but brilliantly co-ordinated)...
Did I enjoy it? Yes, I did. It was one of the zaniest,
sparkiest events I can recall in years, spontaneous,
warm, full of enthusiasm, fun and colour and
precisely the way to end what has been a splendid
festival.[5]

Another little-known work by Berio was
his *Duetti* for violinists of varying ability.
I requested a score, liked the pieces, and to give
their UK premiere invited students from the
polytechnic and Bretton Hall College, young

violinists in Kirklees and pupils from Chetham's
School of Music in Manchester. To make up a
programme, the local Beaumont Park String
Orchestra (consisting of primary-age children)
played Bartók's *Romanian Dances,* and
Chetham's String Orchestra performed Tippett's
Concerto for Double String Orchestra. Wanting
a finale to involve everybody, I decided to write
one myself; and, for no reason that I can recall,
decided that it would be entirely in canon and
sent the brochure to press saying so, having
scarcely composed a note. Come the autumn
I had to work fast, and wrote multiply
superimposed canons of varying difficulty,
partly synchronised, partly not – knowing
that the youngest players would be some
distance from the centre. Structurally I thought
Canons for Strings poorly stitched together.
But I was otherwise happy with the result –
even more so in 2004, when Malcolm Layfield
with the Goldberg Ensemble and groups of
young players, revived it in four workshop-
performances with different groups of
youngsters, held in four different cities.
With one exception, the 1985 festival was
the last to include any of my music. Life had
become too full. Beside so much great music,
my own felt deficient. But I had achieved some
success, winning scond prize in the BBC Young
Composers' competition of 1968 and receiving
a number of broadcasts. Not to compose was
a deprivation. Sometimes, whilst sitting in
a concert, unimpressed by what I was hearing,
my inner ear would take over and begin to
compose something more satisfying.

Spreading wings

The festivals of 1984 and 1985 had been
noticeably more varied. The programmes
encompassed mixed media, electronic music,
music theatre and jazz; and to existing venues
were added Huddersfield Art Gallery, the Afro-
Caribbean Hudawi Centre, the George Hotel
ballroom, Huddersfield Technical College and
the polytechnic drama studio.

Overlapping the main programme in 1984 was
a parallel programme entitled 'PEOPLE AND
PARTICIPATION'. Its highlights were four
days of electronic and video workshops in the
Hudawi Centre and a 'Kirklees Schools Concert
of Music Theatre' in Huddersfield Town Hall.
The latter drew the largest festival audience so
far (see page 212). As well as the music of Berio,

Ken Gray's Man in
static – Mind in transit.

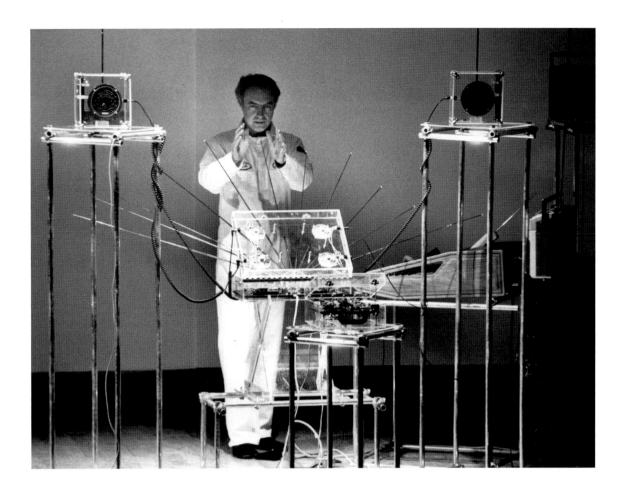

the 1985 festival contained co-promotions with Youth and Music, Live Music Now and the SPNM (a brass composition workshop), and compositions by department of music undergraduates performed by their peers. Among the talks and discussions was a 'Disputation' suggested by Douglas Young, in which he advanced the proposition that 'IRCAM is a total irrelevance'. I persuaded

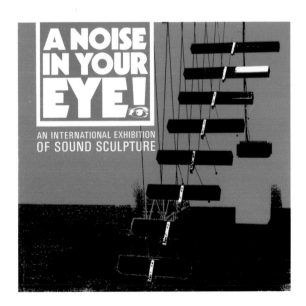

Jonathan Harvey to contest this, which he did with disarming logic, while Douglas's scathing dismissal incited members of the audience to heated interventions. Afterwards, tension was diffused by a late-night confection commissioned from the touring theatre company TNT, with music by John Kenny.

Most remarkable was the exhibition, *A Noise in your Eye,* which filled Huddersfield Art Gallery and included exhibits spectators could play. This was the first ever comprehensive exhibition in Britain of international sound-producing sculptures and acoustic installations, and had been assembled, after three years of planning, for the Arnolfini Gallery in Bristol by Jolyon Laycock. Occupying all five rooms of Huddersfield Art Gallery were the creations of fifteen artists and sculptors, including five from Great Britain. They included Hugh Davies, Max Eastley and Peter Appleton from the UK, Alvin Lucier from the USA, the Baschet brothers from Paris, electronic installation-sculptures by an Alaskan named Ken Gray, the Sonde group from Montreal, and a series of copper, bronze and wooden instruments made by the German sculptor Paul Fuchs. Parties of delighted children visited daily, including some with disabilities. To link the sculptures and concerts, musicians performed in the galleries, and the Appleton and Fuchs sculptures were taken to St Paul's where their creators 'played' them in concert. On the last afternoon, Ken Gray presented his experimental show, 'The Final Catastrophe', in the Great Hall. One piece involved shooting at balloons, causing them to drop pellets onto a set of timpani (after which reparations had to be made to our percussion department). Others implanted everyday objects with electronics. Over this intriguing array Ken Gray presided like a conjuror (see the picture on the preceding page).

The 1985 festival lasted nine days spread across one central weekend. Visitors were now arriving from the continent of Europe, including Scandinavia, and a few from Asia. We were reversing hostile attitudes to new music and attracting local music-lovers. I wrote in the brochure of a festival 'packed with variety yet coherent and purposeful, adventurous yet acceptable, internationally representative yet non-partisan, performed to the highest possible standards yet also inviting the participation of ordinary people, young and amateur musicians.'

The critics continued to write encouragingly. In *The Guardian* Gerald Larner remarked that the difference between Huddersfield and other festivals of contemporary music 'is that Huddersfield attracts an audience'. The presence of Berio, he noted, 'not only filled St Paul's but swamped it... left scarcely a seat in the polytechnic lecture theatre... and crowded the town hall'.[6] Max Loppert's eulogy in the *Financial Times* must have pleased civic officials:

From small, brave beginnings the venture has grown in size, scope and reputation... The 'themes'...are clear and cogent. So is the variety of happenings – musical, verbal, visual, theatrical – collected to embody them. Huddersfield, that handsome, dignified city [sic] of wide vistas and enjoyable walks, is a good festival location. It provides places to meet, listen, talk, eat, and drink; at all events I attended this weekend, the halls were full.[7]

Nor did the polytechnic go unnoticed. Stephen Reeve in *Classical Music* applauded its 'remarkable financial and artistic participation', noting that the role played by the polytechnic in a major festival was unequalled by any other British educational institution.

Sound sculptures by Paul Fuchs.

Cultivating the garden: 1986 to 1989

In 1979 Margaret Thatcher became Conservative prime minister. By the mid-1980s the powers of local government had been much constrained, and the imminent abolition of the metropolitan county councils proclaimed. West Yorkshire MCC had been second only to Yorkshire Arts in its financial support for the festival. But, as we contemplated its demise, from the Arts Council of Great Britain came an unexpected announcement. In a policy document named *The Glory of the Garden,* secretary general Luke Rittner proposed a major devolution of resources. Whether this would help the festival remained unclear and, in an introduction to the 1985 programme book, I voiced anxiety. If unnecessarily alarmist it did no harm, and some national critics rallied to the cause.

In 1986 West Yorkshire's support for arts and community organisations was transferred to a consortium of five urban councils, and the festival grant dropped by half. But the loss was made up threefold by the Arts Council. Around the same time the festival won support for specific projects from the Goethe Institut, Kirklees Council and several charitable trusts. Turnover increased from £46,000 in 1985 to £87,000 in 1986, a rise of almost 90% and beyond all expectation. I decided to use none of it for the administration, although there was good cause to do so. Instead, £3,000 more was spent on marketing, £5,000 more on the increasingly complex technical operation, and the artistic budget almost doubled from £32,000 in 1985 to £60,000 in 1986. Expenditure on artists was now 69% of turnover – and in 1987 even reached 81% – higher probably than in any other major festival. It was the quality of artistic content that brought the public to Huddersfield, and I was convinced that, to remain credible, all other costs had to be minimised. The larger artistic budget made it possible to engage the London Sinfonietta for the first time independently, invite the Northern Sinfonia, and secure the UK debut of Ensemble Modern in three concerts conducted by Heinz Holliger.

The 1986 festival contained twenty-eight concerts, plus a performance by the Natural Theatre Company. There were thirty-four UK premieres and five world premieres, including John Casken's *Salamandra* for two pianos commissioned by the festival. Seventeen other new pieces were aired in six workshops, two of them part of the Young Composers' Competition, and four organised by the Society for the Promotion of New Music. Twenty-three young composers (and others) received bursaries, among them several who would become prominent: Philip Cashian, Michael Zev Gordon, David Horne, Andrew Toovey and Param Vir. A seventh workshop showcased compositions by secondary school pupils at the end of a project involving 120 pupils in eight Kirklees schools. Preparatory work and final sessions for all of these were guided by Simon Bainbridge, John Casken, York Höller and Nigel Osborne, with instrumentalists from the London Sinfonietta and Music Projects/ London, the Lindsay String Quartet, and the clarinet and piano duo of Nicholas Cox and Vanessa Latarche.

In Huddersfield Art Gallery the American cellist Frances-Marie Uitti performed a *Moveable Feast: Gallery tour with solo cello,* pausing to improvise in response to individual works of art. There were two exhibitions. One featured paintings by Colin Rose, a supporter of the festival for most of its history, whose work at that time explored analogous techniques in the music of certain contemporary composers: notably Aldo Clementi, who in 1995 composed a tribute in return, called *For Colin Rose.* The second was a display of graphic notation called *Eye Music,* toured by the Arts Council, which included pages of Cornelius Cardew's iconic *Treatise.* To complement the

exhibition a complete performance of *Treatise* was given by AMM (Eddie Provost, Keith Rowe, Rohan de Saram and John Tilbury), whilst a video about Cardew repeated daily.[8]

There were workshops in improvisation, and a dance and music project in which composers, instrumentalists, dancers and choreographers were invited to participate. Dance featured in two concerts, including a fusion of poetry, painting and dance with music by Steve Lacy, toured by the Network and called *Futurities.* In the Great Hall Mathias Knauer showed his thought-provoking documentary based on Klaus Huber's oratorio *Erniedrigt-Geknechtet-Verlassen-Verachtet (Humbled-Enslaved-Forsaken-Despised),* in which material shot in Nicaragua is interspersed with footage of its Donaueschingen premiere. Knauer had brought with him what was then a pioneering new system to synchronise digital sound with film. The final day culminated in a concert by the BBC Symphony Orchestra conducted by Lutosławski.

But it was the Ensemble Modern and the music of Helmut Lachenmann that provided the intellectual core, in three ensemble concerts, interspersed with chamber performances by the Berne String Quartet, the Holligers and others. The presence of Lachenmann highlighted aesthetic issues that previous festival's had scarcely addressed. Then little known in Britain, Lachenmann's music made a deep impression, hoisting a flag for his work which the festival has flown ever since. Holliger, Höller, Lachenmann, Lutosławski and Osborne engaged in interviews and debate, and Holliger gave a masterclass for young musicians specialising in new repertoire. The whole festival had been a shared voyage of exploration, in which one felt that almost everyone, audience as well as performers, had actively taken part.

The next four festivals continued the trajectory. Berio, who had visited in 1985, and Gubaidulina, Lachenmann and Lutosławski in 1986, were followed by Adams, Ferneyhough and Xenakis in 1987, Andriessen and Stockhausen in 1988, and Boulez, Messiaen and Cage in 1989. Many aspects of these memorable years are covered in the next four chapters, as we consider the orchestras and ensembles that performed and the festival's relationship with major composers. But Huddersfield was not only a platform for big

*Tristan Murail and
Françoise Pellié.*
PHOTO: SELWYN GREEN

names. There were new discoveries, like the Russian recluse, Galina Ustvolskaya, the Polish composer Hanna Kulenty, the Lithuanians and Romanians. There were many smaller events, like Tristan Murail's engagingly instructive lecture-recital on the ondes martenot, ending with a *pas de deux* in which Murial and his wife performed duets for two ondes martenots. Participating regularly as players, and as a lively and (mainly) enthusiastic core audience, were a large number of department undergraduates. Among them, in the late 1980s and early '90s, were several who would have successful careers as composers: Richard Ayres, Joe Cutler, Fraser Trainer, James Saunders and Wayne (now Ty) Unwin, to name but five. Most moved on elsewhere, although James, after studying at the Royal Northern College of Music with Anthony Gilbert, returned to Huddersfied to pursue a PhD, and later joined the full-time composition staff.

Along with my colleagues, I was impressed by what they achieved; but I will cite just one example which gave me pleasure. In his third year as an undergraduate, Fraser Trainer had responded to my suggestion that two of his final compositions might usefully contrast rigorous technical discipline in one piece, sensuous expressionism in the other – a strategy which

we agreed could broaden his palette. Fraser impressively rose to the challenge; and in the November 1989 festival, his strikingly rigorous, yet dramatic *Three Studies for Oboe and Piano* were performed by John Stringer and Fraser himself, in a concert of music by recent graduates that included Richard Ayres's *The Time and Surface Question* for a quartet of two violins, piano and baritone voice led by Alexander Balanescu. Fraser's contrasting and richly expressionist settings of Georg Trakl,

*Kaija Saariaho at
the 1988 festival.*
PHOTO: SELWYN GREEN

Kate Wright and Anne Suggate with the festival's tenth birthday cake.
PHOTO: SELWYN GREEN

scored for the unusual combined sonority of cellos and saxophones, plus voice and percussion, also merited performance. So *Siebengesang des Todes* was heard in a festival concert given by the Polytechnic Twentieth Century Ensemble, superbly sung by another former student, Carol Smith. The concert commenced with a punning series of light-hearted miniatures called *Cereal Music* by another recent graduate, Jim Pywell.

The festival's tenth anniversary in 1988 saw an increased emphasis on multi-dimensional events. A semi-staged performance of Stockhausen's *Michaels Reise (Michael's Journey)* took place under the composer's direction in the town hall. His *Sternklang (Star Sound)* had its UK premiere in Huddersfield Sports Centre, turned into an 'indoor park' to emulate its original outdoor ambience. On the piazza, late one evening in falling snow, Bow Gamelan beat an improbable array of industrial junk instruments, their improvisations interspersed with pyrotechnic explosions. A few evenings later, under a starlit sky, groups of children, assisted by a local community arts group called the Satellites, created an Oriental Lantern Festival beside Huddersfield's Narrow Canal, with music

Margaret Leng Tan performing Cage's piano music in 1989.
PHOTO: SELWYN GREEN

played by a community gamelan. To counter the freezing temperature, hot food was served to all. The following year, again in the piazza but on a warm Saturday afternoon, the Natural Theatre Company constructed an interactive steam sculpture which blew chirpy notes and chords at curious shoppers to cheer them on their way (see the photo on pages 206–7). In the town hall a promenading audience surrendered to the Joycean plurality of Cage's *Roaratorio*, and in the polytechnic drama department, *Enumerations,* Georges Aperghis's beguiling litany of onomatopoeic sounds, actions, lists and objects was performed by his Atelier Théâtre et Musique. All these events are described in more detail later in the book.

4 Orchestras

Constraints of a Victorian concert hall

As orchestral concerts became an annual feature, there was a recurrent debate about what the stage could accommodate. Huddersfield Town Hall had been designed for nineteenth-century orchestras and large amateur choirs. Its semi-circular stage is small, the tiered platforms behind narrow and steep. It had become usual to add a front extension for orchestral concerts, but that did not cater for the large number of percussion instruments in many contemporary scores. The first visit of the BBC Symphony Orchestra (see Chapter 3) had been technically a studio recording, in which the orchestra occupied the 'area' – normally used to seat the public – and an invited audience was confined to the balcony. Years before, I had witnessed Sir Malcolm Sargent conducting Huddersfield Choral Society and the Royal Liverpool Philharmonic Orchestra in a performance of *Belshazzar's Feast*, without any stage extension. Somehow the orchestra had coped, but such cramped conditions were no longer tolerable; and, for the BBC Symphony Orchestra, nor were the narrow tiers.

By 1986 the festival audience had grown, and for self-promoted as well as shared orchestral concerts we needed all available audience seats. The visit of the BBCSO that year, with Lutosławski conducting, was preceded by a tussle with its management about where the orchestra would sit. I argued that it had to play on stage, and promised a larger-than-usual extension and temporary structures over the tiers to halve their number and double their width. Even this was inadequate for the keyed percussion, whose huge dimensions I had been shown by the percussionist Jimmy Holland before a promenade concert in London's Albert

Hall. (The xylophone I had observed in *Belshazzar's Feast* had been a mere toy!) At a site meeting in Huddersfield we agreed the measurements of a temporary structure, and on the morning of the concert I went to inspect it. It was disconcertingly ugly, with raised platforms more like a fortress than a performance space. Arriving for the rehearsal, the orchestra were unimpressed and spent an hour re-arranging themselves. The rehearsal began late, the players disgruntled and uncooperative. Listening in the auditorium, John Casken witnessed their discourteous treatment of Lutosławski with mounting anger, and wrote afterwards to the BBC to complain. The programme contained Lutosławski's Concerto for Orchestra, Double Concerto and Third Symphony, whose rehearsal the composer struggled to complete. But the performances were surprisingly efficient, even exciting, although the critics detected cracks. Re-reading the reviews, I am reminded that Lutosławski had not wanted to conduct two such substantial works as the Concerto for Orchestra and Third Symphony in one concert. I had twisted his arm: 'certainly a miscalculation' according to Robert Cockroft.[1] Gerald Larner, however, was fascinated by the connections between works composed thirty years apart, and happy that 'the festival director got his way', although not unaware of the effort involved:

Like so much else in the Huddersfield Contemporary Music Festival – where the standard of performance has been consistently on the highest level – it was a brilliantly executed concert. Heinz and Ursula Holliger played most imaginatively on the ambiguities and evasions of the Double Concerto. The BBCSO, under the direction of the composer to whom it warmed only gradually, offered some extraordinarily clear and fine detail and eventually found itself so convinced as to surprise itself as much as the audience.[2]

Peter Maxwell Davies at a BBC Symphony Orchestra rehearsal in Huddersfield Town Hall.
PHOTO: KEITH GLOSSOP

Twenty-two years later, in January 2008, the live performance in Huddersfield of Lutosławski's Concerto for Orchestra was issued as a free cover CD with *BBC Music Magazine*.[3]

It was inevitable that, for the orchestra's fourth visit in 1987, the BBC insisted on using the area again. But it remained an awkward compromise and, sensing the players' disdain for the Huddersfield engagement, I thought it was time for a change. The festival's tenth birthday in 1988 boasted two professional orchestras: an opening concert by the BBC Philharmonic co-promoted with Kirklees, and a 'festival finale' performed by the orchestra of Opera North (then called English Northern Philharmonia). Both were familiar with the town hall, and working with them was easy. The following year, however, an opportunity arose, which I had long sought, for Pierre Boulez to conduct the BBC Symphony Orchestra. Discussing the prospect with Aiden Plender (the new Kirklees Music Officer), we agreed to co-promote again, although to accommodate the Kirklees subscribers the orchestra would have to play on the stage. The management accepted this, but it meant that there would be little room for percussion, still less for the quadruple winds in the early Stravinsky ballet which Boulez was scheduled to conduct in London. At Boulez's suggestion, we agreed that the Huddersfield concert would end with Stravinsky's classically-scored *Song of the Nightingale* – a relatively bland substitute. But it would also include Boulez's *Éclat/Multiples* and *Messagesquisse*,

Pierre Boulez rehearsing in the town hall.
PHOTO: SELWYN GREEN

and Messiaen's most recent composition, *La Ville d'en haut*, with the composer's wife, Yvonne Loriod, as soloist. The performance brought Messiaen himself to the festival, and the presence of Cage as well as Boulez led to a historic reunion.

A setback had emerged during the negotiations, when John Drummond – the new BBC controller of music – revoked Ponsonby's financial agreement, citing objections from the commercial orchestras. With the invitation format dead, the public paid for their tickets; but the income did little to defray the enormous cost of transporting a large orchestra 200 miles out of London, as well as the hire fee. It was an expense we could no longer sustain.

Olivier Messiaen acknowledges applause.
PHOTO: SELWYN GREEN

There now developed a close partnership with English Northern Philharmonia based in Leeds, complemented by performances from the BBC Philharmonic in Manchester and the BBC Scottish in Glasgow. None of London's four independent symphony orchestras has performed at the festival – their scale of operation being habitually too expensive – except for one occasion when the Royal Philharmonic Orchestra repeated an all-Maxwell Davies programme one day after playing it in London. In 2005 the Philharmonia's new music ensemble performed a late afternoon concert of Toshio Hosokawa's music, following the pattern of its Music of Today series in London, but it required only around a dozen players. One year later Graham McKenzie engaged the City of London Sinfonia to perform at a similar time, so that the orchestra could return to London the same evening. The arrangement saved overnight expenses; but, scheduled in the town hall at an unusual time of day and without separate marketing, audience numbers were small.

In 1992 Nicholas Kenyon succeeded John Drummond, and Martin Cotton became producer of the Symphony Orchestra. I revived my argument that, in so far as the BBC's purpose was to perform music commercial orchestras were unlikely to attempt, the festival offered an ideal context. Martin promised to advocate the orchestra's re-engagement, and early in 1994 Nicholas agreed to support an extended presentation of Luigi Nono's late works with electronics – a hugely important part of his *oeuvre* not previously performed in Britain. It transpired that neither the BBCSO nor the BBC Philharmonic had sufficient available dates, so the role fell to English Northern Philharmonia. Nonetheless, Nicholas accepted the idea of sharing the project and committed a welcome £25,000. All the Nono concerts were broadcast on Radio 3, and the wider exposure raised their profile.

With any orchestra it is usually necessary to negotiate three or four years ahead. Even then diaries may be full. To find a window in the City of Birmingham Symphony Orchestra's schedule was constantly frustrating, but it happened twice – although without Sir Simon Rattle. The festival's lead-in time was short, influenced by the emerging plans of other partners and by a necessary opportunism: seizing, for instance, the chance to premiere

a work which a year before had not existed. The BBCSO played once more at the festival in 2000, when I believed that only it could do justice to the music of Lachenmann and Rihm. Happily the atmosphere was far more positive, and with Jac van Steen conducting, and a concertmaster, Stephen Bryant, already familiar with Lachenmann's music, the orchestra gave committed and thrilling performances.

The Kirklees subscription series

The arrival of Aiden Plender in 1986 brought new energy to the civic authority's music provision. Having been education officer for the CBSO, Aiden was keen to develop audiences, repertoire and educational projects. Influenced by the festival, he programmed contemporary work throughout the year, both in the orchestral season and a new chamber music series in St Paul's. The latter included a commission from David Sawer, and a project in which primary school children joined the Alberni String Quartet to perform Nigel Osborne's *Lumiere*. At Aiden's suggestion, we introduced a scheme to give music students ultra-cheap admission to the complete orchestral series, allowing them to sit (when available) on the tiers behind the players. I christened the scheme 'A View from the Flight Deck'; the response was gratifying, and every concert was enlivened by a sea of youthful faces.

In 1988 there began an annual co-promotion between Kirklees and the festival which continued for eight years. Besides the BBC Symphony Orchestra concert conducted by Boulez, there were the BBC Philharmonic conducted by Berio, the CBSO with Oliver Knussen, RPO with Maxwell Davies and four concerts given by English Northern Philharmonia. In the Kirklees subscription series, Aiden programmed Gubaidulina's *Offertorium* (which I had failed to achieve) played by Gidon Kremer and the BBC Philharmonic, joined after the interval by Huddersfield Choral Society for Prokofiev's *Alexander Nevsky*. Ten years later, after Aiden's departure, such enterprising programmes disappeared – and, more distressingly, the young audience.

I would dearly like to have offered festivalgoers the CBSO with Sir Simon Rattle, whose musicianship, charisma and commitment to living composers was so persuasive. Simon admired what the festival was doing, but the dates could not be made to work. The nearest we got was a declaration of intent during a conversation in his dressing room after a concert in Leeds, and a brief discussion of possibilities whilst my son, Adam (aged thirteen), who had listened attentively through a long Bruckner symphony, shared his packet of crisps with the maestro.

Through these co-promotions the festival enrolled some of its most dedicated local supporters. Costs were shared – unevenly (to the festival's advantage) – and the collaboration ensured large audiences. Aiden and I regularly discussed our plans, although I devised the joint programmes. Knowing that, for Kirklees subscribers, this might be their only encounter with the festival, I looked for music with an immediacy of impact, and predominantly by major composers. Predictably, some subscribers stayed at home, leaving empty seats in prime positions which in due course we resold. Others were motivated to try further concerts in the festival. I fear that I sometimes strained their forbearance, and when, in 1996, the subscribers were faced with a programme of Reich, Finnissy, Turnage and Henze, Aiden's successor, Rod Birtles, reported that half of them stayed away. On other occasions the enthusiastic applause for such celebrities as Messiaen and Górecki created a *frisson* few could resist.

In 1997 I pushed the boat out even further, with an improbable combination of music by Ives, Lou Harrison, Grisey and Xenakis (see pages 45–47). The ticket statistics recorded an audience of 948 (91% capacity) suggesting that, for subscribers who absented themselves, festivalgoers replaced them. There were a few complaints. But the subsequent withdrawal of Kirklees from further co-promotions had other explanations. Brian Pearson had retired as head of Cultural Services (as it had been renamed); Rod Birtles had moved to Milton Keynes and not been replaced; and, in a round of budget tightening, the council cut its funding support for the orchestral season by a massive two-thirds. The series was franchised to the Hallé Orchestra, which, in return for the ticket income and a fee of c. £25,000, agreed to provide minimal marketing and repeat basic repertoire from its Manchester concerts, requiring little or no re-rehearsal. Content and quality

plummeted, and audience numbers dropped. It was a dispiriting development in which the festival could play no part.

Ironically, we were about to mount our most accessible orchestral concert ever. In November 1998 the Estonian Philharmonic Chamber Choir, Tallinn Chamber Orchestra and Hilliard Ensemble were due to make a Contemporary Music Network tour with music by Arvo Pärt and Erkki-Sven Tüür. I suggested that Cultural Services include it in their season, but all they would agree was to inform subscribers. In the event, the concert sold out and made a sensational impact, with both composers present and rapturously applauded.[4] Meanwhile, to a dwindling audience whose average age had risen depressingly, the Hallé plodded on with its Beethoven and Dvorak, interspersed with safe classics like *The Lark Ascending* and Elgar's *Serenade*.

If I compromised too little, some of my programmes contained too much. My worst excess was a purely festival promotion in 1988 – although Kirklees subscribers were offered discounts. I had engaged English Northern Philharmonia to round off the festival's tenth anniversary, and, as it was also Messiaen's eightieth birthday, invited Jennifer Bate to play a selection of his organ music between the orchestra's two halves, and advertised the event as a 'Gala Concert'. Miss Bate evidently regarded my request for twenty-five minutes trifling: she had, after all, recorded the complete works of a composer not noted for concision. Reluctantly I agreed to five pieces, supposedly short, although a subsequent calculation indicated that they would last at least forty minutes. After the first interval, the audience trouped back, Miss Bate entered, turned on the Father Willis instrument, and began to play with that infinite spaciousness of tempo that Messiaen specially invites. Time dragged on. People yawned and fidgeted, whilst I sat numb with dismay, willing the ordeal to stop. Despite desultory applause there was the inevitable encore. When the orchestra returned after the second interval, two hours had passed and half the audience had left. So over-egged had been my publicity that a recently married gentleman in Holmfirth brought his wife for the treat, although neither had heard a live orchestral concert before. Afterwards Brian Pearson showed me his irate letter, accusing us of nearly destroying his marriage and vowing never to attend such an event again. Brian was characteristically uncensorious, but I wrote an emollient apology offering free tickets for any event in the following festival which I would gladly help him choose. There was no reply.

But there's no accounting for tastes. For several years, three elderly Yorkshire ladies sat in the front row at lunchtime concerts in St Paul's, beaming appreciatively, however fast, slow or 'difficult' the music. Where were they from, I asked? 'Holmfirth' they said, 'We come in the middle of the day so that we can catch the bus. We love it!'

On the penultimate evening of the 1988 festival, an audience in the town hall witnessed three UK premieres performed entirely by young musicians – except for the dancer-choreographer Beppie Blankert, who delivered the narrative in a thrilling performance by the Polytechnic Twentieth-Century Ensemble of Louis Andriessen's *De Stijl*. The concert began with Andriessen's *Symphonies of the Netherlands* played by Kirklees Youth Wind Orchestra,

Barrie Webb rehearsing Threnody *by R. Murray Schaffer in 1988.*
PHOTO: SELWYN GREEN

and ended with R. Murray Schafer's *Threnody*. In this poignant elegy, five children spoke the words of young victims of the Nagasaki atomic bomb, over music sensitively performed by the Polytechnic Symphony Orchestra and a youth choir assembled for the occasion. During its final section excerpts from political speeches are chillingly heard on tape proclaiming the bomb's 'success'. Scheduling this powerful concert on a Saturday evening sprang from my conviction that performances by young people can be as moving and meaningful as those given by professionals, and that they equally merit prime time and a paying audience. Students have more time to rehearse; abnormal instrumentations are more easily resourced; the playing has freshness and commitment. The involvement of both composers in the rehearsals had been demanding, but also inspiring.

I do not believe that participants in such large undertakings have their creativity constrained by serving another's vision, and disagree with those educationalists who assert that only through self-made work is creativity

LEFT:
*Louis Andriessen and
R. Murray Schafer assist
at the final rehearsal.*
PHOTOS: SELWYN GREEN

liberated. Bringing to life an existing work is what professionals do. Why not youngsters? In turning a concept into living sound they too can possess it, share in a collective endeavour, and emerge with imaginations enriched.

The Orchestra of Opera North

After its 1988 debut, English Northern Philharmonia played in every festival between 1990 and 1997. It had been constituted to perform concerts as well as in the pit – a welcome antidote to the repetitiveness of operatic schedules. The players enjoyed the challenge of the festival, and their energy and precision were admirable. In 1990 Gennadi Rozhdestvensky directed a powerfully theatrical all-Schnittke concert, ending with the UK premiere of his *Faust Cantata* sung by Huddersfield Choral Society and four soloists, including John Tomlinson (see page 126). Only on three occasions was Paul Daniel, Opera North's inspirational music director, free to conduct. He did so first in 1991, when Tippett's *Ritual Dances* and recent *Byzantium* framed two formidable scores by Birtwistle: *Endless Parade* and the UK premiere of *Gawain's Journey* – the latter a searing, complex piece (based on episodes in the opera *Gawain*) which Paul steered with devastating raw intensity. Both composers were present and had agreed to engage in a public discussion. It took place in the main polytechnic lecture hall, completely full, and I stood with others at the back. But Tippett was curiously on edge: alternately defensive, pugnacious and flippant. Despite Birtwistle's best efforts, there was no real engagement and I wished that I had chaired the discussion and could have coaxed out of them a serious dialogue. Others remember it as more rewarding.

In 1992 English Northern Philharmonia gave the world premiere of David Bedford's *Stories from the Dreamtime*, commissioned for hearing-

BELOW:
*Three paper collages, made
by Shinagakuen Asashi
gaoka High School in Japan
and presented to Howden
Clough High School in
Kirklees, with the inscription:
'No more Hiroshima. No
more Nagasaki'.*

Ligeti discussing the rehearsal with conductor Elgar Howarth (left) and Ian Ritchie, general manager of Opera North (right).
PHOTO: SELWYN GREEN

impaired youngsters to perform with orchestra by the Huddersfield-based organisation, Music and the Deaf. Participating were groups from schools for the deaf around the country, who arrived in Huddersfield for a residential weekend of final rehearsals, followed by the performance itself, in which their several percussion ensembles encircled the orchestra (see page 217). During the 1995 festival ENP performed twice: first conducted by Paul Daniel in music by Terry Riley, Dillon and Tippett (his final orchestral work *The Rose Lake*, premiered earlier that year); and, at the end of the festival, in music by Schoenberg and Nono. To date the orchestra has played eleven festival concerts – more than any other – most recently in 2002, by which time it had been renamed (as, indeed, it always was) the Orchestra of Opera North.

The orchestral manager, Ian Killick, could not have been more helpful. When I explained that the Nono required the whole string section to be equipped with second instruments abnormally strung and tuned, he was unperturbed. How we would borrow, preferably at no cost, some twenty-two violins, eight violas, six cellos and four double-basses, I had little idea. We decided to approach schools music services, starting in Kirklees, and were surprised to discover that it not only had sufficient instruments in store, but was willing to lend them. Ian undertook their acquisition and restringing as if it were routine. Adept at coping with constricted space, his staff nonetheless appreciated the scale drawings on which I mapped out the orchestral dispositions at other concerts I had attended in the town hall.

The UK premiere of Nono's *Caminantes… Ayacucho* needed bells which the composer had chosen from a foundry in Bavaria. My guide throughout two years of planning had been André Richard, director of the Heinrich Strobel Studio in Freiburg, who had worked with Nono in every performance of his music involving live electronics. André revealed that Nono's decisions in rehearsal had often diverged from the score; indeed, his knowledge of the performance history was crucial. I arranged transport of the bells, which duly arrived for the final rehearsal, by which time I had forgotten that their pitches differed from those notated. The discrepancy was not lost on the conductor, Arturo Tamayo, who immediately alerted Ian. Despite it being a Sunday, within minutes Ian had hired bells to replace them from the Royal Opera in London, and organised their despatch. They were already on the road when André looked up from the electronics console, realised there had been a misunderstanding and explained that the Bavarian bells were indeed those intended. The unused bells from Covent Garden cost an unscheduled £500, but I did not protest. Ian had acted speedily to solve an apparent crisis, and the incident was soon overtaken by the extraordinary impact of the performance. Had it occurred a few years later, mobile phones would have quickly resolved the confusion.

Less assured was the British premiere of Ligeti's Violin Concerto played by ENP in 1993 with Saschko Gawriloff as soloist. Ligeti had completed his final five-movement version earlier that year. But, although premiered in Germany, there was no recording and its intricate textures and non-tempered tunings were strange. Fortunately the conductor was Elgar Howarth, whom Ligeti admired and trusted, and if the performance was no more than presentable, it did not affect the composer's warm regard for the festival. When the Philharmonia played the concerto with Frank Peter Zimmermann in London four years later, he was angrily critical and refused to sanction a planned CD. Since then the work has become familiar, and is now the most widely played and admired of contemporary violin concertos.

In 1994 Hans Werner Henze made a second visit to the festival, and two orchestral concerts featured his music. On the final evening the London Sinfonietta performed his *Requiem,* composed in memory of Michael Vyner and

premiered at the BBC Proms in 1993. As with other major works by leading composers, this was its second UK performance. To repeat pieces for audiences who had not heard them performed live, I considered as important as commissioning, with the added advantage of already knowing their worth. The second concert, given by English Northern Philharmonia, opened with the world premiere of Roger Marsh's *Espace* and ended with a rare revival of Henze's extravagantly monumental *Tristan* for orchestra, pre-recorded tape and piano, with Martin Roscoe as soloist. This was notable for an additional drama, when a trumpeter fainted after a climatic high note – Tristan's 'scream of death' – and fell into the double bass section ten feet below. The audience watched anxiously as one of the bass players bent down to help, whilst Diego Masson and the orchestra continued to the end. The trumpeter was unhurt and, although I feared an explosion of health and safety directives, both he and the orchestra made light of the incident.

The BBC Philharmonic

Major European festivals like Musica in Strasbourg, Ars Musica in Brussels and the Warsaw Autumn commonly contain four or five symphony concerts, several of them given by radio orchestras which shoulder a proportion of the cost. Indeed, the world's oldest new music festival at Donaueschingen was reinstated after the Second World War in a formal association with South-West German Radio, which organises the event, funds commissions and broadcasts all concerts live, including at least two given by the SWR Symphony Orchestra.

Huddersfield's nearest radio orchestra is the BBC Philharmonic in Manchester, but my early proposal of a similar association was firmly rejected. In Britain the relationship between independent orchestras and those funded by the licence fee can be sensitive. Under its manager Brian Pidgeon, the Philharmonic's operation came closer than any other BBC orchestra to the commercial sector, and any perceived undercutting would have been resented. Huddersfield, therefore, with its relatively modest budget, has rarely presented more than two full orchestral concerts in any festival, and in recent years there have been none. Prior to that, the BBC Philharmonic (and its predecessor the BBC Northern) gave a total of seven festival concerts, and had its schedule not been so full there might have been more.

The early concerts were relatively straightforward. But later we encountered problems, although they were never the fault of the orchestra and only once seriously evident to the public. This happened in 1992, when an opportunity arose for Berio to conduct, and we agreed (via his agent) to the pairing of *Ofanim* and his celebrated *Sinfonia*. The latter had been composed in 1968/9 for the New York Philharmonic, Swingle Singers and Leonard Bernstein, but *Ofanim* was more recent. I had been present at its only UK performance in 1990 and greatly attracted to Berio's marriage of the Arab-Bedouin singing of Esti Kenan-Ofri with a children's choir, two antiphonal instrumental ensembles, and trajectories of sound spatialisation transforming and transporting the sounds across and around the audience. To achieve this required the participation of Tempo Reale, the 'real-time' electronic studio set up by Berio in Florence five years earlier. The studio agreed to be involved, but was difficult to pin down. Then, near the end of August after going to press, I learnt of a crisis in Tempo Reale's funding, leaving it with too few staff to deliver the project – even, it seemed, to answer phone calls and faxes. It was later rumoured to have been more of a disagreement between Berio and his staff, but the funding crisis was real enough by 1994, when the Berlusconi government withdrew Tempo Reale's state support. Offering more money might have helped, but the festival had no contingency. We had used it up after Black Wednesday, when Britain was forced out of the European Exchange Rate Mechanism and contracts with European artists suddenly became more expensive. Much disappointed, I agreed to replace *Ofanim* with *Sequenza III*, *Calmo* and another performance of *Folk Songs*.

In Huddersfield the maestro was in a difficult mood. The first half of the concert went well enough, but *Sinfonia* verged on disaster. At the rehearsal, Berio had complained that he could not hear the amplified voices of Electric Phoenix, and insisted that both they and the loudspeakers were moved from front stage to behind the orchestra. The clarity of the text (taken from Lévi-Strauss and Beckett) is always an issue in any live performance of *Sinfonia*. In a complex interaction between words and music, the text is often fragmented and subsumed into the orchestra. Sometimes it is completely submerged, at other times audible, and at key moments it should be crystal clear. Sung it constitutes harmony, texture, timbre and resonance. But the solo male speaker who becomes increasingly prominent in the third movement – reiterating from Becket's *The Unnamable* such phrases as: 'where now?' and 'keep going', and reciting: 'Yes, I feel the moment has come for us to look back, if we can, and take our bearings, if we are to go on', etc – must be clearly heard. To appreciate this richness, I knew that for the audience Berio's decision was unwise. Had I been present at the rehearsal, I would have tried to dissuade him, but there was another event to attend. During the concert, at the end of the first movement, with characteristic Yorkshire directness, a member of the audience called out: 'We can't hear the words'. Berio turned round and a confused dialogue began between conductor and public. Horrified, I froze to my seat until, with speedy presence of mind, Terry Edwards (director of Electric Phoenix) jumped to his feet and assured Berio that everything was fine. But it wasn't. The performance resumed, and I strained to hear the subtleties, associations and humour in Berio's disposition of the text, distressed to think how inadequate an impression listeners would take away.

This was another consequence of the cramped town hall stage. A different challenge arose in 1993, when the BBC Philharmonic and Huddersfield Choral Society performed music by Henryk Górecki. There was no amplification this time; but, besides the large chorus, the orchestra numbered nearly a hundred. I could hardly believe that the uni-dimensional *Beatus Vir* needed thirty violins, twelve violas, ten cellos and eight double-basses to double two or three real parts; but my suggestion of reducing them was rejected. As *Beatus Vir* is also scored for quadruple winds, including four tubas (likewise doubling), no doubt a balanced sonority has to be achieved. The problem was solved by erecting the largest ever stage extension and having the chorus spill over into the balcony. In performance the multiple doublings sounded sonorously magnificent, and the audience were hugely enthusiastic – even some of the sceptics.[5] At the end of a programme that began with Lutosławski and included Górecki's *Concerto-Cantata* for flute and orchestra (like *Beatus Vir* receiving its UK premiere), the composer stood to acknowledge prolonged applause. I would dearly have liked to include *Scontri* – an example of the fiery modernism Górecki had long abandoned – but its abnormal layout and even larger orchestra put it beyond consideration.

The critics found much tedium to bemoan in the Górecki and, up to a point, I agreed with them. However, this undoubtedly successful event demonstrated to a largely local audience that the festival was not to be feared, and with the agreeable addition of the Lawrence Batley Theatre to attract them the following year, there was a significant increase in its local following.

For a BBC Philharmonic concert in 1997 I devised a programme of widely dissimilar pieces, for the simple reason that I wanted to include them all. During his first visit to Huddersfield, Xenakis had given me a recording of *Cendrées* – an extraordinary work for orchestra and chorus requiring a unique manner of singing. At the time, to perform it could only be a dream. But fifteen years later, with turnover eighteen times greater,[6] and the New London Chamber Choir's established expertise in Xenakis, it seemed possible. So did Grisey's 'spectral' masterpiece *Modulations*, which we had been unable to perform in 1992 (see page 130). To precede this esoteric pairing with Lou Harrison's folksy piano concerto may have been foolish. But Lou had just turned eighty, several of his works were scheduled, and I thought (too optimistically) that he would be present. To lovers of Lou Harrison's music, the concerto's rumbustious audacity is uplifting; to others it is brash and bland, despite the orchestra having to retune to the composer's 'favourite temperament', Kirnberger's no 2. To prepare the ground, I decided to begin the concert with a rarely heard masterpiece by Charles Ives, the elaborately polyrhythmic and polytonal *Second Orchestral Set* of c. 1919 – one of his most visionary creations. Its final movement, which recalls the impromptu singing of *In the Sweet By and By* by rush-hour crowds in New York after the sinking of the *Lusitania,* is unforgettably moving.

The conductor, an American called Charles Zacharie Bornstein, had been proposed by Xenakis and was familiar with the Ives.

Nevertheless, he became increasingly alarmed at the task. The prefatory weeks were burdened with long faxes and even longer late-night phone calls in which Charles aired his anxieties, not least about the performing material of the Ives which, he said, was riddled with errors. At one point he confided that he did not understand Grisey's *Modulations,* but would beat time anyway. I feared that the rehearsals would be difficult and, as marriage-broker with the orchestra, felt guilty. But the players behaved with exemplary professionalism, and the principal cellist, Peter Dixon, nobly acted as go-between and confidant.

In the event, the performances were impressive and Joanna MacGregor executed the romping clusters of Lou Harrison's concerto with exhilarating energy. I had not foreseen that the concerto would be so upstaged by the impact of the Ives, and was sorry to hear it derided by some festival regulars. They were predictably receptive to *Modulations,* however.

Huddersfield Choral Society, David Wilson-Johnson and the BBC Philharmonic give the UK premiere of Beatus Vir *by Górecki.*
PHOTO: SELWYN GREEN

*Górecki
acknowledges applause.*
PHOTO: *SELWYN GREEN*

As for *Cendrées*, the performance was as volcanic and elemental as I had imagined, its strange ululations superbly delivered by the New London Chamber Choir. In my terms, *Cendrées* was a triumph. But the programme was tough for some Kirklees subscribers; and, in an unusually disparate festival, I realised that I had stretched my notions of co-existence rather far.

This was the BBC Philharmonic's last major concert at the festival. In 2002 the orchestra gave an open rehearsal and premiered five compositions by postgraduates. There were also concerts that year by the BBC Scottish Symphony Orchestra and the Orchestra of Opera North, making 2002 the only festival in which three professional symphony orchestras have appeared. (A poster for the 1986 festival promised 'six orchestras'; but, as these included the Ensemble Modern, Northern Sinfonia and London Sinfonietta, and only one of the orchestras was professional, this was stretching a point.)

Why, then, have there been no professional symphony orchestra concerts since 2002? The reasons are partly financial, but also due to a change in emphasis. Already, in the mid-1990s programming the new Lawrence Batley Theatre

absorbed funds and attention, whilst developing international relationships increased the role of imported work. Opportunities like sharing with the Barbican the only UK appearance of Harry Partch's unique sculpted instruments, or securing the only UK performance of Heiner Goebbels's *Hashirigaki* – both in the theatre – were prizes indeed. In the town hall, during the late 1990s, I aimed to attract a wider public than the habitual orchestral audience. In 2006 Graham McKenzie engaged the Northern Sinfonia, City of London Sinfonia and Barry Guy's New Orchestra – each numbering between twenty and forty players. But the long tradition of symphony concerts in regional cities was ailing. A genre which had been at the heart of cultural life when I first arrived in Huddersfield had lost its relevance. In recent festivals no orchestras have appeared at all, save one – the emphatically non-symphonic Vienna Vegetable Orchestra.

Other orchestras…

That the Hallé Orchestra, based in Manchester, has never played in the festival seems a strange omission, particularly as it appeared frequently in the Kirklees subscription series, and was for a few years franchised to promote them. Musical standards were declining, however; and by the mid 1990s, after a period of poor financial management, the orchestra was close to bankruptcy. During Kent Nagano's tenure as conductor, programmes and standards improved, if not the financial position; and, during the first half of 1999, towards the end of his contract, I spent five months trying to secure a concert with Kent conducting. Enthusiastically we discussed and exchanged scores, only to be brought up by inadequate rehearsal time. Struggling to build a programme around the UK premiere of Louis Andriessen's *Mausoleum,* we eventually settled on George Benjamin's *Sometime Voices* (which Kent was keen to perform) and Lutosławski's Concerto for Orchestra, because it was 'repertoire', despite the fact that it would be its third festival performance. Although the programme required vocal soloists and chorus, I thought the quotation of £33,150 too high, and I asked the acting concerts manager, Stuart Robinson, to seek economies.

A month later Stuart sent an explanatory breakdown. It revealed that his estimate included £5,000 to reimburse the Hallé Concerts Society for a pick-up band to play a contracted *Messiah,* thereby releasing players to rehearse for Huddersfield. Then he told me that they could not include Lutosławski. Would I accept *Till Eulenspiegel,* which was scheduled for Manchester shortly before and would need no further rehearsal? I was considering this when I was presented with the *coup de grâce.* Stuart had received a message from the Musicians' Union, informing him 'that the 25th December was not Christmas Day!' (because it fell on a Saturday) and it was 'now financially imperative' for the dates planned for Huddersfield to be 'free days'. He was 'very, very sorry to have to say that even if we could reach agreement over the soloists and the covering of the additional *Messiah* costs, we cannot now proceed anyway'.

I half understood the reasoning, which was to do with bank holidays and the entitlement to free days in the players' contracts. But to discover so late was infuriating. In February 2000, following the arrival of John Summers as chief executive, and Mark Elder as principal conductor, I wrote to ask if Mark and the orchestra could appear in November 2001.

The letter expressed a wider concern. A questionnaire given to our latest intake of first year music students revealed that 17% had never attended a professional orchestral concert in their lives. The programme content of the Hallé's Kirklees series had become mummified and moribund – the average age of the music performed being around 150 years old! How could this excite youngsters in the twenty-first century? I urged the Hallé to include in the series, if not contemporary, at least more twentieth-century repertoire, and proposed a reinstatement of the 'Flight Deck' access scheme that had been so successful ten years before. Nothing came of this. A year later I retired from the festival, and Susanna Eastburn reopened discussion with a view to engaging the orchestra for 2003. She met John Summers in Manchester and Susanna continued to email. But the initiative was too one-sided. Despite its near location, the orchestra has still never played in the festival.

In his previous post as manager of the Northern Sinfonia in Newcastle, John had been an enthusiastic partner, during which time the Northern Sinfonia made five visits. The first, in 1986, included music by two composers associated with the Sinfonia – David Blake's *Cassation* and John Casken's *Masque* – and ended with the UK premiere of Schnittke's first Concerto Grosso, which draws on music from his earlier film scores (including one about Rasputin), and featured Ernst Kovacic and Bradley Creswick as appropriately demonic soloists.

When Schnittke himself visited the festival in 1990, Gennadi Rozhdestvensky agreed to direct the Northern Sinfonia, as well as the all-Schnittke concert he was engaged to conduct with ENP and Huddersfield Choral Society two days before. Alerted to its availability by the critic Gerald Larner, we secured the world premiere of Schnittke's *Concerto for Piano Four Hands* to be played by Irina Schnittke and Viktoria Postnikova (Rozhdestvensky's wife). It was ostensibly a coup. But in performance the piece proved disappointingly cerebral beside the fervent spirituality of Gubaidulina's *Seven Words,* whose ghostly dialogue between Vladimir Tonkha's cello and Friedrich Lips's bayan sounded especially haunting in the ambience of St Paul's.

A year later the Northern Sinfonia moved into the town hall to perform concertos by John Casken and Michael Berkeley – the latter a festival commission. The audience was less than half capacity, but too many for St Paul's. Nevertheless, for a more intimate concert in 1998 containing Simon Holt's intense trilogy: *Icarus Lamentations, Daedelus Remembers* and *Minotaur Games*, and a clarinet concerto by Diana Burrell, it seemed better to use St Paul's. In between, I tried unsuccessfully to engage John Adams to conduct, and, on another occasion, to stage Norwegian Ballet's choreography of Arne Nordheim's *The Tempest* in the Lawrence Batley Theatre with the Northern Sinfonia in the pit. This plan foundered after careful measurements revealed that the set would not fit.

When the orchestra returned to the town hall in 2006 it was for the world premiere of Casken's song-cycle *Farness,* complemented by three of Ligeti's compositions to mark his death earlier that year. The Casken had been destined for the newly opened Sage in Gateshead. But an outbreak of 'cautious' programming led the management to suggest its transfer to the festival. Ironically, low key marketing and the unusual start time of 4pm attracted a smaller audience than would probably have attended in the Sage.

Across the country, orchestral programmes have become depressingly risk-averse. Dependence on overworked popular classics contributes to a loss of interest among young and adventurous listeners. The trend accelerates – or, perhaps, it merely accepts – widespread ignorance of the genre, to which the reduction of instrumental teaching in schools, the rise of a techno-based popular culture, and changing social habits certainly contribute. For Huddersfield Contemporary Music Festival too, promoting orchestral music has become problematic.

…and non-orchestras: audience-building

After Kirklees withdrew as a co-promoter, orchestral concerts in the festival required shrewd planning and vigorous publicity. There were no captive subscribers, but equally none to absent themselves. Co-promoted or not, the most effective programmes focused on, at the most, two composers of major stature: Maxwell Davies (1984), Berio (1985) Schnittke (1990), Birtwistle and Tippett (1991), Nono and Schoenberg (1995), Pärt and Tüür (1998), Rihm and Lachenmann (2000) and Lachenmann alone (2005).

The first visit of the Kronos Quartet in 1991 demonstrated, however, that, with energetic marketing, a charismatic string quartet could fill Huddersfield Town Hall. So I increasingly sought non-orchestral events that would attract a predominantly young and diverse audience, yet be compatible with the festival's aims. An all-Reich programme (including the UK premiere of *Hindenburg*) in 1998, Brian Eno's *Music for Airports* performed live by BOAC All-Stars in 1999, and a concert featuring the 'Microtonal Music of Arabia' performed by the Al-Kindi Ensemble in 2000, all drew capacity audiences. They were colourful, even 'popular'; far from the aesthetic of a Rihm or Lachenmann, yet differently mind-opening. The festival was the richer for them – not only artistically.

In 1998 four town hall concerts together raised 35% of a total ticket income of £54,458 generated from thirty-nine events. Two years later four town hall concerts raised 32% of the total, and six events in the Lawrence Batley Theatre another 25%. This meant that 57% of ticket income accrued from just one quarter of that year's programme. The audience-building was as important as income generation, because it demonstrated that, although earned income might be below the level of public and commercial subsidy, a broad constituency benefited. Even in the late 1990s, ticket prices remained relatively low, both to entice the young and encourage attendees to buy into a series of performances through discounted packages. Some came only to the most glamorous. But my ideal was for everyone to encounter as much as possible and take the rough with the smooth. More than most festivals, Huddersfield is conceived as an integrated whole. Capacity audiences in the larger venues spilled over into others; even lectures and interviews were boosted. For an extended afternoon discussion with Beryl Korot and Steve Reich on the day of their concert, 266 people bought tickets. Full halls meant a community of the like-minded. The shared sense of purpose, hum of excitement, appreciation and controversy, made the effort of mounting such a complex operation worthwhile.

Orchestral concerts could themselves be less stereotypical. In 1996 the BBC Scottish Symphony Orchestra gave the world premiere of Tan Dun's *Orchestral Theatre III: Red Forecast* in total darkness (apart from lit music stands), while soloist and conductor moved between spot-lit positions, and a video of 1960s newsreel and animated graphics made by Mike Newman was projected onto a huge screen. This event, and the performance of Tan Dun's opera *Marco Polo*, are described more fully in Chapter 9 (page 162).

Increasingly however, specialist new music ensembles replaced orchestras in the town hall, a trend accelerated by Susanna Eastburn and Tom Service. In 1999 the London Sinfonietta performed Andriessen's *Trilogy of the Last Day* – appropriately enough on the final evening. In 2004 Asko and EXAUDI brought the festival to a close with UK premieres of two zanily eccentric compositions by Richard Ayres: his *No.33 (Valentine Tregashian considers…)* and *No.36 (NONcerto for Horn)* (see page 56). In 2005 Ensemble Modern's stunningly virtuoso performance of Lachenmann's *Concertini* and the earlier *Mouvement (-vor der Erstarrung)* provided that festival's high point and its finale. To end the 2008 festival, Graham McKenzie recreated a notorious concert devoted to the work of John Cage, which had taken place in New York Town Hall fifty years earlier.

5 *Ensembles and soloists*

International visitors

Ever since the debut of Ensemble Modern in 1986, and the UK premiere of Ferneyhough's *Carceri d'Invenzione* by Asko and the Nieuw Ensemble in 1987, performances by international ensembles have been at the heart of the festival's success. Most have visited the UK only to play in Huddersfield, and the expectation of hearing such outstanding musicians became a magnet for the audience.

Between 1978 and 2010 an astonishing number of ensembles from all over the world have appeared, some repeatedly. By 2010 the total stood at 331 different groups, including choirs and jazz ensembles (but excluding orchestras). The majority have been specialists in contemporary repertoire, and most have been instrumental, ranging from the occasional trio to up to fifty players, with the 'sinfonietta' model of around fourteen the most common. Among them have been twenty-seven vocal and choral groups, twenty-three jazz ensembles and big bands, and a dozen dance companies. More than half (177) are, or were, based in the UK; and, although some have been short-lived, it is remarkable how many new music ensembles, both large and small, have managed to exist in what is often perceived to be an unfavourable climate.

Of 154 ensembles from abroad, most have been of Western constitution and character, but with wide stylistic allegiances. The festival has presented some fine representatives of African, Arabic, Chinese, Indian, Indonesian, Japanese, Russian and Tibetan culture. But the ongoing relationships have been with European ensembles, not least because of their proximity and because their governments subsidise foreign touring. So do the governments of Canada and Australia, but not the USA – and in the third world it is rare.

The cumulative total of foreign ensembles jumped from twenty to twenty-eight in 1989 (the twelfth festival), when eight ensembles made festival debuts. These were Arraymusic from Toronto, Accroche Note from Strasbourg, Alternance from Paris, Antidogma from Turin, Amadinda from Budapest (toured by the Contemporary Music Network), the Prazak Quartet from Czechoslovakia, Volharding from Holland and Atelier Théâtre et Musique from Paris. That same year Asko made a second visit, toured by the Contemporary Music Network. Nine international ensemble concerts in as many days set a benchmark for the future.

The Prazak concert was co-promoted with Huddersfield Music Society and, to accommodate a relatively conservative audience, the programme sandwiched an easy-going new quartet by Zdenek Lukás between two works sixty years old – Janáček's Second Quartet and Berg's *Lyric Suite*. Political events, however, gave the Janáček a burning immediacy. Three days earlier riot police had suppressed a peaceful student demonstration in Prague, and by the day of the performance there were half a million protestors on the streets. It was the beginning of the Velvet Revolution. Michael Kennedy heard the news as he drove to the concert, and wrote in *The Sunday Telegraph*[1] that it made the Janáček performance 'especially moving... for searing intensity I have not heard its equal'. Simon Cargill in the *Yorkshire Post*[2] remarked that the Prazaks 'took the place by storm' and, far from sounding reactionary, the 'avant-garde surroundings simply served to emphasize what an astonishing and indeed still under-rated innovator Janáček was'.

The Kronos Quartet and Foday Muso Suso performing at the 1993 festival.
PHOTO: SELWYN GREEN

The next seven festivals saw the British debuts of sixteen major ensembles from Eastern and Western Europe (including Scandinavia), Canada, the USA, Australia and Russia. Another nine, appearing for the first time in Huddersfield, had played elsewhere in Britain, including Les Percussions de Strasbourg, the Vienna Art Orchestra, the Kronos String Quartet, Toimii from Finland and Contrechamps from Switzerland. To secure the Kronos took ten years. An initial proposal came from the quartet's agent in May 1981, too late for inclusion that year. But, as we continued to talk, it emerged that the players preferred always to tour in early autumn, in order to be home in the USA for Thanksgiving. After persistent pleading, they agreed to tour in 1991 during November and December, and did so again in 1993 for a Contemporary Music Network tour, including a concert in the festival. After that their families took precedence.

The Contemporary Music Network

In the early years, with its small budget, the festival depended on the Network to deliver larger ensembles, especially from abroad. Thanks to CMN, between 1978 and 1996 the festival presented Dreamtiger, Music Projects/London, Piano Circus, the Dave Holland Quintet, Gavin Bryars Ensemble, Nash Ensemble, Mike Westbrook Orchestra, Muhal Richard Abrams Band, George Russell's 'Living Time Orchestra', Nexus from Canada, Asko and Hoketus from Holland, the Tokyo International Music Ensemble, Dunya (music from Mali and India), the Warsaw Music Workshop and Hungarian percussion group Amadinda. Also toured by the Network were Northern Stage's production of John Casken's opera *Golem*, Major Road Theatre in Birtwistle's *Bow Down*, two concerts by the London Sinfonietta, the Orchestra of St John's Smith Square, pianists Cecil Taylor and Roger Woodward and a programme of electro-acoustic music. I was briefly a member of the advisory committee, but only for a year, and suspected that Annette Morreau retired members before they could unduly interfere. In fact, I would rarely have disagreed with her choices, which seemed admirable and contributed enormously to each festival's variety.

When Annette retired in 1988, the Network was organised for a few seasons by Judith Ackrill.

But the Arts Council had begun to question its content and purpose, and whether promoting such a series was properly part of its remit. Following a review in 1996, the nature of CMN changed. Serious Productions, which already managed many of the tours, was given a more strategic role, tipping the balance towards jazz, crossover fusions, improvised and world musics. The number of contemporary classical tours dwindled rapidly and, in 1996/97, only Turnage's *Blood on the Floor* represented the genre – albeit infused with jazz. Ensemble Modern's performances were scheduled for the spring, and in Manchester's Bridgewater Hall there where rows of empty seats. I reflected, ruefully, how well the work would have been received at the festival.

Contemporary Music Network publicity for Autumn 1984.

Dunya, toured by the Contemporary Music Network in 1988.
PHOTOS: SELWYN GREEN

A year later, with Beverley Crew at the helm, CMN announced a tour by the Estonian Philharmonic Chamber Choir, Tallinn Chamber Orchestra and Hilliard ensemble. I had heard the Estonian choir singing in Llandaff Cathedral in 1996, and would have engaged them, had I thought we could afford the air fares. The CMN package was larger, promising works for choir and orchestra by Arvo Pärt and Erkki-Sven Tüür, with the cost underwritten by a Virgin recording to be made in King's College Chapel. Promoters would pay more than usual, but it was still a bargain, and, as Beverley had arranged the tour to coincide with the festival, I immediately bid for dates. There were surprisingly few takers, and when in June the planned recording fell through, she telephoned to warn me of the tour's likely cancellation. By then I had negotiated with the agent two additional *a cappella* concerts, and the loss

of all three within days of going to press would have left a gaping hole. Sympathetic to my pleas, the Arts Council accepted that it had an obligation to deliver, and the tour took place, although only to three venues (including the atmospheric ambience of Durham Cathedral). The subsidy must have been huge and I was duly grateful. But in Huddersfield all three concerts were packed to capacity and consistently thrilling (see also page 139).

Under Beverley's stewardship the Network committed itself to 'reaching out to a far more diverse audience' and a 'non-elitist' approach, so that in presenting 'the widest possible selection of contemporary music from many different cultures…there should be as few barriers as possible to people wanting to extend their own spheres of knowledge'. In an interview with Chris Heaton, she argued that as 'the arts are funded by everyone in this country… it would be unfair of us to tailor our output solely to any one group of people'.[3] Such ideals could hardly be gainsaid. Yet, in seeking diversity, it became evident that the Network's earlier advocacy of contemporary classical music would be sidelined. One sensed an anti-intellectualism, that the complex and abstruse were deemed insufficiently inclusive. Western modernity, with its roots in the Renaissance and Enlightenment, had become prey to a peculiarly British hostility towards deeper currents of philosophic thought and artistic individualism. The festival was also concerned with breadth, but its role as a standard-bearer for the serious avant-garde had suddenly become more solitary.

Not that I spurned populism. In 2000 the Network toured La Banda, a 38-piece Italian traditional wind band with international jazz soloists. In Huddersfield Town Hall, the programme's first half sported operatic excerpts by Rossini, Verdi and Puccini, which so infuriated Sally Cavender (promotional manager of Faber Music) sitting beside me, that she left at the interval berating the Arts Council for mis-spending resources that could have supported living composers. Any unease of my own was tempered by the 'designer' garb in which these old chestnuts were decked, the audaciously fruity playing and intriguingly 'dirty' intonation, which had a gratifyingly large young audience bubbling with pleasure. After the interval the band's jazz numbers exploded in improvisatory fireworks, and when the conductor beckoned a member of the audience to take the baton, the players responded to his gestures with uncanny unanimity, provoking peals of laughter and applause. In the *Huddersfield Daily Examiner* Adrian Smith remarked that 'Performance standards were high', but 'the contrived pandemonium of the final moments said it all: this was ultimately show business, not music-making'.[4] My reaction was different. La Banda had reversed many negative preconceptions, and the following day music department students were queuing to buy tickets for other festival events.

Three years later the town hall resonated to a combined Volharding and Icebreaker tour. But by now the 'classical' core, which had been at CMN's heart for almost three decades, had been thoroughly edged aside. After 1996 only one classically-constituted tour coincided with the festival: that of Psappha with Steve Mackey in 2002. Solo artists were now mainly non-Western (e.g. Dhafer Youssef and Evelyn Petrova), and groups accompanied by trendy packaging and fashionable technology (e.g. Kitchen Motors). The banner of high-flown Modernism held aloft by Annette had been furled and put away. Instead DJs, digital beats, folk, 'free noise', grunge, songwriting, dancehall, sound, video and ethnic artists played primarily in clubs, given localised, low-key advertising.

Extraordinarily, during the 2007 festival, a CMN event took place in the Lawrence Batley Theatre simultaneously but separately, since, in Graham McKenzie's view, 'it did not fit into the festival's artistic programme'. Emanating from the Albany in Deptford (a venue in which it may have been more effective), *Speakers Corner* promised 'street sounds and stories' in which seven lyricists, including a rapper, spoken word artist and 'human beatboxer' backed by a house band, would 'expose the slavery that exists in 2007's multicultural generation'. This assertive social agenda failed to attract much support. In 1998 the Network's Estonian tour had drawn an audience in Huddersfield of c.1,000; La Banda two years later drew 558. *Speakers Corner* managed 139. There is nothing new in politicised art. But it was ironic that the Network's displacement of world-class ensembles in favour of social issues had so narrowed its appeal.

The declining relationship with CMN was replaced for a few years by the British Music

Information Centre's Cutting Edge tours, until, in the autumn of 2008, after thirty-seven years under the auspices of the Arts Council, CMN joined the BMIC, Society for the Promotion of New Music and Sonic Arts Network in a newly constituted umbrella organisation called Sound and Music. No further tours took place – neither those previously organised by the BMIC nor by CMN – and the agenda changed drastically to prioritise sound art, although also with a new website including listings of contemporary music and sound art events. There were other negative consequences: the demise of the BMIC's 'New Voices' scheme, which had provided public profile for some forty-five young and mid-generation composers not otherwise represented by a publisher; lost access (although hopefully temporary) to the BMIC's unique library of scores by living and twentieth-century British composer; and the disappearance of all the services so impressively offered by music information centres in other Western countries, and of nearly all the opportunities the SPNM had provided for young composers. Noting these failures, in March 2011 Arts Council England, which had forced the amalgamation three years earlier, cut the budget for Sound and Music by 48%. In a comment made to *The Guardian*, Andrew Clements said that 'The only surprise over the apparently draconian cut... is that [Sound and Music] hasn't been closed down altogether, for so far it has signally failed to fulfil any of the purposes for which it was originally intended'.[5] Meanwhile, the festival's relationships with foreign institutions had grown stronger, and, in a significant development in 2000, the festival joined Réseau Varèse, an association of European new music producers established to share touring projects, funded by the European Union.

Dutch alliances: Asko/Schoenberg, the Ives and Nieuw ensembles

Among international partnerships, that with the Holland's Gaudeamus Foundation has existed the longest. This exemplary new music organisation would have contributed to the very first festival, had not its eponymous string quartet been grounded by fog and unable to travel. Thereafter we continued to correspond, but the first significant collaboration was born at the World Music Days in Amsterdam in October 1985, when I heard Asko rehearsing

Brian Ferneyhough's *Carceri d'Invenzione I.* Dense and intricate, the music's fierce inner rhetoric burned in the mind. Brian was still adding to the *Carceri* (composed between 1981 and 1986), and the complete cycle was due to be performed in The Hague and Amsterdam in the autumn of 1987.[6] Asko agreed to add Huddersfield to its schedule, although the long fifth movement, *Etudes Transcendentales,* would be entrusted to the Nieuw Ensemble, which had given the premiere. Together with two conductors and soloists, this meant over fifty performers, a larger complement of foreign artists than the festival had ever contracted. Excited by the prospect, I worried about its cost; but Willem Hering – Asko's trombonist and agreeably laid-back manager – reassured me. In the event, a subsidy from the Dutch cultural ministry and fees from the BBC meant that, even with addition of a second concert, the final cost to the festival was less than £10,000. To put that in perspective, however, it was three times the *total* turnover of the first festival nine years before.

In Amsterdam I met the staff of Gaudeamus, its director Chris Walraven and assistant Henk Heuvelmans. Gaudeamus had agreed to host the annual showcase of the International Society of Contemporary Music at short notice after the French withdrew, and did so in style, despite having to include some tedious but obligatory national contributions. Our meetings marked the beginning of a warm and fruitful relationship. For a quarter of a century, Asko, the Schoenberg Ensemble,[7] Nieuw Ensemble, Volharding, and later the Ives Ensemble and others, have made regular festival appearances. I admired the openness of the Dutch: their readiness to straddle genres; their cultivation of mavericks like Claude Vivier, Galina Ustvolskaya and Henry Brant; and their welcoming adoption of foreign composers who had chosen to reside in Holland (our own former student, Richard Ayres, and the Greek-Cypriot composer, Yannis Kyriakides, amongst them). In 1991 the Nieuw Ensemble introduced to the West a new generation of Chinese composers, and later composers from the Middle East and Central Asia. It was in the splendidly unstuffy Paradiso – a former church turned into rock, punk, new wave and contemporary music venue – that New York's Bang on a Can All-Stars had their European debut and I first heard them, resulting in the All-Stars appearing at the festival.

Following the tremendous impact of Ferneyhough's *Carceri d'Invenzione* in Huddersfield, Willem kept me informed about future plans. After Renee Jonker joined the organisation, these included both Asko and the Schoenberg Ensemble, with copious faxes from Renee listing an appetising range of projects. The two ensembles had joined forces in the late 1980s to perform Messiaen's *Des Canyons aux étoiles* and thereafter shared offices.

In October 1995 Renee sent the Asko and Schoenberg Ensemble's agenda for the following autumn. There were seven monograph programmes – one each devoted to Henze, Kurtág, Obst, Stockhausen, Ustvolskaya, Vivier and Zorn – plus a programme of music by four Russians. Henze's *Requiem* had already been performed at the festival by the London Sinfonietta. Kurtág's idiosyncratic instrumentations, none of which matched, meant that a portrait concert with only forty-three minutes of music would be very expensive. The Vivier interested me most, but required more than fifty instrumentalists and singers and probably even greater cost. It was a commitment too great to weigh up before the forthcoming festival. But, six weeks later, all the available dates had been taken, and my regret at not acting sooner only deepened when I realised that any revival would be for Huddersfield alone and astronomically expensive. I retained the hope of mounting a substantial Vivier feature, but it was never realised. The Ustvolskaya programme needed thirty musicians, eight of them double-bass players, and was eventually performed in Huddersfield in 1999.

As for Stockhausen's *Orchester-Finalisten* (which Asko had commissioned), it required only thirteen players. I was sceptical about the piece, but thought Asko might carry off Stockhausen's seemingly naïve and repetitive sequence of solo displays. It would bring the composer himself to control the octophonic sound projection, along with new operatic offcuts performed by members of his family. Alas, in Huddersfield *Orchester-Finalisten* proved cringingly embarrassing, and the costumed operatic offcuts verged on the pretentious. To students from around the country who knew little about Stockhausen, he remained a cult figure. But the critics circled like vultures, and both the music and its creator were mercilessly dismembered (see also page 114).[8]

Asko's visit in 2004 highlighted music by Richard Ayres and Michel van der Aa, two relatively young composers newly prominent. Van der Aa's *Here [in circles]* – one of his first pieces to be heard in Britain – seemed spectacularly accomplished. Its final section, in which a soprano soloist 'enters into an emotional, schizophrenic dialogue with the shadows of her own voice on tape', was brilliantly performed by Barbara Hannigan, one of a new generation of contemporary music virtuosi. Richard Ayres had been a student of the polytechnic between 1986 and 1989, and one of an interesting cohort of composers in my analysis class, whose knowledge and enthusiasms made every discussion stimulating. In 1988 he was co-winner with David Horne of the Yorkshire Arts Young Composers' Competition; and the pieces submitted the following summer for his degree displayed some of the flare and eccentricity that would mark him out. After settling in Holland and studying with Andriessen, he found a niche composing with that Pythonesque humour that thrives in British comedy, but too seldom in contemporary music. In April 1999 he sent me some scores and recordings, and that year's festival included two of his pieces.

Asko's two commissions were on a larger scale. By the time Willem proposed the first I had decided to retire, but Susanna Eastburn was equally interested and went to Holland to hear it. Later Willem emailed her, proposing both *No. 33 (Valentine Tregashian Considers...)* and a new Asko commission, *No. 36 (NONcerto for horn)* – 'or as we call it *CORNcerto*' – adding that as, for the full theatrical version, Richard asked for 'some doors (and someone to open them) and maybe a mountain, preferably one of the Alps', Willem had 'immediately thought of the Midlands...'. 'Huddersfield is NOT in the Midlands', Susanna corrected robustly, 'which are generally quite flat, heavily industrial, and around Birmingham/Nottingham!' But about the music she was enthusiastic, remarking that she thought *No. 33* 'a work of genius'. Financial considerations delayed the Huddersfield performances by two years. Meanwhile, commissioned to compose an opera, Richard visited the festival to see Param Vir's *Ion,* which, since its partial premiere at the Almeida Festival, the composer had greatly (and, some thought, 'over') extended. I did what duty would earlier have prevented. During the interval Richard and I repaired to a pub, where we spent a fruitful

hour discussing other ways operas might be conceived. The Asko performances, when they arrived, were a joy. In *No. 33* the ensemble was joined by the choral group EXAUDI. In *No. 36,* although lacking a mountain, the horn soloist dashed nimbly back and forth, running up ramps both sides of the stage like an alpine goat, and disappearing behind the 'door'. Unafraid to indulge pastiche and cliché with the zany hilarity of a silent movie, Richard's quirky invention and non-sequiturs I observed with proud delight.

The Schoenberg Ensemble's portrait of Galina Ustvolskaya five years earlier could not have been more sombre (see also page 127). Her *Compositions Nos 1, 2* and *3* were conducted by Reinbert de Leeuw, who also played the monumental Fifth Piano Sonata. This was the Schoenberg Ensemble's (and Reinbert's) only visit to Huddersfield. After working closely for many years, in September 2008 the two ensembles amalgamated under the single name 'Asko|Schoenberg'. It was a logical development, partly dictated by funding cuts, now affecting even Holland.

Founded in 1986, the Ives Ensemble made its festival (and UK) debut in 1996 in the British premiere of Feldman's last composition, *Piano, Violin, Viola, Cello,* given a wonderfully focused late-night performance in St Paul's. A second concert featured *Themes and Variations* by Christopher Fox, then a member of the music department staff and a composer with whom the Ives has developed a close association. In this extended composition Christopher had

The Ives Ensemble at the 2005 festival.
PHOTO: BRIAN SLATER

The Nieuw Ensemble playing music by Theo Leovendie in 2000.
PHOTO: PAUL HERRMANN

gathered together, as he said, 'some of my favourite things', inspired by the final writings of John Cage and Marcel Duchamp's *boîtes-en-valise* – boxes in which the artist had collected mementos of earlier works and to which Cage, in turn, paid homage. In 2004 the Ives Ensemble gave superb portrait concerts of Aldo Clementi and Gerald Barry. Two more dissimilar composers it would be hard to imagine.

Broader in repertoire and more exploratory, the Nieuw Ensemble's instrumentation of three plucked instruments (guitar, mandolin and harp), along with bowed strings, winds and percussion has earned it a special niche. Joël Bons, the ensemble's founder and artistic director, trained as a guitarist and composer but refrained from using the Nieuw as a vehicle for his own music, instead developing projects with a global remit. A repertoire of several hundred works composed specifically for the ensemble has gone hand in hand with important monograph concerts. At the 1992 festival a Donatoni portrait made an unforgettable impact. In 1999 the Nieuw played music by some of the Chinese composers whom Joël and his colleagues had been instrumental in introducing to the West. In the 2000 festival they played a concert of Theo Leovendie's music and a tribute to Boulez, ending with his magnificent *sur Incises* for three pianos, three harps and three percussionists. Seven years later Joël brought a characteristically eclectic programme of seven UK premieres: two by Dutch, and one each by Chinese, English, French, Japanese and Kuwaitian composers.

The Nieuw Ensemble's return in 2007 marked the beginning of a three-year partnership agreed with Music Centre the Netherlands, the new Dutch umbrella for contemporary music, successor to Gaudeamus. Having lived in Amsterdam, the festival's incoming director, Graham McKenzie, was well placed to curate a range of Dutch notated, jazz and improvised music as well as experimental techno, indie-pop culture and sound art. To celebrate the partnership, some of these were gathered together in *Night of the Unexpected,* a 'multi-sensory experience' based on a Dutch model, which opened the 2007 festival.

Central to the Nieuw Ensemble collaboration was a programme of professional development, set up by the festival in association with the ensemble and northern universities. It enabled emerging young composers to familiarise themselves with the Nieuw's unusual instrumentation, workshop ideas in Holland, and have their completed compositions premiered by the ensemble in 2009 and 2010 – an enormously beneficial process (see also page 229). In 2010 the Nieuw also performed Kagel's *Kantrimiusik:* a partly folk, part-ironic 'pastorale', previously performed at the festival in 1984.

Programme content

An advantage of presenting foreign ensembles was their expertise in specific areas, particularly in works composed for them. In the case of Archeus it was music by fellow Romanians. In the case of ELISION it might be 'new complexity' – both Australian and European. For the Vilnius New Music Ensemble it was the rustic character of Lithuanian new music performed on folk instruments and in costume. But a surfeit of indigenous music could be unpalatable. A substantial Swedish feature at the 1997 festival was underwritten by its state cultural institute, Rikskonserter. I had made myself conversant with the work of leading Swedish composers, and thought I had chosen interestingly, until, in KammerensembleN's two concerts, it became clear that twelve pieces, all of them Nordic and mostly Swedish, actually detracted from each other. 'Swedes with everything,' *The Sunday Times* headed Paul Driver's review. The menu needed variety: to be leavened, perhaps, as Cikada had done in 1991 by mixing Norwegian and British composers (Birtwistle, Dillon and Finnissy) with whom they had a special affinity. Programmes were invariably strengthened by including established contemporary repertoire – Boulez, Ligeti, Xenakis, even Schoenberg – works of proven worth and relative familiarity. The debut of BIT-20 under Ilan Volkov in 2001 proved the point: one concert devoted entirely to the music of their Norwegian compatriot Arne Nordheim (who had turned seventy that year), another combining UK premieres of works by Hans Abrahamsen, Bent Sørensen and Rolf Wallin (three of Scandinavia's finest composers) with Ligeti's Chamber Concerto and *Mysteries of the Macabre*. All were executed with such brilliance that, as Lynne Walker remarked in *The Independent*, 'the performers left no doubt that here were top-rank players teamed-up for the sheer fun of making music'.[9]

A few British composers owe their success as much, if not more, to foreign commissions than to those emanating from Britain. In 1995 the Swiss ensemble Contrechamps arrived with UK premieres of two pieces by Ferneyhough, both commissioned by Contrechamps during the preceding months and performed with dazzling authority. The Dusseldörf-based musikFabrik has been an eloquent advocate of Rebecca Saunders, recording monograph CDs of her music and another of Richard Ayres. Significantly, Saunders lives in Berlin, Ayres in Holland. Only once did I regret accepting a proposal from a continental ensemble to perform British music, when, in 1991, Peter Burwik's Twentieth Century Ensemble of Vienna gave portrait concerts of Birtwistle and Holt. Their imprecision and lack of empathy for both composers' styles was a painful reminder that contemporary music is best entrusted to those fully familiar with it.

Recherche, Ensemble Modern and beyond Europe

It can cost less to bring a European ensemble to Huddersfield than one of equivalent size from London, because the travelling expenses of the former are likely to be subsidised; those of the British ensemble probably not. For the first visit of Ensemble Recherche in 1992, however, there was no subsidy, and the cost of travelling from Freiburg, before the advent of cheap flights, almost exceeded the fee. My invitation was governed by another consideration. Repeated performances – common to the touring schedules of continental ensembles – deepen

the players' understanding, whereas, as I have already observed, the music of foreign composers performed by a British ensemble may only be played once.

I had heard Recherche perform the music of Klaus Huber at an Extasis festival in Geneva, and immediately perceived the advantage of their expertise in articulating his rarefied, microtonal language, with roots in medieval and Arabic music. In Huddersfield Recherche and the mezzo-soprano Magali Schwartz performed six pieces by Huber, four of them UK premieres. Subsequent visits included a portrait of Mathias Spahlinger and the UK premiere of Gérard Grisey's *Vortex Temporum*, both in 1997. With works like the Grisey on offer, my embargo on frequently re-engaging the same artists had to be relaxed; and, as Recherche was a small ensemble with stable membership, warm friendships developed. A nucleus of three winds, three strings, piano and percussion, made the group ideally constituted to play Feldman, as they did in 1996 and again in 2002, when two recently revived film scores and other pieces from the 1940s and '50s were given UK premieres.

Unusually for a chamber ensemble, Recherche has cultivated music theatre, beginning in 1993 with performances of Ligeti's absurdist 'mini-operas' *Aventures* and *Nouvelles Aventures*. In their semi-staged version the schizophrenic eccentricities of the vocalists, Sarah Leonard, Linda Hirst and Omar Ebrahim, were unnervingly arrested by the sudden frozen postures and accusing stare of the instrumentalists, all the more effective for their studied understatement. Ligeti, present at the 1993 festival, had not seen the production and was delighted. In 1996 Recherche brought to the Lawrence Batley Theatre the striking juxtaposition of Feldman's austere *Samuel Beckett: Words and Music* and Dieter Schnebel's concept-score *Glossolalie*. Here the visual gags, casual dress, incongruous props, fragmentary text in several languages and negation of anything recognisably musical grew increasingly anarchic and hilarious – musicians and actors hurling abuse at each other (in impeccable English) – until, having disappeared for a moment, the rear curtain slowly lifted to reveal the players in evening dress, dignified and formal, standing with instruments poised as if to begin a classical chamber concert. It was a stunning *coup de théâtre* crowning Recherche's most extreme music theatre creation.

Sarah Leonard, Linda Hirst and Omar Ebrahim in Ligeti's Aventures *and* Nouvelles Aventures.
PHOTO: SELWYN GREEN

In comparison, Aperghis's *Zwielicht (Twilight),* composed in 1999 specifically for Recherche, seemed at best a courageous failure, and in Huddersfield its impenetrability provoked angry reactions from some of the audience (see page 143). Undaunted, the following morning the players assembled for a purely instrumental conjunction of old and new. At its core was *The 'In Nomine' Broken Consort Book,* consisting of sixteen short pieces based on a well-known sixteenth-century English 'In Nomine', whose composition Recherche had invited, mainly from German and French composers, as a surprise present earlier that year for Harry Vogt, director of the Wittener Tage für Neue Kammermusik. For Huddersfield we commissioned additional treatments from Bryn Harrison, Stuart MacRae and Ian Vine – amongst which the subtlety, restraint and refinement of Bryn's *In Nomine after William Byrd* stood out as especially beautiful. Born in Lancashire, living in the Calder valley, the festival his local new-music hypermarket, Bryn had won categories in the 1993 and 1995 Young Composers' Awards, and had been a finalist in the most recent Gaudeamus Competition. Following the Huddersfield performance, Recherche invited him to compose another 'In Nomine' setting, advancing his reputation on the continent where his music has been increasingly performed. Its rigour and intricacy chime well with European aesthetics. In 2006 Bryn Harrison joined the full-time composition staff at the University of Huddersfield.

For this exquisite concert, performed on the main stage of the Lawrence Batley Theatre on a sunny Sunday morning, I asked for the rear curtains to be drawn back to reveal the curved wall of the original Methodist Mission, its

Zwielicht by Georges Aperghis, performed by Recherche in the Lawrence Batley Theatre.
PHOTO: PAUL HERRMANN

shutters open to reveal the Georgian windows (now triple glazed). I remembered how effectively Opera North had lit the rear wall and shutters for a gala evening during the opening of the theatre. Exposing the glass panes improved the acoustic, and the music seemed aerated by the blue sky beyond.

The much larger Ensemble Modern originated, like Asko, as a student collective motivated to work 'outside the box'. Inaugurated in 1980, it was generously funded by the city of Frankfurt and the Goethe-Institut, which is why the ensemble's UK debut in 1986 cost the festival so little (see pages 33 and 252). Thereafter the subsidies diminished and the quotations escalated. It was only in 2000, after some years of negotiation, that an extensive Ensemble Modern tour made a further visit viable. On that occasion Ensemble Modern's two concerts included an electrifyingly virtuoso performance of Wolfgang Rihm's hour-long *Jagden und Formen*.

During the intervening years, Ensemble Modern dedicated weeks at a time to ground-breaking collaborative projects: notably with Frank Zappa and Heiner Goebbels, whose *Black on White* I saw at the Edinburgh Festival in 1997. Its theatrical brilliance was stunning, the stagecraft of the musicians extraordinary. *Black on White* took the notion of music theatre into unimagined new territory. But the set was too large and the staging too complex for the festival to consider. Happily, in the new century, the partnership of specialist European theatres and festivals under the banner of Réseau Varèse facilitated other collaborations. This resulted in performances at the 2001 festival of both Goebbels's latest creation, *Hashirigaki,* and the Berlin Hebbel-Theater's staging of Sciarrino's *Lohengrin.* In the latter, instrumentalists crawled and crept over an enormous slatted bench, emitting strangely throttled sounds. The symbiosis between the players, Ingrid von Wantoch Rekowski's almost static production, and an Elsa struggling to gulp, whisper and exhale, endowed Sciarrino's non-narrative treatment with extraordinary intensity. Neither work involved the Ensemble Modern. But in 2005 the ensemble returned with two pieces by Lachenmann, including his new *Concertini.* Although the high-point of that year's festival, it was exceptionally expensive, compounding a deficit larger than any previous festival had incurred.

Among other Austro-German ensembles, musikFabrik and Klangforum Wien made UK debuts during the 1990s, then became frequent visitors in the new millennium. Indeed, muskFabrik has appeared in every festival between 2007 and 2011 and has now performed over a dozen programmes in Huddersfield. At least half the repertoire has been by British composers: Birtwistle, Harvey, Rebecca Saunders, and part of Cardew's *Treatise* in 2007, performed with outstanding expertise.

The first visit of Arraymusic in 1989.
PHOTOS: SELWYN GREEN

*The Norwegian trio
Poing at the 2004 festival.*
PHOTO: BRIAN SLATER

The rest has been neither dull nor routine: a recent work by Yannis Kyriakides, a collaborative composition by Enno Poppe and Wolfgang Heinger, arrangements of two pieces by Sun Ra (a pioneer of free jazz not previously performed at the festival), and in 2008 Stockhausen's extraordinary late string trio *'Hope'*, constituting the ninth hour of his unfinished composition *KLANG*, followed by the seventeenth and twenty-first hours in 2010.

The Canadian ensembles Arraymusic, Continuum and Nouvel Ensemble Moderne have each visited the festival twice. Nouvel Ensemble Moderne has retained a relatively strict sinfonietta-size format, whereas Arraymusic's nucleus of clarinets, trumpet, two percussion, piano/synthesiser and double bass has generated a distinctively different repertoire and sound. Its potential was winningly explored by Terry Riley in *Cactus Rosary*, composed for the ensemble in his 'rosary' tuning, and given its UK premiere at the 1995 festival. With text spoken live by the composer, and the periodic interruptions of a peyote rattle, it proved an alluring piece. BIT-20 from Bergen, Ictus from Brussels, Remix from Oporto and mosaik from Berlin have similarly made two visits to Huddersfield. The Ictus Ensemble made its Huddersfield debut performing *An Index of Metals* by Fausto Romitelli in 2004. Billed as a video opera with multimedia projection, this was a tour underwritten by the Réseau Varèse and involving the video artists Leonardo Romoli and Paolo Pachini. In 2009 Ictus gave the UK premiere of James Dillon's *The Leuven Triptych;* and, in two concerts, Remix performed his

Überschreiten, along with two works by Jonathan Harvey and three by Emmanuel Nunes. This was the first time Portugal's leading composer had been featured in Britain.

When ELISION arrived from Australia in 1996, it was to make its British debut amid other European engagements. The ensemble's three concerts featured Australasian composers and such English exemplars of 'new complexity' as Richard Barrett, Brian Ferneyhough and Michael Finnissy. The UK premiere of Barrett's *Negatives* instigated a developing association between the ensemble and the composer, resulting in six more pieces from Barrett being performed by ELISION at the 2006, 2009, 2010 and 2011 festivals. Commissioned by the City of Liverpool, *CONSTRUCTION* (2011) is one of the longest works ever performed at the festival, lasting two hours and formed out of four interlocking five-part 'cycles', involving twenty-two musicians and a sixteen-channel sound installation.

The ensemble's Huddersfield debut in 1996 also featured the work of Liza Lim, including the magical *Garden of Earthly Desire* originally composed for performance with puppets. Liza had commissions from Ensemble Modern and InterContemporain, but this was an important introduction to her music in the UK. Twelve years later she was appointed to the University of Huddersfield as a research professor of composition, and her relocation from Brisbane to the North of England with her husband Daryl Buckley, founder of the ensemble, led to ELISION becoming ensemble-in-residence at the university, and making regular appearances at the new King's Place music and arts complex in London and annually at the festival.

Smaller groups have made a strong impression in the last decade, such as the Norwegian trio Poing, combining accordion, saxophone, bass and electronics, which has performed three times since 2004. Latterly, the festival has introduced more young ensembles engaged in experimental and crossover styles and live computer processing. Laptops and leads criss-cross the stage; and their titles (as often as not in fashionable lower case) convey the character of the approach: mosaik, ascolta ('listening'), zeitkratzer ('time-scraper'), cranc (and Crank), Insomnio, [rout], the house of bedlam, The Letter Piece Company, Ensemble Klang, The New String Theory, etc.

Explosions in November

Tiere stitzen nicht (Animals don't sit), *a 'creative adventure' devised by Enno Poppe and Wolfgang Heiniger in collaboration with musikFabrik, given its UK premiere in the Lawrence Batley Theatre in 2009. A unique feature was the integration of all the instruments owned by musikFabrik and its members.*
PHOTO: BRIAN SLATER

Pipes, drums, fiddles, carrier bags and the spoils of war

Processed sound can be strangely levelling and its sonic promise illusory. Yet younger composers are understandably drawn to hands-on control, preferring an ubiquitous, easily transported hardware to the plethora of percussion which pervaded much twentieth-century music. For audiences, the miracles of co-ordination achieved by virtuoso percussionists can be as fascinating to see as to hear. Inspired by Cage's use of everyday objects, percussionists are always adding to their armoury. The Hungarian group Amadinda played in St Paul's in 1989, already with an exotic range of instruments. Returning in 2000, their further acquisitions overflowed the performance space like some fantastic sculpture. To employ them, most of the music had been composed by the players themselves. The highlight, however, was a work written for Amadinda by Ligeti: the UK premiere of his amazingly 'youthful' late work for mezzo soprano and four percussionists: *Síppal, dobbel, nádihegedűvel (With pipes, drums, fiddles)*, alluringly sung by the mezzo-soprano Kátyá Karolin. Ligeti's instrumentation is never indulgent. But the sixth song requires four marimbas, and for the duration of the fifth each percussionist plays a mouth organ. In Huddersfield, they performed the latter from memory, standing in a semi-circle around the singer and bathing the voice in a halo of glowing harmonies.

It is to be assumed that percussion ensembles of five or six players, like Nexus, Kroumata and Les Percussions de Strasbourg, will need a lot of space. Kroumata brought the largest load, although their huge keyed instruments and drums in multiples of sixes were more conventional than exotic. We had agreed that Kroumata would appear in three contexts, but this also meant three venues: an evening concert in Huddersfield Town Hall, a workshop-demonstration in the Recital Hall the next morning and a performance with the Per Jonsson Dance Company in the theatre that evening. I had watched Kroumata play in Stockholm, but had seriously underestimated the number, size and weight of the instruments, not to mention their flight cases. The arrival of a huge pantechnicon revealed the enormity of the task. Moving in and out of venues six times in less than two days (not least from

street to stage in the town hall), was an unwonted extra burden on our technical team and required the urgent hiring of extras to help shift gear during the night. The interaction of the players and dancers was interesting, while in the town hall Kroumata were joined by the trumpeter Håkan Hardenberger and trombonist Christian Lindberg, perhaps the finest living exponents of their instruments. But, despite their excellence as performers, some of the predominantly Scandinavian music played seemed unremarkable.

Their programmes did include Xenakis's 'Peaux' from *Pleïades,* and *Zythos* (a Kroumata commission). Most ensembles offered at least one of Cage's *Constructions* from the 1940s, whose metric symmetry and modest instrumentation (despite the inclusion of 'found objects' like brake drums and a conch shell) give them an appealing clarity and almost classic perfection. In 1992 the young Helios Quartet from Paris performed five of Cage's early compositions, after which children from six primary schools arrived with Simon Limbrick and Kevin Renton to play their own 'constructions' on instruments they had made themselves. The Helios joined them for a 'jam session' and then, to an awestruck mass of delighted children sitting cross-legged on the floor, performed Giorgio Battistelli's *Heliopolis Primo* (a co-commission between Huddersfield and Musica in Strasbourg) with mime and clownish masks (see the illustrations on pages 218–19). Another success with a youthful audience was the duo-recital in 1999 by Colin Currie (BBC Young Musician of the Year finalist) and our own former student, Julian Warburton. Playing almost entirely from memory, and in a crowded St Paul's packed with students, their finely-nuanced musicianship and breathtaking dexterity won a tremendous ovation. For the *Examiner* critic it was: 'Fabulous! Hair-raising! Mind-blowing'[10]

After a Lontano concert in 1985, I had been irritated to receive what I considered an excessive invoice from Lontano's percussionist for hiring his own instruments: three triangles at £15 each... and so on down the list. I resolved to avoid large percussion specifications until the practice changed. (It did.) So my heart warmed to Ensemble Bash's idea of commissioning composers to write only for what could be transported in four carrier bags. Their lunchtime concert in 1996 was less restricted but not

*Dean Drummond and
the cloud chamber bowls.*

He had already established an ensemble
called Newband to perform microtonal
music, and now embarked with its members
on learning to play the Partch instruments and,
crucially, how to tune them. In 1990 they made
a sensational appearance at New York's Bang
on a Can festival.

One year later I attended a Newband
performance with the instruments in Oslo.
But the cost of transporting them was
enormous, and the ensemble's next European
tour planned for 1993 would take place in the
summer. There things rested for a further five
years, until Alex Poots, with whom the festival
was collaborating on a Tan Dun project,
telephoned from the Barbican to say that he was
negotiating a visit from Newband and to offer
Huddersfield a performance. The terms were
generous, but at twice the price I would have
accepted. In November 1998 Newband and the
instruments duly arrived. Magnificently arrayed
on the stage of the Lawrence Batley Theatre
were the chromelodeon, kithara, diamond
marimba, gourd tree, cloud chamber bowls and
spoils of war, poised to recreate Partch's vision
in one of the most entrancing concerts ever to
take place there.

The Arditti String Quartet

Of the numerous contemporary music
ensembles that have played in Huddersfield,
the most enduring has been the Arditti String
Quartet, which, in fourteen visits spread over
twenty-eight years, has given twenty-three
concerts – more than any other ensemble.
The Ardittis, like the London Sinfonietta,
first performed in 1982, since when both
have presented such essential repertoire to
such dizzyingly high standards, that the festival
would have been the poorer without them.

My early intention that no performers should
be habitually re-engaged was based on the
simplistic logic that an organisation devoted
to new music should showcase each year
a new roster of artists and composers.
With the Ardittis it was soon evident that any
such restriction was self-defeating. Indeed,
Huddersfield is the only British context in
which the quartet's unique achievement has
been consistently celebrated. Their accumulated
repertoire, mostly composed specifically for
them and by the world's leading composers,

spendthrift either, and the ingenuity and wit
with which they made music from everyday
objects won over another audience
predominantly of students.

When, soon after his graduation, Julian
Warburton performed James MacMillan's *Veni,
Veni, Emmanuel* with the University Symphony
Orchestra at the 1995 festival, I was struck
by the way his timing, stance, and 'journey'
between groups of instruments underscored
the dramatic narrative of the music.[11] It was
a movingly sensitive interpretation which
contributed to his adoption by the Young
Concert Artists Trust as the first percussionist
the trust had represented.

Percussion instruments are intrinsically
theatrical. The American maverick Harry
Partch (1901–74) famously exploited this
attribute by building his own percussion and
reed orchestra, tuned to a forty-three-note scale,
each instrument conceived for its timbral and
visual contribution to a musical and dramatic
ritual. My interest in his work had increased at
the University of Illinois, where I met the
composer Ben Johnston who had assisted
Partch. Three years later Partch died, and with
him, it seemed, any hope of further performances;
until, in 1986, Dean Drummond, one of
Partch's original players, succeeded in having
the instruments transferred to New York,
undertook their restoration and, because many
were fragile, had replicas constructed.[12]

contains an increasing body of acknowledged masterpieces, and our programmes aimed to balance the immediacy of the new with what had already become canonical.

Irvine Arditti would suggest, or I would enquire, what premieres were available. Our choices included new works by Birtwistle, Dillon, Ferneyhough, Carter and Xenakis which had been premiered abroad, alongside, for example, the world premiere of a first quartet by Benedict Mason. From the quartet's foreign repertoire we chose selectively, and only in the first year did I regret accepting a work by the comparatively unfamiliar René Koering, whose influential position at Radio France and later as artistic director of the Montpellier festival probably helped secure him performances. After a tough and intense quartet by Vic Hoyland, and the UK premiere of Takemitsu's delicately refined *A Way a Lone,* Koering's dry cerebralism strained my patience, and the subtle beauties of Dutilleux's *Ainsi la Nuit* which followed, with its chain-like structure (and parentheses of music prefigured or recollected) my antennae could hardly register. According to Desmond Shawe-Taylor there was 'no dead wood in the programme';[13] but neither he nor other critics considered the Koering worth a mention. They did remark on Irvine's sangfroid after his E string snapped towards the end of the Dutilleux, and he continued to play without it. 'Virtuoso could go no further' wrote Nicholas Kenyon admiringly in *The Times.*[14]

The next morning the Ardittis gave coruscating performances of all Xenakis's string chamber music in the presence of the composer – music with which they had become authoritatively familiar. The concert was given 'in the round' in the music department Recital Hall, so full that members of the audience were almost elbowing the players. A year later the Ardittis played Carter during the first of his two visits to Huddersfield. None of his existing quartets had been composed for the Ardittis, but there was no point in asking any one else to play them.[15] Carter's Second and Third Quartets were followed by Xenakis's new *Tetras,* dedicated to the Ardittis, and the concert began with a quartet by James Dillon – his first commission (and only the festival's second).

Thereafter the Arditti Quartet usually returned every other year. In 1985 it was to premiere a rhythmically complex microtonal quartet by

Michael Finnissy, and play Jonathan Harvey's (at that time) only quartet, along with Donatoni, Rands and Sciarrino. In 1987 it was for British premieres of Ferneyhough's Third Quartet, Gubaidulina's Second and a new Piano Quintet by Xenakis, rounded off with Carter's Fourth Quartet. In 1989 the Ardittis again gave two concerts, including first performances of Ben Mason's First Quartet and *Four* by Cage, plus the UK premiere of Lachenmann's Second Quartet, composed for the Ardittis.

Four years elapsed before, their next appearance. In between were concerts by the Allegri (with clarinet and extra viola), the Balanescu, Brindisi, Kronos and Mondriaan quartets. When the Ardittis returned in 1993 it was in the midst of criss-crossing the globe, flying into Manchester late in the evening from France, performing the next morning at 11.00am and flying that afternoon to Mexico. A typically high-voltage programme included three UK premieres: Benedict Mason's Second Quartet, Kagel's Fourth, the first three of Birtwistle's *Nine Movements*, and ended with a masterly performance of Ligeti's Second Quartet – arguably the finest of late twentieth-century additions to the genre. Neither of Ligeti's quartets had been written for the Ardittis, but they had become his preferred interpreters. Ligeti heard the rehearsal but found little to 'correct' – which was hardly surprising. After playing the Second Quartet at a Ligeti festival in Dublin in November 2007, Irvine told me that it had been the Ardittis' 268th performance of the work. Repeatedly Ligeti promised to compose a new quartet for them; but, although he wrote down ideas (in words) in his planning book, no music ever resulted.

Exceptionally, in 1995 Irvine spent four days at the festival: as soloist in Nono's *La lontananza nostalgica utopica futura*, as duo partner with Mieko Kanno, in an Arditti trio playing Rihm, and finally with the quartet in Kagel, Rihm, Dillon and Nono. Afterwards he wrote to say how much he had enjoyed participating, noting that it was the first time in all his visits to Huddersfield that he had been able to get an overview, and 'even with a busy schedule, taste some of what others were doing,' adding, 'It is a pity that you are the only person in this country doing a job that is more common in Europe'.

By now the Ardittis had become an inseparable component of the festival, their concerts eagerly anticipated, and to celebrate the quartet's twenty-fifth anniversary in 1999 I invited them to play four concerts on four successive days. Any fears that the audience would be spread thinly were dispelled when ticket sales topped 1,000. The oldest piece was Schoenberg's Second Quartet of 1908, with its prophetic Stefan George text conjuring 'airs from other planets' sung by Claron McFadden. Elsewhere were works by Cage, Carter, Dillon, Ferneyhough, Harvey, Ligeti, Rihm, Sciarrino and Xenakis; while the fourth programme featured younger composers from five countries: Thomas Adès, Toshio Hosokawa, Hilda Paredes, Bent Sørensen and Guo Wenjing, in whose quartet with bamboo flute (commissioned by the festival) the Ardittis were joined by Dai Ya from Beijing.

Since the early 1990s I had been wondering how to entice György Kurtág. A large-scale tour emanating from Budapest had fallen through because the pianist, Zoltán Kocsis, was unavailable and Kurtág would accept no one else. On a visit to Berlin in 1995 I called on the composer, but we did not then know each other and it was an inconclusive meeting. Kurtág's reluctance to travel could only be overcome if he was actively participating, with several days of rehearsal in the performance venue itself – a requirement not easily met. In 2000 Irvine told me that Kurtág had composed a string quartet with live electronics together with his son, and wanted to work with the Ardittis on a new version. I wrote offering four days of uninterrupted rehearsal in Huddersfield

Irvine Arditti at the 2010 festival.
PHOTO: BRIAN SLATER

Town Hall, around which there would be performances which Kurtág had already heard and approved, or could rehearse in Huddersfield. Satisfied with this, that November the composer, with his wife Márta, and György Kurtág junior, duly arrived. Their joint composition, *Zwiegesprach,* was only partly successful; and, unlike his compatriot Ligeti, Kurtág senior would not engage in public discussion. But he attended concerts with evident pleasure. And he and Márta crowned their presence with a wonderful late-night recital of piano duets from *Játékok,* given in the area of the town hall with the audience on three sides. Performing with the most sensitive control of soft dynamics, and with charmingly visible affection, the music was both playful and witty, radiating beneficence.

Live electronics on a higher plane distinguished Jonathan Harvey's Fourth Quartet, given its UK premiere in 2003. This too required extended preparation and rehearsal in the performance space, equipment brought from IRCAM, and the participation of Gilbert Nuono, Jonathan's assistant in Paris. The result was a strikingly beautiful and sophisticated synthesis of live and transformed sounds, a testament to Harvey's long (probably unmatched) experience composing at IRCAM, above all to the spiritual elevation of his music. It ended an exceptionally fine concert, which began with Ferneyhough's String Trio of 1995 (its second festival performance), and included the UK premiere of Dillon's *the Soadie Waste* with Noriko Kawai – an evocation of an old dance hall on the outskirts of Glasgow.

Three years went by without the Ardittis, and it seemed as if the festival might be moving away from the intellectually and technically demanding notated art with which they were identified. But in 2007 the quartet returned, and from then on annually. A concert in 2008 ended with Birtwistle's *The Tree of Strings* – a thirty-minute work of subtly evocative and intricate beauty. In 2009 the quartet gave the world premiere of Dillon's Fifth Quartet. A typical programme in 2010 contained four UK premieres, ending with Ferneyhough's Sixth Quartet, a co-commission between the Donaueschingen Musiktage and the BBC for performance in Huddersfield, which won the Royal Philharmonic Society award for chamber-scale composition that year. A second concert featured music by the Norwegian crossover violinist and proponent of 'extreme' sound-art, Ole-Henrik Moe. Moe himself should have taken part, but was indisposed. His place was brilliantly filled by the ELISION violinist and former Arditti Quartet member, Graeme Jennings.

New music ensembles in Britain

The 1970s and '80s were fertile years for British ensembles dedicated to performing the work of living composers. Tours were organised not only by the Contemporary Music Network but, for the few years of its existence, by a Regional Contemporary Music Network set up to tour smaller groups. The Cheltenham Festival focused on new music and living composers – mainly British. Bath and Edinburgh staged major features and commissions. Sir William Glock continued to run Dartington until succeeded by Maxwell Davies in 1980. Glasgow's Musica Nova was flourishing, the new Huddersfield and Almeida festivals expanding, and in London Adrian Jack ran an important series at the ICA. All included ensemble concerts, while general festivals like Brighton gave plentiful space to new music.

Of over ninety ensembles (including string quartets) which visited the festival between 1978 and 1990, Dreamtiger, Lontano, Music Projects/London and the Arditti Quartet performed most frequently. Created by Douglas Young to explore music that bridged East and West, Dreamtiger courted exoticism. A key member was the Sri Lankan cellist Rohan de Saram, who had in 1977 also joined the Arditti Quartet, and whose eloquence was evident in Dreamtiger's first festival concert devoted to music by George Crumb. In 1983 Douglas and Keith Swallow gave the UK premiere of *Three Quarter-Tone Pieces for Two Pianos* – exploratory late Ives, so rare and beautiful I was loath to have the pianos restored to A440. The following year Douglas proposed a programme entitled 'Bali and Beyond…', which interspersed gamelan transcriptions made in the 1930s and 1940s by Colin McPhee with music by Dieter Mack and James Wood. Mack was a Ferneyhough pupil, and an authority on the twentieth century gamelan style called *Kebyar*. This concert ended with the first ever public performance of transcriptions by McPhee for the unusual combination of three pianos, celesta, percussion, two cellos and double bass.

Lontano had been founded by its conductor Odaline de Martinez, known to everyone as Chachi. Their mission was the exploration of Latin American music, but none appeared in its Huddersfield programmes, unless one counts Henze's dramatic tale of a runaway Cuban slave, *El Cimarrón,* performed in 1981. That year I asked Chachi to play music by Balassa and Birtwistle – both present – and to workshop shortlisted pieces for the Young Composers' Competition. Lontano undertook similar ensemble categories in 1985, and again in 1987 when the winner was Gordon McPherson. His *Prosen,* which hauntingly multiplied a single line played by six solo strings, was the first of several increasingly impressive pieces by Gordon presented at the festival. Performed in a public concert, *Prosen*'s elegantly simple concept mediated between the polarities of Brian Ferneyhough's *Funérailles* and John Adam's *Shaker Loops* on either side.

More varied in size and repertoire was the ensemble founded by Richard Bernas in the same year as the festival. Like Dreamtiger and Lontano, Music Projects/London presented its own annual series in London, played regularly in the Almeida Festival and broadcast on Radio 3. As only the London Sinfonietta received sufficient Arts Council funds to afford a fully-fledged management, Douglas, Chachi and Richard did most of their own administration, and when Douglas and Richard developed wider careers their ensembles ceased to function. Richard's faxes were admirably to the point. 'From the Department of Computing Errors' one was headed, and another: 'From the Department of Loose Ends'.

Music Projects/London made its festival debut in 1985 – along with Lontano, Spectrum and the Ardittis – playing music by the three British composers featured that year (Finnissy, Harvey and Rands), plus a clutch of Italians. This was the eighth festival; but there was as yet no influx of foreign ensembles, the only one in 1985 being Divertimento from Milan. Richard's American upbringing, and the flexible composition of the ensemble, made Music Projects ideal for a programme of American West Coast pioneers in 1987. As so often, I wanted it to serve several ends, and the combination of pieces by Henry Brant, Cage, Cowell and John Adams required not only two solo pianists – Alan Feinberg and Yvar Mikhashoff – but four conductors: Richard himself, Brant and Amy Schneider (his assistant and partner), and Adams, who directed his own *Grand Pianola Music* (see his comment on page 102).

In 1989 I invited Richard with an enlarged Music Projects to give the British premiere of Cage's ballet music *The Seasons*. Composed in 1947 for Merce Cunningham, this is Cage's only work scored for 'classical' orchestra and, for that reason rarely performed, although it is characteristic in every bar. I had obtained a copy from the publishers, and was intrigued by this apparently forgotten pearl from an exceptionally productive decade. The performance marked the beginning of a ten-day residency by Cage himself, and the concert ended with part of *Socrate* by Erik Satie, the composer probably closest to Cage's heart. Restrained but poignant in its austere self-denial, the vocal line, with its simple narrative manner, was beautifully sung by a former music department student, Carol Smith.

In the 1980s there was no northern equivalent comparable to the leading London new music ensembles. This changed when the freelance percussionist Tim Williams (who had been briefly a student in Huddersfield) founded Psappha, after graduating from the Royal Northern College of Music in 1991. With a core of six musicians and Sir Peter Maxwell Davies as patron, Psappha took as its model the defunct Fires of London, reviving its repertoire with flair and authority. Its first festival engagement in 1994 was in a quasi-Fires programme, ending with one of Max's finest Orkney creations: *Image, Reflection, Shadow*. Around the same time, Psappha launched into music theatre, and persuaded Max to compose a new work specifically for them, *Mr Emmet Takes a Walk*, which was staged in a production by David Pountney (also its librettist) at the 2001 festival. Drawing on players based primarily in the North West, Psappha was able to expand without compromising quality, and with the advantage to the festival of no overnight expenses. An example was the effective pairing in 1999 of Cornelius de Bondt's *Het gebroken oor (The Broken Ear)* and an imaginative new work by Gordon McPherson called *Detours*.

A younger ensemble than Psappha, Noszferatu is a music collective working across a range of genres, which made its debut at Oxford Contemporary Music in 2001. Noszferatu performed in Huddersfield for the first time in 2004, and again in 2005, on both occasions featuring works mainly by mid-generation British, or Britain-based, composers. In 2010 it returned with music by Howard Skempton and Frederic Rzewski, including a fine performance of Rzewski's celebrated *Coming Together* of 1971, with its powerful text by Sam Melville describing the passing of time in prison superbly narrated by Skempton. To date, Psappha has performed eleven times at the festival, Noszferatu on three occasions and the Nash Ensemble only twice. Considering its long existence and outstanding reputation, one might have expected the Nash to have appeared more. But its repertoire is not solely contemporary, and its focus amongst the living on composers at the heart of the British establishment (admirably given repeated performances), made the Nash a lower priority than ensembles playing less familiar repertoire.

The London Sinfonietta

To have postponed until now consideration of Britain's premiere new music ensemble may seem strange; but for over a decade it was an elusive beast. The Sinfonietta's quality and enterprise under Michael Vyner I greatly admired, but its London operations allowed little scope for regional appearances and Michael de Grey, the administrative director, showed no inclination to facilitate an engagement. His first quotation was far higher than the festival could afford, augmented by ancillary charges I thought excessive. An education project devised in 1986 with Gillian Moore changed the tone, and her visit to discuss it left us buoyant with anticipation. Its structure followed the model Gillian had pioneered in London, and would culminate in a concert by the ensemble. To fund it I negotiated a tripartite package in which Yorkshire Arts, the Arts Council of Great Britain and Kirklees each contributed £5,000 – annually as it turned out after the scheme was extended for two more years. Its success owed much to the inspirational charisma of the project leaders – all prominent composers or performers – who began each stage with a day or more for teachers, and then visited schools to stimulate creativity (see page 213).

But it was still difficult to contract the Sinfonietta separately, and throughout the first fourteen festivals we succeeded

only once, as part of the 1986 project.
Two further appearances occurred as part of
CMN tours. Late November was peak time for
its London promotions, soon to be harnessed
to the contemporary agenda of Nicholas
Snowman, one of the Sinfonietta's co-founders
who, in 1986, had become artistic director of
the new South Bank Centre (see pages
105–106). In 1991 for example, the Sinfonietta
was due to perform in the South Bank's 'Henze'
series, giving three concerts between 26
November and 11 December preceded by
rehearsals. As already remarked, it was easier
and cheaper for Huddersfield to engage
ensembles from abroad.

In 1992 the obstacles suddenly disappeared.
The Arts Council may have instructed the
Sinfonietta to extend its remit. But it was
Paul Meacham, its new general manager,
who effected the change. Paul had worked
previously for the Royal Liverpool Philharmonic
Orchestra, knew the festival well and was keen
to collaborate. Not only would he provide the
Sinfonietta for no more than the cost of a
concert and general rehearsal; the festival
could have new programmes before they
were performed in London. Repetition spread
costs and effectively doubled the audience.
Nevertheless, I appreciated the offer. Paul took
the initiative, and, although the festival could

not accept his every proposal, there's nothing
like a menu to whet the appetite. In autumn
1992 the festival hosted the world premiere of
Contraflow by Colin Matthews, a Sinfonietta
commission to which the festival made a modest
contribution. The concert cost £7,573, around
half previous quotations and less than it cost
to bring the Nieuw Ensemble from Holland
or Alternance from Paris. Similarly *O-Mega*
by Xenakis and Simon Holt's *eco-pavan*
(commissioned by the BBC) received their
world premieres in Huddersfield before being
heard in London.

The relationship became closer still when
Cathy Graham succeeded Paul as general
manager in 1997, with Jane Williams as artistic
administrator, and when a year later Gillian
Moore became artistic director. I had worked
with all three in their previous posts, and our
similar aspirations were reinforced by
friendship. Holt's bleak *eco-pavan*, with
Rolf Hind articulating the skeletal solo piano
part as if enacting a sombre ritual, made an
extraordinary impression in St Paul's. But the
increasing scale of Sinfonietta concerts needed
Huddersfield Town Hall. Henze's Requiem in
1994, Gubaidulina and Feldman in 1996,
Lindberg's *Related Rocks* with Andriessen's
Trilogy of the Last Day in 1999 – all involved
much larger forces and attracted substantial

*The London Sinfonietta,
Sinfonietta Voices and New
London Children's Choir
about to perform Louis
Andriessen's* Trilogy of the
Last Day *in 1999.*
PHOTO: PAUL HERRMANN

audiences. In 1999 the audience numbered 700, augmented by guests for the festival's final evening. Among them were the Earl and Countess of Harewood. As president of the festival, Lord Harewood (who died on 11 July 2011) took his role seriously, and throughout the 1990s he and Lady Harewood made regular visits. His extensive career directing successive festivals and opera companies informed his interest in the Lawrence Batley Theatre as well as the festival as a whole. In 1994, Hans Werner Henze – already a friend – stayed with the Harewoods, and Lord Harewood himself never failed to write after a visit, or, indeed, if he had been unable to attend. His letters were touchingly warm, personal and appreciative.

In 2000, resurrecting its association with Opera Factory, the Sinfonietta staged Turnage's precociously accomplished first opera *Greek*. Superbly acted, sung and played, it was ideal in scale for the Lawrence Batley Theatre. This was the sixth festival finale to be entrusted to the Sinfonietta. Toured with financial support from the Arts Council and charitable trusts, the staging of *Greek* cost each promoter only £6,000. One year before, assembling Magnus Lindberg's *Related Rocks* and Louis Andriessen's *Trilogy* for Huddersfield alone cost £39,462. The Sinfonietta had performed both pieces on different occasions, but they needed to be re-rehearsed. Andriessen's hour-long *Trilogy* employs forty-one players, female choir, children's choir, ten soloists and conductor. *Related Rocks* inflated these already high costs, because it involved live electronics and four additional performers (on two pianos and percussion). This was the largest outlay ever spent by the festival on a single event – more than for any orchestra, three times more than the average paid for an ensemble.

But both were commanding and important pieces: visionary, audacious, monumental. I would never have considered pairing them, but for problems dogging another project on the verge of collapse. In early summer, the festival still had insufficient funds for the Andriessen. But suddenly the picture changed, and on 2 June I wrote to Jane Williams:

Since we spoke, my long-standing plans for the Hallé and Kent Nagano to give the final concert of this year's festival have run into the buffers. Just like that... Bang! – I'll explain sometime. So the way is clear to invite the London Sinfonietta.. for *Related Rocks* followed by *Trilogy*.

The frustrating outcome of months of negotiation with the Hallé Orchestra (described on pages 47–48) released both the final evening and its allocation in the budget. The change had to be approved by the Dutch Cultural Fund to which the festival had applied for financial support. This meant another month of uncertainty during which the Sinfonietta could not finalise its contracts with the players.

Before retiring, I acceded to one more Sinfonietta initiative, although it would not be realised for three years. The proposal from Gillian was that the festival should host the UK premiere of a major new work by Birtwistle. It was a generous arrangement, considering that this would be the first work Harry had composed for the Sinfonietta for many years. All the more so, as the festival was not asked to contribute to the commission, which would be funded by a syndicate of the Sinfonietta's own commissioning circle, the South Bank Centre, the Ruhr-Triennale festival supported by the American arts philanthropist Betty Freeman – and not least Ensemble Modern, whose input earned them the world premiere. Conceived for between thirty and forty-five players with two conductors, even without contributing to the commission, the cost was a potential time-bomb for my successor. But Susanna Eastburn confirmed the commitment within days of taking over. In the event Harry wrote for thirty-two players, and the concert (which included, besides the new *Theseus Game*, *Tragoedia* and the first UK performance of *Wind Sequences* by Péter Eötvös) cost £18,700 – less than anticipated.

If I have dwelt on performance costs, it is because for any arts manager they perpetually gnaw at the mind. Money is a constant obsession, and as constantly inconstant. It is true that, for most of the 1990s, the festival's core subsidy remained static. But, to keep pace with inflation and fund new ideas, along with other organisations we had to bid for project monies and persuade funders to support them. Bidding is competitive, and the funds raised implicitly finite. In the new millennium, several well-funded projects had run their course, and the cost of engaging the London Sinfonietta again became an issue. Not only the cost. A preference for non-conventional formats, interactive technology, non-notated music and sound art shifted the emphasis away from straight concert-giving, and for five years the Sinfonietta did not appear.

In 2009 the London Sinfonietta returned, now to Bates Mill, to mark the seventieth birthday of Jonathan Harvey and the fiftieth birthday of Richard Barrett. The programme contrasted Harvey's *Bhakti* of 1982, a product of his early association with IRCAM, with a Sinfonietta commission, *Mesopotamia*, from Barrett – both repeated in London five days later. The two pieces spanned twenty-seven years of electroacoustic development. In *Bhakti,* music played live alternates with pre-recorded and transformed sounds heard on quadraphonic tape; in *Mesopotamia* computer software replaces the fixed methodology of tape, and the (now amplified) ensemble is heard both live and simultaneously sampled and transformed. At the 2010 festival the Sinfonietta performed a major new piece by Rolf Wallin – *Appearances,* for an ensemble of twenty-five players – at the end of a concert which began with Lachenmann's *Pression* for solo cello. Superbly played by Oliver Coates and strongly lit against a black background, its effortful, grinding opening had a visceral physicality.

Apartment House, Maciunas, Cardew and graphic scores

Founded by the cellist Anton Lukoszevieze, Apartment House takes its name from a piece by John Cage. The ensemble first played at the festival in 1999, but had already given concerts for the university. Initially I had reservations, less about repertoire than about its standards of performance and presentation. My successors had no such scruples, and in the new century I came to admire the players' dedication to the experimental currents of twentieth-century music, not only its major figures but the unique perspective of someone like Helmut Oehring (child of deaf-mute parents), whose music was featured in 2003.

The pairing of two Lithuanians in 2007 was, perhaps, the most engaging of Apartment House's offerings. The unfamiliar Rytis Mažulis (b.1961), a younger exponent of the Lithuanian minimalism encountered at the 1990 festival, was represented by three UK premieres; but

Piano piece no. 13 (Carpenter's piece) *by George Maciunas.* PHOTOS: BRIAN SLATER

the works of George Maciunas (1931–78), the notorious founder of Fluxus, are scarcely better known. Drawing on his own Lithuanian roots, Anton brought an empathy to Maciunas's music that endowed its zany iconoclasm with unexpected depth. The final *Piano piece no. 13 (Carpenter's piece)* had Anton and the pianist Philip Thomas daubing with red paint and otherwise bedecking an upright piano, at which Anton sat methodically hammering nails into its keyboard. As the strings resonated to the blows, their strangled cries – processed in real time by Mathew Adkins – acquired a strange disembodied beauty, with the piano itself gradually metamorphosing into art installation, slowly but inexorably silenced.

In the 'hallowed' surroundings of St Paul's, Apartment House's 2001 tribute to Cornelius Cardew seemed unduly reverential for a composer so famously subversive. On several occasions – some would say too many – the festival has revisited Cardew's radicalism. In 1986 *Treatise* was performed by AMM in Huddersfield Art Gallery. A concert in 1991 marked the tenth anniversary of the deaths of both Cardew and Bill Hopkins (the lives of each ended tragically young). In 1994 the twenty-fifth anniversary of the Scratch Orchestra was marked by performances of Paragraphs 2 and 7 of *The Great Learning,* whose preparatory workshops anyone could join and be guided by Michael Parsons and John Tilbury, two of the Scratch Orchestra's founders. Other paragraphs were performed as part of the festival's 2001 tribute. Graham McKenzie included work by Cardew in all his first three festivals. In 2006 Apartment House performed Paragraph 5 of *The Great Learning* with EXAUDI singing its 'Ode Machines'; whilst showing continuously in Huddersfield's Media Centre was a new film about the Scratch Orchestra, called *Pilgrimage From Scattered Points,* made by Luke Fowler. In 2007 musikFabrik gave one of the finest performances of pages from *Treatise.* No one, however, worked so closely with Cardew as Tilbury. And, when his long-awaited book on the composer was published in 2008, it was appropriate that its launch should take place during the festival, at the end of a piano recital introduced and performed by Tilbury himself.

Cardew's radicalism earned him admiration outside the UK. But the most far-reaching repositioning of music undoubtedly emanated from Cage – so widely regarded as an *agent provocateur* that the spiritual and philosophic depth of his ideas is easily overlooked. To close the 2008 festival, making its eighth appearance in ten years, Apartment House re-enacted a legendary all-Cage concert given fifty years earlier in New York Town Hall. The original event had been organised and paid for by Cage's friends, notably Jasper Johns and Robert Rauschenberg, and attended in a spirit of solidarity by virtually all the New York avant-garde. But the performances had been all but drowned by protests from the audience, and sabotaged by some of the musicians. In Huddersfield Town Hall, as in New York, the main work was the *Concert for Piano and Orchestra,* but now treated with the dedication such a masterpiece of graphic musical art deserves. Pages from the score had been displayed in Huddersfield Art Gallery as part of the Arts Council's *Eye Music* exhibition in 1986. In 1992 a performance was given by Roger Woodward and the Italian ensemble Alpha Centauri; but, on that occasion, the unscripted entrance of Franco Donatoni holding a teapot, which he threatened to empty into the bell of a large tuba, introduced an unseemly levity. It was timely that the festival should properly pay tribute to Cage's extraordinary score, and Philip Thomas and the instrumentalists explored the interpretative ambiguities of its notation with sensitive rapport.

Graphic scores have featured more often than the audience was probably aware, and others have been exhibited as visual art. When in 1992 Barry Guy, Evan Parker and the musicians of Gemini performed Barry's *Bird Gong Game,* large sheets of its visually intriguing score were displayed on the walls of the Recital Hall. Like *Sundance* in the same concert, their realisation requires spontaneity and improvisation. To the limited extent that I programmed other improvised music, the performers were usually individual artists and mainly keyboard players: Howard Riley in 1980, Cecil Taylor in 1987, Slava Ganelin in 1990, Terry Riley in 1995 who, during a late-night recital, held a huge audience in thrall as he performed first on a piano in equal temperament and then one in just tuning. It was not until 2006 that Graham McKenzie introduced a range of improvising ensembles, and invited for the first time such established British artists as Simon Fell and John Butcher.

Recitalists

Perhaps the festival should have presented more top-rank soloists, such as the pianist Maurizio Pollini, whom I regretted never inviting. A recital in 1982 showed that musicians primarily identified with mainstream repertoire can be persuasive interpreters of the new. Fresh from his success at the Tchaikovsky Competition in Moscow, Peter Donohoe agreed to perform a formidable contemporary programme flanked by sonatas by Beethoven and Prokofiev. Brilliantly executed, this two-and-a-half hour marathon followed a strenuous morning playing compositions shorlisted for the Young Composers' Competition. For Desmond Shawe-Taylor writing in *The Sunday Times*, it was 'one of the most remarkable piano recitals to have come my way'.[16] Two winners had emerged from the workshop, Mark-Anthony Turnage and Andrew Ford, both of whose 'decidedly interesting pieces' Donohoe performed in the concert, alongside George Benjamin's early sonata and a first complete performance of Nicholas Maw's *Personae I, II & III*. This was the last time such an extensive evening concert was entrusted to a single artist. After that, ensembles and other genres took precedence.[17]

Solo recitals thereafter were less gargantuan, and usually scheduled during the day or late evening. Most have been given by specialists in new music, often in particular areas of repertoire. It is easy to underestimate the challenges such artists face. Berio's fourteen *Sequenzas*, composed between 1958 and 2002, each for a different solo instrument, famously set the pace. Nearly all have been performed at the festival, some several times.[18] Xenakis's solo works present more daunting challenges: to interpretation and virtuosity, even to what is physically possible. The solo works of composers like Ferneyhough and Barrett embody other difficulties: extreme rhythmic intricacy, exaggerated contrasts of register and dynamic, dense multilayered activity, and notation so minutely detailed as to demand intense mental and technical preparation. At an opposite pole, the indeterminate works of the 1950s and 1960s raise many issues of interpretative decision-making. The considerations involved in playing such music were addressed in an issue of *Contemporary Music Review* edited by Barrie Webb, with contributions from Christopher Redgate, Mieko

Kanno, and Philip Thomas.[19] That both Webb and Thomas were respectively a professor and senior lecturer (now reader) at the University of Huddersfield is evidence of the close partnership between its research and performance, and between the festival and university.

The majority of recitalists have been pianists, among them prominent Americans like Alan Feinberg, Anthony de Mare, Yvar Mikhashoff, and the Singapore-born Margaret Leng Tan – a specialist in the prepared piano, Cage and oriental music. One of the most compelling performances was of Schnittke's Piano Sonata, played by the Russian pianist, Viktoria Postnikova (wife of the conductor, Rozhdestvensky), in the presence of the composer in 1980. Writing in *The Observer*, Nicholas Kenyon described its

twenty-eight riveting minutes, which seem to accumulate all the desolation and struggling against odds of a Russian lifetime... it is difficult to disentangle the piece itself from the astonishing performance it received from Viktoria Postnikova. Intoning a high, brittle, chant at the very top of the keyboard, weaving folk-song-like melodies around the piano, alternating impassioned, growling dissonances with luminous, serene chords, and finally tumbling into a horrible cluster of despair at the very bottom of the register, this was a display of totally committed, un-self-advertising piano playing.[20]

In complete contrast, Márta and György Kurtág's late-night performance of pieces from the composer's *Játékok* in 2001 was serenely enchanting (see also page 67). Most solo pianists, however, have been British: notably

Nicolas Hodges.
PHOTO: BRIAN SLATER

Claire Edwardes.
PHOTO: BRIAN SLATER

representing the twenty-four hour day, of which Stockhausen had completed twenty-one 'hours' at the time of his death. Its long silences punctuated by grandiose chords, stretched over two hour-long recitals, seemed formulaic and hollow. Nicolas gave his best. But how incomparably richer had been James Dillon's *Book of Elements,* whose fifth volume he premiered in 2002, and which Noriko Kawai performed complete in 2005 in a spellbinding late evening *tour de force.* It is hardly surprising that such complex music is rarely played from memory. So when the American, Marc Ponthus, making his UK debut in 1995, played Boulez's Second Sonata, *12 Notations* and Stockhausen's *Klavierstücke X* entirely without music, the sense of well-honed precision driving the dramatic spontaneity of performance was immensely exciting.

Andrew Ball, Peter Hill, Rolf Hind, Nicolas Hodges, Joanna MacGregor, Philip Mead, Sarah Nicolls, Ian Pace, Philip Thomas, John Tilbury – and one might reasonably add Noriko Kawai, although she was born in Japan. Some of their performances, covering a wide range of repertoires, are described elsewhere in this book.

One of the most talented, Nicolas Hodges, arrived inconspicuously to accompany Trug Opera in 1993. Five years later he stood in for Rolf Hind when the latter was indisposed. That year Hodges and Richard Casey gave a two-piano recital featuring the European premiere of John Adams's *Hallelujah Junction* and George Crumb's *Celestial Mechanics,* with Crumb in the audience. In the years since, Hodges has given six solo recitals and three duo recitals, now seeming, like the Ardittis, virtually indispensable. In 1999 he played Sciarrino's Sonata no. 5 (originally composed for Pollini) and the complete world premiere of *Four Nocturnes,* one of them dedicated to Hodges after Sciarrino heard him play in London. In 1985 I had failed to entice the composer to Huddersfield. Now, although uninvited, Sciarrino came.

In the last decade, Hodges's programmes have been unflinchingly modernist: Dillon, Ferneyhough, Lachenmann, Neuwirth, a monograph portrait of Walter Zimmermann, world premieres of *choler* by Rebecca Saunders (with Rolf Hind) and Finnissy's *Whitman* song cycle (with Kirsten Blaise), and the UK premiere of Birtwistle's *The Axe Manual* (with Claire Edwardes). In 2008 he played Stockhausen's *Naturliche Dauern,* part of the cycle *KLANG*

Of other instrumentalists, violinists and cellists have appeared most often, with and without piano. I have mentioned Frances-Marie Uitti's *Moveable Feast: Gallery tour with solo cello* in 1986. At the same festival she performed an impressive late-night recital in the relatively intimate Venn Street Arts Centre. It began with Bernd Alois Zimmermann's seminal Sonata for Solo Cello of 1960, and ended with Uitti using two bows to sustain four-part chords in a composition of her own. Also included was *Le Fleuve magique* by Scelsi, who had entrusted to Uitti many of his short solo works. After Mieko Kanno's remarkable solo debut in 1994, Mieko played frequently in Huddersfield. A recital in 2005 containing music by Sciarrino, Jo Kondo, Aaron Cassidy and Scelsi was wholly 'entrancing', wrote Ivan Hewett in *The Daily Telegraph,* despite 'a hard-line modern aesthetic and a very restricted aural palette, at an hour when concentration tends to flag'. Her sensitive playing 'was revealed to maximum advantage by the fabulous acoustic of St Paul's Hall'.[21]

St Paul's is attuned to such concentration. But I thought audiences should sometimes relax after a full day, perhaps with something light-hearted. A late-night duo for double bass and dancer in 1985 began with the double bass player, Sophie Preston, performing Tom Johnson's *Failing,* which famously requires the bassist to read a 'commentary' on his or her performance whilst attempting to play ever more demanding music – a task that becomes increasingly hilarious. More whimsical was *For Love of the Double Bass* by the American

James Sellars, which Robert Black and Anthony de Mare performed in 1989. Here bass player and double bass mimic flirtation, dating and dancing, leading to 'Touch Music' and 'Nocturne' with both in close embrace lying on top of a grand piano. In 1987 Tom Johnson related his *Bedtime Stories*, originally written for Australian Radio, illustrated by the clarinettist Roger Heaton. This late-night event commenced with Trevor Wishart's entertainingly mystifying *Fidelio* for actor, six cassette recorders and six suitcases – one of which conceals an instrumentalist. Wishart's was a refreshing voice in the music of the 1980s. In 1980, the tuba player Melvyn Poore ended a recital with his *Tuba Mirum:* a vision of the Last Judgement culminating in an explosion of lights, and a bouquet of flowers and fireworks emerging from the bell of the tuba.

Wishart was also influential in electronic music. In 1987 the festival mounted a presentation of the 'Composers Desktop Project', in which he played a significant part. The project sought to make sophisticated sound transformations, comparable to some of the work being undertaken at IRCAM, available on an Atari computer. That year his *Vox 3, 4 & 5* were performed by Electric Phoenix, and in 1980 his

allegorical tape piece *Red Bird* – in which live recordings are fused and metamorphed through intricate tape splicing. Roger Heaton himself gave a fine late-evening clarinet recital in 1994, assisted by Chris Bradley and Tim Williams in Feldman's *Bass Clarinet and Percussion,* and in Gavin Bryars's *Three Elegies for Nine Clarinets* weaving an opulent multi-track texture of pre-recorded melodies.

Relatively little was composed for solo winds before the second half of the twentieth century, when the lure of extended instrumental techniques, and the possibility of a viable career, led to an explosion of solo pieces and duos, some with tape or electronics. Two concerts in the 1985 festival, which illustrate the trend, were given by the same three Italians: the flautist Roberto Fabbricciani, clarinettist Ciro Scarponi and pianist Massimiliano Damerini. Ten pieces spread over the two recitals included the UK premiere of Nono's *Inquietum* for bass flute and contrabass clarinet, the UK premiere of Ferneyhough's *Lemma-Icon-Epigram* for piano, and the European premiere of Scelsi's *Ko-Lho* for flute and clarinet. There was a further duo, and two pieces for flute and tape, one of them *Fantasia* by Aldo Clementi, a guest of the festival that year. In none did all three artists

FAR LEFT:
Daniel Kientzy.
PHOTO: SELWYN GREEN

LEFT:
Carol McLaughlan in
Crown of Ariadne *by*
R. Murray Schafer.
PHOTO: SELWYN GREEN

play together. But in Clementi's *Duetto con eco,* Fabbriciano and Scarponi were echoed by students playing off-stage in a haunting four-part canon.

The French saxophonist Daniel Kientzy required no partner, arriving in 1989 with no less than seven saxophones, from tiny sopranino to a serpentine contrabass, all to be played in one recital. We had chosen eight UK premieres from his vast repertoire. But, despite the variety of instruments, in performance they sounded curiously undifferentiated, and I decided that successive wind soli can quickly pall.

Twenty years later, too many unaccompanied pieces by a new generation of composers unwittingly repeat what has already been done. Or composers hide behind frenetic speed and virtuosity, saying very little. It takes rare imagination to make something distinctive. Changing fashions have made it harder to sustain a solo career as a wind player. But there are exceptions. In 2003 the supremely accomplished Italian flautist, Mario Caroli, interleaved Ferneyhough's four pieces for flute and piccolo with two by Dillon and two by Finnissy in a long solo recital that was wholly dazzling. Starting at 10pm and running (with an interval) for ninety minutes, it was, as Michael Dervan reported in *The Irish Times,* 'an occasion on which some of the most demanding of contemporary composers were matched by the sort of transcendent virtuosity that Liszt put so firmly on the map in the nineteenth century'.[22]

In the new millennium, soloists are more likely to be accompanied by tape, live electronics and other media. Two recitals by the American-born, Amsterdam-based violinist Monica Germino, in 2007 and 2010, demonstrated how far the genre had changed, and in pieces employing violin, electric violin, and voice, how important can be the creative partnership with a sound engineer – in this instance Frank van der Weij. The composers invited to write pieces for Germino's second recital had been encouraged to 'deviate' and be 'daring'. One result was an extraordinary new piece by the Bang on a Can composer Julia Wolfe. It was a far remove from the Canadian harpist, Carol McLaughlan, performing the UK premiere of R. Murray Schafer's *Crown of Ariadne* in 1988, whose extended sonorities consisted of hand-held percussion and bells attached to her ankles.

A *festival of pianists*

In 2009 Graham McKenzie presented a virtual festival-within-a-festival of piano music performed by eleven professional pianists. Geneviève Foccroulle played Anthony Braxton, Frederic Rzewski his own *Nanosonatas,* Sarah Nicolls world premieres by Michel van der Aa and Atau Tanaka involving wrist and arm sensors, voice and film. There were Ralph van Raat in Harvey and Boulez, Noriko Kawai in Nunes's large-scale *Litanies du feu et de la mer,* and Rolf Hind in Liza Lim's *The Four Seasons (after Cy Twombly).* Richard Utley played works by British composers, and Philip Thomas music by younger experimentalists in Britain and their mentors in the States. Employing piano, cassette, recorders and keyboards, Sebastian Berweck performed works by five radical young Germans, studiously '(mis)using the piano and other veritable instruments' in order 'to escape the romantic piano'.[23] Whilst every day at 11am, in the atrium of the Creative Arts Building, Thomas played pieces selected by chance methods from Michael Pisaro's 1998 composition *pi (1-2594),* 'setting' different decimal places from the Archimedes constant. During a day devoted to Louis Andriessen, the piano duo of Gerard Bouwhuis and Cees van Zeeland joined Icebreaker and others in two concerts devoted to his music, and Andriessen's seventieth birthday was marked by the launch of his piano book, *Image de Moreau.* In another concert in Huddersfield Town Hall, fifty pianists played twenty-five pianos simultaneously in a performance of *Piano Phasing* by Kristoffer Zegers (see the further description and photos on pages 227–28).

In praise of the piano tuner

The festival has been fortunate in having free use of the keyboard instruments owned by the university and Kirklees, it being agreed early on that it would only pay for their tuning. From 1978 to the present, all the pianos and harpsichords used have been serviced by Barry Hynes, making him the only person employed by the festival throughout its history. An accredited Steinway technician, Barry worked for many years in the piano department of the West Yorkshire music retailer, Wood and Sons. Becoming self-employed in the new millennium, he continued to maintain the music department's many instruments, plus those of Kirklees and other institutions throughout Yorkshire, and to attend to the festival's requirements each November. Doing the latter has been far from routine.

During the late 1980s and '90s the density of the programme and almost continuous use of venues required careful scheduling, and tuning had often to be done very early or very late. The first unusual task arose in 1983, when the festival staged the UK premiere of Charles Ives's *Three quarter-tone pieces for two pianos* – a work virtually unknown except by reputation, although by then sixty years old. Ives had carefully calculated the ratios between the resultant overtones, and two of the three movements are relatively slow to give listeners time to absorb them. Barry re-tuned one piano a few days earlier so that it could settle, and the precision of his final tuning produced a quarter-tonal clarity that was strangely alluring, yet always otherworldly. I am not aware that these remarkable pieces have been performed on any other occasion in Britain.

Nor can we recall whether the altered piano was tuned a quarter-tone higher or lower. But it was almost certainly lower. In the late 1980s, when the festival increasingly featured foreign ensembles, their addiction to high pitch worried colleagues charged with care of the department's instruments. Only later did we realise that tuning an expensive concert grand to A444 would not destabilise it. Initially cautious, I would agree with incoming ensembles from central Europe (the main drivers of pitch inflation) that, yes, we would raise to A444; knowing that Barry intended to tune to A442 and that, despite the visiting ensemble's keyed percussion being (supposedly) built at A444, nobody appeared to notice the discrepancy. During the 1990s the problem increased, as more ensembles followed one another in St Paul's requesting different tunings. Andrea Smart, the administrator, warned them that 'it is difficult to keep tuning pianos up and down during the festival because there is so little time between concerts and it is not good for the instruments.' Meanwhile, the UK stuck resolutely to A440, until British concert halls succumbed to the trend.

Initially there was no precedent for this situation, and we learnt what it was feasible to do by doing it. On rare occasions problems were exacerbated by baroque pitch. Thus, a fortnight

before the 1993 festival several urgent faxes between Andrea and Asko addressed the pitch of the Department's Woolley harpsichord, which for 22 November had to be tuned to A=415 for a recital with baroque flute, for 25 November restored to A=440 and, in between, raised to A=442 to match Asko's celesta. Not surprisingly, Barry advised that it could not take the strain. It then transpired that for Asko's all-Ligeti programme a modern harpsichord was required, and, thanks to the ferry between Rotterdam and Hull, Asko brought its own.

After John Cage famously invented the 'prepared piano', many composers followed his initiative. 'Preparation' became a familiar component of contemporary piano music, and an ever-expanding range of objects were placed on, woven through, used to 'stop' harmonics or otherwise mute the strings. Already, in the first festival, Crumb's *Voice of the Whale* and *Makrokosmos II* required rosined twine to be pulled through the strings, nodes to be marked with crayon, and a 5/8th inch chisel to be slid along one string – reassuringly 'with a smooth cutting edge', as advised by the composer. At first, we did these things unquestioningly; indeed, Crumb maintains that his techniques inside the piano do no damage. Understandably, however, modern concert halls forbid such treatment. The music department also needed to protect its concert instruments, and we decided to employ an older, little used Chappell grand to be 'prepared' or re-tuned, leaving the precious Steinways unassailed.

The 'honky-tonk' uprights required for Maxwell Davies were easily provided. More perplexing was how to achieve 'gamelan' tuning for the UK premiere of Lou Harrison's *Concerto for Piano with Javanese Gamelan* in 1988. Faxes sped to and fro between Huddersfield and California, with Lou indicating the appropriate ratios for tuning 'in just intonation of a Javanese kind.' We were still scratching our heads when he revealed the truth. Few gamelans are tuned alike and all shift with time. What we should do was to install the gamelan in the venue – on this occasion Gamelan Sekar Petak from York – and let Barry tune the piano to it.

I have already referred to the UK premiere in 1997 of Lou's rumbustious *Piano Concerto with selected orchestra,* and its requirement of a rarely used temperament, 'Kirnberger No 2'.[24] The concerto is accompanied by only those orchestral instruments without fixed keys, and so able to play in the same temperament – hence its title. As all musicians know, equal temperament, which has underpinned most Western music since the time of Bach, is an 'impure' compromise. Yet deviations from its levelling democracy may not be for the queasy. In *The Observer* Fiona Maddocks remarked that:

Harrison's outrageous, elephantine piano concerto, originally written for Keith Jarrett, was played here with evident delight and ease by Joanna MacGregor... Harrison instructs the piano to be tuned to a more natural temperament than usual, which confuses the ear by sounding out of tune but also uncovers a beguiling range of colours and instrumental relationships.[25]

Perhaps with an eye for entertaining copy, Gerald Larner took a more jaundiced view:

While Harrison did not like equal temperament, he seemed not to like Kirnberger No 2 much either. Certainly, after an oddly insipid beginning, he introduced a second movement of such percussive ferocity that the fine tuning was distorted within minutes. Specially equipped with an octave bar designed to strike eight white keys or six black keys at once. Joanna MacGregor performed an extraordinary feat of brilliantly choreographed, precisely calculated and relentlessly sustained

rhythmic violence. After that, there was no way that the concerto could return to Kirnberger No 2 dullness. Its bland temperament had been irretrievably wrecked and all it could do was stagger through a bewildered slow movement to an unconvincingly brief end.[26]

He had conveniently overlooked the fact that, because the octave bar distributes weight evenly, each string receives less impact than when struck individually. Two hours earlier, a concert in St Paul's given by Recherche required two pianos, both with a third 'sostenuto' pedal. On one of them, four pitches had to be tuned a quarter-tone lower for the UK premiere of Gérard Grisey's *Vortex Temporum*. By now this was a familiar procedure, but it had to be done two days earlier to allow sufficient time for the tuning to stabilise, during which period the piano could be used for nothing else.

In 1995 a concert was planned in which the six members of Piano Circus would all play grand pianos, instead of the electronic keyboards they normally used. To join the town hall's two concert grands, four more arrived from Steinways, and our main concern was whether the stage would bear their weight. The concert included the first performance of a piece for six pianos by a former composition student, Roland Freeman-Taylor. For the finale, the pianists

Andrew Ball and assistants.
PHOTO: SELWYN GREEN

joined forces with ten percussionists – past and present students of the department of music – for a rare performance of George Antheil's legendary *Ballet mécanique* of 1926. Fourteen years later the hall witnessed the performance (already mentioned) of Kristoffer Zegers's *Piano Phasing*, played by fifty student and amateur pianists on twenty-five upright pianos – the culmination of an imaginative education project (see also pages 227–28). The first rehearsal was held in the showroom of Besbrode Pianos in Leeds, and the company then lent twenty-five instruments for the concert. Despite arriving by road, Barry reported that tuning so many pianos in a short space of time was surprisingly easy.

Other abnormal situations had little to do with tuning. In 1999 Andrew Ball played the world premiere of Benedict Mason's highly original *Six Studies*, the fifth of which – 'Steinweg nach Hamburg', a tribute to the Steinway company – uses harmonics that can only be played on a Model D full-length grand. The composer instructs that 'fixed harmonics on the strings of the lower half of the piano (chosen for ergonomic and microtonal considerations) are prepared by nine assistants who retain their finger positions throughout the performance'. Whether intended or not, the black-clad assistants standing motionless round the piano seemed to evoke some strange ritual.

Stockhausen's *Mantra* – performed by the Dutch duo, Ellen Corver and Sepp Grotenhuis, in 1996 – uses the relatively old technology of ring modulators, enabling pitches, once struck, to glissando and drift apart in dreamlike resonances. No physical retuning is involved. Nor was it for Sarah Nicolls's remarkable recital in 2007 which featured five world premieres in which live sounds were captured and changed electronically. In Jonathan Green's *Into Movement*, for instance, wrist sensors worn by the performer are used to 'bend' the struck pitches so that, discreetly amplified through hidden loudspeakers, they, too, seem mysteriously to glissando up and down (see page 265).

Organs and voices

Festival regulars frequently wondered why the organ in St Paul's was rarely heard. In the ill-funded early years I begrudged the expense of tuning its reeds. Organ music has its fraternity, contemporary music another; the combination – like new music for brass band – can be unpopular with both constituencies. Messiaen apart, there is a dearth of organ music by major twentieth-century composers. Nevertheless, in 1981, Gillian Weir gave a fine full-evening recital on the St Paul's organ that included

Kevin Bowyer at the
St Paul's Hall organ.
PHOTO: BRIAN SLATER

Ligeti's *Volumina*. In 1984 Christopher Bowers-Broadbent played Casken, Maxwell Davies and Tavener. In 1986 the organ lent its noble voice to Gubaidulina's *In Croce,* given an impassioned UK premiere by the cellist Timothy Hugh and organist Graham Barber. I have already described my ill-considered addition of organ pieces by Messiaen to an orchestral concert in 1988 (see page 40). Even less satisfactory, I fear, was the UK premiere in 1992 of Xenakis's only organ work, *Gmeeoorh,* which I had persuaded Timothy Bond to attempt on the town hall's Father Willis instrument. He wrestled valiantly with its near-impossible demands, but its 20-minute duration was an ordeal. Not until 1999 did the St Paul's organ feature again, when Kevin Bowyer played works by Donald Bousted, Diana Burrell and Ferneyhough. A decade later Graham McKenzie commissioned David Fennessy to compose *Big Lung* for organ with percussion, and Bowyer brought his habitual flair to its first performance.

If voice and piano recitals have also been few, it is partly because a genre so identified with the nineteenth and early twentieth centuries has, for contemporary composers, been problematic. Six vocal recitals during the festival's first decade (one of which also involved a violinist) contained – amazingly – almost nothing contemporary, little even by living composers. After that, no more voice and piano recitals took place for almost twenty years, when Kirsten Blaise and Nicolas Hodges premiered Finnissy's ambitious cycle *Whitman,* commissioned by the festival and the BBC in 2006.

The partnership of voice and instruments has seemed more congenial: whether with a single instrumentalist – as in Gubaidulina's *Galgenlieder* for soprano and percussion, commissioned by the festival in 1996 – or with a mixed ensemble. The latter has attracted a lexicon of extended vocal and instrumental techniques, Boulez's *Le Marteau sans Maître* of 1953–55 being an early model. There followed Berio's *Circles,* Crumb's *Ancient Voices of Children,* Carter's *A Mirror on which to Dwell,* Gruber's *Frankenstein,* Harvey's *Song Offerings,* Ligeti's *Aventures* and *Síppal, Dobbal, Nádihegedüvel,* Maxwell Davies's *Eight Songs for a Mad King,* Vivier's *Bouchara* – all of them now relatively celebrated, and all performed at the festival. A procession of fine international singers was led by Jane Manning, whose duo-recital with Barry Guy in 1979 featured the

British composers she has consistently championed. She gave another recital in 1985 containing two pieces with piano (including the UK premiere of Finnissy's *Anninnia*) and two with tape (Simon Emerson's *Time Past IV* and Harvey's *Nachtlied*).

Choirs

During the second half of the twentieth century, the ever more exacting standards of concerts and recordings caused the gradual displacement of amateur choirs by professionals. The search for authenticity in early music, and the extreme technical demands of new work, hastened the trend. In England, the 1960s and '70s saw the creation of professional groups like the Monteverdi Choir (1964), Tallis Scholars (1973), John Alldis Choir (1962) and London Sinfonietta Voices (1978) – the last two created specifically to perform new music. Amateur chamber choirs continued to promote specific repertoire, but new music had become largely the preserve of professionals.

Nevertheless, the first choir to perform at the festival was the New London Chamber Choir, hand-picked amateurs brought together by James Wood specifically to tackle contemporary repertoire. Invited to sing in Henze's *Cantata della fiaba estrema* at the 1983 festival, the choir perfectly captured its airborne lyricism. The following day they gave a hugely impressive *a cappella* programme, whose towering centrepiece was the UK premiere of Ligeti's *Drei Phantasien nach Friedrich Hölderlin,* surmounting its difficulties with a precision and tonal unanimity rare among professionals. This was the first of ten visits to Huddersfield. In 1995 NLCC joined the professional Freiburg Solistenchor for the 1995 UK premiere of Nono's *Caminantes… Ayacucho,* and in 1997 – more demandingly – partnered the BBC Philharmonic in the UK premiere of Xenakis's *Cendrées,* whose glottals, whoops and strange ululations they mastered as if their daily fare. The choir's familiarity with Xenakis's choral works, and Wood's involvement in microtonal music, were here huge advantages. The latter found an outlet in his creation in 1992 of the Centre for Microtonal Music, whose eponymous ensemble joined NLCC for an Arts Council tour the following year, bringing to the festival music by Scelsi and Xenakis, plus Harvey's *Valley of Aosta* and Wood's own *Phainomena.*

The day after NLCC's performance in *Cendrèes*, the choir gave a remarkable concert in St Paul's containing the UK premiere of Harvey's *Ashes Dance Back* and Wood's *Séance*. Both works involved live electronics, with a microphone for each singer feeding into will-o'-the-wisp transformations – evoking the 'surreal spirits' of *Séance*, and in the Harvey spatialising individual phonemes so that they seemed, in Jonathan's metaphor, to be scattered 'by wind, fire and water'. This was the first of Harvey's compositions performed at the festival with live sound transformation and diffusion. The Fourth String Quartet was another, performed by the Arditti Quartet in 2003. Two years later NLCC made its final appearance directed by Wood in a concert devoted to Giacinto Scelsi, a composer they had notably promoted. Then, in 2009 conducted by his successor, James Weeks, NLCC gave a stunning performance of Harvey's *The Summer Cloud's Awakening*, composed eight years earlier for the choir's twentieth anniversary. With live electronics engineered at CIRM in Nice and eight-channel spatialisation, its 'clouds' and 'mists' surged and whirled sensationally above and around the audience. In this evolving medium, Jonathan's long experience, and his unique marriage of spiritual and technical dimensions, have earned him wide regard.

In 2010 the choir performed with the Raschèr Saxophone Quartet (making its first festival appearance since 1987). The concert was a co-production with November Music in the city of 's-Hertogenbosch – part of Graham McKenzie's collaboration with Dutch institutions – and contained joint commissions of music by Peter Adriaansz and Michael Finnissy and

an entertaining late work by Kagel. The UK premiere of Finnissy's *Gedächtnis-Hymne* was particularly striking, with the winsome, incantatory lines of the saxes linking passages from the choir.

Meanwhile Weeks's professional vocal ensemble, EXAUDI, had become a frequent visitor, performing every year except one between 2003 and 2008, including two concerts devoted to the music of Christopher Fox and another to Kagel and Stockhausen. Flexible in size, EXAUDI can change from a handful of soloists and music of madrigalean intimacy to a larger chamber choir. A similar ensemble was Singcircle which performed at the festival in 1982. The more extrovert Electric Phoenix, which also performed during the 1980s, consisted of four or five solo voices with sound diffusion in the hands of John Whiting. Its first concert ended with a zestful performance of Berio's *A-Ronne*, and its second with three of Trevor Wishart's adventurous *Vox* cycle (two being first performances). There followed the Hilliard Ensemble, King's Singers and Orlando Consort, the BBC Singers on three occasions, and three vocal groups from Paris, including one constituted in 1992 to perform in Xenakis's *L'Histoire d'un Faust*, which subsequently became Les Jeunes Solistes.

Neue Vocalsolisten Stuttgart in Stockhausen's Stimmung.
PHOTOS: BRIAN SLATER

In 2001 an ensemble founded the previous year made its festival debut. This was Neue Vocalsolisten Stuttgart: seven singers using live electronics who have since made further Huddersfield appearances. Besides postwar classics like *Stimmung* and *A-Ronne,* they have presented UK premieres of works by Aperghis and Sciarrino and, in 2010, Rolf Wallin and Rebecca Saunders. Amateur choirs have continued to play a part: the Pegasus Chamber Choir in 1988 and Joyful Company of Singers in 2000, the youthful fervour of the National Youth Chamber Choir in 1994, and Huddersfield Choral Society on three occasions (described elsewhere). In 2001 London's multi-ethnic The Shout, with singers from different traditions, gave an earthy and corporeal mixture of improvised, gospel, jazz, operatic, early and contemporary classical styles. Then they provided the core for a 'nautical extravaganza' devised by its founders Richard Chew and Orlando Gough, with 200 singers from local amateur and youth choirs, staged to striking effect in the town hall (see page 224).

Whether amateur or professional, none could match the tonal richness of the Nordic choirs which appeared between 1998 and 2003, with their sonorous male voices and full-bodied deep bass notes. The three concerts by the Estonian Philharmonic Chamber Choir are described on page 139. The Latvian Radio Choir, which performed in 2000, may have lacked some of the Estonian's charisma, but were in no way inferior either vocally or musically. Billed as 'Choral Excellence from Riga', for David Fanning the description 'proved to be an understatement'.[27] There were stirring pieces by Peteris Vasks and two astonishingly powerful works by a less familiar Latvian, Maija Einfelde. Unlike the Tapiola Chamber Choir's concert in 2003, the programme extended beyond compatriots, to include Ligeti, Scelsi and Casken, a striking *Es ist genug* by Sven-David Sandstrom – and ended, magically, with an improbably effective transcription of the final movement of Messiaen's *Quartet for the End of Time.*

Tapiola Chamber Choir.
PHOTO: BRIAN SLATER

KAGEL

3.00pm

Film marathon; MATCH HALLELUJAH,
LUDWIG VAN

8.00pm
Concert: SCHLAG AUF SCHLAG, CON VOCE
UNGIS INCARNATUS EST, REPERTOIRE.

The London Music Digest
at the Mermaid Theatre, May 26th 1974.

6 *The shock of the new*

RIGHT:
Paul Steinitz.

Disturbing encounters

At school in the 1950s I was encouraged to
compose, and could play records, whenever
I wanted, from the director of music's collection.
Despite having been a chorister immersed in the
liturgical music of the sixteenth to nineteenth
centuries, I was instinctively drawn to what he
possessed by Stravinsky, Bartók, Shostakovich
and other twentieth-century composers, and
came to regard Stravinsky with particular
veneration. When my father, the conductor
Paul Steinitz, was preparing his London Bach
Society to give the first British performance of
Stravinsky's *Canticum Sacrum* in St Martin-
in-the-Fields in 1956, soon after its Venice
premiere, the imminent arrival of the composer
struck me with the sort of awe I imagine
Catholics might experience at the Second
Coming. Stravinsky had suffered a minor
stroke while conducting in Berlin, so the
London performance was directed by his
assistant Robert Craft. Both Stravinsky and
his wife were in the audience, but whether ill
or well, I would hardly have dared to
approach him.

Although known for his pioneering Bach
performances, my father regularly programmed
contemporary compositions to leaven his
twenty-five-year progress through the complete
Bach cantatas. They included other works by
Stravinsky, the UK premieres of Maderna's
Three Greek Lyrics and Dallapiccola's *Canti di
Prigionia,* the London premiere of Maxwell
Davies's *Veni Sancte Spiritus,* and pieces by
Schoenberg, Glasser, David Matthews, Maw,
Milner, Newsome, Rawsthorne, Rubbra and
Tavener, several of whom the London Bach
Society commissioned. On the staff of the Royal
Academy of Music and Goldsmiths College,

he taught or befriended young firebrands
such as Cale, Tilbury and Cardew – the latter
contributing an analytical guide to help the
choir learn the *Canticum Sacrum.*

My father's juxtaposition of music by, for
instance, Schütz, Bach, Mozart and Brahms
with the work of living composers echoed the
ideals of William Glock. But it was done with
a passionate conviction that undoubtedly
influenced my own.[1] It was in Cambridge
that I became more familiar with the Second
Viennese School, and played all Craft's boxed
set of Webern recordings, following the music
in Universal Edition's recently published
miniature scores. The emerging younger
deities of the avant-garde I viewed with similar
timidity, distanced by the daunting intellectual
fire surrounding their serial Valhalla. Nevertheless,
the late 1950s and early '60s were heady days
for new music, and by my early twenties I knew
and loved a great deal.

Yet it could be perplexing. In July 1969, an
all-Xenakis concert in the Royal Festival Hall
aroused my anger. The main work, *Strategie,*
pitted two orchestras against each other in a

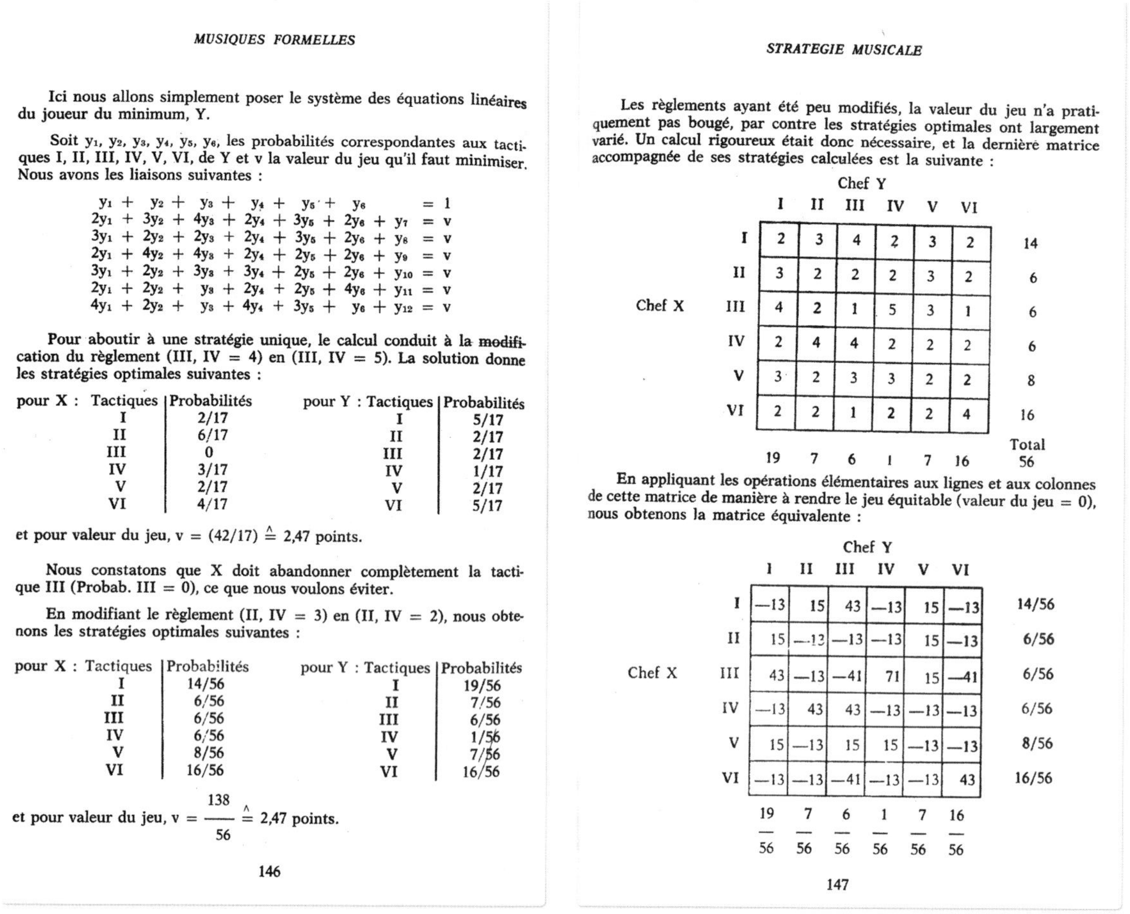

MUSIQUES FORMELLES

Ici nous allons simplement poser le système des équations linéaires du joueur du minimum, Y.

Soit $y_1, y_2, y_3, y_4, y_5, y_6$, les probabilités correspondantes aux tactiques I, II, III, IV, V, VI, de Y et v la valeur du jeu qu'il faut minimiser. Nous avons les liaisons suivantes :

$$\begin{aligned} y_1 + y_2 + y_3 + y_4 + y_5 + y_6 &= 1 \\ 2y_1 + 3y_2 + 4y_3 + 2y_4 + 3y_5 + 2y_6 + y_7 &= v \\ 3y_1 + 2y_2 + 2y_3 + 2y_4 + 3y_5 + 2y_6 + y_8 &= v \\ 2y_1 + 4y_2 + 4y_3 + 2y_4 + 2y_5 + 2y_6 + y_9 &= v \\ 3y_1 + 2y_2 + 3y_3 + 3y_4 + 2y_5 + 2y_6 + y_{10} &= v \\ 2y_1 + 2y_2 + y_3 + 2y_4 + 2y_5 + 4y_6 + y_{11} &= v \\ 4y_1 + 2y_2 + y_3 + 4y_4 + 3y_5 + y_6 + y_{12} &= v \end{aligned}$$

Pour aboutir à une stratégie unique, le calcul conduit à la modification du règlement (III, IV = 4) en (III, IV = 5). La solution donne les stratégies optimales suivantes :

pour X : Tactiques	Probabilités	pour Y : Tactiques	Probabilités
I	2/17	I	5/17
II	6/17	II	2/17
III	0	III	2/17
IV	3/17	IV	1/17
V	2/17	V	2/17
VI	4/17	VI	5/17

et pour valeur du jeu, $v = (42/17) \triangleq 2{,}47$ points.

Nous constatons que X doit abandonner complètement la tactique III (Probab. III = 0), ce que nous voulons éviter.

En modifiant le règlement (II, IV = 3) en (II, IV = 2), nous obtenons les stratégies optimales suivantes :

pour X : Tactiques	Probabilités	pour Y : Tactiques	Probabilités
I	14/56	I	19/56
II	6/56	II	7/56
III	6/56	III	6/56
IV	6/56	IV	1/56
V	8/56	V	7/56
VI	16/56	VI	16/56

et pour valeur du jeu, $v = \frac{138}{56} \triangleq 2{,}47$ points.

146

STRATEGIE MUSICALE

Les règlements ayant été peu modifiés, la valeur du jeu n'a pratiquement pas bougé, par contre les stratégies optimales ont largement varié. Un calcul rigoureux était donc nécessaire, et la dernière matrice accompagnée de ses stratégies calculées est la suivante :

Chef X \ Chef Y	I	II	III	IV	V	VI	
I	2	3	4	2	3	2	14
II	3	2	2	2	3	2	6
III	4	2	1	5	3	1	6
IV	2	4	4	2	2	2	6
V	3	2	3	3	2	2	8
VI	2	2	1	2	2	4	16
	19	7	6	1	7	16	Total 56

En appliquant les opérations élémentaires aux lignes et aux colonnes de cette matrice de manière à rendre le jeu équitable (valeur du jeu = 0), nous obtenons la matrice équivalente :

Chef X \ Chef Y	I	II	III	IV	V	VI	
I	−13	15	43	−13	15	−13	14/56
II	15	−13	−13	−13	15	−13	6/56
III	43	−13	−41	71	15	−41	6/56
IV	−13	43	43	−13	−13	−13	6/56
V	15	−13	15	15	−13	−13	8/56
VI	−13	−13	−41	−13	−13	43	16/56
	19/56	7/56	6/56	1/56	7/56	16/56	

147

Xenakis considers the application of game theory to the conductors' tactics in Duel *(1959), prototype of* Strategie *(1962) – both for two orchestras – in the original edition of* Musiques Formelles.

contest governed by elaborate rules, their two conductors choosing from 'stochastic' structures computed on the 7090 IBM in Paris, the success (or not) of their tactics being assessed by umpires who, at intervals, held aloft large score cards. As sound it seemed wholly alienating. Music from this rigorously calculated period of Xenakis's career I still find problematic, whilst admiring its radicalism. This adverse impression was not improved when I tried to grasp the formidable mathematical concepts of *Musiques Formelles*, published in an English translation as *Formalized Music* in 1971.[2] I mention this because, as will already be evident, Xenakis became one of the composers I most loved and revered.

Persistence repays. In London there were many opportunities to hear new work and, when possible, I seized them. In April and May 1974, the Second London Music Digest helpfully took place on Sundays when I could visit London, with a day devoted to Xenakis, another to Kagel. The Kagel included the rare treat of the composer and Cologne New Music Ensemble performing *Repertoire*, the opening tableau of his legendary *Staatstheater*. In this 'scenic concert for five performers', music is but one ingredient of an inventive visual 'theatre', whose amusing iconoclasm the audience responded to with delight. The Xenakis concert at the Roundhouse was seismic. I still have the notes I wrote afterwards, overwhelmed by the 'profound grandeur' of *Bohor*, and the five brass players in *Eonta* standing at the rear of the stage, 'swinging their bells from side to side, like the trunks of prehistoric mammals or antennae of radio-telescopes calling to each other... the hard glitter, brilliance, toughness and strength of this music... its texture, sonority, density and (at times) harmonic tension'.

During a year at the University of Illinois (1972–73) I discovered the music of Crumb and Carter, witnessed experiments at the frontiers of computer technology, lay on the floor in a 'Dream House' whilst La Monte Young intoned to the accompaniment of mesmeric drones and Marian Zazeela's abstract shapes rotated above, joined a voyeuristic throng as Charlotte Moorman played the cello half naked with two tiny television monitors strapped to her breasts showing images created by Nan June Paik, heard the Black Earth Percussion Group's glittering performance of Rzewski's process piece, *Les moutons de Panurge,* whose success paradoxically relies on the inevitability of failure.

Fascinated by all this, I am ashamed to recall how badly I reacted to early 'minimalism'. Back in England, I took my future wife to Steve Reich's *Drumming* in a depressingly empty Huddersfield Town Hall. The following year, we drove to Keele to hear Philip Glass's *Music in Twelve Parts* – also very sparsely attended. Both these early works were performed by their composer-led ensembles and toured by the Contemporary Music Network in 1974–75. On each occasion I failed to register their inner 'processes'; and, lacking any conventional signposts of time passing (and concerned by the 'ordeal' I was imposing on Nan), after twenty minutes of monochrome repetition, in which 'nothing "happens" in the usual sense',[3] I could have screamed. Numbed by incessant quavers and exceptionally loud amplification, we quitted Glass at the interval. As a student in Cambridge, I had even misjudged Schoenberg's First String Quartet, half-listening to a broadcast while doing something else, and irritated by its apparent dissonance. A year later, listening again late one evening with the score, I could hardly believe that this expressive music, so palpably ardent and beautiful, could ever have seemed irksome.[4]

Through years of teaching and planning, I never forgot these uncomprehending first encounters with music I came to love; and that, if you look only for attributes which happen not to be present, you fail to hear those which are. It was a lesson to remember as the festival developed its mission: which was (once I recognised it) similar to that of the great Sir Henry Wood – ie. to bring the best music to the greatest possible number of people, except that in Huddersfield this was qualified by the adjective 'contemporary'.

Moulding expectations

Time-scale, type of discourse, density of information, continuity, content, manner, process. The elements of music are treated so variously by composers that listeners need to be able to adopt several different modes of reception. To assist them, without being overtly pedagogical, the festival tried to be informative. The initial brochure was key to shaping expectations, and, even when the festival had an executive team, I preferred to write copy myself. How can anyone who does not intimately know a piece of music convincingly introduce it?

In the programme book I tried to moderate the wilfully obscure and pretentious, and ensure that notes and essays were pertinent, clear and literate, and biographies (however compressed) conveyed ideas as well as facts. An unfamiliar piece may contain few clues to its structure, even fewer to its length. Perceptions of time passing are relative and, as we know, partly governed by habit. Faced with the unfamiliar, it helps to be forewarned. So, from 1986, durations (if sometimes speculative) were printed in the programme for every piece. We were rewarded when Gerald Larner, in *The Guardian* Arts Review's 'Top 10 listings for 1988', cited Huddersfield 'for the clarity and breadth of information in the programme book'.

The tone and style of the brochure were crucial. To be informative, demystifying and enticing was one thing. It needed to be intellectually substantial, yet witty and a little anarchic, both to convey vitality and set the stage for novelty. Its visual appearance increasingly absorbed me. Text, image and design were key to conveying the flavour of a particular festival, and we worked hard on their interaction. We tried to be slightly enigmatic, tapping a vein of curiosity, whilst media endorsements helped dispel suspicions that the festival would be incomprehensible and dry.

After the appointment of a full-time administrator in the early 1990s, the production of print became more collaborative; and, as it was now digital, we would share long shifts sitting with the designer at a computer. I admired practice in other disciplines, believing that pictures of people, especially faces, exercise a powerful magnetism. So the A5 brochures between 1998 and 2001 were modelled on theatre and contemporary dance (which habitually draw larger audiences), with full-page photos and a pithy slogan on the left of each double-page spread, and listings and explanatory copy on the right. Full colour was introduced in 1999, but the tone was still quizzical, with a photo showing the concourse at Charles de Gaulle airport, but with artists, composers and events listed on the 'Arrivals' board instead of airports and planes. That for 2000 showed a burning hut on a beach, and a man in half-length boots, holding a violin case, about to enter.[5] They were the festival's most successful publicity in attracting the public, as audience statistics confirm, although supported by additional leaflets, commissioned by Maria Bota, the festival manager, highlighting the most engaging town hall and theatre performances.

Explanations and ideas

Gathering together the work of a single artist in any medium can be revealing. More of it makes more impact. Hence the thematic nature of most Huddersfield festivals. What the composer has to say is nearly always illuminating, and for that reason interviews in the 1980s and '90s were generally unhurried, with ample time for the exposition of ideas, to laugh, digress, probe and pursue whatever might arise. This resulted in some exceptionally deep and sympathetic encounters – and, occasionally, more combative. Such conversations were prized by the festival audience, and many lasted well over an hour. That between George Benjamin and Pierre Boulez in 1989 continued for nearly two, despite starting late in the evening. Unfortunately, I never asked for any to be recorded, but some were, and a volume of transcripts is to be published separately.[6]

With my background as a teacher I viewed the festival as broadly explanatory. Lectures and discussions were components from the start. An early landmark was Trevor Wishart's illustrated lecture on 'Sound Transformation and Aural Music-theatre' – issues which his music ideally exemplified. In 1984 Maxwell Davies spoke eloquently of his experiences as a school teacher in Cirencester, and of the liberating power of music and innate musicality, 'in nine out of ten people,' waiting to be released. Nigel Osborne extolled 'the increasing power and influence of music over other art forms', and his vision of music theatre as 'the torch of theatrical development'. Mauricio Kagel gave a lecture on his television productions.

The following year, in conversation with David Osmond-Smith and in response to questions

Brochures for the 1998 and 1999 festivals.

from a large gathering on the afternoon of his first concert, Luciano Berio, remarkably eloquent in English, was 'bracing and calming, vigorous and unflappable', revealing 'a mind every bit as lucid and richly textured as his music'.[7] Delivered one morning during the 1987 festival, Tom Johnson's *Lectures with Audience Participation* were a playful, yet thought-provoking, diversion. Later that day Henry Brant, Carleton Clay, Yvar Mikhashoff and Stephen Montague shared memories of Henry Cowell, 'the neglected pioneer', after Montague and the polytechnic orchestra had revived his Piano Concerto, which had lain virtually forgotten for fifty-seven years. The polytechnic's Symphonic Wind Band and Twentieth-Century Ensemble also performed that year, and the active participation of so many students increased their interest in what was happening, not least because it was generally shared. At £28, a student season ticket for the whole festival still cost only a quarter of the price for adult tickets purchased separately.

It was at this festival that Stephen Albert, invited as part of an American focus, delivered his withering condemnation of twentieth century European music (see page 100).

It sounded even more insulting after Xenakis, in conversation earlier in the festival, had displayed such sensitivity, humanity and far-sighted vision.[8] In 1987, an illustrated lecture on Piranesi's *Carceri d'Invenzione* was given by the art historian John Wilton-Ely. With a set of the original prints on view in the Art Gallery, and Ferneyhough explaining his musical response to Piranesi's 'incompatible co-existent perspectives', the artist's drawings became a fascinating subject in themselves. Some who came to Wilton-Ely's lecture did not bother with the concert. For others, it was an illuminating preparation for the UK premiere of Ferneyhough's complete *Carceri* cycle.

In 1988, Stockhausen's pre-concert introduction to *Michaels Reise* was 'sane and practical',[9] 'a model of lucidity'[10] – unlike his talk eight years later, whose inflated pomposity was castigated by the critics. I wish that I had asked more composers to give talks, but busy composers often agree only to be interviewed. For many years, Ligeti had taught annually in Darmstadt, but when he visited Huddersfield in 1993 he had no time to prepare. Instead, I interviewed him twice; and, after an illustrated lecture by the Bremen mathematician, Hans-Otto Peitgen, the relationship between fractals and music was explored by Ligeti and Peitgen together. One of the most riveting of all lectures was given by Feldman's close friend, Bunita Marcus, in 1996.

A lively late-night discussion between George Benjamin and Pierre Boulez.
PHOTO: PETER LAWSON

All these were part of a daytime diet of interviews, discussions, masterclasses, films, installations and participatory workshops. After 1996, formal lectures became rarer; but, in the new university lecture theatre in Canalside West, there were some extended and fascinating interviews: notably with Brian Eno, Helmut Lachenmann and Wolfgang Rihm, and Nuria Schoenberg-Nono (daughter of Schoenberg and Nono's widow). In the new millennium such interviews have been shorter, and consequently less probing. But there have been broad-based symposia, as in 2004, when a panel of producers, journalists, marketers and others led a debate on 'How contemporary music can win new audiences without compromising its integrity'. A similar Sound Circuit symposium took place in 2005. In 2008 the festival hosted the General Assembly of Réseau Varèse, and began a relationship with the British Council that has brought practitioners to Huddersfield from many other countries.

Educational projects were linked to festival themes, and we encouraged participants to hear other concerts not linked to their projects. With experience, I designed events for different audiences. Some might be complex, intimate and esoteric, aimed at the *cognoscenti*; others bolder public statements (in the town hall, perhaps), or dance, theatre, puppetry etc., in the Lawrence Batley Theatre. Themed weekends focused on emblematic large-scale concerts and premieres likely to attract international visitors. Weekdays might be geared more to local and regional audiences as well as students, with participatory daytime activities.

All these strategies were intended to assist understanding and fire enthusiasm. None did so more effectively, however, than the presence of the composers themselves.

LEFT:
One of the trapeze artists
performing in L'Histoire
d'un Faust *by Xenakis in*
Huddersfield Town Hall.
PHOTO: SELWYN GREEN

7 *Composers*

Xenakis and the UPIC computer

When Xenakis arrived in 1982, he revealed a warmth, humanity and generosity I had not expected. Sitting on the platform in an empty St Paul's, on the morning following a day filled with performances of his music, Iannis took from his bag a lavishly illustrated book about the 'polytopes', his striking site-specific installations of the 1950s and 1960s. Inside he had written my name, and under it his thanks and best wishes for my 'wonderful action in favour of the music of today'. I didn't think I had done much and was touched. Delving further, he produced copies of *Musiques Formelles* and his book on music and architecture, then an LP which he had also inscribed. It introduced me to *Cendrées* for chorus and orchestra, a seething, molten, volcanic composition propelled by huge glissandi erupting in the orchestra, and ululating wails from the chorus unlike anything I had heard. Listening to it triggered a deep desire to programme *Cendrées,* an aspiration which, as we have seen, was eventually realised in 1997.

Five years later I called on Iannis in Paris, meeting him in his top-floor composing loft in rue Victor Massée. Although crammed with books, scores, boxes and artefacts, the room looked orderly and purposeful. Xenakis worked like the novelist Trollope, standing at a tall desk. On a low coffee table lay Heinz-Otto Peitgen and Peter Richter's newly published *The Beauty of Fractals.*[1] We discussed bringing over the UPIC drawing computer for what would be its first UK appearance. Xenakis had conceived the idea in 1953, whilst transcribing his graphic drawings for *Metastasis* into musical notation. Twenty years later, developments in technology and computer science had caught up with his

dream. By then his own research, and that of colleagues specialising in electronics, software and signal processing, was concentrated in the Centre d'Études de Mathématique et Automatique Musicales (CEMAMu), located at the Centre National d'Études des Télécommunications (CNET). The system they created they called Unité Polyagogigue Informatique du CEMAMu, producing the acronym UPIC.

The purpose of the UPIC was to enable composers to create sounds directly by moving an electromagnetic 'pencil' across a sloping sensitised 'drawing board', and to hear the results almost immediately. It thus united the visual and aural domains of Xenakis's career both as architect and composer. Without knowledge of programming or mathematics, even of conventional notation, any user could manipulate the basic musical constituents, and build them progressively into a composition. Iannis invited me to visit him the following day on the seventh floor of the Telecommunications Centre where the computer was housed. He was busy finishing *Taurhiphanie,* and told me, with a conspiratorial smile, how the premiere of this, his second tape composition using UPIC, in the Roman amphitheatre in Arles, would be accompanied by wild bulls and white horses from the Camargue galloping round the arena.

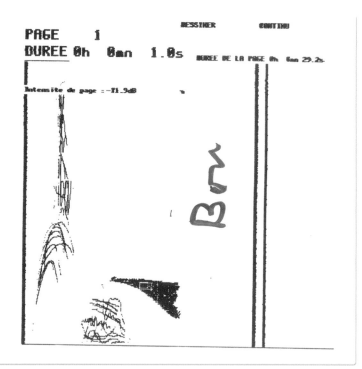

Unfolding the computer print-out, he showed me successive pages of its 'score', each containing graphic formulations – visualised sound one might say. On one he had written *'Bon'* in red, presumably a mark of approval; on another superimposed ascending curves simulated the whoop-like bellowing of the bulls. Iannis had to leave for a meeting, but suggested I stay and try my hand. It was surprisingly easy, and during an intoxicatingly happy hour I drew a shape, copied, stretched, shrunk and rotated it, whilst listening to the results.

My original plan to bring the UPIC computer to Huddersfield in 1982 had stalled when President Mitterrand's emergency economies cut the French cultural budget. But the delay had advantages, both regarding the festival's better resources and improvements in the UPIC software, enabling the drawn sounds to be

ABOVE:
Two UPIC print-outs
for Taurhiphanie.
The second represents
the bellowing of bulls.

LEFT:
Interviewing Xenakis
in Huddersfield.

heard virtually in 'real time'. Xenakis made much of the system's accessibility, which allowed composers – indeed anybody, including children and the physically impaired – to create their own electronic soundscapes without prior experience either of composition or computers. In 1985 he established a pedagogic team to run courses using duplicate hardware; and it was these personnel, along with the Scottish composer Peter Nelson, who installed the UPIC in Huddersfield Art Gallery in November 1987. During two weeks of workshops they taught composers, students, amateurs and children (some of them disabled) arriving from both sides of the Pennines, with a public demonstration held every day at noon. On the gallery walls were displayed Xenakis's schemata, polytope designs, photographs and drawings. Surrounded by these and an attentive audience I engaged

LEFT:
UPIC workshop in
Huddersfield Art Gallery.
PHOTO: *HUDDERSFIELD*
DAILY EXAMINER

Xenakis in a revealing discussion which, thanks to a recording made by the BBC, survives and will be published.[2] Later that afternoon Nouritza Matossian lectured on 'Xenakis: Master of Chaos', after which Claude Helffer with the Arditti String Quartet and Spectrum played a portrait concert. It included *Ikhoor, Dikhthas, N'Shima,* the UK premiere of *Akea,* and ended with *Eonta,* as did the first festival concert in 1978, but now more thrilling in the encircling acoustic of St Paul's.

The composer's music and his presence in person were immensely stimulating. Every five years between 1982 and 1997 the festival featured his music. Xenakis attended all of these except 1992, although that year included his music-theatre spectacle, *L'Histoire d'un Faust,* assembled by the composer out of existing works with linking additions. The idea had come from meeting a young Parisian percussionist, Roland Auzet, and his partner Véronique Bétourné, a trapeze artist in Le Cirque d'Hiver. Iannis forged warm bonds with dedicated interpreters. His controversial and difficult emergence as a composer lay far in

the past, and he had become a beacon for the young. Creating a theatrical sequence for a dazzling young percussionist and circus performers appealed to him, and the concept developed to include Roland Auzet playing the part of Faust, the bass Nicholas Isherwood as Mephistopheles, two trapeze acrobats representing Margeurite and La Bohème, and a vocal ensemble. I learnt about the production from Marc Dondey, previously Pierre Audi's assistant at the Almeida Festival and now programming Strasbourg's 'Musica', a model I greatly admired. Marc would phone to tell me about Strasbourg projects he thought Huddersfield might like to repeat, and only once asked us to share a modest commission fee. With its aerial *mise-en-scène, L'Histoire d'un Faust* required a month of rehearsals, but the cost was underwritten by sponsors in France and the fee requested of Huddersfield only £6,000. It was a bargain, even after John Major's government was forced out of the ERM and the £6,000 increased to £7,651 – although with travel and accommodation the final total rose to £13,687.

UPIC Sketch *drawn on the UPIC computer by Colin Rose. The different colours represent left and right channels.*
© *COLIN ROSE 1992*

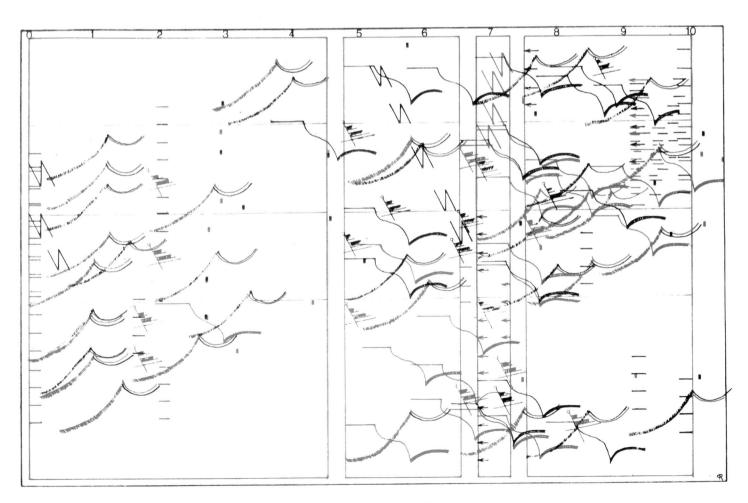

Roland Auzet and the stage manager visited Huddersfield, and after careful inspection, we agreed that the trapeze artists could be suspended from the stucco ceiling. I had not forgotten how we nearly killed Stockhausen, when a wooden plug attached to one of the rigging holes fell onto his mixing desk. For *L'Histoire d'un Faust* the trapeze ropes were attached above the stage. But as Véronique and her partner ascended during the performance, they started to swing further and further over the audience. Sitting beside Brian Pearson, I watched them spiralling ever more alarmingly, each held by a loop of rope around one ankle. With no safety net, and adrenalin raised by the ferocity of Roland's drumming, the aerial gymnastics grew ever more audacious and terrifying, generating a tension never forgotten by anyone who witnessed it. If anything went amiss, I knew that Brian, as Head of Cultural Services, would be blamed; but he maintained his usual *sangfroid*. Afterwards Jenny Lockwood, the ever helpful and efficient manager of the Kirklees halls, was characteristically charming and unruffled. Only years later, when I met Jenny at a function and reminded her of the event, did she admit that the following morning she had received an extremely irate phone call from a disapproving official, and had to promise never to allow anything like it to happen again.

Four years later, approaching Xenakis's seventy-fifth birthday, Paul Meacham, manager of the London Sinfonietta, suggested that we jointly commission a work for Evelyn Glennie and the Sinfonietta; and, although the festival's contribution would be small, offered Huddersfield the premiere. From Paris however came disturbing reports of illness, a dimming of creative energy, perhaps also of Xenakis's mind. Concerned, I flew to see him, and Françoise, his wife, invited me to lunch along with Radu Stan, Iannis's publisher and a long-standing friend. I had never visited their home and felt privileged. The meal was simple but graciously served; the apartment spacious and welcoming, filled (like Cage's in New York) with exquisite art and artefacts, some ancient and doubtless very valuable, others personal gifts to Xenakis from living artists. In their unostentatious arrangement, they complemented and enriched each other.

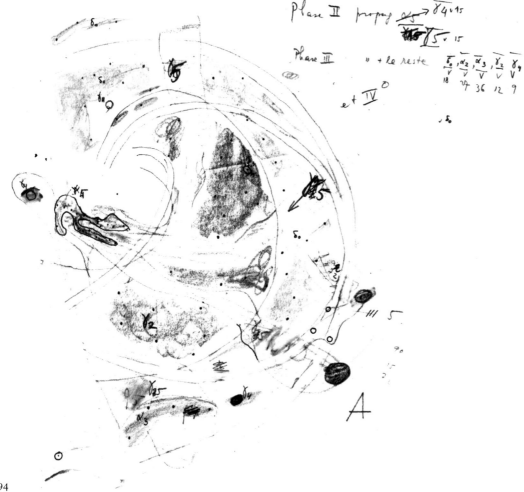

One of Xenakis's sketches on tracing paper for the Polytope de Montréal *(1967). The drawing shows one effect of the phased lights positioned along five nets of cables.*

Iannis was lucid, warm, dignified, entertaining and fastidiously courteous. But his sentences were short and there were things he could not remember. He spoke of being tired and having difficulty composing. Moved to be with him, saddened to think that this courageous creative spirit might have little more to give, I returned home. During the summer and early autumn reports remained worrying. Suddenly, against our expectation, a few pages arrived, but only twenty-eight bars of music scored for variously pitched drums and small ensemble, spare in gesture and dynamics, and pointedly titled *O-Mega*, the last letter of the Greek alphabet. It was, indeed, his final work. Iannis arrived in Huddersfield shepherded by Françoise and Radu. The festival included the British premiere of *Cendrées* played by the BBC Philharmonic, its primeval choral part superbly delivered by the New London Chamber Choir and its total effect extraordinary. Afterwards Xenakis went on stage to warm applause. The next day I had scheduled a short public discussion, but it was one of the hardest interviews to conduct, as I had constantly to prompt and fill in what he could not recall. The sadness was felt by everyone. Like Ligeti, Iannis declined slowly, his death in 2001 depriving the world of a wise, warm and wonderful person whose courageous vision and daring produced music of extraordinary originality. Defiantly working at the margins, no composer better epitomised Modernism.[3]

Gubaidulina, Holliger and Lachenmann

There could hardly be a more different approach to the plasticity of sound than the music of the Russian composer, Sofia Gubaidulina, whose relative isolation and Tartar background has given her music a mystical, fleeting spirituality; whereas that of Xenakis is formidably concrete. Like him, Gubaidulina came to Huddersfield three times: in 1986, 1990 and 1996. I was introduced to her work at the offices of Boosey & Hawkes in London. Music publishers naturally advocate their house composers, and, now that Huddersfield was a significant platform, the relationship with the publishers had become close. Meetings with their promotional staff were stimulating and fruitful, and from my somewhat detached viewpoint nearly 200 miles from London, it was helpful to hear at first hand about performances both in the UK and abroad,

in assessments that were never unduly partisan. These became long and valued friendships, opening up many new paths and accompanied by an unstinting supply of information, scores and recordings. They arrived without obligation. I had to be convinced.

Gubaidulina's music was managed by the Hamburg publishing house Sikorski, specialists in the Russian avant-garde. As agents, Boosey & Hawkes had no direct contact with the composer, but stocked scores and tapes. I was shown into a listening room, invited to sample whatever I wished, and, after listening to several works culminating in the violin concerto *Offertorium,* found myself unexpectedly moved. I made notes and took home a copy of Sikorski's work-list and a score of 'chamber works' published the previous year by Sovetsky Kompozitor in Moscow. The volume included a work for cello, bayan and strings called *Sieben Worte (Seven Words)* – as I only discovered later. For it was not so named, the Soviets having suppressed Gubaidulina's religious titles (including *Offertorium*), renaming this piece *Partita*.[4] Janis Susskind, head of promotion, arranged for me to receive the quarterly magazine *Music in the USSR*, published by Gosconcert, the state music organisation, whose spring 1985 edition contained an article on Gubaidulina. She also put me in touch with Gerard McBurney, UK expert on Soviet music who had studied in Russia and knew most of its composers personally. I postponed an earlier intention of approaching Kúrtag, and wrote a letter to Gubaidulina (translated into Russian) inviting her to the 1986 festival, with a further letter to the powerful head of the Composers' Union, Tikhon Khrennikov. There was no reply from either.

Meanwhile I had met Heinz Holliger, not only a fine oboist, but a significant composer – although unknown as such in Britain – and invited him to participate as performer, teacher and composer. I had not yet learnt that he was also a gifted conductor. To perform his music Heinz suggested that I contact Karsten Witt, manager of the Junge Deutsche Philharmonie and its recent offshoot Ensemble Modern, already making an impact in Europe.

Karsten replied positively, and at the 1985 ISCM World Music Days in Amsterdam we met and I heard Ensemble Modern give performances of Walter Zimmermann's

Saitenspiel and Helmut Lachenmann's *Mouvement (-vor der Erstarrung)*. The energy of the playing was continuously gripping, the individuality of both pieces astonishing. But the Lachenmann outshone everything. I still have my notes of this first encounter scrawled on the back of the programme:

Startling, electrifying effect, dance-like with the fun of not knowing what we'll hear next. Riveting piece… extreme and total use of novel playing devices…their fascinating and ultimately sensational assembly into teasing, alluring and exhilarating formations, paced with consummate skill… a *tour de force* of ensemble playing in which new instrumental sounds, so over-exploited in solo pieces, were thrown together in a brilliant mosaic of unpredictable yet exciting and satisfying events.

Subsequently I came to understand *Mouvement* better, but this baptism was revelatory, firing a commitment to Lachenmann's music which Huddersfield, alone in Britain, maintained for two decades. Meeting on various occasions in Italy, Spain and England, we became friends, and Helmut's return to Huddersfield in 2000 was a special pleasure, this time with Wolfgang Rihm, during which they engaged in a long and lively public discussion.[5] In the 2005 festival, Tom Service programmed the UK premiere of the new *Concertini*. It was Ensemble Modern's seventh performance of *Concertini* since giving the world premiere three months earlier. Brilliantly inventive, virtuoso and dramatic, it is one of Lachenmann's most dazzling creations.

In Amsterdam Karsten had proposed that Holliger conduct Ensemble Modern in Huddersfield; so I met Heinz again to discuss content, particularly the music of Gubaidulina and others behind the Iron Curtain about which he was impressively knowledgeable. Three Ensemble Modern concerts were agreed, although only one piece by Lachenmann, *Mouvement (-vor der Erstarrung)*, the only one at that time in their repertoire. There would be two works by Holliger, two by York Höller and one each by seven other composers, mostly from the Eastern bloc. I would dearly like to have included the whole of Holliger's *Scardanelli-Zyklus*, which had recently been premiered in Donaueschingen, but to programme more than part of it was impractical. Also in the festival were Lachenmann's *Pression, Gran Torso* and *Salut für Caudwell*, plus *Kinderspiel* for piano played by Helmut himself. Of Gubaidulina we agreed *Detto II* (its UK premiere), and *Garden*

Sofia Gubaidulina being interviewed at the 1987 festival.
PHOTO: THE SUNDAY TIMES

of Joy and Sorrow played by the Holligers with Aurèle Nicolet and Jean Sulem in a chamber concert. Elsewhere were *De Profundis, In Croce* and *Fatselya. Quasi Hoquetus* replaced a scheduled new string quartet after we heard that it would not be ready. To complete this Gubaidulina portrait, Music Projects/London performed *Concordanza*.

I had already committed the only professional orchestral concert to Lutosławski conducting the BBC Symphony Orchestra in his own music. But two years earlier the Polytechnic Symphony Orchestra had given a very creditable account of Nigel Osborne's *Sinfonia No 2* under Barrie Webb's direction. Now we weighed up Holliger's much more difficult and highly innovative *Atembogen* and decided that – despite notation, instrumental techniques and sonorities far removed from students' experience – it was worth attempting. An intensive rehearsal schedule was carried through with dedication, and the performance itself was a triumph.

Holliger, who missed the performance, seemed pleased with the recording. Disappointingly, it looked as if Gubaidulina would not be coming at all. She had been allowed out of the USSR on only one previous occasion, and less than a week before the festival there was still no reply

Brian Ferneyhough.
PHOTOS: *SELWYN GREEN*

from Russia. Then, with just two days to go, Gerard phoned to say that she was on her way, and soon after they arrived together, Gerard acting as translator.

Of the eighteen works by Gubaidulina, Holliger and Lachenmann performed that year, fourteen were new to Britain. Of the sixteen compositions by Gubaidulina presented by the festival in 1986 and subsequently, nine have been UK premieres and one a world premiere. None were orchestral, although *Jetzt immer Schnee (Now always Snow)* was performed in 1996 by an enlarged London Sinfonietta, with the Sinfonietta Voices positioned around the audience as a metaphysical extension of the musical space. On the final day of the festival, when this concert was due to take place, snow did indeed fall. The rehearsal had taken place in the morning, and during the afternoon some of the players drove to the Showcase multiplex near Leeds, emerging later to find themselves snowbound in its car park. In Huddersfield Town Hall we waited anxiously to begin the concert, eventually thirty minutes late. The audience was already depleted by the weather, but there was a more tragic consequence. Whilst driving back to London, the CoMA double bassist, Paul Servis, who had played in the festival that afternoon, was killed on a treacherous section of the M1.

Simmering polarities

The 1987 festival featured not only Gubaidulina and Xenakis, but a more than usually broad spectrum of composers of widely differing aesthetic standpoints. Believing that there are many ways in which creative artists respond to the world, I was instinctively non-ideological, asking only that, of whatever persuasion, the music should be good of its type, performed as well as possible, and that, in the spirit of Cage, listeners should be open-minded. I thought often of the Zen doctrine cited by Cage: 'Imitate the sands of the Ganges who are neither pleased by perfume and who are not disgusted by filth.' This, he said, 'is almost the basis of oriental philosophy and could be the basis for any useful ethic we are going to make for a global village. We are going to have to get over the need for likes and dislikes.'[6] Yet I also empathised with Schumann's aphorism in *Neue Zeitschrift für Musik*: 'Never play bad compositions and never listen to them when not absolutely obliged to

do so.'[7] Despite their contradictions – and never having attended Germany's famously polemical courses in Darmstadt – it seemed somehow possible to live by both.

Thus, when the arrival of Xenakis was followed by Ferneyhough, Stephen Albert and John Adams, the polarities that emerged took me by surprise. I had intended no confrontation, approaching everything with equal curiosity – a quality that Huddersfield audiences appeared to share. Stephen Albert's music had prompted some doubts, but it effectively embodied the contemporary-romantic mainstream in America. It had earned him a Pulitzer prize and, I thought, deserved hearing. The animosity that erupted has become part of a Huddersfield mythology. But the story needs correcting. Among the annals of famously disrupted premieres, fisticuffs and bloodshed, it was a minor disturbance. And protest was provoked by and directed at Albert – not Adams – as I explain below.

Ferneyhough's reception

Presenting the first complete performance in the UK of Brian Ferneyhough's *Carceri d'Invenzione* was central to this plurality. I was well aware of its importance and, indeed, it made the most impact. Yet Ferneyhough's music was controversial, shunned by listeners and by the establishment. The festival also included his three *Time and Motion Studies* performed for the first time as a cycle, the UK premiere of his Third String Quartet and *Funérailles* for strings. Ensemble Exposé gave a concert entitled 'Darmstadt and Beyond: Ferneyhough and Pupils', wholly devoted to 'new complexity' apart from a piece by Kaija Saariaho. The young Scottish composer-pianist James Clapperton, an entrant for the Young Composers' Competition, offered to play *Lemma-Icon-Epigram* and gave a brilliant impromptu performance one afternoon in the Recital Hall. The presence of Brian himself was stimulating. For however conceptualised the music, he was an insightful and incisive speaker. This long-overdue exposure in Britain acted as a magnet to young composers, who were also drawn to the opportunity of working with Xenakis's UPIC computer. That year we awarded bursaries to thirty-eight unsalaried individuals: mainly young, but including one lady in her seventies, mainly British, but including some from Holland, New Zealand and the USA.

Brian appeared not to notice – or at least did not remark – that I had judiciously rewritten his programme notes for the *Carceri*, in an attempt to make them clearer and more grammatical. Evidently I had altered too little. Robert Cockroft of the *Yorkshire Post* complained that they remained 'extravagantly impenetrable'.[8] Peter Heyworth in *The Observer* accused Ferneyhough of 'verbal obfuscation', blaming his years in Germany for a tendency to 'invent a non-word like "suggestionality" without blushing'.[9] For Malcolm Hayes, however, writing in *The Sunday Telegraph*,[10] the composer's introductory talk was 'articulate and fascinating', and the performance itself 'truly wonderful', especially the soloists. As well as the 'sensational virtuosity' of Irvine Arditti, Harrie Starreveld's playing of the piccolo, concert, alto and bass flutes was 'something close to genius'.

Overall, the *Carceri* benefited from a performance which was not only inspirational, but appeared to be extraordinarily accurate, amounting to a searing vindication of an achievement applauded in Europe, still viewed with perplexity in England. In complete contrast, the three *Time and Motion Studies*, heard seven days earlier, seemed weighed down by their technical complexity, as Paul Griffiths reported despairingly in *The Times*:

Brian Ferneyhough is like one of those artists who invent fantastic scripts and fill whole volumes with hieroglyphs that nobody can decipher. His is an absurdism become decadence: in the face of a hopelessness about communication, the music plays on and on, awesome and even heroic in its continual racing after more and more total bewilderment. Sunday night in Huddersfield provided the rare opportunity of being at once numbed and amazed for an hour, when his three *Time and Motion Studies*, written in the 1970s, were played consecutively for the first time. They show the inappropriate complexity of Ferneyhough's style carried to a point of unhinged musical glossolalia. First a bass clarinettist streams breathless through ten minutes of almost non-stop excitability; then a cellist battles for more than twice as long against the obstacles of ferociously demanding notation and crudely demeaning electronic adjuncts; and finally sixteen vocalists whisper, groan and ululate through webs of unmeaning. Performances in these cases have to be judged not by the success with which they present

some musical ideal but by the intensity of their unsuccess: in such terms the evening was a triumph.[11]

A week later he underwent a Damascene conversion:

This festival will surely be remembered for the music of one composer who is in dark days carrying the torch forward: Brian Ferneyhough. Last week I suggested that Ferneyhough is the last of the absurdists; it is no contradiction to say that he is also one of the last of the Romantics, convinced that music can still be made in new ways. After Saturday's astonishing performance by the Asko and Nieuw ensembles of his *Carceri d'Invenzione* cycle, one can only agree, not without pleasure and relief, that indeed it can... Nobody could be freer than Ferneyhough from the wearied, wearying regurgitations of this retro age... His is music bright enough to dazzle without a foil... each of the seven pieces in the new cycle keeps spinning off new reasons for awe as it proceeds along its particular tightrope. Together they make a concert of quite extraordinary energy.[12]

The focus on Ferneyhough increased press attention, already attracted by the festival's variety and a more-than-usual mix of apparently quirky and bizarre happenings. The effect on the audience was electric, causing Nicholas Payne of Opera North to declare: 'We must commission an opera!' It was not an idle jest. In 1992, after we had jointly mounted Robert Saxton's opera *Caritas* and were considering further ideas, I wrote to Brian with a proposal. But he was juggling his teaching in San Diego with several existing commissions and had no time. Nor had he decided on a scenario.[13]

Adams and other Americans

Woven throughout the 1987 festival were different facets of American music. Seven composers took part personally – John Adams, Stephen Albert, Henry Brant, Michael Gordon, Tom Johnson, Michael Torke and the jazz pianist-composer Cecil Taylor – against a background of earlier pioneers.[14] The pianist Alan Feinberg gave world premieres of Milton Babbitt's *Time Series* and a sonata by Charles Wuorinen, and there was music by Antheil, Cowell (four pieces), Ives, Varèse and Lou Harrison, including the UK premiere of his flamboyant Concerto for Organ and Percussion Ensemble. Torke was represented by the first performance of *Adjustable Wrench*,

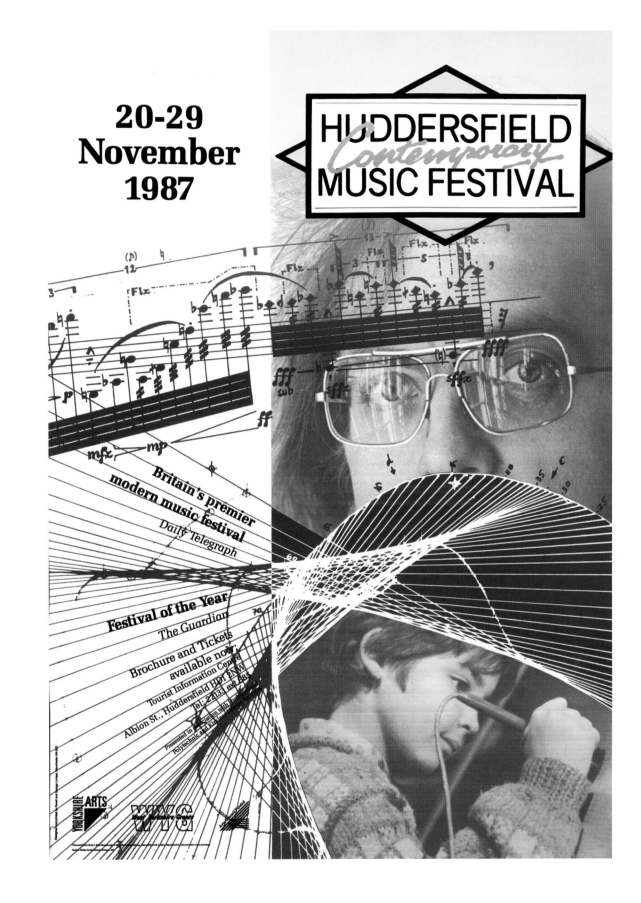

commissioned by the festival and the start of a continuing relationship with the composer. His *Rust* received its world premiere in Huddersfield in 1989, followed by UK premieres of *Overnight Mail* and *Flint* in 1998. There were also UK premieres of works by William Albright, John Corigliano and William Duckworth.

The diversity of style reflected the vastness of America, and the different upbringings, experience and inclinations of its composers. John Adams was, to my mind, the most striking and original, whose music we represented in performances of *Grand Pianola Music* and *Shaker Loops,* and UK premieres of *Phrygian Gates* and *Harmonielehre.* I had wanted to include *Harmonium,* undoubtedly one of the finest choral works of the late twentieth century, which had not yet been performed in Britain. But I feared that amateurs would find it difficult to sustain and count its long high notes, held bar after bar above metrically-shifting pulses. I doubted whether Huddersfield Choral Society could manage, and there was no viable alternative. Had there been a professional chorus available of adequate size, we could not have afforded it. When the CBSO Chorus eventually gave the British premiere in Birmingham under Sir Simon Rattle, even they sounded uncomfortable, although a second performance televised the next day from Warwick was thrillingly assured.

In a public forum with Wilfrid Mellers, it was evident that John himself felt ill at ease at a European festival on an academic campus, where, as he said, 'it seems that every time I turn corners I see huge posters of terrifying notation and composers leering at me'.[15] I had not foreseen that he might feel vulnerable. The critical responses to his early music had largely passed me by. Liking its *joie de vivre* and celebration of the American vernacular, I considered the style entirely valid and a refreshing antidote to Xenakis and Ferneyhough. My juxtaposition of *Funerailles* and *Shaker Loops* in one programme, with their similar instrumentation, seemed to me rather inspired. If their very different modes and procedures activated different neurological paths in the brain, so much the better.

Surfeited on European Modernism, some prominent UK critics had already dismissed Adams's music. As his visit to Huddersfield

followed the world premiere of his first opera *Nixon in China* by only five weeks, European audiences were yet to discover its brilliance. But, in conversation with Mellers, John was eloquent: his answers insightful, his remarks on other composers thoughtful and restrained, his vision sincere and persuasive. The audience instantly warmed to him. But few, if any, of the press were present. Three days earlier, in another pre-concert discussion, Stephen Albert had provoked a hostility so far unknown at the festival, through a forthright condemnation of European music since Schoenberg – whom he accused of taking a wholly 'wrong' direction – and an even more abusive denunciation of the avant-garde. Odaline de la Martinez, who had proposed Albert's music, had warned me that I would find his acerbic manner disconcerting; indeed, that it might be prudent not to invite him. Nevertheless, I was shocked.

John Adams.

Albert's chamber cantata *Into Eclipse* was the main work programmed that evening. Technically adroit, its post-Copland, post-Stravinskian manner is emotive, dramatic and vividly scored, and, in a fine performance from Peter Hill and Lontano, appeared to be enjoyed. That it could also be regarded as clichéd and facile, for those most insulted by what Stephen had said, only confirmed their repugnance. During the performance a group of students and composers sitting near the back (among them Richard Ayres and Andrew Toovey) slowly tore strips off their copies of the text. It was an effective protest, typically English and understated: irritatingly audible to a few people nearby but unnoticed by the majority. The boos at the end were unmistakeable, however. A disapproving David Fanning labelled the protesters 'the Disgusteds of Darmstadt'.[16]

The BBC Symphony Orchestra concert on the final afternoon contained UK premieres of *Rain Music* by Albert, Corigliano's Clarinet Concerto and *Harmonielehre* by Adams. This was the second time the orchestra had occupied the area of Huddersfield Town Hall instead of its relatively cramped stage; and, with a larger audience in the balcony and poor sightlines, the arrangement was not ideal. After the last chord of Albert's *Rain Music,* a cry of 'rubbish', or similar, upstaged the applause. The perpetrator was the artist, Colin Rose, for whom aesthetic integrity is a serious issue, and who has reminded me that it was 'Albert's boorish behaviour at the young composers' workshops, as opposed to Ferneyhough's warmth and suavity, that upset the composers more'. Indeed, I recall the discomfiture I felt on their behalf, and my twinge of disappointment on finding that the interjection had been deleted from the Radio 3 broadcast.

Also deleted was a more withering insult from Peter Heyworth, distinguished music critic of *The Observer*, who arrived after the interval, following a leisurely lunch in The George Hotel, just in time to hear *Harmonielehre*. The work's title is taken from Schoenberg's treatise on harmony, and the piece is a deeply thoughtful study of *fin de siècle* musical language and its dissolution – an obsession common enough among early twentieth-century composers, but frowned upon in its self-conscious second half. More controversially, Adams approaches late-romanticism through the portal of developmental minimalism – 'a conceit' he acknowledges, 'that could only be attempted once'.[17] The first movement of *Harmonielehre* begins with pounding E minor chords which subside, during a long middle section, into a yearning, 'roaming' melody. As the movement ended, Heyworth rose noisily from his seat, protesting 'forgery, absolute forgery!' and stormed out, to embarrassed titters from his colleagues. The disturbance destroyed concentration, and appeared to affect the players and conductor, Richard Buckley, between whom there was already little rapport. My own faith in the work was shaken, and only restored when I heard John himself conduct a magnificent performance of *Harmonielehre* in Manchester at the end of an all-Adams Hallé concert some ten years later.

The critics were brutal. Heyworth could comment on only one movement, but it was sufficient for him to write of 'empty-headed process music' and 'offensive opportunism', and of his 'repugnance at this shameless attempt to put other men's ideas to illicit purposes'.[18] My relief that the composer had left for California before the concert took place ended when I heard that Boosey & Hawkes had sent him the reviews – for had they not, Janis Susskind explained, John would have requested them. Compounding a personal distress, because his father was dying, the reviews left a bitter taste. In Huddersfield I thought that John's reception had been friendly; there had certainly been a warm response to *Shaker Loops* and *Grand Pianola Music*.

ut subsequent invitations failed to entice him. At first I sensed reluctance; later he was too busy. Meanwhile, the festival gave the UK premiere of *Road Movies* in 1997, the Chamber Symphony and European premiere of *Hallelujah Junction* in 1998, and staged *I was looking at the ceiling and then I saw the sky* in 1999.

After the festival I wrote to Heyworth – the only time I ever reproached a critic – explaining that the concert had been part of a subscription series aimed at a general, not a specialist audience, that Americana was a multi-faceted culture which it was valid to represent, and that the concert had been attended by the largest audience of that year's festival. My hope was to win over a public alienated from new music, not to programme Ferneyhough's *La Terre est un homme,* for example, 'to an uncomprehending, two-thirds empty hall'. If not those pieces, what would Heyworth have chosen? He replied courteously, even warmly, but declined to add or subtract anything. Years later I might have cited what I heard Jonathan Miller say in a radio discussion: 'The making of almost any art involves looting.' Rather than mere plagiarism, 'it becomes art when you take components and then recompose them into new configurations... A great deal of the history of art is the history of looting and reconstruction from the debris of the past.'[19]

It is appropriate to add that *La Terre est un homme*, which had been widely regarded as unapproachably dense and impenetrable since its ill-starred premiere in Glasgow in 1979, was magnificently rehabilitated by the BBC Symphony Orchestra and Martin Brabbins at a Barbican Total Immersion Day on 26 February 2011. Discussing the work on BBC Radio 3's 'Hear and Now' later that evening, Tom Service spoke of its 'seismic, cosmic, literally transcendental' quality, saying that what the performance did was 'wrench the piece from history', that it was 'absolutely one of the essential experiences of late twentieth-century music'. Ivan Hewitt remarked that it had been 'raised from a thirty-year sleep'. Perhaps Huddersfield should have attempted an earlier awakening. But the orchestra numbers nearly a hundred players, and I had accepted the work's negative reputation.

Critical opinion, in the last two decades, has swung in Adams's favour. It is not unqualified, but his standing in London, as elsewhere, is high. Most of those who reviewed the 1987 festival assumed that my programme 'deliberately embraced extremes', that I had positioned 'Ferneyhough to stand for High Modernism and musical complexity, while an American theme largely amounted to putting the case against'.[20] It was a reasonable assumption viewed from the aesthetic high ground, but took no account of my broader concern to overcome the isolation of so much new music, and face up to the challenge of audience building. The festival's publicity that year did not place themes in opposition, merely side by side, and the denigration of the critics, like other famous historical rejections, has been eclipsed by Adams's subsequent success. A festival showcase is an appropriate context, however, in which to debate new musical directions. Demonstrative reactions might be deemed too rare among British audiences. On this occasion, the dispute between the Albert and Ferneyhough camps continued in the American musical press. But not for long. Stephen Albert was killed in a car accident on Cape Cod in December 1992. He was fifty-one.

Following his Huddersfield visit, I occasionally met John at concerts of his music in London, as well as at the premiere of his second opera, *The Death of Klinghoffer*, in Lyon. We had not communicated for many years, however, when out of the blue, in October 2010, an email arrived. Prompted by his son Sam, now also a composer working in Brooklyn, he had been discovering 'some wonderful music by Georg Friedrich Haas, Salvatore Sciarrino, and other Europeans I had not spent much time with'. He had also become involved with, 'and humbled by', the late music of Ligeti, and wrote appreciatively of my book on the composer, and its brief comments about his own music.[21] We exchanged further warm emails, myself expressing regret that his visit to the festival had been painful, John expressing embarrassment that he had declined my repeated invitations to return, and discussing the position of musical languages in the general cultural dialogue. I sent him the first dozen pages of this chapter, and he replied that he thought them fair; remarking, however, on the difference in the quality of the performances of his music in Huddersfield, and of Ferneyhough's – which was performed, as we have noted, by specialists who had played it many times. He suggested that, 'perhaps even without intending it, you start from an

assumption that the European avant-garde is the gravitational center of the Huddersfield festival, and your invitation to us Americans was a gesture of inclusiveness, a kind of "big tent" impulse'. It was not something with which he had a problem, since there are few such contexts in which such work can be heard, and 'here in the US it's nearly impossible to hear anything at all by Stockhausen or Xenakis outside of very sporadic performances in New York.'

Regrettably, concentration on the completion of this book left me unable (for the moment) to continue an interesting conversation. To the 'gesture of inclusiveness' we shall return in a moment. Adams is still sensitive to poor UK reviews, and he still considers that my combination of *Funerailles* and *Shaker Loops* 'made little sense'. I still think it was valid. But that's fine! Whilst relishing the different cuisine served up by contemporary composers, I recognise that which dishes combine most agreeably is a matter of taste.

Michael Gordon, Tom Johnson, Henry Brant and Robert Ashley

The raw mix of systems and New York rock performed by the Michael Gordon Philharmonic (actually six players) was hard-edged and visceral. But their debut at the 1987 festival nearly did not happen. This was their first engagement in Britain at a time when foreign musicians required work permits. Busy with numerous preparations, I had posted the application precipitously late, with the result that, on arrival at Heathrow and finding no permits, Michael and his colleagues were on the point of being returned to the United States. In desperation he telephoned Steve Martland, his one contact in London, who alerted me and jumped into a taxi to render support. Steve's remonstrations had little effect, and with growing horror I realised that, it being a weekend, there might be nothing I could do. Scrabbling for Foreign Office phone numbers, I made repeated calls without raising anyone in authority. Trying number after number, after thirty minutes or so, somebody who was neither a janitor nor a cleaner answered, admonished me for my tardy paperwork, but promised to send a fax to Heathrow. Disaster was averted, and late that evening the tired and chastened musicians arrived in Huddersfield. Michael subsequently became a driving force behind

Henry Brant.

Bang on a Can, whose All-Stars performed with panache in Huddersfield in 1993.

The older Tom Johnson and Henry Brant were differently removed from the American mainstream. For years Tom had lived in Paris, where I called on him in his converted butcher's shop near the Bastille. A performance artist, logician and ultra-minimalist, his widely performed *The Four Note Opera* had been

BELOW:
Forearm clusters in the first movement of Henry Cowell's Piano Concerto.
© *EDITIONS MAURICE SENART*

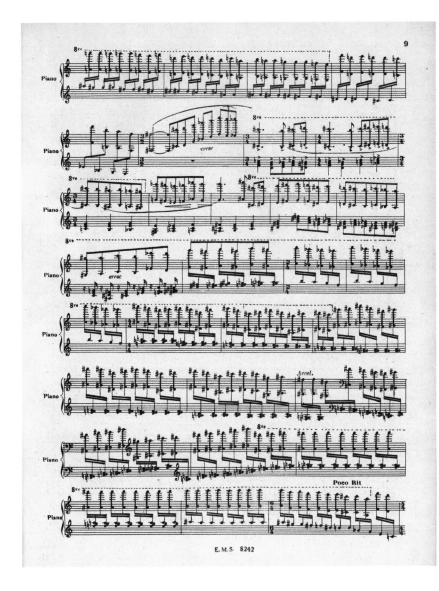

staged by the Huddersfield music department's opera class, and his witty *Failing* – 'a very difficult' piece for a talking double bass player – performed at the festival in 1985. Tom's is a music of game-playing, in which the pleasure derives from making audible simple deductive processes. I asked him to deliver his *Lectures with Audience Participation*, and to narrate *Bedtime Stories* with Roger Heaton playing the clarinet – their first concert performance. Most memorable was his *Nine Bells* which required the suspension of nine second-hand burglar alarm bells above the St Paul's performance area so that Tom, clad in jeans, T-shirt and trainers, could pad purposefully between them – a 'three-mile walk' he claimed – tracing, with impressive stamina, figures-of-eight, interlinked-circles, a clover leaf, an eight-point star and other choreographic patterns, during an intriguing hour of 'change-ringing'.

By now performance art had become a regular component of the festival. In Huddersfield Art Gallery, also in 1987, a performance artist called Charlie Hooker created a site-specific installation piece called *Parallel Beams*, in which dancers and musicians moved across a luminous three-dimensional musical score, and through changing light patterns, out of a background of pitch darkness. The audience included the manager of the nearby Victoria Wine shop, who explained that he had been attracted by the artform and its location. Anything in a concert hall or on the campus he would not have considered. Five years later Tom returned to play and narrate *Music for Eighty-eight,* a series based on numerical conundrums and composed in 1988 for the eighty-eight keys of the standard grand piano. Later I considered a performance of his *Bonhöffer Oratorium,* but recoiled from its two-hour-long austerity.

I learnt of Henry Brant in the Netherlands, where in 1984 the Holland Festival had devoted a week to his music, culminating in a commissioned piece employing four barges (each carrying twenty-five flautists and a percussionist), jazz and brass bands, antiphonal choruses and the joyful ringing of Amsterdam's several carillons.[22] Brant was a habitual experimenter, for whom the spatial separation of the performers and the unscripted collision of different musics was a preoccupation. Curious, I wrote to the composer, and received twelve typed pages of proposals with detailed specifications and drawings of their dispositions.

He also sent recordings. From these and telephone discussions I chose four pieces which would all be UK premieres, and invited groups from Huddersfield Technical College, Leeds College of Music and the polytechnic music department to take part. Hardest to persuade was Barrie Webb whom I had asked to share the conducting with Brant and his partner and assistant, Amy Schneider. Henry himself, I explained, would be wearing his usual concert dress of a bright yellow suit and matching sunshade. Barrie doubted whether the music was worth the effort, and didn't care for co-conducting with someone dressed like Donald Duck. But he had been mollified by the inclusion of Varèse's *Arcana,* which concluded the concert in an outstanding performance by the Polytechnic Symphony Orchestra under his direction.

The score of *Instant Huddersfield,* which opened the programme and which Brandt had devised for the occasion, looked superficial on paper, and in performance proved to be uninterestingly haphazard. But his other three pieces were less eccentric and not without originality. Far more arresting, however, was Henry Cowell's piano concerto, bristling with forearm clusters and played with great panache by Stephen Montague. There had been only one performance in America since the concerto's premiere in Cuba in 1930 with Cowell himself at the piano. For most of the intervening fifty-seven years the performing material had been gathering dust in the basement of Salabert in Paris. 'An entertaining and dazzlingly scored essay in brutalism,' as Robert Cockroft described it in the *Yorkshire Post,*[23] it was well worth reviving and should be heard more often.

'Cowell, the neglected pioneer' was the subject of recollections shared between Montague, Brandt and others, on a day which contained three lecture-discussions, five concerts and a late-night theatre performance. The main concert, given by Music Projects/London, contained Brant's *Inside Track,* Cage's *Concerto for Prepared Piano and Chamber Orchestra,* Cowell's *26 Simultaneous Mosaics* – the Brant and Cowell each written for groups spatially separated and unsynchronised – and ended with Adams's gloriously extravagant *Grand Pianola Music* conducted by the composer. In discussion John had been defensive about *Grand Pianola Music,* but I thought it needed no apology. The music department New Music Ensemble relished reviving it on more than one occasion.

About *Grand Pianola Music* the critics were scornful. But they applauded the festival's 'remarkably comprehensive and courageous survey' (*The Daily Telegraph*)[24] in which the 'labyrinth of contemporary music has been explored with astonishing thoroughness' (*The Times*).[25] Paul Driver noted that the 'response to the concerts – three or four a day, interspersed with talks and workshops – has been astonishing: every concert I attended was virtually sold out, and its audience passionately keen and predominantly young' (*The Sunday Times*).[26]

The following year I tried to persuade Lou Harrison to come, but he had been offended by the Conservative government's anti-gay legislation, and refused to set foot in Britain. In 1997 I tried again and we exchanged several letters. Lou was now eighty, had impaired health and disliked flying. Moreover, he was preoccupied with building a straw-bale house in the Mojave desert. I thought that he had reluctantly agreed, and scheduled a discussion with him. Finally he said that he could not undertake the flight, and the discussion had to be cancelled. But he put me in touch with Larry Reed's shadow theatre in San Francisco which, together with York University's Gamelan Sekar Petak, contributed to a beautiful tribute in the Lawrence Batley Theatre.

Robert Ashley performing one of his text compositions for amplified voice and tape in 2007.
PHOTO: BRIAN SLATER

Robert Ashley had hovered in the margins of my planning for several years. His innovative use of video, culminating in the TV opera *Perfect Lives*, was part of a worldwide explosion of video art in the 1980s. Other video operas followed, but I thought the technical cost of presenting any of them in Huddersfield would be too great. Circumventing these, in 2007 Graham McKenzie brought Robert himself to perform some of his text compositions, both solo and in collaboration with the Dutch ensemble MAE. American composers have a propensity for 'composing' speech: one thinks of Copland, Reich, Rzewski, Johnson, the Fluxus-inspired prose compositions of the 1960s, Glass in *Einstein on the Beach* and, of course, Cage. Ashley's treatments, reminiscent of Gertrude Stein, revealed a phonetic musicality latent in the words. The grainy lilt of his voice was attractive and engaging – as he was also in an interview with Robert Worby which probed revealingly Ashley's arms-length relationship with the American establishment.

Alarming developments – planning ahead

Margaret Thatcher's abolition of the six English metropolitan county councils in 1986 accompanied her more politicised assault on the Greater London Council. Under its leader Ken Livingstone, the GLC was a provocative adversary in City Hall, opposite the Houses of Parliament just across the Thames. The GLC was abolished, City Hall sold, and the Arts Council inherited responsibility for the Royal Festival Hall, Queen Elizabeth Hall, Purcell Room and Hayward Gallery next door. In April 1986 they were consolidated into the 'South Bank Centre' with an annual subsidy of c. £9 million; and Nicholas Snowman, who with David Atherton had founded the London Sinfonietta and since 1972 had been running IRCAM for Boulez in Paris, was appointed its artistic director. He soon let it be known that he would feature living composers – several each year – in a mega-procession of commissions, premieres and festivals starting in 1988. The South Bank's programmes needed invigorating and the emphasis on new music was timely. But the scale of Snowman's intentions was alarming. He telephoned, proposing that we meet to discuss our plans and that we should collaborate. But his manner sounded aloof.

Apprehensively, in December 1986 I took a train to London. The meeting was disturbingly one-sided. Nicholas listed a series of projects that would leave barely a chink for Huddersfield. New works would be reserved for the South Bank. Their composers would take part and so be disinclined to appear elsewhere. Furthermore, the South Bank would mount a large-scale festival of contemporary arts in the autumn of 1988, whose musical component would peak in late November. He did not ask, nor seemed interested in what I had in mind, so I didn't tell him. But in fact I hardly knew. Nicholas was planning for two years ahead and beyond. I had to devise a festival in 1987.

This was exclusion, not collaboration. Compounding the usual post-festival blues, I felt uncommonly deflated. Pondering the problem on the train journey north I made a decision, and the following day went into Huddersfield's principal stationers and purchased a 150-page exercise book with marbled covers. If Nicholas was planning two years ahead, we would have to leap-frog him. Cutting the right-hand edge of the pages like an address book, I divided the book into ten sections, one for each year from 1987 to 1996. Each was subdivided, with headings assigning successive pages to 'Anniversaries', 'Featured Composers', 'Themes', 'Premieres', 'Performers', 'Orchestral ideas', 'Polytechnic Ensembles', 'Educational Projects', 'General Events' etc – and (crucially) 'Other Festivals'. After this modest exercise I felt better. Mechanical activity can be therapeutic and stimulate thought. Next I entered all the anniversaries I could think of, and began devising 'themes'.

This became the first of two handwritten Ten-Year Planning Books. The second overlapped the first, running from 1992 to 2000, and contained more pages, forty of which I used to list composers and their works, potential UK premieres, useful comments and my private up to five-star ratings. On the first page I wrote a subtitle: 'The known, the less known and the unknown', unwittingly anticipating Donald Rumsfeld. This planning book, and then its successor, accompanied me everywhere, providing an instant overview of long-term strategy. Each I indexed, so that information could be located or added more quickly than on a computer – which, in any case, at first we could not afford. When the festival purchased computers in the early 1990s, the general availability of laptops was several years ahead. So I pasted a printout of each festival's budget adjacent to its programme-planning grid, and both were to hand wherever I might be.

In the 'Other Festivals' section for 1988 I entered Snowman's plans: Schoenberg, Brahms and Messiaen festivals; a new series called 'Perspectives' involving Boulez, Lutosławski, Reich and Stockhausen; a 'New Music Digest' of younger composers. In the same year Birtwistle would be extensively featured at the Barbican; Finnissy and Kagel at the Almeida. The London Sinfonietta would perform new commissions from Abrahamsen, Birtwistle, Denisov, Holloway, Holt, Xenakis, Osborne, Sallinen, Takemitsu and 'three younger unknowns'. In 1989 the South Bank would celebrate Lutosławski's seventy-fifth birthday in February, Berio in conjunction with the UK premiere of *Un re in ascolto* at Covent Garden, and Ligeti in October. There would be a 'New Music Review', a Canadian festival, a Greek festival, 'Music from Latin America' and three days in June devoted to electroacoustic music (the proposed National Studio). Boulez would be the subject of the BBC/Barbican festival in January; the Almeida planned a Soviet survey, and in the autumn another festival of Soviet artists and composers would take place in Glasgow.

The 'threat' posed by the South Bank was felt elsewhere. Pierre Audi, artistic director of the Almeida Festival, crossed swords publicly over the UK premiere of Ligeti's Piano Concerto. After hearing it in Vienna in 1986, he had invited the commissioners, Mario and Anthony di Bonaventura, to give the British premiere at the Almeida in 1987 during a Vienna retrospective which would also feature the new piano études. Working closely with Ligeti's London agent Allied Artists, Snowman was determined to reserve any Ligeti not yet performed in Britain for the South Bank's festival in 1989. The impression of a conspiracy was heightened because he and Allied's two directors, Andrew Rosner and Robert Slotover, had attended the same preparatory school; and in the late 1960s Rosner, Snowman and David Atherton – co-founders of the London Sinfonietta – had shared a house with Antony Pay, from which they ran 'the Sinfonietta as a cottage industry'.[27]

On 3 January 1987, *The Guardian* printed a lengthy feature by its music critic, Tom Sutcliffe, in which Huddersfield and Aldeburgh were cited alongside the Almeida Festival in 'a David and Goliath contest with the hugely wealthy South Bank Centre, threatening to determine both the scale and variety of many promotions and smaller arts organisations in the capital and elsewhere'. All felt constrained, he said, by exclusive agreements between Snowman and the South Bank's resident orchestras and ensembles. Among them was the Sinfonietta, whose general manager Michael de Grey had admitted, according to Sutcliffe, that 'if we are invited to perform elsewhere in London, we discuss it with the South Bank to ensure that we aren't doing anything against their interests. They are being fairly aggressive in their presentation of contemporary music. If they didn't like what we proposed I think they could try to stop us'.

Pierre Audi, who had asked the Sinfonietta to play, and hoped Ligeti would attend, was told that the composer would be unavailable. Nor would he attend Aldeburgh where he was also invited. But the rancour was damaging and Nicholas had to give ground. The Almeida had its premiere – without Ligeti present – although, as he had by then decided to extend the concerto, so eventually did the South Bank which, in 1989, claimed the final five-movement version in a lavish series of ten concerts containing more than thirty of Ligeti's compositions. Certainly, no other organisation could have presented such a feast.

In Huddersfield the festival board discussed the issue on 26 February 1987, and agreed that 'the decision to programme the South Bank event in Huddersfield's traditional late November slot was at best careless and at worst infamous'. It resolved to write a letter to Snowman, sending copies to the Arts Council and the press, which, without being confrontational or bitter, would forcibly state the festival's case.[28] As it happened, the hegemony rapidly became less hegemonic. A shortage of funds to deliver such ambitious plans, and a very public dispute between the South Bank Centre and the Philharmonia and London Philharmonic Orchestra – both competing for 'resident' status – muddied the waters. Other composers kept their distance. 'Stockhausen, whom I deal with, is definitely not being reserved,' Slotover asserted. But, then, Stockhausen was never beholden to anyone, and chose between supplicants himself.

Negotiating with Stockhausen

Soon after Snowman's appointment, Anthony Sargent joined the South Bank as artistic projects director, bringing the same readiness to collaborate which I had appreciated when he was at the BBC. We discussed our shared interest in Stockhausen, and Tony suggested that I join him on a visit to the composer in Kürten. Early in 1987 we boarded a flight to Cologne, where Tony had hired a car and we set off on a winding country drive, pleasantly interrupted at Peter Eötvös's timbered farmhouse where he and his partner gave us lunch. At Kürten Stockhausen was welcoming. We sat at a round table by windows opening onto the garden, discussing possibilities, whilst tea and sweetmeats were regally dispensed by the composer.

Tony had been involved in the BBC's *Music and Machines* at the Barbican in January 1985, the most extensive concentration of Stockhausen's music in Britain so far. That September Covent Garden staged *Donnerstag*, the first of the seven-part *Licht* cycle, and the impact of both the opera and Barbican performances had stoked my desire to present a major Stockhausen project in Huddersfield. Top of the list was *Momente*, a huge, passionate, semi-autobiographical composition unperformed in England since the 1960s. It had undergone radical restructuring, culminating in the 'Europa-Version' of 1972. Tom Sutcliffe exaggerated, however, by asserting that Huddersfield and the South Bank were in a 'tug-of-war' over its performance. There were many unsolved questions: who would take part, whether Stockhausen would release the material, whether he would direct and control sound projection, what venues could free up sufficient time both to rehearse and perform. Tony was equally interested in *Mixtur* or *Hymnen* which, although both performed at the Barbican three years before, required orchestras and so better suited the South Bank's priorities.

As we weighed up ideas, Stockhausen countered with a suggestion. What about a semi-staged performance of *Michaels Reise (Michael's Journey)*, the middle act of *Donnerstag*, which he had recently recast as an extended 'trumpet concerto' for his son Markus, with nine solo players replacing the original orchestra? Newly rehearsed, it would be touring in the autumn of 1988, performed entirely from memory, and would be in Metz prior to Huddersfield and could go afterwards to London. Having succumbed to the spell of the opera, I readily assented. Later we agreed to add *Tierkreis, Telemusik, Zyklus, Kontakte,* four of the *Klavierstücke* and five instrumental off-cuts from subsequent operas, all of which would be UK premieres. Played by the same musicians plus Bernard Wambach (piano), they would fill three successive evening concerts in Huddersfield Town Hall, preceded by a day of preparation and rehearsals.

Tony was still considering the larger pieces, until it became clear that the South Bank had too little unallocated time in its schedules to satisfy Stockhausen's rehearsal requirements. I was not privy to the deliberations, but one year later the composer sent a characteristic letter, handwritten in green ink:

Stockhausen

febr. 25th, 1988

Dear Richard Steinitz,

many thanks for your letter to Suzanne (February 11th, 1988) which I must answer because she has too much work.

HYMNEN – rehearsals cannot take place between Nov. 18th and 28th or later.

LUZIFERs TANZ needs full 12 days of rehearsals. Also SIRIUS, need much more time and preparation!

I also cannot work during this period for MOMENTE.

Please realise that I will be working now NON-STOP daily until November in rehearsals and performances and cannot work with conductor and director in spring.

Please understand: we plan very carefully everything at least a full year ahead of time and are completely engaged until June '89. Only MICHAELs REISE would have worked after Metz. Purcell Room is excluded for KATHINKAs GESANG.

friendly yours
Stockhausen

With Stockhausen you had to accept his current preoccupations. Complex earlier compositions he had no time to revive. As for the later pieces, without his personal direction they could not be performed. The South Bank could not accommodate him, so Huddersfield would have Stockhausen to itself.

Star sounds

And there would be an interesting addition. In Kürten I had tentatively proposed that we should give the British premiere of *Sternklang (Star Sound): Park Music for 5 groups,* explaining, however, that as it would be November it would have to be performed indoors. To my surprise, Stockhausen was encouraging. The piece had had an eventful history. Meditative, ritualistic and drawn out, *Sternklang* had been composed for the Berliner Festwochen in 1971 for performance 'during the warm summer weather' under the stars, where its premiere in the English Gardens of the Berliner Tiergarten had been attended by around 4,000 people. The five groups of performers were widely separated, and listeners could wander between them, whilst sound-runners, guided by torch-bearers, carried musical 'models' from one group to another. Stockhausen's visionary idealism was in tune with the times: he was revered by rock and pop musicians; young people flocked to his concerts, others to work with him. Two of the five groups which had taken part in all previous performances (plus the recording) were English: Gentle Fire led by Hugh Davies, and Intermodulation co-founded by Roger Smalley, Tim Souster and Peter Britton. I was in touch with Peter; and, given his knowledge of the piece, Karlheinz was happy for him to oversee the British premiere.

The Berlin performance barely escaped being rained off. At the last moment the clouds opened and Stockhausen's injunction that the constellations be 'read from the sky and integrated as musical figures' could be observed. Later that year a performance took place at the Festival of Arts in Shiraz. The police had difficulty controlling a crowd of some 8,000 Iranians who, dissatisfied with the inadequate space cordoned off for the audience, climbed the speaker towers and nearly swamped the musicians, until tension was diffused by the calming effect of the music. *Sternklang* had

received one indoor production in July 1980 in Bonn, when prolonged bad weather caused Stockhausen to move from the Rheinauenpark into the Beethovensaal, hastily decked out with 350 potted plants and trees. After this he was willing to approve indoor performances, and as no others had yet taken place, liked my proposal to transform Huddersfield Sports Centre into an indoor park. That our efforts pleased him is clear from his use of a photograph of the performance on the cover of the Stockhausen-Verlag CD.[29] We agreed that the participants would be drawn from educational institutions in Cambridge, London and Huddersfield, that Peter would prepare and direct them, and that Karlheinz would join us for the final rehearsals.

Stockhausen approves the arrangements. He habitually used programmes of other performances in which he was involved on which to write messages. The 'Greeting' to which he refers was for the festival's tenth birthday to be printed in the programme book.

CAISSE DES DÉPÔTS ET CONSIGNATIONS

10.
X.
88

KARLHEINZ STOCKHAUSEN
CYCLE DE MUSIQUE DE CHAMBRE

Yes, dear Richard Steinitz, these 11 concerts were protected by our angels! I send you the Greeting. Cowbell: O.K. Rooms at "George" O.K. I will bring ear plugs. Program: FINE. **OPERA COMIQUE** *Contract: signed.*
26 SEPTEMBRE - 6 OCTOBRE 1988
Yours, Stockhausen ♡dially

108

In Huddersfield we installed Stockhausen, Suzanne Stephens and Kathinka Pasveer in the best suite at the George Hotel, recently occupied by Princess Anne. I warned Karlheinz that it faced the railway, to which he replied 'Don't worry. I'll bring earplugs'. Some weeks before, Stockhausen's German sound engineers arrived to assess the town hall, returning at the start of the festival with a van full of equipment, including large loudspeakers. I had thought to reduce the expense by using our own expertise and resources. But the result convinced me that, when sound projection is so integral to a concept, the best result may only be achieved by the composer's trusted technicians using their own equipment. This was particularly true of Stockhausen, whose whole career had been concerned with sound diffusion; and who, with his engineers, produced to my ears a more satisfactory balance throughout all three levels of the town hall auditorium than anybody else. Before he returned in 1996, the same engineers assessed the Lawrence Batley Theatre, this time communicating by fax. The theatre has few places where additional speakers can be attached. Measuring carefully, and exchanging drawings, we settled on many small speakers positioned behind the rear seats and attached to staircase railings so as to not contravene regulations.

The three town hall concerts were unforgettably impressive, not least for the virtuosic brilliance of the playing. Markus Stockhausen excelled in *Michaels Reise*. Simply staged on platforms of differing height, the music sounded pungent and vivid released from the confines of the orchestra pit, while stylised gesture and mime conveyed the confrontation between Michael and Lucifer. Indeed, all ten soloists performed superlatively, playing from memory whilst moving elegantly on stage: a dimension which had not been part of the opera production. Reviewing the festival for *Contact*, Christopher Fox wrote of their 'extraordinary musicianship', with the members of Stockhausen's family 'as committed as ever as the central characters [while] Lesley Schatzberger and Ian Stuart (clarinets and basset-horns) gave delightful performances as a pair of clowns. The fluent grace of their movements as, in the closing stages of the piece, they mimic a love duet between Michael and Eve, made a charming contrast...'. Fox was also impressed by the outstanding playing of Bernhard Wambach and Andreas Boettger in *Zyklus*, *Klavierstucke V, VII, VIII and XI* and, together, in *Kontakte*, noting that 'Boettger played *Zyklus* from memory – a feat in itself – and after the interval proceeded to do the same with *Kontakte*. The resulting performances took the interpretation of postwar music to new heights.' [30]

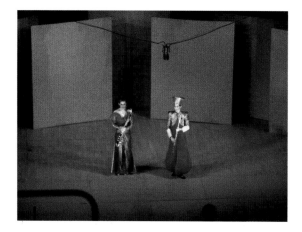

Reviewing *Michaels Reise* in the *Yorkshire Post*, Robert Cockroft marvelled at 'the sheer beauty and excitement of the music, its physical, visual and dramatic impact, its amazing ability to arrest and hold the ear', adding that he thought it 'amongst the finest concerts the festival has ever mounted' and that it 'yielded some of the best playing ever heard here'.[31] Something of the magic can be relived on the CD recording made the following year.[32] A further revelation was *Tierkreis* which, in its first publication as a collection of twelve melodies with harmonic accompaniment, had appeared lightweight. In 1984 Markus, Kathinka and Suzanne developed their own sophisticated realisation, which they now performed from memory, gracefully regrouping to underline different instrumental alliances, with and without piano (played by Markus), on an otherwise bare stage. Elegant and supremely 'musical', with its well-ordered symmetries *Tierkreis* struck me as an inventive addition to the classical canon, worthy to join a chamber music tradition stemming from Haydn.

Preparation of the main Sports Hall was undertaken by Steve Taylor, who had lit previous festivals; and now, in the role of technical and stage manager, enjoyed the challenge of realising Stockhausen's conception. I had booked several days for the preparation and rehearsal of *Sternklang* in situ, agreeing to compensate the Sports Centre for loss of earnings in its largest interior space. Steve hired green matting to cover the white-lined floor. Plants were borrowed from Pennine Garden Centre, which had already provided French earthenware flowerpots for *Komboi* in 1982. The *coup de théâtre* was his acquisition of plantation samplings and Christmas trees to give the appearance of a park. Scruples were appeased because the saplings were due to be thinned and the Christmas trees would be given

afterwards to schools in Kirklees. The numerous trees and shrubs, and skilful lighting produced a far more convincing effect than in Bonn. Sound projection was entrusted to Ian Dearden. That there was no night sky mattered not: Stockhausen had transcribed the constellations into his music.

The performers consisted of two groups from Huddersfield Polytechnic, and one each from City University, the Guildhall School of Music and Drama, and Cambridgeshire College of Arts and Technology where Peter Britton taught.[33] Karlheinz was demanding, awe-inspiring, appreciative and encouraging. During the

ABOVE LEFT:
Suzanne Stephens and
Kathinka Pasveer after
giving the UK premiere
of Ave *for flute and*
basset horn.
PHOTO: SELWYN GREEN.

ABOVE:
Kathinka Pasveer.
PHOTO: COURTESY
OF HUDDERSFIELD
DAILY EXAMINER

BELOW:
Rehearsing Sternklang *in*
Huddersfield Sports Centre.
PHOTO: SELWYN GREEN

performance he, Suzanne and Kathinka sat on a box near the middle, and then moved to chairs against a wall. The audience wandered quietly among the trees, sat cross-legged or lay on the floor. Candle-bearers led processions of white-clad musicians from one group to another. Paul Griffiths, music critic of *The Times,* brought his dog which, despite plentiful opportunities to raise a leg against a tree, behaved impeccably, sleeping contentedly through most of the evening. In the open, the five groups might be so far apart that in no position could one hear the whole. Here, as one moved around the 'hall-park' the aural perspective changed, but one could also hear the collective sound. Although damped by matting and trees, the acoustic remained warm and benign.

Support for the Stockhausen events worth £10,000 came from the Goethe-Institut and BBC Radio 3 which, through Stephen Plaistow, had agreed to broadcast the town hall concerts as co-producer. Before the first of them a queue for tickets stretched round the outside of the hall. In the programme book I described the first decade of the festival's development as 'a tale of stealth and ingenuity, incessant begging and diplomacy, the chipping away at resistance, forging of partnerships and discovery of an ever-growing circle of stalwart friends, generous allies and eager participants; more recently, of changing attitudes and a heart-warming growth of interest and enthusiasm from the public at large'. It could be measured by the box office income, which from 1986 to 1987 had risen substantially. Now it increased again. The participation of Stockhausen earned previews in *The Guardian, Yorkshire Post* and *Huddersfield Daily Examiner.* Displays, posters and leaflets bedecked the town. Wanting to humanise the broadcasts with snippets of *vox pops*, the BBC producer, Edwina Woolstencroft, carried a portable tape-deck into the streets to record what ordinary folk thought of Stockhausen's arrival in town. None of her eighteen interviewees had heard of him, although one suggested that he had been a First World War flying ace.

The performance of Sternklang in Huddersfield. The framed platform containing a large gong (not visible), is at the centre of the 'indoor park'.
PHOTO: SELWYN GREEN

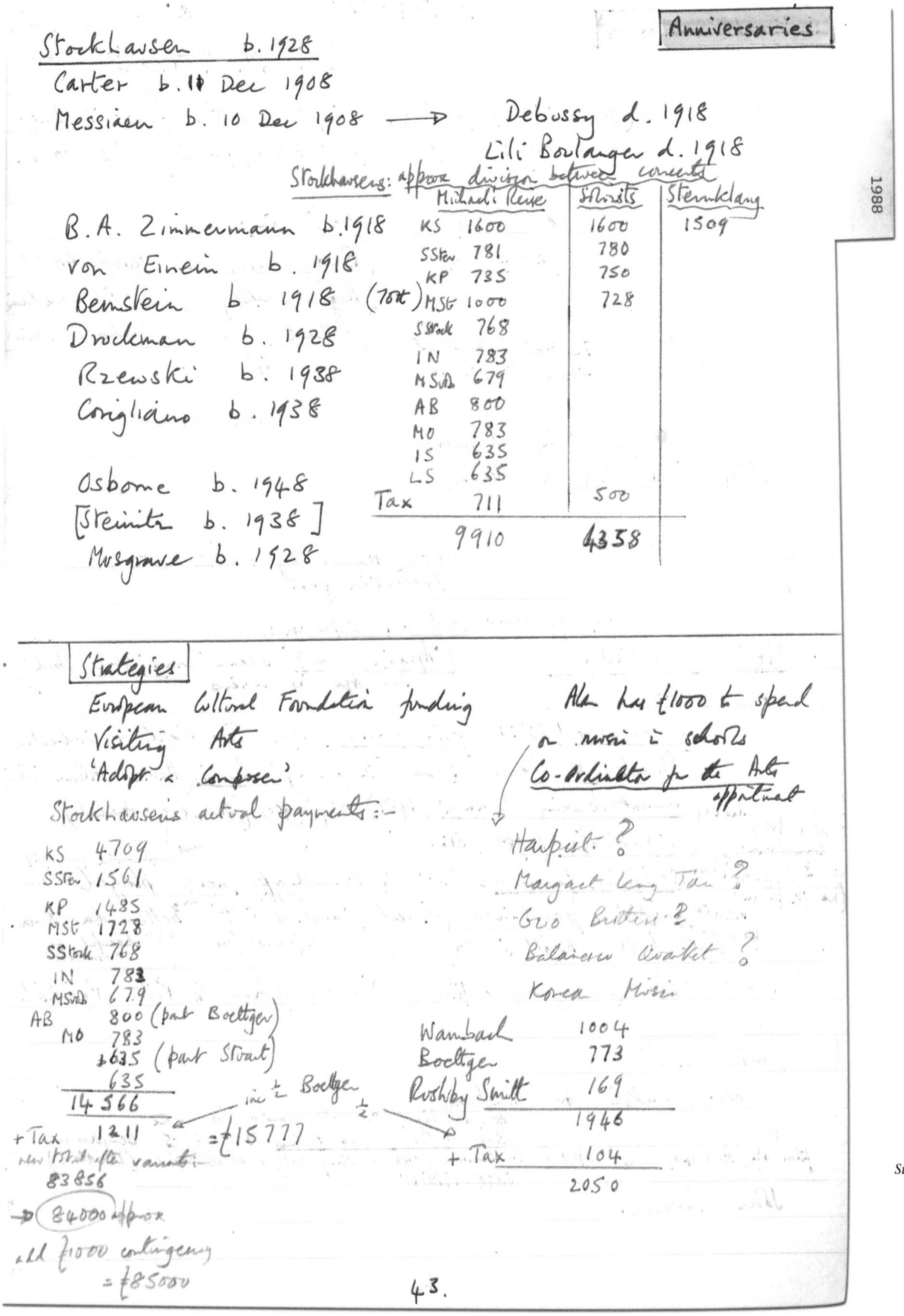

Stockhausen   b.1928

Carter   b. 11 Dec 1908

Messiaen   b. 10 Dec 1908   ⟶   Debussy d. 1918

Lili Boulanger d. 1918

[Anniversaries]

Stockhausen: approx division between concerts

	Michael's Reise	soloists	Sternklang
KS	1600	1600	1509
SSten	781	780	
KP	735	750	
MSt	1000	728	
SStock	768		
IN	783		
MSvb	679		
AB	800		
MO	783		
IS	635		
LS	635		
Tax	711	500	
	9910	4358	

B.A. Zimmermann b.1918

von Einem   b. 1918

Bernstein   b. 1918   (70th)

Druckman   b. 1928

Rzewski   b. 1938

Corigliano b. 1938

Osborne   b. 1948

[Steinitz   b. 1938]

Musgrave   b. 1928

[Strategies]

European Cultural Foundation funding

Visiting Arts

'Adopt a Composer'

Stockhausen's actual payments :—

KS 4709
SSten 1561
KP 1485
MSt 1728
SStock 768
IN 783
MSvb 679
AB 800 (part Boettger)
MO 783
    ±635 (part Stoart)
    635
    14 566 ← inc ½ Boettger ½
+ Tax 1211 = £15 777
new total after variants
    83 856
⟶ 84000 approx
add £1000 contingency
    = £85000

Alan has £1000 to spend on music in schools

Co-ordinator for the Arts appointment

Harpist ?
Margaret Leng Tan ?
Gio Britten ?
Balanescu Quartet ?
Korea Music

Wambach	1004
Boettger	773
Rushby Smith	169
	1946
+ Tax	104
	2050

43.

Updated payments to Stockhausen and his musicians, noted on some spare space in my planning book. The amounts are in sterling, and a revised total for artistic expenditure is written below. Most of the actual payments were made in Deutschmark notes.

On the Monday morning I was alerted to an incident that could have been disastrous, and hurried to the town hall where Karlheinz was rehearsing. He had been standing at his mixing desk in the centre of the hall when a plug from the stucco ceiling, lowered on its chain two days before so that microphones could be suspended, inexplicably dropped the full height of the auditorium and hit the mixer within inches of his head. I expected Karlheinz to explode with anger, and so he apparently had before I arrived – at the BBC technicians, as Don Hartridge, the recording engineer, told me much later. Some suspected the BBC of malicious intent. Unlikely, I thought. But why the missile had launched itself at that precise moment remained a mystery. To my apologies the composer replied philosophically, making light of the incident and only concerned about the loss of a knob that had fractured on impact. I promised that we would pay for repairs. Perhaps the composer who once dreamed that he came from Sirius, and expected one day to return there, was relieved to find himself still on Earth.

There was an exaggerated impression that Stockhausen was difficult to deal with, and his demands excessive. Neither artistically, technically nor financially did I think them unreasonable. He was autocratic, stubborn, insistent on certain performing conditions, unwilling to compromise. He would not come unless his family, trusted performers and sound engineers came too, all paid fees. In negotiation he was given to brinkmanship. But he was precise and practical, sure of his goals and how to achieve them, disciplined in regulating an immensely busy life. In rehearsals he was a charismatic and inspirational mentor – as the students who participated in *Sternklang* felt privileged to experience. Afterwards he could be touchingly warm and appreciative, and for several years after his two visits sent me signed mementos or presents of new publications. Those who accused him of exorbitant fees failed to appreciate his role as a performer. If, as sound director, he was paid the equivalent of a concerto soloist, why not? He would argue that a similar level of technical and artistic skill was involved, and Stockhausen in this role was arguably unrivalled. His family were uniquely authentic exponents of his concept of music theatre: consummate soloists performing long and complex pieces from memory. Few performers of contemporary music do likewise.

But there were bizarre requests, not least that the entire entourage be paid cash in their own currency. I can still visualise laboriously counting sheaves of grubby Deutschmarks in the crush bar of Huddersfield Town Hall with the Kirklees officer handling festival payments, and Karlheinz and Markus stuffing them into bulging back pockets. During an agreeable late-evening Indian meal at the end of their visit, I took Stockhausen gently to task (one was never less than diplomatic) about the perceived high level of their fees. He replied that they lived simply and paid themselves very little. Most of their earnings financed documentation and publication. It was a credible argument: for since 1970 Stockhausen had published all his own music, with more copious documentation about the actuality of performance than provided by any other composer. An early example (albeit published by Universal Edition) is the minutiae of technical detail in the score of *Kontakte*. Excessive it may seem, but Stockhausen's documentation was not without humour. After his liner-notes for the recording of *Klavierstücke I–XI* have described the venue, its temperature and humidity, the type of microphones and attentions of the piano tuner, he continues with the account of a squeaky piano stool and what Aloys Kontarsky ate for breakfast.[34]

Some of them were grasshoppers[35]

By 1996, when Stockhausen revisited Huddersfield, his dominance of the new music scene had declined. Two decades devoted to his massive seven-opera project *Licht* had removed him from the every day. Yet he remained an extraordinary figure, and when our fearless (but reassuringly sane) Dutch friends offered a performance of *Orchester-Finalisten* from *Mittwoch* (the section of the cycle on which Karlheinz was currently engaged) I was curious. In June I attended Asko's premiere in Amsterdam and, although sceptical, decided to accept a package that would include Kathinka, Suzanne, and Markus (who would also give a masterclass). With the addition of Annette Meriweather they would perform off-cuts from the recent operas in the Lawrence Batley Theatre. We would also show Frank Scheffer's film of Stockhausen's most eccentric composition to date, his *Helicopter String Quartet*. Performed during the Holland Festival in 1995, it involved the Arditti quartet playing in four helicopters flown by the Royal Netherlands Helicopter Display Team 'The Grasshoppers'. Meanwhile Karlheinz had mixed film of the musicians, and the sounds of their playing, with the noise of the helicopter motors for an audience on the ground.

Projected onto a large screen, the film was striking, if more sensational than musical. The festival included some earlier masterpieces: *Mantra* played by the Dutch piano duo Ellen Corver and Sepp Grotenhuis, and *Klavierstück X* whose spectacular wrist glissandi Corver executed with thrilling authority. Stockhausen had imagined *Orchester-Finalisten* as a staged music competition encouraging 'new methods of interpretation when playing from memory, and a personal style of movement and individual aura'. The concept may have been interesting; but, in performance, the sequence of thirteen solos minimally accompanied by electronic tape seemed tediously thin and formless. Festival regulars had their tolerance stretched and the critics were, without exception, scornful, reserving the most stinging condemnation for the events in the theatre. 'Stockhausen in depressing decline' ran a headline in *The Irish Times*. 'A hero falls' pronounced *The Guardian* above a review by Andrew Clements in which he accused Stockhausen of 'astonishingly inept dramatic packaging… with negligible musical results', of 'embarrassing choreography… ludicrous, degrading costumes… tiny musical ideas tricked out with cheap, naïve pantomime'. Tellingly, Clements contrasted the concert-lecture given in the Lawrence Batley Theatre with

a lecture Stockhausen gave just over a quarter of a century ago to Cambridge undergraduates, which remains possibly the most memorable single musical experience of my life: there was a man literally carving out musical history, and communicating his excitement in a spellbinding way. To compare that with the composer who confronted us in Huddersfield, totally bound up in his own increasingly limited world, indulging his fantasies and whims without a hint of self-criticism, was more depressing than I could have imagined.[36]

A purpose of the festival is to present music as it exists, and – as Cage might advocate – not too judgementally. Many who came to hear the Stockhausen were young people, who knew his reputation but little of his work. Few had attended the festival before, and they were touchingly attentive, moved and stimulated to think. Among the best-informed was Björk. Long fascinated by Stockhausen, they were kindred spirits of a sort. Indeed, she had recently interviewed him for the culture magazine, *Dazed and Confused*.[37] Andrea Smart, the festival administrator told me during the interval of the Asko concert that Björk was present, and I heard that she stayed for the *Helicopter String Quartet*. But festival directors have obligations and our Dutch performers were about to depart. Afterwards I much regretted not having introduced myself and asked Björk to perform at the festival. I phoned and wrote more than once, but failed to break through the protective shell of agents, minders and assistants. It was an opportunity missed.

John Cage

Anniversaries were, perhaps, an over-obvious peg on which to hang a strategy, but there was a birthday we could not overlook. In 1987 John Cage would be seventy-five. I wrote to invite him. Cage replied by hand on a sheet from his personalised message pad, as he did in all subsequent letters – a curious method which he did not use as intended. Its pages in triplicate consisted of a yellow sheet for the writer to retain, white and pink carbon copies to be mailed to a recipient who was supposed to return the white copy with a response in the column headed 'Reply'. Cage only mailed the white copy and, if he needed more space, would write in both 'message' and 'reply' columns. His first letter was brief and explained that, as he would already be abroad for most of the autumn preparing the premiere of *Europeras 1 & 2* in Frankfurt, he 'hoped another year would be mutually feasible'. As fate would have it, an arsonist set fire to the Frankfurt opera house a few days before the premiere. 'Isn't that beautiful,' Cage is reported to have said as he watched the conflagration – not unlike the playwright/manager Richard Sheridan, who, when encountered drinking a glass of wine in the street while watching his Drury Lane Theatre burn down, is reported to have said, 'A man may surely be allowed to take a glass of wine by his own fireside.'[38]

The performances of *Europeras* were postponed, and for Huddersfield the delay was advantageous, as we had plenty planned for 1987 and Stockhausen to accommodate afterwards. Following the latter's departure,

John Cage's letter of 27 December 1988.

JOHN CAGE

101 WEST 18 STREET (5B) • NEW YORK, NEW YORK 10011

I wrote to Cage again. This time he replied at greater length, remarking on our 'beautiful programs', and telling me of his plan to finish the immensely difficult *Freeman Etudes* for solo violin, which by 1990 might be ready for Irvine Arditti to premiere in Huddersfield. I knew, however, that in that year, Cage had accepted an invitation to Glasgow's Musica Nova. It would be better if he visited Huddersfield the previous November. I telephoned his agent to arrange a meeting, and in April flew to New York.

Visiting Cage in his loft apartment in West 18th Street was an unforgettable privilege. After we had talked for a couple of hours, John offered to make lunch, a macrobiotic stew already partly prepared. He apologised that he had to leave for an afternoon meeting, but invited me to stay so that I would not have to hurry. I finished eating and walked slowly around his large open-plan studio breathing in its atmosphere – the functional furniture, the plants and numerous pictures, the bare wood floor and large windows flooding everything with light, a tray of rounded stones which he had collected from New River

in the Appalachians, a chess set arrested in mid-game, and to water the plants an open stepladder… Could this be the very ladder from which Cage had read in 1952, whilst Cunningham, Rauschenberg, Tudor *et al* performed 'concerted actions' in the world's first ever 'Happening' at Black Mountain College? Probably not, but it was an agreeable thought.

On the walls hung priceless works of abstract art by his New York friends, and among them etchings and watercolours by Cage himself. He had dabbled in art in his youth. Years later, in 1978, responding to an invitation from Kathan Brown, Cage began making annual visits to her Crown Point Press in San Francisco to create his own etchings. A year before I met him, he had painted a series of watercolours at the Mountain Lake workshop in Virginia, set up specially for him by Ray Kass. The results were beautiful. Many of them had interlocking circular patterns drawn around stones, an idea inspired by the Zen-style Ryoanji Garden in Kyoto. I wanted to show this unfamiliar aspect of Cage's work in Huddersfield. But most of the watercolours were touring in North America (Cage had given me a catalogue), and, on phoning Crown Point Press, I learnt that the etchings were destined for an exhibition in Japan that exactly coincided with the festival. In the event, they stayed put. The San Francisco Bay earthquake on 17 October disrupted transport and a shipment could not be made. Cage's visual art finally arrived in Britain in 2010, in a retrospective exhibition presented by the Hayward Gallery and toured to other centres, including Huddersfield Art Gallery during the 2010 festival (see pages 198–200).

But Cage himself would come. Along with smaller pieces, we discussed the possibility of a large multi-dimensional performance. One idea, HPSCHD, had been premiered in the vast Assembly Hall at the University of Illinois in 1969. Three years later, when I spent two semesters at the university, memories of the spectacle were very much alive. It had lasted five hours and involved seven harpsichordists, fifty-two tape-recorders, numerous amplifiers and loudspeakers, over 6,000 slides (mostly from NASA) using sixty-four projectors, plus multiple cine films shown on twelve screens. Cage had envisaged an environment with so many components that no single medium would dominate. But one could employ fewer.

Another possibility was *Roaratorio – An Irish Circus on Finnegans Wake,* lasting one hour. Originally a radiophonic piece commissioned by WDR, *Roaratorio* had a similarly wide embrace and could also be performed live, but required fewer resources. At its core were Cage's 'mesostics' derived from *Finnegans Wake.*[39] Enveloping them was an encyclopaedic collage of thousands of environmental sounds, recorded at locations in Ireland mentioned in the *Wake,* by Cage and John Fullemann (sound consultant for the Merce Cunningham company), mixed with other recordings from around the world. These they assembled at IRCAM on sixteen simultaneous tape tracks, to which were added, for the broadcast, recordings of 'the king of Irish singers', Joe Heaney, singing in Gaelic, plus contributions from other Irish folk musicians.

Three live performances of *Roaratorio* had taken place involving the Merce Cunningham dancers, including one during the 1987 BBC Proms. The plurality of both pieces attracted me, but the soundscape of *Roaratorio* especially. We booked the Irish musicians, but not the dancers, who were in any case unavailable.

John Cage's apartment in New York.
PHOTOS: RICHARD STEINITZ

During the ensuing months, Cage made further programme suggestions. The then festival administrator, Jocelyn Williams, found him a ground-floor flat within walking distance of the town centre, where he could do his own cooking, and we learnt where to source macrobiotic ingredients. With greater difficulty, we located a sixteen-track tape recorder. When John arrived, I drove him to the flat, he declared his approval, and we took a short walk up New North Road looking out for mushrooms in the front gardens. Cage stayed for the whole festival – unlike all other 'great' composers featured in Huddersfield – during which he attended virtually every concert, whether or not his music was played, listening with interest and encouraging any composer who spoke to him.

His kindness, warmth, humour, gentle demeanour and pleasure in everything spread a benign aura over an unforgettable ten days.

His other music I chose selectively, so as to show Cage's achievement as a composer of at least partially organised music. It is an achievement often underrated, as is the amount of choice he applied to works that are ostensibly random. So the festival presented ten compositions from the fertile years between 1939 and 1950: some familiar, like *Imaginary Landscape I, Forever and Sunsmell,* and the iconic *Amores* and *Second Construction* for percussion; others less so, like the short but dramatic *In the Name of the Holocaust* given its UK premiere, and UK premieres of three remarkable and more substantial pieces – at least in their duration.

Four Walls for solo piano had been written for a 'dance-play' devised by Merce Cunningham in 1944. Lasting an hour, and using only the white keys of the piano, its gradually changing repetitions anticipate minimalism. The piece had been rediscovered by the pianist Margaret Leng Tan, and Cage had heard a performance for the first time only one year before coming to Huddersfield. His 1947 ballet score *The Seasons,* scored for an orchestra of forty-three players, had also been choreographed by Cunningham, but had fallen into obscurity. Performed by Music Projects/London, its isolated sounds, tiny arabesques and fragments of melody – without either rhetoric or functional harmony – perplexed some listeners, unable to appreciate their Eastern, almost calligraphic neutrality. I thought both pieces beautiful. But the finest was undoubtedly the *Three Dances* for two prepared pianos, which requires the most complex preparations Cage ever devised, with sometimes as many as six objects altering the sound of a single note. Its rhythmic intricacy, and the skill and panache with which Cage handles his uncharted sound world, Michael Tilson Thomas describes as 'a testament to compositional technique, imagination, and taste'.[40] It was given a thrilling performance by Gerard Bouwhuis and Cees van Zeeland – amazingly the first time the *Three Dances* had been played in Britain.

I did not programme *Variations I–IV,* for instance, or other works in which Cage so radically eliminates 'self' that creative identity, despite chance procedures, is largely ceded to the performers. Not that I thought them insignificant; but I preferred the more structured work. Four works stood out: all partly notated and partly indeterminate. One was *Roaratorio,* in which specific materials are freely combined.

John Cage in the audience at St Paul's Hall. Sitting behind him is Fred Booth and in front John Stringer, then a student at the polytechnic. On Cage's right are myself and the author and critic Paul Griffiths.
PHOTO: SELWYN GREEN.

Another, composed for the Ardittis and given its world premiere, was *Four,* in which pitches are notated, but durations, repetitions and silences are decided (within fixed time frames) by each player. Then there were two sets of studies: *Etudes Boreales I-IV* for solo cello (in which the range constantly changes) and *Freeman Etudes* for solo violin (which exploits both extremes of the instrument virtually simultaneously). The interface between notated and indeterminate parameters produced strikingly different results – almost superhuman bravura in *Freeman Etudes*, the stilled tranquillity of *Four* – and I was inclined to think that the touch of their creator controlled rather more than is often assumed.

Only once did I see Cage perturbed, after the premiere of *One²*, which he had composed at the request of Margaret Leng Tan to perform on up to four pianos, all with their sustaining pedals depressed. Using the freedoms inherent in the score, Margaret had made 'an installation/theatre piece using three pianos as sound sculpture' to generate a perspective stereophony in which sounds would 'interpenetrate but not impede each other'.[41] But the triangular arrangement of the pianos, the ritual of walking between them, and the repetitive cycles of chords verged on the tiresome. Afterwards, as I drove John to his flat he was uncharacteristically distressed.

The periodicity and almost irritatingly insistent ceremony were far from what he had imagined. He would ask Margaret to change her interpretation.

But by the third set of traffic lights the cloud had lifted. He would accept the performance. It was a part of life. He couldn't upset her. He would move on. *Four* achieved that elevated serenity which had been absent in *One²*. I was surprised by the quartet's harmoniousness, learning only later that, influenced by James Tenney and Pauline Oliveros, Cage had acquired a new interest in 'harmony without theory'.

But the musical and spiritual centrepiece was *Roaratorio*, its galaxy of environmental and live sounds as wonderful as I had imagined. Seated at the side of the stage, John intoned his mesostics lit by a single anglepoise. Dotted around the town hall, each of the Irish folk musicians played for one third of the time, contributing whatever and whenever they thought fit, and otherwise remaining silent. There was no planned convergence, but one sensed an intuitive empathy. Seats had been

John Cage reading his mesostics in Roaratorio.
PHOTO: COURTESY OF HUDDERSFIELD DAILY EXAMINER

Peader Mercier playing bodhrán at the rehearsal of Roaratorio.
PHOTO: COURTESY OF HUDDERSFIELD DAILY EXAMINER

removed from the area, where the audience wandered at will, soaking up the experience from different perspectives. On one perambulation I encountered David Williams, a former composition student. We were both in a state of heightened rapture.

Interviewed for a broadcast during the interval of the 1987 Prom, Paeder Mercier, the bodhrán player, was asked what it felt like to play in *Roaratorio*.

Well, I can tell you quite frankly: when I first heard it, I really thought it was the weirdest, most astonishing, most unacceptable cacophony that I had ever heard. And now I love every moment of it. And I'm waiting there for sounds that are my pet sounds. There's a blackbird which sings; the waterfall which comes tumbling down at the back of your neck; there's the car revving up on O'Connell Bridge; there're the seagulls all down over the tower in Sandy Mount. And it's quite, quite wonderful. And there are times – little magic moments – when all the cacophony seems to cease and all you hear is John's intonation. And then that precious moment is gone, and down comes the clamour and cacophony again. And to say that I love it now, and that I absolutely thought it was dreadful the first time, is a clear indication of what beauty lies [within], if you look for it.

On the final weekend of the festival the weather was crisp and bright. My wife, Nan, and I took John and our three children to watch the Natural Theatre Company build an abstract

Gathering mushrooms with Emily and Adam Steinitz.
PHOTO: RICHARD STEINITZ

steam sculpture on the piazza, after which the actors, who had been dressed as construction workers, reappeared as archetypal business men and women, with brief cases and rolled umbrellas, who then improvised musical responses to the notes and chords blown by the sculpture, to the bemused delight of shoppers (see the illustration on pages 206–207). Enjoying the warm sunshine, we drove John to the woods behind Castle Hill to hunt for fungi. With Emily, Adam and Ben, he had an instinctive affinity, and I thought what a wonderful grandfather he would have been, had he had other than musical progeny. Finding some handsome boletus, we took them home and John cooked them, introducing the family to fungi hunting, from which we have so far survived.

An historic meeting: Boulez, Cage and Messiaen

During the festival's final weekend none of Cage's music was performed. It held for him, however, a different promise in the arrival of Pierre Boulez. More than anyone else, he and Boulez had transformed musical aesthetics in the mid-twentieth century. They had met in Paris in 1949, where Cage spent several months during his first postwar trip to Europe, and where he also met Messiaen. After Cage returned to New York, he and Boulez had maintained a close friendship through correspondence, sharing confidences and aspirations, exchanging information about their compositions and promoting each other's music. But in 1953 Cage's embrace of indeterminacy, and Boulez's rejection of 'chance as a component of a fully developed work,' caused an acrimonious parting of the ways. Boulez, the more ideological, could not accept Cage's laissez-faire liberalism, and on a visit to New York in 1962 engaged in vituperative argument that left Cage feeling hurt. Since then, they had met but briefly.[42]

Relatively late in my planning it emerged that, because Boulez would be working with the BBC Symphony Orchestra in London, but with some time to spare, he and the orchestra could add a performance in Huddersfield. Programme choices were constrained by the limited rehearsal time and, more frustratingly, by a lack of space on the town hall stage. But we could include Messiaen's new *La Ville d'en Haut* with his wife, Yvonne Loriod, as piano soloist. I had invited Messiaen on the occasion of his eightieth birthday the previous year. Messiaen had declined and, knowing that he was growing frail, I had not repeated the invitation. So it was a surprise to hear in the middle of the festival that he intended to come. As we considered how to arrange transport from London, Tim Sledge – engaged to manage front-of-house and later the festival's first (nearly) full-time administrator – made a suggestion. He would hire a limousine and, to keep costs down, drive it himself. The proposal was accepted and Tim left for London. 'The surreal experience of driving Pierre Boulez, Olivier Messiaen and Yvonne Loriod from London to Huddersfield, and the conversation in the car with Loriod feeding me with hotel biscuits', Tim later wrote, was the 'highlight' of his time with the festival.[43]

Cage would like to have engaged with Boulez in a public forum, but Pierre would have none of it, and I sensed John's disappointment. Instead, Pierre agreed to be interviewed by George

Boulez and Cage leaving St. Paul's.
PHOTO: SELWYN GREEN

Benjamin, although it could only take place after he had rehearsed the orchestra on the Saturday evening. Thus, after Asko had finished their concert and St Paul's had been cleared, the public trekked back, filling every seat and hanging onto every word. Beginning at 9.30pm, George and Pierre talked and disputed until 11.20pm. A year before, I had interviewed George (then still in his twenties) and given him a 'hard time' – so he said. George agreed to interrogate Pierre no less rigorously, secure in

The historic meeting between Cage, Messiaen and Boulez on 26 November 1989.
PHOTO: SELWYN GREEN

the strength of their friendship and mutual regard. The result was fascinating: animated, combative but good humoured, and theatrical, as the audience responded with laughter and applause for a remark well aimed. It was the longest interview ever to take place at the festival and one of the most riveting.[44]

Sitting in the audience was Cage, soon noticed by Boulez who remarked: 'I see my friend John Cage here.' Afterwards, they left the building together, Pierre with a hand on John's arm. The next day they met at the final reception. Selwyn Green, the festival photographer, caught a historic handshake as they greeted each other, a beaming Olivier Messiaen looking on, glass in hand. But this meeting was also their last – an encounter of hearts but not of minds. John would have liked more. Boulez still adhered to the view he had expressed to Morton Feldman: 'I love John's mind, but I don't like what it thinks.'[45]

Sur Répons d'Avignon

Throughout the 1990s I tried assiduously to woo Boulez back. We met in London, Birmingham, and at his apartment high up in Perspective 2 overlooking Paris, between Radio-France and the Eiffel Tower. The *grand projet* was to present *Répons,* which, inexplicably, has still not been mounted in Britain since an early, shorter version was performed at the BBC Proms in 1982.

Commissioned by South West German Radio, *Répons* received its (partial) premiere at Donaueschingen on 18 October 1981. During the next six years Boulez extended the piece and developed increasingly sophisticated real-time electronic processing using the 4X computer at IRCAM. Performances of successive versions culminated in *'la version définitive'* created at the Festival d'Avignon in July 1988, and performed eight times in the dramatic outdoor setting of the Carrière Callet à Boulbon – an old quarry first used as a performance space for Peter Brook's *Mahabharata* in 1985. Twenty-four members of the Ensemble InterContemporain (EIC) sat on a stage in the centre of the audience, which was in turn surrounded by six soloists on separate platforms. Lighting and loudspeakers were suspended from a specially constructed grid held up by eighteen supports and covering 1150 square metres. The enormous cost of the enterprise was underwritten by the new Louis Vuitton Foundation, created specifically to support contemporary music and opera.

Although announced as 'definitive', the version performed in Avignon appears to have been structurally identical with the 'third version' performed in Turin in 1984 and lasting around forty minutes. This version of *Répons* was reprised in Basle, Metz, Paris and Baden-Baden in 1985, and on tour to five American cities in 1986. Interviewed during July 1988 in Avignon, however, Boulez confessed that recent technological developments at IRCAM, 'especially in the last three or four years', had 'compelled [him] to integrate these discoveries'. But it was also – as in his other works – a Proustian process, and he had in mind to add further 'chapters'.[46] According to Jean-Jacques Nattiez, writing in *Le Combat de Chronos et d'Orphée* in 1993, 'the composer envisages a new, long, and slow insertion that would take the length of the work to seventy minutes'.[47]

No further insertions have yet appeared. But already, *Répons* is arguably the most important achievement of its composer and the research institute he initiated. In a preface to Boulez's collected writings, Nattiez suggests that *Répons* is 'the true completion of earlier works unfinished... the single, total work which, in a sense, cancels all the others and makes the completion of the unfinished ones pointless'.[48] Considering Boulez's stature, the absence in Britain of any performance, since the shorter 1982 version, is strange. But to perform *Répons* is hugely expensive, and the few London institutions that might be able to afford it lack an appropriate venue with flat floor and no fixed seats. In Huddersfield we had hired the Sports Centre for *Sternklang* in 1988, and were about to do so again for Grisey's *Le Noir de l'Étoile* in 1992. The Grisey demonstrated that the Sports Centre roof could support the weight of heavy speakers and lighting, and that, if *Répons* was to be performed there, we would not need to import IRCAM's expensive freestanding grid. By the mid 1990s there were also more compact alternatives to the bulky 4X.

With Alain Jacquinot and Risto Nieminen at IRCAM I drafted a technical schedule, and with Boulez a programme of performances. There were to be one, or possibly two concerts in the Sports Centre and one in St Paul's, all given by

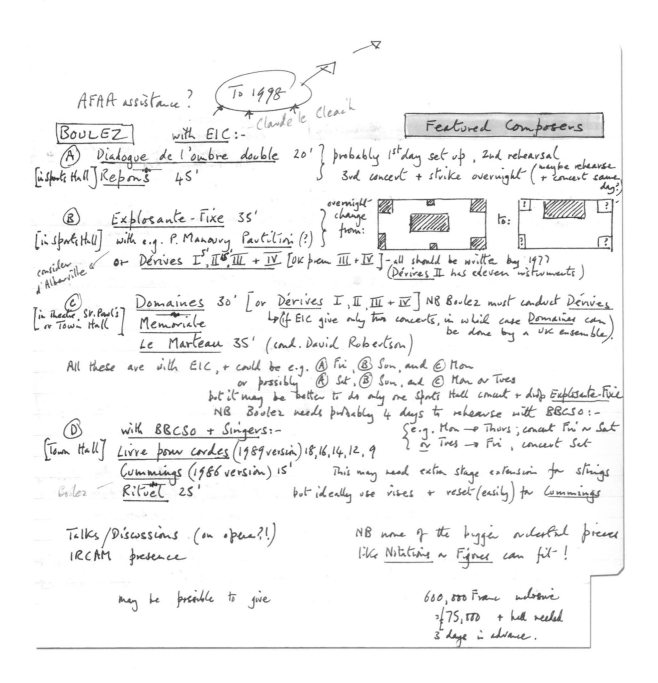

AFAA assistance?   To 1998
                    — Claude le Cleach

BOULEZ   with EIC :–   [Featured Composers]

(A) Dialogue de l'ombre double 20' } probably 1st day set up, 2nd rehearsal
[in Sports Hall] Répons 45'   } 3rd concert + strike overnight (maybe rehearse + concert same day?)

(B) Explosante-Fixe 35'   overnight change from:
[in Sports Hall] with e.g. P. Manoury Partition (?)   to:
consider d'Albarville   or Dérives I', II', III + IV [UK prem III + IV] – all should be written by 1977
                                                                                 (Dérives II has eleven instruments)

(C) Domaines 30' [or Dérives I, II, III + IV] NB Boulez must conduct Dérives
[in theatre, St. Paul's or Town Hall] Mémoriale   (if EIC give only two concerts, in which case Domaines can be done by a UK ensemble)
           Le Marteau 35' (cond. David Robertson)

All these are with EIC, + could be e.g. (A) Fri, (B) Sun, and (C) Mon
                    or possibly (A) Sat, (B) Sun, and (C) Mon or Tues
but it may be better to do only one Sports Hall concert + drop Explosante-Fixe
         NB Boulez needs probably 4 days to rehearse with BBCSO :–
                                         { e.g. Mon → Thurs; concert Fri or Sat
                                         { or Tues → Fri, concert Sat

(D) with BBCSO + Singers :–
[Town Hall] Livre pour cordes (1989 version) 18, 16, 14, 12, 9
        Cummings (1986 version) 15'   This may need extra stage extension for strings
Boulez   Rituel 25'   but ideally use risers + reset (easily) for Cummings

Talks / Discussions (on opera?!)   NB none of the bigger orchestral pieces
IRCAM presence   like Notations or Figures can fit!

        may be possible to give   600,000 Francs welcome
                                         = £75,000 + hall needed
                                         3 days in advance.

Projections in my planning book for a major Boulez feature.

the Ensemble InterContemporain with direction shared between Boulez and David Robertson. In a fourth town hall concert the BBC Singers and Symphony Orchestra would be conducted by Boulez. Besides *Répons*, the programmes would include *Dialogue de l'ombre double*, '...explosante-fixe...', *Dérive I–IV* (*III* and *IV* being UK premieres), *Mémoriale*, *Le Marteau sans maître*, *Livre pour cordes*, *Cummings ist der Dichter* and finally *Rituel: in memoriam Bruno Maderna*. The cost of bringing the IRCAM technology, plus EIC, six soloists and two conductors would be 500,000F–550,000F. An enormous sum. But Nicholas Kenyon, newly appointed controller of BBC Radio 3, expressed enthusiasm for a co-production, and there had

been positive indications of support from AFAA (the cultural department of the French foreign ministry).

The biggest problem was Pierre's diary, especially in November when he was habitually occupied as guest-conductor of the Chicago Symphony Orchestra. The plans agreed in 1992 could not be realised until 1997. But Pierre was also enthusiastic. It would be the festival's most magnetic concentration on the music of one composer, and worth waiting for.

Then in July 1993 came a bombshell from Boulez's assistant, Astrid Schirmer:

Dear Richard

I have the terrible task to tell you of Pierre's sabbatical year in 1997... Pierre's schedule for 1995 and 1996 is so full that he realised it was impossible to continue like this. Not only will he have no breathing space at all, but there will be no time for composing whatsoever. Also, little health problems keep turning up here and there whenever he is doing too much, increasingly so with increasing age...
It was, therefore, decided that a sabbatical year was the only solution. Unfortunately, this does not seem possible in the immediate future, so 1997 is the big year. Pierre is very adamant about it, and I have had to cancel all projects for that year, and even a few during 1996... I hope you will understand that this was not an easy decision... Pierre sends all regrets to you... He sends also his best thanks for the photo you sent of him, Cage and Messiaen.

Yes, I understood. But I was keenly disappointed, and wrote back seeking to reschedule the project. Matching dates, although problematic, looked hopeful, and in 1994 we established that Pierre could conduct two concerts with EIC in November 1998, although he had neither time, nor 'the inclination to conduct also a symphony orchestra'. But a year later this, too, foundered. After his sabbatical, Astrid explained,

Pierre wants to work only for 4–6 months in the years that follow.... His regular commitments in Cleveland and Chicago, as well as the LSO and some recording engagements in Berlin and Vienna have already filled his schedule for 1998 and 1999 much more than he intended. Pierre now feels that he has to let go of Huddersfield and hopes you may wish to continue the *Répons* project with David Robertson and the EIC.

I am very sorry indeed having to tell you this. We have plotted this Festival for so long and you have been so patient...

My wish had always been to have Boulez present. Without him I felt that so ambitious a project would lack its intellectual core, and less easily engage co-producers. By now we had other irons in the fire, and the financial challenge of funding staged events in the theatre. Unless we short-changed these new priorities, we would have insufficient funds.

It was, perhaps, an uncourageous decision. Composers are mortal and their work eventually has to be presented without them. Ensemble InterContemporain remains the only major European new music ensemble never to have appeared in the festival. Nor was any of

Boulez's music performed in Huddersfield between 1995 and 2000, in which year the Nieuw Ensemble gave a seventy-fifth birthday tribute ending with his superbly imagined *sur Incises*. The concert took place in Huddersfield Town Hall before a disappointingly small audience of 370. Had Boulez been present, there would surely have been double that number, perhaps more.

Glasnost and Eastern Europe

During the 1980s, what was happening musically behind the Iron Curtain became an absorbing fascination. Among concert promoters in the West, Schnittke eclipsed Shostakovich as cult figure of the moment. Meanwhile Leo Feigin, a Russian émigré working for the BBC World Service in London, had commenced his own record label as a vehicle for hundreds of smuggled tapes of jazz and improvised music received from the Russian 'underground'. Enclaves of new music in Eastern Europe were becoming better known – one of them to Barrie Webb, who from 1986 travelled regularly to Romania as guest trombonist and conductor, and became one of the Romanian composers' most committed advocates. In 1986, as we have seen, the festival succeeded in bringing Sofia Gubaidulina on her first visit to Britain, and only her second outside the Soviet bloc.

From the many ideas in my planning book, I was tending towards a more substantial Russian theme, with invitations to Schnittke and again to Gubaidulina. There were numerous works by both of them unperformed in Britain, despite performances of Schnittke's music in Glasgow, London and elsewhere. I was already negotiating with Huddersfield Choral Society, English Northern Philharmonia, Rozhdestvensky and the composer to mount an all-Schnittke concert on his fifty-sixth birthday, 24 November 1990, when the extraordinary historic events of early November 1989 unfolded. Despite the imminence of that year's festival, like everyone else I was mesmerised by the live television broadcasts as the Berlin Wall was breached, and sat riveted and in tears during Barenboim's televised open performance with the Berlin Philharmonic of Beethoven's *Eroica* two days later, before hundreds of East Berliners who had crossed into the West for the first time in their lives.

The longing for freedom was spreading fast, and in December the Romanian dictator Nicolae Ceausescu was overthrown and executed. I decided to broaden the focus and, with Barrie as go-between, invited Ensemble Archaeus from Bucharest to perform at the 1990 festival, accompanied by four Romanian composers: Calin Ioachimescu, Adrian Iorgulescu, Doina Rotaru and Liviu Danceanu, who was also the conductor. In the event, Ioachimescu was unwell and unable to travel. The members of Archeus, when they arrived the following November, looked, not surprisingly, slightly down-at-heel, but the quality of the playing was excellent. The music of Rotaru proved especially imaginative and included the UK premiere of *Clocks,* written specifically for Archeus, to which we added UK premieres of her Flute Concerto and Second Symphony, played by the Polytechnic Symphony Orchestra. Nearly all the Eastern bloc music heard at the 1990 festival was new to Britain; and all the ensembles – Archeus, Trio Syrinx from Romania, the New Music Ensemble of Vilnius, Orkestrion and other artists from Russia's musical 'underground' – were making UK debuts. The festival touched briefly on the music of Stefan Niculescu, the senior composer still resident in Romania. Later I met him in Bucharest and he showed me Ceausescu's infamously grandiose architectural projects, and the medieval church which the dictator had ordered to be rolled out of the way intact, not daring to demolish it. I grew to know and admire more of Niculescu's music, and when Ligeti, whose first twenty years had been lived in Romania, came to the festival in 1993, he was pleased that I was also planning to invite Niculescu.

Besides the Russians and Romanians, there was music by Eisler and Górecki, and the world premiere of a string quartet by one of Poland's most distinctive young composers, Hanna Kulenty – who for Ben Watson, writing in *The Wire,* was 'the most exciting discovery at Huddersfield this year'.[49] Arguably, the three most interesting composers in 1990 were all women: Gubaidulina, Kulenty and Rotaru – to whom one might add the British composer, Erika Fox, whose full-length 'puppet music drama', *The Bet,* was performed by the Feinstein Quartet and Norwich Puppet Theatre. After the main concert one evening, Polish food was served in the town hall by some of the town's Polish community, and the audience invited to join in folk dancing, led by a local Polish dance group with music played by Troika.

With Bulgaria and Moldova there was still little contact. Hungary, on the other hand, had been well represented in the West by the publisher Editio Musica Budapest, whose urbane and charming Balint Varga (later employed by Universal Edition) had accompanied Balassa and Bozay to Huddersfield in 1981. There was less need to include its music.

The arrival of the Lithuanians was due to a chance meeting. In March 1990 my wife and I spent two days at Ars Musica in Brussels, where a meeting of European contemporary music festivals had been convened. Waiting for a bus to take us back from a reception at the Palais Stoclet, Nan could not resist asking the couple sitting opposite why they were conversing in English, although neither appeared to be British. Violetta Tovianskaite, we discovered, was a young Lithuanian living in Holland, her partner Wim Loman a composer and producer at Dutch Radio – their common language English. In reply to my questions, Violetta described an unexpectedly vibrant musical scene in Vilnius, and promised to send me a recording by its New Music Ensemble. The cassette arrived and I was captivated, but to follow it up one had to overcome difficulties. The Russians had cut off the oil; a plane flew to Vilnius once a week, but only from Berlin; there was no fax; mail took six weeks, and phone calls (quite apart from the language barrier) had to be 'pre-arranged'. I asked Violetta to contact Šarūnas Nakas, director of the ensemble, who suggested we communicate via telex. Telex? Surely it was obsolete? But, no. It still functioned and, much to my surprise, somewhere in the bowels of the polytechnic there was a telex printer.

Through telex and a couple of phone calls we set up a visit by the Vilnius New Music Ensemble, accompanied by two composers: Osvaldas Balakauskas and Bronius Kutavičius. I wrote also to invite the recently elected president of Lithuania, Vytautas Landsbergis, a distinguished musicologist who had written extensively about Kutavičius. But the Baltic states were busy negotiating their independence from Russia, and it was no surprise that he did not reply.

The music of the Lithuanians had an individuality unlike anything else. Embedded in

folklore, its revolving cycles combined ritual and a kind of rustic minimalism, with such refreshing novelty that their Sunday afternoon concert in St Paul's was a delight. Performing mainly from memory and dressed in long white robes, the twelve musicians stood in a circle facing each other as if in some ancient ceremony: playing pipes, zithers, tuned stones and clay drums; bowing nail-violins and blowing into huge, bellowing wooden horns. Most interesting were the two compositions of Kutavičius which occupied two thirds of the programmes – one of them, *Magic Circle of Sanskrit*, a world premiere composed for the occasion – whose aura of ritual was underlined by the occasional regroupings of the musicians.

The Lithuanians travelled from Vilnius to Huddersfield by train; the Romanians drove in their battered East European cars; the Russians flew on their comradely but austere state airline, Aeroflot, from a Moscow suffering severe food shortages. Nothing, however, impeded their artistry. Friedrich Lips, one of the finest accordionists in the world, made his UK debut, producing astonishing colouristic effects and an organ-like grandeur. His partnership with the cellist Vladimir Tonkha in the UK premiere of Gubaidulina's *Seven Words* involved esoteric extremes of sound production, unvoiced, seemingly human 'breathing', and chant-like unison melodies of eloquent solemnity.

Earlier, one of the strangest concerts featured the celebrated Russian gypsy singer, Valentina Ponomareva, garishly lit in red, mauve and purple, and accompanied by electronics. She was followed by Orkestrion, an abrasive, avant-garde group from Stalingrad whose members included the poet Sergey Karsaev, a vocalist, a percussionist, and a multi-instrumentalist playing 'scrapyard' instruments culled from garbage tips. Ponomareva's 'wailing, whistling and otherwise vocalising into a microphone' entranced some and alienated many. Ben Watson thought it 'artless and crucifyingly boring'.[50] But for the jazz critic of the *Huddersfield Examiner*, Chris Strachan, her 'instrumental' vocalisations, to the accompaniment of pre-recorded tape and projected images, were 'exciting', 'mercurial' and 'formidable'. Orkestrion's 'grim impression of life in the USSR', and Natalia Pshenichnikova's often 'harsh and shrill' improvisation, using voice, flutes, and 'strange metallic trills coaxed from a scaffolding tube', created a 'sombre mood of anguish and oppression'. 'Altogether not a comfortable evening,' he concluded, 'but one which gave a fascinating taste of new Russian music.'[51] Both Ponomarave and Orkestrion owed their reputation in the West to the records released by Leo Feigin, and Leo himself was present to talk about 'Jazz in the Soviet Union' with the Leningrad commentator Alex Kahn.

A birthday cake for Alfred Schnittke

The high point of the 1990 festival was a spectacular choral and orchestral concert devoted entirely to the music of Schnittke, whose fifty-sixth birthday fell that day. For the UK premiere of *Ritual* four sets of tubular bells were required, two behind the orchestra and one on each side of the balcony, entering at the climax with the same melody played (characteristically of Schnittke) in close four-part canon. Composed in memory of the victims of the Second World War and lasting less than ten minutes, the piece made an unforgettable impression: 'a whole world of sublimated grief' (Nicholas Kenyon in *The Observer*),[52] 'progressing from subterranean brass growls to a tremendous climax with bells and organ added to the full orchestra' (Michael Kennedy in *The Sunday Telegraph*),[53] but which seemed 'to glow with life-affirming light... in the exalted transfiguration of wonderfully played high bells and crotales' (Simon Cargill in the *Yorkshire Post*).[54]

The concert's climax was the UK premiere of Schnittke's *Faust Cantata*, in which Huddersfield Choral Society took part along with English Northern Philharmonia, conducted by Rozhdestvesnky, and with four soloists headed by John Tomlinson as Faust. This was the Choral Society's first participation in the festival. Having conducted a Yorkshire choir myself, knowing many of the Choral Society members but aware of its somewhat staid reputation, I took care to engage enthusiasm and address practical issues encouragingly. When rehearsals started, I wrote to every singer to welcome their involvement, raise anticipation and alert them to an imminent BBC2 television programme on Schnittke, which helpfully included a five-minute excerpt from the Faust Cantata.

The world premiere, due to take place in the Tchaikovsky Hall in Moscow on 23 May 1983, had been banned by the Soviet authorities – nervous about the participation of Russia's most famous 'rock' singer, Alla Pugachova, as Mephistopheles. It was eventually allowed to be given in Gorky. In Huddersfield, Pugachova's role was taken by Fiona Kimm, who entered midway from behind the audience in the area in a *coup de théâtre*, singing Schnittke's demonic tango into her radio mike as she slinked towards the stage. The subsequent depiction of Faust's

death was as thrilling as it was chilling. Schnittke's use of parody and pastiche for dramatic effect was never more telling. After music of such formidable power, the sight of the frail composer effortfully ascending the podium to acknowledge tumultuous applause was breath-catching. The chorus, who had excelled themselves and for whom this was an unusual excursion into new music, were visibly moved. One of their older members remarked to Natalie Wheen on Radio 4: 'It was the first time I've seen a standing ovation in the town hall in thirty-five years.'

Anne Suggate from the festival team organised a birthday cake to carry onto the stage with fifty-six lighted candles as Schnittke received the applause – another affecting moment. We had hoped it might reappear at the party held in the Mayor's Reception Room afterwards; but the Schnittkes and Rozhdestvenskys had arrived from a country in the grip of famine. The cake was not seen again. English Northern Philharmonia had also performed impressively, earning Michael Kennedy's approval in *The Sunday Telegraph* as 'now one of our best orchestras'.[55] For Christopher Bradley, principal percussionist – who with a section of eight players and four sets of tubular bells spilling over into the balcony had plenty to do – it was their most memorable participation in the festival.

A few days later Gerard McBurney introduced two of the animation films for which Schnittke and Gubaidulina had composed music in order to earn income. One was Schnittke's *The Glass Harmonica* – a fable about 'the impossibility of combining totalitarian government and human spiritual needs'. Even more telling of life during the Brezhnev era were the testimonies of various Soviet musicians filmed in *The Unreal World of Alfred Schnittke*, made for BBC TV by Donald Sturrock and shown earlier in the festival.

Having toyed with several titles for the festival's East European theme, I settled on 'The Curtain Rises'. It symbolised for me not only the Iron Curtain, but the *frisson* of expectation as a theatre curtain rises, and, more profoundly, curtains in the mind. Ron McSweeney's design for the publicity leaflet showed a large red curtain, its lower edge slightly raised revealing swathes of fabric interwoven with barbed wire. On the reverse, he had raised the curtain (still with its barbed wire) to the top of the page, below which explanatory paragraphs told festivalgoers what to expect. The following February a substantial review appeared in Russian in the *Musical Newspaper of the USSR*. Across the top of the two pages containing the article, swathes of curtain taken from our leaflet were also draped. Printed in a single colour, the barbed wire was invisible.

'The lady with the hammer': Galina Ustvolskaya

As an addendum to the 1990 exploration, the 1993 festival included a small portrait of the seventy-three year old St Petersburg composer, Galina Ustvolskaya. A rarely seen recluse, she was identified with music of such idiosyncratic and uncompromising severity that, up to 1990 (when Sikorki published a catalogue), little of it had been heard in Russia, let alone in the West. A turning point occurred in April 1991 when six works were performed in a concert entirely devoted to Ustvolskaya's music in the St Petersburg Spring Festival. Afterwards an article entitled 'The lady with the hammer' appeared in *Vrÿ Nederland,* and then in a collection of essays, in which the Dutch musicologist and critic Elmer Schoenberger described the tremendous impact of that occasion.[56] Performances followed in Holland, and in 1993 I was able to sit with scores and tape recordings, again in the offices of Boosey and Hawkes in London, and assess the music

for myself, struck by its relentless 'gouging of the soul' as Schoenberger described it, its strength and bleak honesty, its 'hammering on the anvil of truth'.[57]

To fit into an already full festival I chose three pieces, all UK premieres: the *Grand Duet for Cello and Piano*, the *Duet for Violin and Piano*, and *Composition No 1: Dona Nobis Pacem* for the eccentric combination of piccolo, tuba and piano. The last two were performed in a newly found venue, St Thomas's Church just outside the town centre, another fine Victorian edifice whose interior had recently been reconfigured and redecorated. Ustvolskaya had said that her works, although not religious in a liturgical sense, 'are infused with a religious spirit, and best suited to performance in a church'.[58] Late in the evening under its neo-gothic arches, with the performers spotlit in a side aisle, and all but the fourteen stations of the cross in semi-darkness, the effect was spellbinding (see the photograph on page 174).

Two years later Ustvolskaya was persuaded to make a rare trip outside Russia to hear performances by the Schoenberg Ensemble and Reinbert de Leeuw at the Amsterdam Concertgebouw, and afterwards stood diminutive and bent, shy and retiring, astonished, it seemed, by the ovation. When in 1999 Willem Hering offered us a similar concert (what would be de Leeuw and the ensemble's UK debut) I gladly accepted, although there was no chance that the composer herself, now aged eighty, would come. It enabled us to present *Compositions Nos 1, 2* and *3* (1970–75) in sequence as a triptych as she had intended, although their bizarre scoring (eight double basses, piano and a 'thick plywood cube played with wooden hammers' in *No 2*; four flutes, four bassoons and piano in *No 3*) is anything but straightforward. Hard, brutal, lacerating – the grim yet passionate spirituality of the music was compelling. Ustvolskaya's music had been honed and hidden during years of cultural oppression. Now all this had changed. Communism and censorship had gone. Such draining defiance belonged to the past.

'There is no pathway, there is only travelling itself' – Luigi Nono.

Ustvolskaya was, at least, alive. She might be an elderly recluse who had ceased composing.

RIGHT TOP:
Galina Ustvolskaya on the stage of the Concertgebouw in 1995.

RIGHT BOTTOM:
With Reinbert de Leeuw before the world premiere recording of her Second Symphony in 2005.

But being alive, it seemed to me, was a reasonable prerequisite for inclusion in a festival of contemporary work. So my decision to focus on the music of Nono three years after his death caused some heart-searching. The justification was simple. Few of the compositions of his final decade had been performed in England and, as a fiercely honest expression of modernist sensibility, they had a powerful resonance. I had written to Nono in 1987 but he had not replied. I should, have visited him, except that with a young family and full-time teaching, there was no time to do so. Four years later he was dead.

Nono was always a controversial figure. The memory remains vivid of developing prints in my brother's photographic darkroom on the evening of 13 April 1961, whilst listening to the world premiere, broadcast live from La Fenice in Venice, of Nono's opera *Intolleranza 1960,* and the rush of adrenalin as the jeering right-wing *claque* in the gallery repeatedly halted the performance, followed by angry exchanges with Bruno Maderna in the pit. Far from there being any decline of interest, Nono's posthumous stature seemed only to have increased. Throughout Europe festivals honoured his memory, and performances proliferated, led by the Music Biennale in Venice itself, the city in which he had been born and died. In June 1993, juggling assessments and exam boards, I earmarked five days when I could visit, staying perforce on the Lido and crossing the lagoon daily to attend the concerts.

In the serenity of Venice, with its absence of automobiles, its mutable reflections and omnipresent bells, Nono's music sounded especially beautiful and transcendent.[59] Presiding over its live electronic transformations was André Richard, director of the Heinrich Strobel Experimental Studio for Acoustic Art in Freiburg, who had worked closely with the composer throughout the 1980s. As we have observed, Nono's collaborative approach to the realisation of his final works resulted in scores that are (or were) only partial guides. André's knowledge of actual practice was indispensable, and I had arranged to meet him to discuss the outline of a project in Huddersfield. It was soon evident that for Nono's summatory achievement, *Prometeo,* Huddersfield had no suitable venue, and its complex requirements were beyond our means. But there was no lack of other possibilities, and our provisional choices mapped out in Venice changed little, as

we met to flesh out details three times in three different countries during the next two years.

The poignancy of Nono's late music, with its fragility and ambivalence, its sense of pained isolation, interior listening and infinite space, I found especially meaningful. The inscription which Nono discovered on a monastery wall in Toledo – 'Caminantes, no hay caminos, hey que caminar' ('Traveller, there is no pathway, there is only travelling itself') – and which underpins so many of his compositions, describes the journey of any truly original artist, or lone explorer without map or mobile, or individual facing death in an age of unbelief.

The festival board did not need me to tell them that, despite its humanity, the uncompromising nature of Nono's work would draw smaller audiences than we had built in previous years. But there was no dissent. All agreed that this was something the festival should, and that only the festival could, do. I approached Nicholas Kenyon at the BBC, who agreed to co-promote the Nono events, contributing to the cost and broadcasting them on Radio 3, despite the fact that, because of its extreme quietude, discontinuity and diffusion through space, Nono's music more than most gains from being experienced live, and would challenge the BBC engineers. Ticket sales did indeed fall in 1995, but by only 8% – a small blip in their otherwise continuous increase throughout the 1990s. And those who came brought a degree of a dedication that endowed each concert with a sense of intense spirituality.

There were, in fact, only three UK premieres. But two of them, *Das atmende Klarsein,* in which André Richard conducted the Freiburg Solistenchor, and *Caminantes… Ayacucho,* with its two choirs, orchestra and soloists, were substantial undertakings. The Arditti Quartet's performance of *Fragmente-Stille, an Diotima* followed the first British screening of Edna Polititi's prize-winning film, *Le Quator de possibles,* which shows the Ardittis rehearsing with Nono against the backdrop of Venice. In St Paul's, Irvine Arditti performed *La lontananza nostalgica utopica futura,* a 'madrigal' for wandering violinist. Its gentle figurations, multiplied by André's live electronics, seemed to float polyphonically as if 'raining violins from on high', and 'glowed with depth and feeling', as David Murray remarked in the *Financial Times.*[60] The composer's widow,

Nuria Schoenberg-Nono, contributed to a forum on 'The mind of Luigi Nono', and André, along with Roberto Fabbriciani and Roger Heaton, gave a 'Micro-surgery on real-time sound transformation,' in which flute and clarinet students took part. Irvine joined Mieko Kanno to play new violin duos submitted for the Young Composers' Award (won by Bryn Harrison with *Frozen Earth*), and to perform a duo recital featuring the world premiere of James Dillon's first book of *Traumwerk*.[61]

The programme had been planned to allow time for the Freiburg equipment to be installed first in St Paul's, then transferred to Huddersfield Town Hall, where the final concert took place. A regret was the indisposition of Wolfgang Rihm, whose *Sphere* for solo piano, percussion and winds (placed stereophonically around the hall) made an electrifying impact. *Caminantes…*

Ayacucho also required antiphonal placements: horns positioned around the balcony, choruses and two soloists right and left, above them the organ, and at the centre the orchestra with the exceptionally deep bells chosen by Nono himself and imported from Germany. Its forty minutes of delicate whispers, microtonal clusters, lustrous soprano solos and bass flute, assailed by angry outbursts of brass and percussion, were both gripping and strangely cathartic. As John Warnaby wrote in *Musical Opinion*,

The latter was a revelation, refuting the suggestion that in the introspective late works Nono abandoned his Marxist convictions. It was an anguished protest at capitalist exploitation in the poorest regions of the world, and it brought the festival to a sombre and thought-provoking conclusion. Yet it was also exhilarating, proclaiming creative principles to which Nono adhered throughout his career, and which have produced some of the finest music of the past half-century.[62]

Afterwards there was a modest reception. Late that night Anthony Sargent drove home to Birmingham and at 2.00am sent me a fax (see left).

Looking back seventeen years later, I still regard the Nono performances, and this concert in particular, as amongst the most important during my tenure as artistic director.

Remembering Morty

The success of the Nono led to the celebration of another dead composer. In 1996 Morton Feldman would have been seventy. I knew his earlier music, but it was Richard Ayres who triggered my interest in the late works. He had attended Feldman's classes in 1986 at Darmstadt and Dartington, and the experience influenced his own decision to pursue a career in music. It seemed careless of Morty to have died before I got round to inviting him; or maybe I was needlessly laggard. But, like Nono, his posthumous reputation soared; numerous CDs appeared and, in the early days of planning, whilst listening to the late works late at night, I succumbed utterly to their rarefied beauty.

In the event, Feldman's unostentatious music was slightly upstaged at the 1996 festival by the larger than life presence of Stockhausen, although I suspect that most festival regulars preferred the former. There were ten pieces by Feldman: three of them from the last year of his

life. René Berman and Kees Wieringa played *Patterns in a Chromatic Field* with a sensitivity that held a late-night audience spellbound. Recherche performed five of Feldman's ensemble pieces, and then, in the Lawrence Batley Theatre with three speaker/actors, presented the bleak and searing *Samuel Beckett: Words and Music* – originally a radio play for a revival of which Beckett had invited Feldman to compose music. The regard Feldman had for Beckett was manifest earlier in the festival when an expanded London Sinfonietta performed *For Samuel Beckett*. In another late evening concert the Ives Ensemble gave the UK premiere of his last completed composition, the 80-minute long *Piano, Violin, Viola, Cello*.

In 2002 Recherche returned with six UK premieres of early 'unknown Feldman', including two compositions written for films about Jackson Pollock and De Kooning, both projected in St Paul's and accompanied by the music. Later that evening, Nicolas Hodges gave a rapt performance of Feldman's late masterpiece for piano, *For Bunita Marcus*. Its dedicatee had herself been present at the 1996 tribute, and in the newly transformed West Mills lecture theatre had delivered one of the most fascinating lectures given at the festival.

In 2006 Graham McKenzie devised a more extended Feldman strand running throughout his first festival. It included all twelve of his compositions for piano and strings, played by John Tilbury and the Smith String Quartet, in concerts spread over nine days. The University New Music Ensemble added three further pieces, in what was the first ever festival concert performed by students to be broadcast on Radio 3 – although others had surely deserved to be. Only four out of the ten works by Feldman performed in 1996 and the fifteen in 2006 were duplicates. St Paul's proved again a perfect context for his timeless art. Unlike the Kronos recordings, the Smiths used no vibrato, and their adoption of baroque bows the composer would probably have approved. For their tenth appearance in the final concert of the festival, John Tilbury and the quartet gave a superbly poised performance of *Piano and String Quartet* – Feldman's favourite among his works, and one of the most original and audacious compositions of the last century.

Latterly, Huddersfield has featured more dead composers than I would have deemed appropriate, but it has also hidden the 'contemporary' in its title by using the acronym 'hcmf'. One could argue that Cardew, Feldman, Ives, Maciunas, Nono, Partch and Varése, in being so boldly experimental, were more contemporary in attitude than many composers living now. With the death of Berio, Cage, Kagel, Ligeti, Stockhausen and others, around whom earlier festivals were built, it could be tempting to mount further retrospectives.

Grisey and Dusapin

Gérard Grisey died younger than any of them, but not before we had presented some of his most important compositions. I first met Gérard at Oslo's Ultima festival in 1991, when what I knew of his music came from scores and recordings, plus a live performance of *Partiels* heard one year before. Although composed in 1975, *Partiels* had never been played in Britain; nor, indeed, had most of Grisey's medium-scale and larger compositions. Talking with the composer intensified my desire to programme *Modulations* for thirty-three musicians; but it turned out to be unexpectedly expensive. My Ten-Year Planning Book lists twenty-six pieces under discussion with English Northern Philharmonia for a concert in November 1992. Against Klaus Huber's *Tempora* I had noted that it was 'excellent'. But only to Grisey's *Modulations* and *Le temps et l'écume* had I given 'four-star' rating. Above the list is a reminder in red: 'CAUTION – Consider percussion platform set-up!' Evidently, a conversation with ENP's manager revealed further impediments: 'Can't do *Three Screaming Popes* because of approx 6 extra players!' I wrote. 'Can't do *Modulations* or *Tempora* because of chamber music rates'.

The Huber needed only nine string players, the Grisey twelve. But, because each player would be reading a separate part, they would be contracted as soloists, and the whole orchestra would be eligible for solo rates. This we could not afford. (To undertake *Les Espaces Acoustiques*, the cycle to which *Partiels* and *Modulations* belong – and which gradually expands from solo viola to large orchestra with four solo horns – would have been far beyond our resources. It received its UK premiere in London only in October 2008 performed by an enlarged London Sinfonietta further augmented with students from the Royal Academy of Music.)

The orchestral programme eventually agreed contained nothing by Grisey (although it did include Turnage's *Three Screaming Popes*). But, after a late injection of funds from the European Arts Festival, my attention turned to an extravagant multi-media piece which Gérard had described to me in Oslo. *Le Noir de l'Étoile* is the kind of audacious flight of the imagination to which composers sometimes aspire; although, with its unusual staging requirements, elaborate lighting and a live pulsar signal transmitted from outer space, there is a risk that any realisation will not match the composer's vision. In Huddersfield our preparations were frighteningly thrown askew when, only days before the performance, a serious accident befell the festival's technical director. What happened, how we dealt with it and the nature of Gérard's concept are described in Chapter 9 (see pages 149–51).

If *Le Noir de l'Étoile* seemed slightly portentous, Grisey's mastery of instrumental

Gérard Grisey in 1997.
PHOTO: SELWYN GREEN.

sonority was impressively evident in *Périodes* and *Partiels* (its UK premiere) performed also in 1992. Five years later, as we have noted, *Modulations* was played by the BBC Philharmonic, again in Gérard's presence, along with *Talea* and *Vortex Temporum I-III* (another UK premiere) both played with dazzling artistry by Ensemble Recherche. They were a thrilling confirmation of Grisey's status as the leading exponent of 'spectral' music, and the musical world was shocked when, one year later at the age of fifty-two, he suddenly died of an aneurysm.

A very different voice, although no less distinctive and original, I found in Pascal Dusapin – born in 1955 and comparatively overlooked in Britain, despite a growing reputation in France. Unlike Grisey, Dusapin represents no 'school' and has been neither a polemicist nor a teacher. But his neglect owes more to the tendency for Boulez, Messiaen, Grisey and Murail – and Kaija Saariaho who, although Finnish, is another Parisian resident – to dominate discussion. More existentialist than Grisey and more melancholic, Dusapin's music is affected by his immersion in text and language. Passionate, lyrical and sensual, with a masterful command of colour and texture, his work is rare among contemporary composers for the primacy given to the voice. Many of his earlier works involve singers, six of them quasi-operas. I was introduced to his music by the French publishers Salabert, as well as by two Parisian ensembles: Alternance which performed at the festival in 1989 and 1992, and 2é2m, conducted by Paul Mefano – an ensemble I considered inviting but never did, suspecting, perhaps wrongly, that it had lost its earlier energy.

Few of Dusapin's stage works are conventionally operatic; rather they are dramatic tableaux, and for that reason seemed easier to attempt. Choosing from those completed during the 1990s, *Medeamaterial* ruled itself out because it used a period orchestra. *Roméo et Juliette* attracted me because of the richness of its music and multilingual text, and because, as Antoine Gindt describes it, the piece 'can be seen as a conflation of the composer's career' up to the late 1980s.[63] Unfortunately, the festival's semi-staging in 1997 was, like *Le Noir de l'Étoile*, less than ideal. There was fine singing by the French soloists, Vox Nova and London Sinfonietta Voices, and playing by English

Northern Philharmonia conducted by Luca Pfaff. But, on the town hall stage the production looked awkward, the tubular lights which marked out the acting area alienating and unatmospheric. At the mixing desk in the area, Pascal's chosen audio engineer failed to diffuse the work effectively for other levels of the hall. It did not prevent some listeners being drawn to Dusapin's colourful palette. But for others, baffled by the production, and struggling to hear and understand the poet Olivier Cadiot's deconstructive narrative, the experience was too confusing.

One could draw parallels between Dusapin's *Roméo et Juliette* and Berio's *Un re in ascolto,* another non-narrative stage-work, which Berio calls an *'azione musicale'* rather than an opera, and whose text by Italo Calvino and Berio himself derives from *The Tempest.* Cadiot's text is more mannered, and now seems more dated. It was expecting rather much, perhaps, for this multilayered work to succeed with our limited resources. But I was sad not to serve the composer better. Disappointment was mitigated, however, by the quality of a related educational collaboration, *Exploring Romeo and Juliet,* whose 'outcome' performance in St Paul's was effectively staged and designed, and powerful in its impact. It is described in Chapter 13 (see pages 222–23).

A concert devoted to Dusapin's ensemble music revealed a composer of striking individuality. Seeking the most persuasive advocates, I settled on Ars Nova, the ensemble founded by Marius Constant in 1963 to counteract the narrower aesthetic of Boulez's Domaine Musicale. Ars Nova had become more-or-less inactive, until revived in the 1990s under the direction of Philippe Nahon. Now, relocated in La Rochelle and consisting of younger players, it had taken into its repertoire all of Dusapin's ensemble works. In Huddersfield the players were joined by soloists from Accroche Note, and their joint portrait concert containing five works, all new to Britain, was immensely rewarding. A further piece, *Quad,* for violin and ensemble was performed by Clio Gould and the London Sinfonietta.

Elsewhere in Britain there appeared to be little interest. None of Dusapin's major works had received performances in London, where, apart from *Niobé* programmed by the Almeida Festival in the early 1980s, and repeated in

Julian Anderson's 'Music of Today' series in 2007, his only advocates were the Arditti Quartet. Then, in April 2011, the BBC announced UK premieres of two substantial orchestral works at the forthcoming Promenade concerts. The first, *Morning in Long Island (Concert No 1 for large orchestra)* – a co-commission between the BBC and Radio France – was warmly received by an audience of several thousand in the Albert Hall on 18 July 2011. The second owes its existence to Irvine Arditti, who, over many years, had urged Dusapin to 'compose a quartet with orchestra'. The result is a hybrid: *String Quartet No 6, 'Hinterland' ('Hapax' for string quartet and orchestra).*

Dillon, Harvey and Rebecca Saunders

For one of the UK's most individual living composers, James Dillon has also received patchy recognition in London, although repeatedly commissioned abroad. Like Dusapin, his early music was programmed at the Almeida festival and, starting in the 1990s, Radio 3 commissioned four works for the BBC Proms which, in 2010, also heard the UK premiere of *La navette,* nine years after its Donaueschingen premiere. Shamefully, the London Sinfonietta has played nothing by Dillon since it commissioned *Überschreiten* in 1986. In Scotland the BBC has been as committed as in London and, in November 2010, to mark James's sixtieth birthday, mounted the first ever complete performance of *Nine Rivers,* the huge cycle of nine differently scored compositions on which James had worked throughout the 1980s and 1990s. *Nine Rivers* won the 2010 Royal Philharmonic Society's award for large-scale composition, making Dillon, with four awards, one of the two most frequently honoured individuals in the society's history – the other being Birtwistle. Yet none of the award winning works had been premiered in London.

The festival's relationship with James goes back to 1978 when *Dillug-Kefitsah,* the earliest work in his catalogue, won the Young Composers' Competition (see page 11), and, five years later, we commissioned his First String Quartet. Richard Bernas, who had been involved in the Almeida performances, was a keen advocate when, whilst planning a Nono retrospective, I was looking for an opportunity to feature Dillon's music more substantially. The two ideas came together in 1995. It was already clear that

Richard and Music Projects/London should be involved, and Richard suggested *Windows and Canopies* which they had recorded for NMC in 1991. Our eventual choice was *La femme invisible* and *Überschreiten* in a programme which included Rihm's *Chiffre III*, Webern's Songs op. 14 and Birtwistle's *Nenia on the Death of Orpheus* sung by Alison Wells.

The density of the two Dillon pieces required ultra-attentive listening, but back in London Richard wrote to me commending the audience's 'extreme concentration' – a phenomenon which St Paul's particularly induces. Later in the festival, *Vernal Showers* was given its UK premiere by Cambridge New Music Players, its demanding violin solo played with superb musicianship – and from memory – by Mieko Kanno. A Belgian duo, Bureau des Pianistes, gave the world premiere of *black/nebulae*, and Accroche Note from Strasbourg the world premiere of *Redemption*, plus the UK premiere of *L'évolution du vol* with its unexpectedly charming modal folk

Noriko Kawai performing the complete Book of Elements *by James Dillon.*
PHOTO: BRIAN SLATER

In the new millennium the festival has continued to premiere James's chamber compositions which, like his orchestral works, embody developments in style that have often been surprising. In 2003 *the Soadie Waste* received its UK premiere from the Ardittis and Noriko Kawai. Two years later Noriko gave a superbly nuanced performance of the complete *Book of Elements,* the third of Dillon's works to win a Royal Philharmonic Society award. The 2009 festival contained the world premiere of the Fifth String Quartet and the UK premiere of *The Leuven Triptych* – the latter receiving an uncharacteristically poor performance from the Belgian ensemble Ictus, which had arrived with little time to rehearse.

If Jonathan Harvey's name has appeared regularly through this book, it is because his works have been performed more frequently than those of any other composer, with the exception of Cage, Stockhausen and Xenakis (who heads the list with over seventy performances). The tally includes none of Harvey's large-scale pieces, but the numerous works in other genres (ensemble, choral, string quartet etc), along with Jonathan's exploration of live electronics, evidence an exceptional creative mind, internationally admired. The festival's early choices were relatively minor, until in 1985 the music of Harvey, Michael Finnissy and Bernard Rands was celebrated with significant works by each. Those by Harvey included the ensemble pieces *Inner Light I, Concelebration* and *Song Offerings* (with Rosemary Hardy, soprano) and the First String Quartet performed by the Ardittis. His fiftieth birthday in 1989 saw performances of the

Visual Kitchen's video accompaniment to Jonathan Harvey's Mortuos Plango, Vivos Voco.
PHOTO: BRIAN SLATER

qualities. The Ardittis played the Second String Quartet – another UK premiere, and Irvine and Mieko joined in what turned out to be the first 'book' (just completed) of *Traumwerk* for violin duo.

Deeply impressive, this remains the most substantial portrait of Dillon's music ever to have taken place in Britain (with the possible exception of the complete *Nine Rivers* in Glasgow); and it reinforced my belief in the music's exceptional quality. The language had become richer, more direct, less easily typecast. It was broader, more varied and transparent – as if the densely compacted lines of *helle Nacht* (Dillon's first orchestral score of 1987) had been thinned, like saplings enabled to grow unimpeaded. In a concert given by English Northern Philharmonia and Paul Daniel, *helle Nacht* itself received a blistering performance – but in curious company. I had invited Terry Riley, the co-founder of minimalism, and wanted to include a recent example of orchestral music, which, if not his natural medium, was one in which I thought he had something to say. In the event, the folksy amiability of *The Sands* sat uneasily between the formidable *helle Nacht* and Tippett's luminous last orchestral piece, *The Rose Lake*. My nonchalant notions of coexistence were over-strained.

Second String Quartet, *Valley of Aosta* and *Nataraja*; and, in 1994, the festival featured eight works, including the groundbreaking *Bhakti* for ensemble and tape.

To mark his seventieth birthday in 2009, Harvey became the festival's first composer-in-residence and the University of Huddersfield awarded him an honorary doctorate. Throughout this festival the celebrated tape composition from 1980, *Mortuos Plango, Vivos Voco,* played continuously in St Thomas's Church. Projected onto the floor was an abstract video by the Belgian duo Visual Kitchen, commissioned by Lieven Bertels for the Gaida Festival in Vilnius, and for four hours each day the nine-minute loop recycled: the music repeating, the images subtly changing. In other programmes, the Dutch pianist Ralph van Raat provided an overview of Harvey's complete piano music, and the Ardittis repeated the rarefied Fourth Quartet with real-time electronics, which had made such a profound impression at its UK premiere in 2003 (see page 67).

Jonathan Harvey thanks Enno Poppe and the members of musikFabrik after the UK premiere of Sringara Chaconne.
PHOTO: BRIAN SLATER

Harvey's *Sringara Chaconne* of 2009, a ravishing ensemble composition given its UK premiere by musikFabrik, exemplified a recent penchant for weaving shimmering textures around simple chords. Recalling Harvey's second opera *Wagner Dream*, Ivan Hewitt observed that 'the harmonies took the magic garden in Wagner's *Parsifal* and transported it to an Eastern heaven.'[64] That the opera had been a tripartite commission between Netherlands Opera, the Grand Theatre, Luxembourg, and IRCAM in Paris, is a testament to the composer's international standing. Not yet staged in Britain, it is due to receive a concert UK premiere at the Barbican in January 2012.

Harvey is one of the most accomplished users of computer controlled spatialisation and transformation, and his pre-eminence was memorably demonstrated in the New London Chamber Choir's performance of *The Summer Cloud's Awakening* in 2009. In this superb thirty-five minute piece, Buddhist temple instruments played by the singers, solo flute and cello, and eight channel spatialisation (evolved

with the sound designer Carl Faia at CIRM in Nice) produce music of sustained spiritual elevation. The choir sing Buddhist texts. The music, Harvey explains, 'is based on the relationship of a brief phrase from Wagner's *Tristan and Isolde* to the Buddhist vision of reality.' Indeed, the motif 'is stretched out from twelve seconds to five minutes – the "longing" of the Wagnerian phrase so achingly long that it seems almost motionless'. Stretched out it may be, but the control of musical time is masterly, and for many listeners this was the high point of the 2009 festival.

In 2010, Rebecca Saunders followed Harvey as composer-in-residence, with one world premiere and two UK premieres, culminating in the remarkable site-specific *Chroma*. Although first performed in 2003, through successive mutations *Chroma* amounts to a summation of her preoccupations to date and, in two successive performances made a deeply memorable impression (see pages 271–4). After studying with Nigel Osborne in Edinburgh in the 1990s, then with Wolfgang Rihm in Karlsruhe, Saunders settled in Germany where she has become increasingly prominent, in 2009 being appointed composer-in-residence for Staatskapelle Dresden. Impressed by what I had heard on tape, in 1999 I programmed the UK premiere of *CRIMSON – Molly's Song 1*, her

most substantial and intriguing ensemble piece at the time, and commissioned a duo for viola and percussion. Five years later *choler* for two pianos was commissioned for Huddersfield by the BBC, and seven other works were heard in a feature devised by Susanna Eastburn. Most of them were performed by musikFabrik and Recherche, both ensembles having developed close relationships with Saunders, and both returning for Graham McKenzie's further feature in 2010. As so often, Huddersfield has been the principal British showcase for an increasingly important British composer resident abroad.

Ligeti

Before Ligeti came to Huddersfield in 1993, we had performed surprisingly few of his pieces for so important a composer. They included the *Three Pieces for Two Pianos* in 1979, and the UK premiere of *Drei Fantasien* in 1983, but neither of the string quartets, despite regular appearances by the Ardittis. I first met Ligeti at Glasgow's Musica Nova in 1973, and had written an article about him for *Music and Musicians*.[65] Ligeti had sent an appreciative card, but that had been twenty years before and he had probably forgotten me. So, on 10 March 1992, I flew to Amsterdam for a concert given

Rebecca Saunders at the 2010 festival.
PHOTO: PAUL GREENWOOD

by Asko and the Nederland Kamerkoor in which Ligeti's music shared the bill with that of Claude Vivier. In a pre-concert talk, he brushed aside his own music, extolling instead the prematurely dead Vivier. After the concert I joined Ligeti and members of Asko for dinner and the following morning shared a taxi to the airport with the composer, his assistant Louise Duchesneau and a 'girl friend' (Ligeti's, not mine!). On the way, we planned an outline programme. Ligeti later said that he liked the way I thought about his music. Perhaps that clinched the deal. He also admired the festival's character: its stylistic plurality, openness, interweaving of different strands and risk-taking; and praised my readiness to include 'bad' music as well as 'good' – which did not prevent him striding backstage after a Kronos Quartet double-bill, during his 1993 visit to the festival, to berate the players for their 'terrible' choice of programme. The pieces by Georgescu, Yanov-Yanovsky, Zograbian and Kancheli had most irritated him. But he admired (and shared) the players' interest in world musics.

At the centre of Ligeti's visit were three wonderful concerts by artists as fine as one could engage. Ensemble Recherche's simple but telling staging of *Aventures* and *Nouvelles Aventures*, already described (see page 58), formed the second half of a concert that began, rivetingly, with the UK premiere of Galina Ustvolskaya's *Grand Duet* for cello and piano, eloquently played by Lucas Fels and Sven Thomas Kiebler. One day earlier, dazzlingly accomplished performances of the Chamber Concerto, Cello Concerto, Piano Concerto and *Melodien* were given by Taco Kooistra, Pierre-Laurent Aimard and Asko. The British conductor, Jonathan Nott, who had directed the concert in Amsterdam, was on this occasion making his professional UK debut. Ten years later, Ligeti entrusted Nott with recording his large orchestral scores with the Berlin Philharmonic, so rescuing the complete CD edition of his music which had been suspended after he vetoed further recordings by the Philharmonia.[66] In an even more astounding chamber concert (for the music was still little

*Ligeti talking
about his music.*
PHOTO: SELWYN GREEN

known), Aimard played the first two books of Piano Études (including UK premieres of *Entrelacs* and *Coloana infinit*), then joined in performances of the *Three Pieces for Two Pianos* and Horn Trio. Their brilliance in such virtuosic and dramatic music was unforgettable. In the town hall, on another evening, the Kings Singers gave the first complete performance of Ligeti's *Nonsense Madrigals*, including the world premiere of its last movement.

In total, eighteen of Ligeti's works were performed during the 1993 festival, in concerts supported by discussions, films and presentations more varied and extensive than for any composer previously featured in Huddersfield. In a pre-concert introduction and an hour-and-a-half interview, Ligeti talked about his outlook and aspects of his technique. Most fascinating was an illustrated lecture by the Bremen mathematician, Heinz-Otto Peitgen (a pioneer in the graphic representation of fractals), followed by a discussion with Ligeti about the relationship of fractals to musical pattern formation.[67] Ligeti's interest in the festival's interweaving strands extended to the educational programme, about which he was effusively complimentary (see pages 218–219). I saw nothing of the brusqueness to which he was prone. A diffident Michael Gordon introduced himself in the interval of a concert: 'I so admire your music,' said Ligeti, leaving

Michael astonished that the exchange had been this way round. In fact, Ligeti knew the work of the Bang on a Can composers and admired their resolute forging of an independent pathway.

The following year I was considering writing something more substantial about contemporary music than I had done before, and phoned Louise to ask whether anything on Ligeti was due to be published in English. The only existing book was a slim volume by Paul Griffiths, then ten years old. Not as far as they knew, she said. A moment later Ligeti himself picked up the phone and said, 'I would like you to write one.' 'But I don't read German,' I protested, thinking of the many books and articles about Ligeti in that language. 'It doesn't matter,' he said, 'none of them are any good.' It is true that the polemical nature of German musicology was not to his taste, although he was even more scathing about American dissertations. But I was to find the dismissal characteristically unjust. Fortified by Ligeti's encouragement, I began work on my book.[68] Soon persuaded of the importance of key German texts, I struggled to understand them.

Arvo Pärt

Around 1980, Universal Edition sent me a cassette of music by a composer of whom I had never heard. It was Arvo Pärt, whom UE had recently signed. On one side was a version of *Fratres* played on Renaissance instruments; on the other *Tabula Rasa*. Although Alfred Schnittke was listed playing the harpsichord, I did not then realise its significance; for, by booking him to play in *Tabula Rasa* and his own Concerto Grosso No 1, Gidon Kremer (organiser of the 1977 tour during which the recording was made) had enabled Schnittke to revisit Vienna and the West for the first time in thirty years. The insistent A minor modality of *Tabula Rasa*, its figurations reiterated without any hint of chromaticism or even modulation, sounded so far removed from what the festival embraced, that I could hardly conceive how to programme it. The music was strangely addictive, however, and I played both pieces repeatedly, but then put the cassette aside, never envisaging that within less than a decade Pärt's music would be a worldwide cult.[69]

When Pierre Audi opened the 1986 Almeida Festival with three days devoted to Pärt, I realised that I had missed a trick. Pärt's asceticism polarised opinions, but it clearly had a niche. So in 1990 when, in the wake of *glasnost* and the fall of the Berlin Wall, the festival featured Eastern Europe and Russia, Pärt's music appeared in three programmes. The performers included his most persuasive advocates, the Hilliard Ensemble, plus the New London Chamber Choir in the British premiere of 7 *Magnificat Antiphons*.

In 1998, as we have seen, the Contemporary Music Network toured a concert of music by Pärt and Erkki-Sven Tüür, performed by the Estonian Philharmonic Chamber Choir, Tallinn Chamber Orchestra and Hilliard Ensemble, to which we added two *a cappella* concerts specifically for Huddersfield. The first included folk and shamanistic pieces by Veljo Tormis performed from memory and in national costume, the singers in St Paul's moving and regrouping, and in one piece advancing ominously towards the audience. The other contained the UK premiere of Pärt's unaccompanied *Kanon Pokajanen (Canon of Repentance)*. Resonant and intense, its soaring eighty-five minutes of sonorous choralism is reminiscent, at times, of Rachmaninov's *Vespers*. But it was deeply impressive on its own terms, and, despite a few sceptical reviews, I thought it one of Pärt's finest compositions.

All three concerts were packed to capacity, predominantly with local people. Knowing that Pärt himself was shy, retiring, and had limited English, I had not invited him. Some ten other prominent composers would be attending and the budget was overstretched. So it was a surprise when Pärt arrived unannounced before the *Kanon Pokajanen* performance, at the end of which the audience gave both choir and composer an ovation, and he was visibly moved.

Afterwards, Michael White wrote in the *Independent on Sunday* that

At festival time, the world's leading composers arrive in this unlikely place by every train – heading straight for the thermal underwear department of Marks & Spencer – but none the less pleased to be there. And on an average day at Huddersfield's M&S this week, you'd have found any or all of the following: Arvo Pärt, Elliott Carter, Steve Reich, Terry Riley, George Crumb, Tan Dun, stocking up on long-johns and investigating blizzard-wear. The Pennine cold in late November always comes as a surprise to visitors.[70]

I thought of answering this slight on my adopted town, particularly as in Huddersfield the temperature was a healthy 5°C, whereas in Berlin, from where Pärt had flown, it was well below zero. But Michael was unstinting in his praise of the festival and, as thermal underwear probably costs less in Yorkshire, I held my peace. Wisely, it would seem. Recently Sally Groves, Head of Contemporary Music at Schott Music, London – Hans Werner Henze's publisher – sent me a recollection of Henze and his Italian 'Jeeves' arriving from warmer climes via Henze's house in Knightsbridge.

I will never forget Hans and Fausto arriving at the George Hotel in sleety weather, and Fausto advancing on the hapless spotty youth behind the bar demanding Bloody Marys and then rejecting the poor boy's efforts. I ended up drinking the rejects and Fausto got behind the bar and showed the boy how to make a proper one. Then the next morning, he sallied forth in his black silk cloak lined in scarlet, looking for warm underwear for Hans, and accosting the startled citizenry of Huddersfield with the question, 'Where is your 'Arrods?' We did, in fact, find a gentleman's outfitters of the lovely old-fashioned kind with yellow paper against the windows, where we found row upon row of long-johns and long-sleeved T-shirts. Fausto came back to the George in triumph.

8 *Premieres and commissions*

Apart from instrumental solos and duos, there were few world premieres in the early festivals. The more substantial were clarinet quintets by David Blake in 1979 and Harrison Birtwistle in 1981, David Bedford's *Sun Paints Rainbows on the Vast Waves* for the Polytechnic Symphonic Wind Band in 1982, string quartets by James Dillon and Michael Finnissy in 1983 and 1985, John Casken's *Salamandra* in 1986, Michael Torke's *Adjustable Wrench* and Trevor Wishart's *Vox 3* in 1987, Kaija Saariaho's *From the Grammar of Dreams* in 1988, Vic Hoyland's Piano Trio in 1989 and Gavin Bryars's Second String Quartet in 1990. Only two of these were for more than five instruments and only eight of them festival commissions – a surprisingly low total for the first twelve years. Huddersfield, however, was becoming an increasingly important showcase for commissions brokered elsewhere. Indeed, after the demise of both Glasgow's Musica Nova and London's Almeida festival in the early 1990s, it was the only place in Britain where you could annually keep pace with the latest music from abroad.

The 1986 festival contained only one festival commission, but forty-nine premieres – thirty-three of them UK premieres. Little public money was available for commissioning. But, as so much that was created abroad did not otherwise reach Britain, the festival could take a lead in performing it. This had the advantage of being able to evaluate scores and recordings and know that one's choices would be worth hearing. Nor were these UK premieres only of works by foreign composers. In 1987, as we have seen, Huddersfield mounted the momentous first performance in Britain of Brian Ferneyhough's complete *Carceri d'Invenzione,* and presenting major UK premieres continued to be an important *raison d'être.*

Aside from premieres, my programming was motivated by the unfashionable imperative of reviving what deserved to be more widely known. In the transient medium of musical performance, it was important to assert the canonicity of contemporary music's finest achievements and promote their assimilation into the general culture. Some of the works that made the greatest impact had received only one or two performances – perhaps not wholly successful, like Maxwell Davies's *Worldes Blis.* Some had been performed in Britain but never in the North, like Cage's *Roaratorio.* Some were archetypical contemporary pieces like Birtwistle's *Punch and Judy,* but new nevertheless to many of the audience.

Orchestral premieres are at the core of Donaueschingen and other continental festivals served by radio orchestras, whose brief includes commissioning. Consequently some of their most interesting new work has been large-scale. Readers may be surprised to learn that Huddersfield has never commissioned a full-size orchestral score. To fund it might have meant losing two or three smaller concerts. Only occasionally did any festival contain two orchestral concerts, and it was usually one – or even none. I used these limited opportunities to introduce music central to an appreciation of composers such as Grisey, Lachenmann, Nono, Rihm and Xenakis.

British composers were represented, but less frequently than board members would have liked. A concert in 1994 included the world premiere of Roger Marsh's *Espace,* but it was a score composed for no specific occasion which nobody had commissioned. In 1991, Birtwistle's *Endless Parade* and *Gawain's Journey* (its UK premiere) were sandwiched between Tippett's

Ritual Dances and *Byzantium* (its second UK performance) – a stunning *tour de force* from English Northern Philharmonia conducted by Paul Daniel. Two years later Benedict Mason's *Lighthouses of England and Wales* opened a concert which contained UK premieres of Stefan Niculescu's *Cantos* and Ligeti's finally completed Violin Concerto. Commissions for chamber orchestra were easier to fund, and for a concert by the Northern Sinfonia in 1991 the festival commissioned a Clarinet Concerto by Michael Berkeley to perform alongside music by John Casken and Robert Saxton.

Premieres from abroad enhanced the festival's reputation and attracted an international audience. By avoiding the narrow ideology of Donaueschingen or Darmstadt, the catholicity of Huddersfield made it a destination for anyone broadly interested in the new. For example, between 1988 and 1999 the festival gave UK premieres of twelve works by Louis Andriessen, several of them substantial. Starting in 1988, whilst London's South Bank Centre was reserving for itself forthcoming world premieres (see page 105), Huddersfield announced forty-five UK and European premieres. Among them were six by Andriessen including *De Stijl*, Stockhausen's *Sternklang, Michaels Reise* and five more of his pieces, eight works by Isang Yun, six by R Murray Schafer, four by Kaija Saariaho, two by Lou Harrison, one by Tōru Takemitsu and around a dozen others. Apart from a short vocal duet by Saariaho (later included in *The Grammar of Dreams*), none of these were world premieres. The festival was being less of an instigator than an advocate.

There were world premieres, of course, including a handful by major composers: if modest, like Cage's *One²* and *Four*; or due to good fortune, like the sixth of Ligeti's *Nonsense*

Dedicated to Simon Carrington and Alastair Hume
VI. A Long, Sad Tale
(from Lewis Carroll's: "Alice's Adventures in Wonderland"
and "Original Games and Puzzles")
Comissioned by the King's Singers

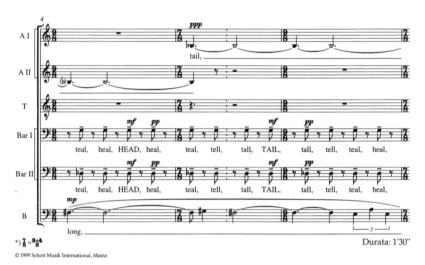

Madrigals which had been commissioned by the King's Singers and happened to be ready for their Huddersfield concert; or extremely spare, like Xenakis's *O–Mega*. In the 1990s the festival commissioned new works from Michael Berkeley, Simon Holt, Colin Matthews (in partnership with the London Sinfonietta), Stefan Niculescu and Julia Wolfe amongst others. And there were its three substantial opera commissions (discussed in Chapter 9), albeit three or more years apart.

This balance was rarely questioned, except in a joint appraisal by Yorkshire Arts and the Arts Council of England in 1996, which drew attention to the low number of world premieres, and proposed more collaborative commissions with other partners. The point was well made, but was undermined the following year, when the Arts Council terminated its music commissioning budget. In fact, there were some joint commissions – with Musica in Strasbourg, for example – and opera productions were necessarily collaborative. In November 1996, whilst the appraisers were preparing their report, the world premiere took place of Tan Dun's *Orchestral Theatre III: Red Forecast,* jointly commissioned by the festival, Radio 3 and BBCTV. The festival's contribution was funded by the Arts Council/British Gas Working for Cities Award which it had won two years earlier.

As a direct client of the Arts Council of Great Britain, the Cheltenham Festival spent annually around £10,000 on commissions, mostly using funds provided by the Arts Council. In the thirty years between 1968 and 1998 fifty-one of its commissions were Arts Council funded. Huddersfield, on the other hand, was initially entitled to apply only to the regional arts association, which had a very much smaller budget set aside for commissioning. Rarely could we place more than one commission a year, and generally only for a work of chamber proportions. In 1991 the balance of responsibilities was reviewed and ACGB agreed to consider applications from Huddersfield. This led to both ACGB and Yorkshire Arts helping to fund the composition of Robert Saxton's opera, performed in 1991, and HK Gruber's opera in 1994. Then, in partnership with Opera North, an £8,000 grant was achieved from the Arts Council to commission Simon Holt's *The Nightingale's to Blame,* premiered in 1998, which the festival 'topped up' out of revenue.

The commissioning consortia of interested individuals, established by the London Sinfonietta and Birmingham Contemporary Music Group (BCMG), were far-sighted initiatives, but in Huddersfield would have required more attention than a hard-pressed team had time to give. Instead, we enrolled friends and benefactors to help fund performances, although a few also funded commissions. Similarly, applications to trusts and foundations were mostly in aid of performances. Thus, when the festival and the London Sinfonietta jointly commissioned Xenakis's *O-Mega* in 1997, Huddersfield contributed only £1,000, the Sinfonietta £4,500. The previous year, I had succumbed

to Stockhausen's proposal that Huddersfield should commission *Bijou* for alto flute, bass clarinet and tape, paying £5,455 (DM12,000) entirely out of revenue. This was unusual, and I soon concluded that it was a mistake, particularly as the piece existed in a previous incarnation in *Donnerstag* from *LICHT.* The agreement, however, was part of a more complex negotiation to secure Stockhausen's return to Huddersfield for a package which would include other UK premieres.

Towards the end of the 1990s the proportion of world premieres increased: twelve in 1996, thirteen in 1997, five in 1998, eighteen in 1999. But few were festival commissions. Some were gifts, others paid for out of foreign cultural budgets. After the East German composer Steffen Schleiermacher arrived with Ensemble Avantgarde, I was embarrassed to find that, for an exquisitely conceived piece he had composed for the occasion, he was expecting a fee. Steffen had proposed the programme, for which he said that he would write a new piece; but there had been no discussion of a commission, nor any mention in our contract with the ensemble. The festival budget was fully assigned, and I stood my ground, uneasily aware that life was still financially difficult for residents of the former East Germany

Risk is a given when commissioning new work. Compositions may be incomplete at the time of going to press, production processes hardly begun, performers from abroad unheard and unassessed. Of the festival's own commissions one could be reasonably confident. But if work was still in production elsewhere there could be many unknowns. Such was the case with Georges Aperghis's *Zwielicht (Twilight)* in 1999, to which we were already committed before I attended its premiere at the Marstall theatre in Munich that July, and found myself sickeningly unconvinced by both the concept and its performance. Despite my regard for Aperghis and the musicians of Recherche, the combination of music, text and stilted action manifestly did not work. With long passages of Goethe, Kafka and Klee spoken in German, many of the Huddersfield audience would be alienated. My pleas for an English version or surtitles were rejected, and it is true that to provide them would have been complicated and costly. There were, indeed, some angry complaints from festival regulars. But to withdraw from the network that had underwritten the production would have been seriously unwise. It had been funded from the Kaleidoscope programme of the EU through a collaboration that, in 1999, was formalised as Réseau Varèse, under whose auspices some of the finest international work seen in Huddersfield has been delivered.

There were other events I would not have contracted had there been opportunity to evaluate them in advance. But many premieres exceeded expectations. The variety of tone-painting, humour and vernacular references in Kagel's complete *Die Stücke der Windrose* could hardly have been guessed from the few sections that were already known. Performed in Huddersfield by musikFabrik, conducted by the composer, twenty-four hours after giving the world premiere in Berlin on 24 November 1995, this *tour de force,* two hours long, deservedly won an ovation. Similarly, Wolfgang Rihm's finally completed[1] *Jagden und Formen,* given a stunningly high-octane performance by Ensemble Modern in November 2000, proved a far more impressive masterpiece than one would have expected from its preliminary components. *Jagden und Formen* won that year's Royal Philharmonic Society award for large-scale composition. This was the first time Ensemble Modern had returned to Huddersfield in fifteen years. In the meantime its fees had escalated enormously; but, by attaching two concerts onto the end of a European tour, the cost was just manageable.

Another revelation was the superb production of Vivier's chamber opera *Kopernikus* in 2000. I had met Thom Sokoloski, the artistic producer. But he could tell me little about its staging until his company, Autumn Leaf Performance, came together in Banff in the summer of 2000. By then the festival brochure had gone to press and I had agreed to a performance without knowing the technical costs. As the production took shape the specification grew alarmingly. Demands became imperious, exchanges more fraught, and there was near mutiny among the festival's technical team. Tim Garbutt, technical manager since 1998, stoically resolved differences, and the performance was exquisitely beautiful. The difficult high vocal lines were sung with breathtaking purity, and the staging had a poise and luminosity that engraved images on the mind. With Pascal Rophé and Stanilas Nordey as the music and stage directors, I should have expected no less. Proud that the

The only UK performance of the Canadian production of Vivier's Kopernikus, *shown at the festival in 2000.*
PHOTO: PAUL HERRMANN

festival had presented the only performance of this near perfect production in Britain, I wished also that more people could have seen it.

That year (2000) witnessed the world premiere of Deirdre Gribbin's *Celestial Pied Piper* – a millennium commission from her publisher, Faber Music. In 2001 two of the finest music theatre productions seen in the Lawrence Batley Theatre – Salvatore Sciarrino's *Lohengrin* and Heiner Goebbels's *Hashirigaki* – received UK premieres. Like the Aperghis, their tours were co-ordinated by Réseau Varèse, but we had been better able to assess them. Four days before a Réseau meeting in Brussels, *Lohengrin* had opened in Berlin, and had now transferred to Brussels where the delegates could see it. The previous autumn, *Hashirigaki* had been premiered at the Théâtre Vidy-Lausanne in Switzerland. The technical requirements were clear, but not the cost. I had thought *Hashirigaki* too expensive, but at a further Réseau meeting it appeared possible, especially when other members agreed to accept our lower contribution.

Both Susanna Eastburn and Graham McKenzie have placed more emphasis on the festival's own commissions: Susanna partly perhaps because, as promotion manager for Chester Music, she had been engaged in securing composers a livelihood; Graham because his view of the festival is that it should be more proactive in the creation of new work. Apart from featuring Per Nørgård in 2002, Susanna Eastburn prioritised UK composers, with world premieres of BBC orchestral commissions from Joe Duddell and Stuart Macrae, and the UK premiere of Birtwistle's *Theseus Game* performed by the London Sinfonietta in 2003.

In 2002, with funds provided by the Arts Council and a festival benefactor, six pieces were commissioned to receive world premieres from Psappha in a concert of Twenty-fifth Birthday Festival Commissions. The composers chosen were Jonathan Powell, James Saunders, Ariene Elizabeth Sierra (the only women, and first American to win the Toru Takemitsu International Composition Prize), Ian Vine, Jennifer Walshe and Joe Cutler – whose *Symborska Settings,* spectacularly sung by Sarah Leonard, Joe had touchingly dedicated to me. That same year Susanna also collaborated with the BBC Philharmonic, enabling five UK postgraduates to have compositions premiered and subsequently broadcast by the orchestra. For the final concert of 2002 she programmed the UK (concert) premiere of the second act of Gerald Barry's opera, *The Bitter Tears of Petra von Kant* (till then performed only in Ireland), whetting appetites for its subsequent production by English National Opera three years later. In total, the 2002 festival contained twenty-four world premieres, including Christian Wolff's *Apartment House Exercise* and James Dillon's *Book of Elements (Volume 5).* Most, however, were by younger UK composers. The following year works by Gavin Bryars, James Clarke, Michael Finnissy, Simon Holt and Helmut Oehring were premiered.

Arriving in 2006 as the festival's first *full-*time artistic director and also its chief executive, Graham McKenzie brought his experience as artistic director of Glasgow's Centre of Contemporary Arts to extend the network of collaborations, engaging a wider range of international co-producers to share projects and commissions. His first festival included world premieres of works by John Casken and the Bolivian composer Agustin Fernández, performed by the Northern Sinfonia: a composition for piano and electronics by

Carlos Sandoval performing Mosaicos *with ensemble mosaik in 2007.*
PHOTO: BRIAN SLATER

James Saunders; pieces by Anna Meredith and Jennifer Walshe as well Michael Finnissy's hour-long *Whitman* song cycle. On stage in the Lawrence Batley Theatre the brilliantly impassioned Trio Fibonacci from Canada performed several of Finnissy's musical 'commentaries' to silent films screened during the concert, and a new 'unofficial soundtrack' commissioned by the festival from Albert-André Lheureux.

The 2007 festival contained twenty-four first performances, five commissioned by the festival and others in association with the BBC, the Netherlands Culture Fund and various Dutch institutions. Three of them each occupied a concert, their creators – Simon Fell, Evan Parker and Tomoku Mukaiyama – indicative of Graham's interest in the border between structure and improvisation, as well as innovative multimedia (see the photo on page 140). Experimental electronics featured in a concert by the Berlin-based ensemble mosaik conducted by Enno Poppe, whose four world premieres included a festival commission from Sam Hayden and a theatrical concept piece composed and performed by Carlos Sandoval, using a pair of gloves with pressure sensors to trigger pre-recorded sounds. A piano recital by Sarah Nicolls with live electronics consisted entirely of first performances, and in Huddersfield Art Gallery an absorbing interactive sound installation by Janek Schaefer was another festival commission (see pages 264–65).

The following year, along with UK premieres, the festival commissioned substantial new works from Richard Barrett, John Butcher, Christopher Fox and Bryn Harrison, and a number of smaller works instigated collaboratively, including five co-commissioned with the BBC. In 2009 and 2010 the collaborative web of co-commissioning and co-production had grown exponentially, with partners including Réseau Varèse, Muziek Centrum Nederland, the Danish Composers' Society, KölnMusik, November Music, Elvermose Concerter, Musikforeningen Cecilia, the Royal Liverpool Philharmonic Orchestra, Neue Ensemble, Transit and Ictus Ensemble, Donaueschingen Festival, MaerzMuzik/Berliner Festspiele, Wundergrund Festival, Besbrode Pianos, Kettles Yard Cambridge, the Henry Moore Foundation, Sound and Music, German Federal Foreign Office, University of Huddersfield, British Council – and, of course, BBC Radio 3.

9 *The festival in the 1990s*

A *decade of growth*

During the 1990s the festival grew more ambitious. The opening of the Lawrence Batley Theatre in 1994 enabled it to branch out into opera, dance, and more varied forms of music theatre. There was a greater engagement in performance art, installations, cross-disciplinary and site-specific events. An outstanding example was *HOUSE,* created for the 1998 festival in two derelict cottages close to the theatre by Louise and Wils Wilson, with four actors, poetry by Simon Armitage and music by Scanner (see pages 191–93). Concerts were often bold in conception and technically complex. There were new opportunities to bid for money. Throughout the decade the festival's evangelising mission was vigorously pursued, and, intrigued by its growing reputation and adventurous programmes, audience numbers steadily increased.

Only in its second decade could the festival afford a basic executive, consisting of an administrator (in effect the general manager), administrative assistant, and one person dealing with both education and fund-raising. All were part-time until 1992, when Andrea Smart was appointed the first full-time administrator.[1] In 1994 Bill Vince became the first member of the team exclusively engaged on education and outreach, although still a half-time appointment. In 1991 the festival won a Sainsbury's Award for Arts Education, in 1992 the Prudential Award for Music, and in 1994 the Arts Council/British Gas Working for Cities Award. Most gratifying was to receive two Royal Philharmonic Society awards in one year (1999) – for 'Concert Series and Festivals' and 'Education' – the only time this has happened in the history of the RPS awards.

Turnover, which in 1990 stood at £159,674, steadily increased, until in 1999 it reached £481,359. Here it peaked until 2009, when – after declining at the start of the new millennium – the award of 'Thrive' from the Arts Council, the achievement of other project grants, and a further input from the Arts Council's anti-recessionary Sustain fund, brought it to around £600,000. The steady improvement throughout the 1990s made possible a threefold increase in the artistic budget, a threefold increase for administration, two-and-a-half times more on marketing and a fivefold increase in the technical budget. The opening of the theatre and frequent complexity of other events inevitably escalated technical expenditure. But it still consumed only 6% of the total. Marketing absorbed 9%, administration 19%, and 60% was spent on artists and composers. (In 2010, the festival's 'investment of c. £345,000 in the creative sector' similarly represented around 60% of turnover.)

During the 1980s I had spent around 70% on artists. Indeed, in 1987 it had been 81%, with administration consuming only 9%, marketing 4% and the technical budget 6%. This extreme disparity – unmatched by any other festival – arose from my determination, given limited funds, to spend the maximum possible on artistic content. Holding down other costs seemed essential to achieve a worthwhile programme. The frugality of those lean years required a hands-on attention to many details of delivery; but with a part-time administrator and a modicum of paid and voluntary assistance these festivals, too, were remarkably successful.

Despite the threefold increase in turnover, core revenue (i.e. public subsidies) rose between 1992 and 1999 by only 20%. The increase in

The Lawrence Batley Theatre.
PHOTO: PAUL HERRMANN

147

turnover came partly from ticket income, which in 1998 topped £50,000, more than four times where it had stood ten years before. More significant were new funds raised from charitable trusts and commerce by the festival's first development directors, Pamela Bone and Stella Murrell. Pam's success was crowned by the five-year sponsorship of the Halifax Building Society as it metamorphosed into a bank. When this came to an end, the Performing Right Society assumed the role of title sponsor, although only for one year (1999). Particularly helpful were two new sources of grant aid. In 1997 the festival won a three-year allocation from the Foundation for Sport and the Arts worth £81,000.[2] The following year, following a second application, the National Lottery awarded a three-year grant worth £140,000, primarily for staged productions in the theatre. In 1999 these were augmented by £42,000 from the Netherlands government to support Dutch components of the programme. But by definition, all such project funds were short term. By 2000 most had run their course and others were running out, leaving a bleak prospect ahead.

An unexpected bonanza

Development directors need specific ideas to sell, and my frequent prevarication must have been frustrating. How late the artistic content could change was exemplified in 1992. The previous December, prime minister John Major surprised the arts community by announcing that, during the second half of 1992, Britain would mount a European Arts Festival to mark its presidency of the European Union. Rumour had it that he had not told the Treasury. Certainly there was little time to get organised. Most of the designated £6 million was to be given to existing organisations across the country, and in January John Drummond retired from the BBC to effect its distribution. Proposals were invited. I submitted one, and on 3 March met him in London. Within a month the festival had been offered £39,487, and ideas too extravagant to contemplate had suddenly grown wings. We had just three months in which to ensure that they could fly.

Meanwhile the prime minister called a snap general election, unexpectedly won, and appointed David Mellor as secretary of the newly named Department of National Heritage,

with responsibility for culture and sport. The amalgamation of arts and sports in one department was a characteristically British fudge. In France the minister of culture has his or her own department and a seat in cabinet. In the Netherlands, as in many other European countries, responsibility for culture is combined with education and science. Among ministers appointed to the UK equivalent, Mellor was undoubtedly one of the best qualified. A known arts devotee, he was equally passionate about classical music and football, and boasted financial acumen honed in his previous post as Chief Secretary to the Treasury. He also had the advantage of genuine friendship with the prime minister. On 13 July Major and Mellor held a reception at 10 Downing Street. I was invited, and found a gathering of leading arts organisers, very different from the popular celebrities later preferred by Tony Blair. To enter through that famous front door and ascend the stairs to a suite of unexpectedly spacious and elegant formal rooms was inspiring. After most of the guests had left, I went over to speak with the prime minister, who was sitting on a *chaise longue* with Mellor at his elbow. The conversation was a transformation from the negative tone of the Thatcher years. The outlook looked rosy. But, alas, euphoria was short-lived. Less than two weeks later an extra-marital affair between Mellor and an actress was exposed in *The People*, followed by further scandals throughout the summer. He held on as long as he could, but on 24 September resigned. Eight days earlier occurred the financial disaster of Black Wednesday, after which Major's authority gradually drained away.

The European Arts Festival took place nonetheless, although the devaluation of sterling made everything European more expensive. In Bradford, Anamaria Wills, general manager of Bradford theatres, mounted an extraordinary feast, among which were performances by Le Thèâtre du Soleil in a specially converted mill, and Nederlands Dans Theater with music by Mozart and Janáček performed live by a piano soloist, full orchestra and the Bradford Festival Choral Society. These dazzling indulgencies reputedly left a deficit of £1 million, and the city's already sceptical councillors resolved never to have anything to do with High Art ever again. Or so it appeared.

A multimedia extravaganza

In Huddersfield I used the additional money to
fund three multimedia events more ambitious
than any we had undertaken – with the
exception of Stockhausen's *Sternklang*.
Xenakis's *L'Histoire d'un Faust* (already
described on pages 93–94) was the most
straightforward, despite our having to suspend
trapeze artists from the town hall's stucco
ceiling. Georges Aperghis's *H, litanie musicale et
égalitaire* was due to open during the summer at
the Théâtre des Amandiers on the outskirts of
Paris. Performed by his own group of actor-
musicians, Atelier Théâtre et Musique (ATEM),
its subject matter, typically of the composer,
consisted of lists of words and objects all
beginning with 'h' – 'by far the best and most
interesting letter' according to Georges, 'on
which to base musical games'. It was also a
letter unpronounced in both France and
Yorkshire: a curiosity upon which the actors
made play during their performances in
Huddersfield. The set for Aperghis's earlier

Enumerations, seen in 1989, had been compact
and simple. Since then, the company had moved
from its first home in the intimate Théâtre de
Villette to the large modern auditorium in
Nanterre. For *H* they had a created an elaborate
mise-en-scène, with a hinged set that, when
open, would be problematic to accommodate.

The most complicated undertaking was Gérard
Grisey's *Le Noir de l'Étoile,* which had already
been performed in Brussels and Strasbourg.
Over coffee with Gérard in Oslo, during Ultima
1991, he had explained his concept of an
enormous indoor space, with the audience
sitting in concentric circles, beneath a large
white canopy of triangular sails suspended from
tall poles. Around and outside them were
positioned the six members of Les Percussions
de Strasbourg, responding to live pulsar signals
beamed from space. There was a computerised
lighting plot, although it had been only half
completed. Intrigued, I had put *Le Noir de
l'Étoile* to the back of my mind. But Major's
largesse made it possible. In Huddersfield we

The set for Le Noir de
l'Étoile *in Huddersfield
Sports Centre.*
PHOTO: SELWYN GREEN

would have to hire the Sports Centre for several days (as we had done for *Sternklang),* cover the floor with sand, erect the tent-like canopy and enlist the collaboration of Jodrell Bank. These were not inconsiderable challenges, and, at the end of the day, neither the production of *H,* nor that of *Le Noir de l'Étoile,* were entirely successful. But as multidimensional experiences they lifted the festival to a new level.

As soon as the funding was confirmed we made preparations. The festival's technical manager, Steve Taylor, visited Paris to establish what had to be brought from the Théâtre des Amandiers, and took stock of the University Great Hall. It was a disagreeable space which I loathed, but, at the time, was the only venue with total blackout into which the set would fit. Steve had created the 'indoor park' for *Sternklang,* and now made contact with Grisey's production team for *Le Noir de l'Étoile.* We learnt that they wished to measure the reverberation time in the Sports Centre's large hall, and an acoustician, Otton Schneider, flew from Strasbourg to assess it. In his bag was a rifle, which customs at Heathrow predictably impounded. But they missed the starting pistol in his pocket, and we arranged to interrupt several dozen table-tennis players, while Otton fired blanks from the periphery and we measured the delay before the report registered on the other side of the hall. The data from this bizarre 'happening' would be fed into a computer programme controlling sound diffusion, which, in some miraculous way that I never understood, would make the pulsar signals and the individual percussionists appear to synchronise wherever any of the audience sat.

On 9 July I visited Jodrell Bank, and was met by the astronomer Ian Morrison. Ian tuned in to pulsar waves from various parts of the sky, and played me their different characteristics, transformed into sound through an instant decoding process. Gérard had confided that, because the French observatory at Nancy could not receive pulsar signals at the time of the performances, in Strasbourg and Brussels the pulses had been surreptitiously replayed on tape. I was determined to do better, and wrote to the head of British Telecom, citing a mutual friend. To my delight, he promised that BT would relay a live signal by satellite from Jodrell Bank during our performance.

One week before the start of the festival we heard terrible news. Steve Taylor had been hit by a car while crossing the North Circular road in London and was unconscious in King's College Hospital. His file was in his flat, his computer at his family's home in Shropshire, some information in the festival office. In three days time, two lorries (or was it three? – we were unclear how many) were due to collect the set, props and equipment for *H* from Paris. We had no list of precisely what, nor did the theatre seem to know. In the event we authorised the third lorry to bring several enormously heavy counterweights which only Steve knew were unnecessary.

For a small organisation in which each person has a unique responsibility, to lose a key member of the team is a major disaster. Shattered by the blow, the festival administrator, Andrea Smart, and I considered what to do. The greatest challenge was how to rig the Sports Centre and prepare the set and installation. Within forty-eight hours we needed to find and appoint a replacement technical manager for this alone. I phoned every contact I could think of, including all the theatres in the region and Opera North. Only one person appeared to be qualified and available: a former lighting director for the opera company. The next day Andrea and I interviewed him, and at the weekend he began work, supported by his partner. That was the easy part. There followed protracted briefings, requests to purchase equipment, hire extra staff, solve problems (real and inflated) and arbitrate between our anxious stand-in manager and a volatile French lighting designer, whom Gérard had chosen to replace the designer who had failed to complete his task. We were constantly fighting fires. Just before the festival opened, Andrea and I held a difficult late night meeting in the Sports Centre. Leaving at 1.30am, drained and immensely tired, she fought back the tears. It was her first festival.

In the Great Hall there were further problems. Steve's memorandum specified a lighting grid weighing no more than 550kg. The efficient young lady I had promoted from his team calculated 3,750kg (approx 3½ tons). What we didn't realise was that Steve had no intention of using the counterweights which accounted for much of the load, and which we had unnecessarily brought from Paris. The polytechnic authorities became understandably concerned. A Kirklees structural engineer was brought in as a consultant and, through him,

Franco Donatoni being interviewed by David Osmond-Smith in 1992.
PHOTO: SELWYN GREEN

Ove Arup and Partners. After their assessment, and two days before the first performance, the polytechnic insisted that we obtain increased indemnity insurance.

Despite these hurdles, all the performances took place, and the public appeared to be unaware of our difficulties. In many respects, all three productions were remarkable, especially *L'Histoire d'un Faust* in Huddersfield Town Hall (see the photo on page 90). In the Sports Centre, the French lighting designer produced disappointing results. Gérard was apologetic, and I knew that, had Steve been present, he would have ensured that the lighting was more evocative. The pulsar signals, too, sounded unexpectedly bland. 'Gutsy little bleeps', wrote Michael White in the *Independent on Sunday,* observing that they had travelled for 7,500 years, but questioning whether it had been 'worth the journey'.[3] Too often they were submerged in an onslaught of percussion which, for such a normally fastidious composer, sounded surprisingly crude. In the Great Hall, ATEM installed their set, taking up most of the floor space. There was little room for the public, but, performed twice, *H* provided for those who saw it some rewarding delights. To our great relief, Steve arrived towards the end of the festival and, although bandaged and subdued, was slowly on the way to recovery.

These complex undertakings were part of a varied festival which included a visit by the eccentric doyen of Italian music, Franco Donatoni. Performed by Alpha Centauri, Ensemble Alternance, the London Sinfonietta

and the Nieuw Ensemble (whose 'Donatoni portrait' included four UK premieres), his music captivated everyone present. It was difficult to credit that this portly, affable humorist could craft such musical jewels.

Opera

In the Lawrence Batley Theatre (LBT) the festival at last had a venue for opera. Not that opera had been wholly absent. Stockhausen's *Michaels Reise* is, after all, merely a revised version of Act II of his opera *Donnerstag.* Restaged for the concert hall, it demonstrated how fluid can be the distinction between opera and music theatre. In 1991 John Casken's powerful first opera *Golem,* commissioned two years earlier by the Almeida Festival, was toured by the Contemporary Music Network. The new production by Northern Stage Company and the Northern Sinfonia worked well enough in St Paul's, except that a third of the audience had an impaired view, and the production had the appearance of camping out in a church. Two years later Music Theatre Wales made a strong debut with its production of Philip Glass's opera *The Fall of the House of Usher,* its compact, free-standing set effectively installed in Huddersfield Town Hall.

The Fall of the House of Usher in Huddersfield Town Hall.
PHOTO: SELWYN GREEN

As early as the autumn of 1986, the general administrator of Opera North, Nicholas Payne, and I met to consider a shared project. Who had taken the initiative I don't recall, but the allure of greasepaint took hold of me as soon as I entered the workaday lift backstage at Leeds Grand Theatre. Nevertheless, I was surprised to find Nicholas so receptive, hardly expecting a large opera company to consort with a relative minnow that had neither a theatre nor resources. Our joint tenth anniversaries were looming, however; and, although based in Leeds, Opera North was funded by all five West Yorkshire metropolitan areas and needed to broaden its remit. Both Nicholas and Paul Daniel, its young music director, wanted to commission new work. Perhaps I failed at first to recognise the strength of their commitment; for, despite our positive meeting, in the Ten Year Planning Book I began that December, with its sections dedicated to different attributes of each festival, there was no page headed 'Opera'.

Prior to a second meeting in January 1987, I prepared a shopping list of nine potential composers plus existing recent works. Four of the composers already had commissions, the products of which we would either have to share or restage. To commission afresh was more attractive; and, after further soundings, we chose Robert Saxton. Initially I imagined we could present a new chamber opera every year, beginning in 1988. That was too soon for Robert, and the idea of an annual production was wholly unrealistic. Three co-promotions did ensue: Robert Saxton's *Caritas* with a libretto by Arnold Wesker in 1991, HK Gruber's *Gloria: a pigtale* in 1994, and Simon Holt's

The Nightingale's to Blame with a libretto by Amanda Holden in 1998.

Huddersfield still awaited its theatre, and I welcomed Payne's suggestion of giving the premiere of *Caritas* in Wakefield's Theatre Royal and Opera House, instead of, as we had originally assumed, in St Paul's. This small Frank Matcham theatre, if a little dowdy, suited the opera's chamber dimensions. Coaches transported the festival audience, and Collins Classics recorded the work for a CD. The performances attracted plenty of attention and generally approving reviews, although some questioned the effectiveness of the stage set (designed for touring) and whether the story itself, and Robert's finely crafted music, sufficiently struck gold.

It had been a satisfying collaboration; and, with the Lawrence Batley Theatre due to open in 1994, we met to consider a second project. The list of potential composers had grown, and of some we made enquiries. I wrote to sound out Brian Ferneyhough and Peter Sculthorpe (could we have chosen composers less alike?), but neither had a subject ready, nor time to write an opera. The choice fell on the Austrian, HK (Nali) Gruber, whose famously successful *Frankenstein!!* – a 'pan-demonium for chansonnier and ensemble' – was a persuasive calling card. He already had a scenario and, more crucially, a potential German co-producer.

Nali's one-act libretto was being adapted from a German children's literary classic, *Gloria von Jaxtberg,* by its author Rudolf Herfurtner. His co-producer was Big Bang Theatre in Munich,

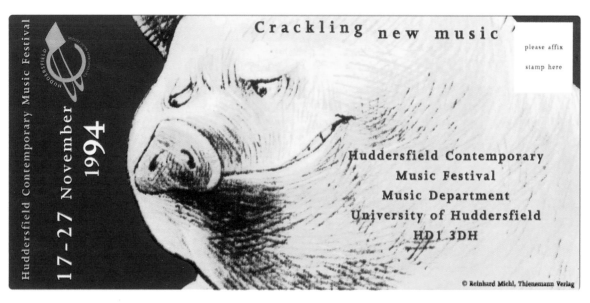

Returnable card listing 1994 highlights and offering respondents the full festival brochure.

a small company – in effect one man, Helmut Danninger, who had instigated the whole idea. We invited Helmut to Leeds and agreed that he should direct with his usual stage designer Marc Deggeller, and that the opera would be premiered in Munich by Opera North prior to four performances in Huddersfield. Amanda Holden was engaged to make an English translation, renamed (the first of many puns) *Gloria: a pigtale*. All went well until 1993, when Helmut relayed the news that his company had lost its funding.

Although a joint commission and a co-promotion, *Caritas* had been materially resourced by Opera North. Nicholas had accepted a maximum contribution of £27,500 from the festival, leaving us spared further financial anxiety. For *Gloria* I had promised £35,000, but this time responsibility for the budget was shared, and it was already a headache. At a gloomy meeting after Helmut's announcement, the project came within a whisker of cancellation. Reluctant to accept defeat, we agreed to meet again. Although the work could no longer be staged in Munich, Helmut was willing for the UK performances to take place, and a corner was turned when the Contemporary Music Network, then managed by Judith Ackrill, agreed to tour the opera and contribute to the production. The Orcofi Foundation helped fund its commission; but

there was still a shortfall. This was plugged when the Halifax Building Society, approached by Opera North, agreed to support the production.

It was a timely association, for the Halifax was about to demutualise. In 1986 the Conservative government loosened regulation of the financial markets, enabling larger building societies to become banks. The Abbey National led the way, and between 1995 and 1999 eight others followed. Of these, the Halifax was the biggest, and, conscious of its impending elevation, wanted to affirm its local roots through more visible sponsorship. That its head office was neither in London nor Leeds but in a neighbouring mill town was a rare advantage. Unlike potential sponsors in Leeds, it was keen to engage with the whole of West Yorkshire. Its executives and their wives evidently enjoyed their visit to the Lawrence Batley Theatre, and, in 1995, the Halifax became title sponsor of the festival, remaining until 1998 and contributing up to £30,000 annually.

Most of the audience appeared to enjoy *Gloria* too, although its Bavarian humour was at times heavy-handed. To my ears, the orchestral balance was skewed by Gruber's inclusion of a tuba, whose 'oomphs' emerged from the pit with uncomfortable regularity. But the quality of the cast, stylish staging and lighting brought

House, Covent Garden, and was succeeded in Leeds by Ian Ritchie. Whilst shoring up the funds for *Gloria,* Ian, Paul Daniel and I began to discuss a third collaboration; and, with their approval, in January 1994 I met Simon Holt to sound out his interest. The festival had performed several of Simon's works, including the world premiere of *Lilith* in 1990 and a substantial portrait concert in 1991. Although fundamentally eclectic, with its dramatic, gestural manner and imaginative coloration, his music was strikingly distinctive, shaped by an affinity with Spanish culture and classical mythology. Its passionate intensity and dark shadows, invoked not only in his settings of Lorca, suggested a composer ready to write an opera. Simon was keen, and soon chose for a scenario Lorca's play, *The Love of Don Perlimplin for Belissa in the Garden.* We agreed a target date for the premiere of November 1997.

to the theatre and festival both glamour and pizzazz. The critics were divided. Holden's entertaining text 'throws in every sausage joke you can imagine, and a few you'd rather not,' wrote Michael White in the *Independent on Sunday*, admitting that 'perhaps it's just my puerile sense of humour, but I found the pathos, pantomime exuberance and sheer silliness of *Gloria* enchanting'.[4] A 'surfeit of piggery jokery' countered *The Times* headline disapprovingly.[5] It was one of those occasions which, having been close to the project from the start, I watched nervously, concluding that the opera's breathless pace (Nali had composed in a hurry) left one feeling short-changed. Paul Driver, writing in *The Sunday Times,* also thought that it 'somehow leaves one asking for more: more developments, more meaning'. On the other hand,

…this is a real opera, not one of those all too familiar, drily half-sung, half-declaimed plays with music. There is a splendid quartet in which an expressive arching line for Gloria (hitting a top C) is accompanied by a trio of male-voice croaking frogs; a droll 'doobee doo' duet for oxen; and a good deal besides of genuine *musical* fun. Writing so adroitly for his nine-piece folkish-cabaret band that it often sounds like a medium-sized orchestra, Gruber is forever teasing the ear, passing a note from pizzicato violin to harp so that you can only just tell the difference, suddenly reducing the texture to a single high note or surprising silence.[6]

In 1993 Nicholas Payne left Opera North to become opera director at the Royal Opera

As usual, assembling sufficient funds proved difficult. To find even the commission fee was a challenge. Simon intended to spend two years composing the piece, which the fee needed to reflect. Meanwhile, Opera North was addressing an accumulated deficit. To justify the financial outlay and give the work wider exposure, the company decided to present the opera as part of its main season, with performances in the spring following the Huddersfield premiere.

After the cumbersome collaboration required for *Gloria,* neither Ian nor Paul were keen to involve another European co-producer. But within months, an approach came from an unexpected quarter. In the spring of 1988, with the support of its mayor and cultural officer, Hans Werner Henze had initiated a biennale in Munich, committed to staging world premieres of music theatre and opera, mostly by composers making their debuts in the medium. The first biennale had launched Mark-Anthony Turnage's hugely successful *Greek.* The fourth in 1994 had included *Playing Away* by Benedict Mason, a co-production between Opera North and Munich, conducted by Paul Daniel. Now Henze planned to extend the biennale to include an autumn season, and wanted to buy into Simon's opera with which to open it.

The 1994 festival happened to include two of Henze's orchestral works, and I had invited him to give a talk about them. Over lunch in

Huddersfield he explained his plans for Munich, saying, however, that he wanted the biennale to have the premiere, and that it would pay for the commission. I thought Hans was being over-acquisitive, and expressed reservations. But we parted on good terms and negotiations began. They proved endlessly complex. We agreed to co-commission, but the biennale insisted that the world premiere was a condition of the collaboration, and in December 1995 I conceded it, aware that, in any case, the Munich dates preceded Huddersfield, and that without a co-producer we could not stage the opera. Budget meetings ensued, and tedious exchanges concerning clauses in the contract.

The following spring Tilmann Broszat, our contact at the biennale, warned me that the city of Munich was facing a 'severe financial situation'. He could make no firm commitment until the city announced its budget. On 20 July the city council held its meeting and Henze's request for further funds was rejected. The autumn programme would not take place and the biennale could no longer be a partner, although it would honour its contribution to the commission. This was a serious setback. Richard Mantle had now succeeded Ian Ritchie as general director of Opera North, but was no less committed to the project. Simon was already composing the prologue and his vision of the piece was exciting, although he would welcome extra time. We agreed to postpone the production until 1998, and rigorously pruned the budget. I promised a contribution of £50,000 – but we had first to find the money.

At this stage the National Lottery, launched by John Major in 1994, became a potential saviour. In the spring of 1997 the festival made an application and was turned down. In November we made another and were awarded £140,000 spread over three years. Its purpose was to support different planks of the programme, but principally help to finance three operas: in 1998 *The Nightingale's to Blame*, as Simon's opera was now called; in 1999 a new production of Judith Weir's *A Night at the Chinese Opera*; in 2000 the world premiere of *God's Liar* by John Casken.[7]

Early in 1998, before the announcement of the lottery awards, Simon phoned with a *crie de coeur*. He had been working on the opera day after day for two years, accepting no other commissions. Unlike many composers, he did not supplement his meagre royalties with regular teaching. He needed the remainder of his fee, and I took steps to get it released. In the autumn, planning gave way to pleasure when rehearsals began and I first heard the music. I thought it consistently fine: sinewy and intense, but also lyrical and sensuous, funny, touching, strongly characterised and imaginatively scored so that every pitch and timbre made an effect. The colourful production, directed by Martin Duncan and designed by Neil Irish, suited LBT – although it looked even better in Leeds the following April, where the music, now conducted by Richard Farnes, seemed to breathe more spaciously. In Huddersfield the reviews were mixed, although all praised the quality of the cast and their delivery of the demanding vocal lines. Criticism mostly centred on a perceived lack of action. But there are many operas in which little actually 'happens'. What does unfold is the musical discourse. Simon's agile, intricate and precisely conceived score was full of riches not, perhaps, instantly perceived. But in an expansive and glowing review in *The Observer*, written with knowledge of his other music, Fiona Maddocks hailed it as an 'outstanding new opera'.[8] The third performance of *The Nightingale's to Blame* was broadcast on Radio 3 – a rare live broadcast from the festival and the only occasion from the main auditorium of the Lawrence Batley Theatre.

Despite the vicissitudes, working with the personnel of Opera North had been rewarding, and I never wavered in my immense regard for the company. Whilst we were jointly coping with the birth-pangs of *Gloria* and *The Nightingale's to Blame*, the festival presented single performances of three fine productions toured nationally by Music Theatre Wales. Two were classics of music theatre about whose quality there could be little doubt: *The Lighthouse* by Maxwell Davies and *Punch and Judy* by Birtwistle. To assemble and present each in a single day was happily unproblematic, and the reputations of both MTW and the pieces ensured full houses.

The plans to revive Judith Weir's *Night at the Chinese Opera* and give the UK premiere of John Casken's *God's Liar* both came to grief. My motivation to stage the Weir arose partly from failing to see it during its hugely successful initial production by Kent Opera. More objectively, I admired its refreshingly quirky

character and humour, although the size of the cast and orchestra were potential problems. City of Birmingham Touring Opera (CBTO) had expressed an interest in collaborating, but in 1998 failed in its bid for support from the Arts Council's New Audiences Fund to underwrite a UK tour.[9] I approached Opera Factory, Scottish Opera and Opera North without success, and there remained an open question of whether even a reduced string section would fit in the pit.

John Casken's second opera had been commissioned by Northern Sinfonia as a culmination of the composer's long relationship with the orchestra, brokered by its chief executive, John Summers. As musical ideas and a scenario began to emerge, a collaboration between the Northern Sinfonia, Huddersfield Contemporary Music Festival, and the Théatre Royal de la Monnaie in Brussels took shape. Four performances in Brussels would be followed by two in Huddersfield, one in Newcastle and others elsewhere in Britain. During 1998 John Casken used a sabbatical to concentrate on its composition. The following year, John Summers was appointed chief executive of the Hallé Orchestra, and was succeeded in Newcastle by Andrew Bennett, previously administrator of CBTO. Throughout the first half of 2000 Andrew fleshed out both the schedule and budget. We knew that he was seeking other partners to make it balance, but he sounded optimistic. The opera had been cast, and the director, Keith Warner, was developing ideas for its staging. Everything appeared to be moving forward. On 1 May John completed the score, and on 5 May went to Brussels with the director and designer to give a presentation, and to play parts of the opera to the directorate of the theatre. There was no warning of the bombshell that arrived from Newcastle by fax on 16 June, signed by Andrew and preceded by a phone call just in time for a festival board meeting the previous day:

In the past few days efforts to maintain the viability of the *God's Liar* opera project in autumn 2000 have come to a head. Despite much constructive discussion between partners in the production, Northern Sinfonia has reluctantly decided that it is not possible to continue with the project... Several elements of the budget had been rising, reflecting mainly the desire of the creative team to do justice to the quality of the opera on a stage as prestigious as La Monnaie. There would have been a colossal deficit on the project had it gone ahead... the Society is not able to expose itself to risk on such a large and potentially worsening scale.

The statement acknowledged that, besides the financial commitment of the three co-producers, funding had been secured from the Arts Council of England's National Touring Fund and the Northern Arts Regional Lottery Programme. The Northern Sinfonia was responsible for the overall budget, and on 11 June, as we learnt, Andrew had produced a 'restructured budget' showing a deficit of £119,616. But the decision was not only precipitous, not only at the eleventh hour when La Monnaie had already announced the opera premiere and cast in its next season's brochure. It had been taken unilaterally without consultation. The lack of discussion and lateness of the announcement gave no time to consider other strategies, or, for instance, for Bernard Foccroulle, director of La Monnaie, to attempt a rescue. This is not the place to apportion blame; merely to illustrate the difficult process of originating work, the hazards of collaboration, and to draw the moral that an orchestra may not be best placed to manage an opera production.

Despite the loss of *God's Liar* so late in our planning, the 2000 festival programme had no holes. Nor did it lack staged opera. We replaced *God's Liar* with a production of Vivier's *Kopernikus* created in Banff during the summer, about which I had only recently received information. There would be Michael Berkeley's *Jane Eyre* performed by Music Theatre Wales; Turnage's *Greek* in a new production by London Sinfonietta Opera, and *Bitter Fruit* by John Woolrich, a work with no text, but combining the physicality of Trestle Theatre (using masks, mime and puppets) and a score

Frederic Rzewski contributing to the Minimalist Marathon in 1993.
PHOTO: SELWYN GREEN

played by Birmingham Contemporary Music Group. All these were single performances of touring productions. *Kopernikus,* staged by Autumn Leaf Performance, Toronto, cost £25,000 less than we had committed to *God's Liar.* Ticket income held up (a concert of microtonal Sufi music from Arabia took £8,250) and I was able to bequeath a surplus on the year of nearly £60,000 to my successor, Susanna Eastburn – useful in view of the reduced project funds anticipated in the new millennium.

God's Liar was rescued by Almeida Opera and performed in London and Brussels in 2001. We hoped that the UK tour, which the Arts Council had agreed to fund in 2000, would be deferred, and that we would stage it during the 2001 festival. But the Almeida's application was rejected in favour of two other productions. One of them was a revival of MTW's *The Lighthouse.* Excellent though it was, it had already been seen at the festival in 1994.

A feast of styles and genres

It might appear that we were preoccupied with opera. In fact, the festivals of the 1990s explored a plurality of genres and ranged widely across styles. Woven into the 1993 programme were different strands of minimalism: both the archetypal minimalism of Riley, Reich and Glass, and the diverse treatments of Andriessen, Górecki, Lang, Pärt, Torke, Volans, Wolfe, assorted Scandinavians and other composers. There were concerts by the Kronos Quartet, Piano Circus and Bang on a Can All-Stars, plus a 'Minimalist Marathon' based on Bang on a Can's model in New York. This was far from the wall-to-wall modernism with which Huddersfield was often associated – so far, indeed, that Keith Potter spoke for several critics when he questioned why Górecki 'was being presented in the festival at all', and urged Huddersfield to return to the challenging work that was 'its original, and surely true, purpose'.[10] Against this backdrop, the eighteen works by Ligeti, performed during (mainly) the second half of the 1993 festival, combined supreme musicality and a questing intelligence before which one could only be in awe. This festival also introduced the thought-provoking work of Galina Ustvolskaya, represented by three UK premieres (see page 127).

After the theatre opened in the autumn of 1994, people naturally wanted to see the building and attend performances. It was an ideal opportunity to attract new predominantly local audiences – and not only to opera. There were 'animated theatre', films, concerts, workshops, discussions, music theatre, and dance which, after years without an appropriate venue, I was impatient to present. For the first time we had a suitable acoustic for amplified groups, jazz ensembles and big bands. The theatre's opening coincided with the launch of the National Lottery, and I collaborated with LBT's director, Ron McAllister, to submit a joint bid. The money received underpinned both the festival programme and that of the theatre throughout the year, jointly marketed so that audiences for one would be tempted by the other. In 1995, for example, we offered a 'Double Opera Deal' for Crystal Clear Opera's *The Tragedy of Carmen* in September, and the festival's community production of Judith Weir's *The Black Spider* in November.

Inaugurating the festival's presence in the theatre were the four performances of Gruber's opera, *Gloria – a pigtale.* It made sense if we could actively involve composers in performances, and Gruber excelled them all. He joined the University Twentieth-Century Ensemble for the opening concert, giving a vivid portrayal of the deranged George III in Maxwell

Davies's *Eight Songs for a Mad King,* then appearing as chansonnier in his own *Frankenstein!!* The next day he introduced the opera in a pre-performance talk, and attended its premiere. The following morning he flew to Austria to play principal bass in four concerts with the Vienna Tonkünstler Orchestra (his 'day job'), returning to Huddersfield at the end of the week to conduct Klangforum Wien.

In between, festivalgoers could choose a concert for player piano (pianola), a study morning on Cardew's *Great Learning,* a Nexus workshop on African drumming, the Vienna Art Orchestra's jazz-theatre homage to Jean Cocteau (*Beauty and the Beast*), Laurie Booth's Dance Company with live music from the Gavin Bryars Ensemble, and the production of Davies's *The Lighthouse* by Music Theatre Wales. They could watch music by four SPNM composers being choreographed by the Siobhan Dance Company, hear local artist David Blackburn introduce his one-man exhibition, and take a guided tour of the Henry Moore sculptures in the Yorkshire Sculpture Park. In St Paul's they could hear ensembles from Austria, Canada, Denmark, Switzerland and the UK.

A highpoint was a rare semi-staged performance of Stockhausen's autobiographical

Laurie Booth and his dancers in Wonderlawn *in 1994.*
PHOTO: SELWYN GREEN

Stockhausen's
Momente *performed*
in St Paul's in 1994.
PHOTO: SELWYN GREEN

all except its last few minutes. That same evening, coinciding with the Stockhausen, Lord and Lady Harewood and various festival sponsors were due to attend the second performance of Gruber's opera. I had witnessed the rehearsals and premiere of *Gloria*, but it was my duty to join the festival's guests. I have yet to hear a complete performance of *Momente*.

The next year's concentration on more esoteric concert music was a calculated antidote. But, if the focus of the 1995 festival was more rigorous than in other years, the polyglot umbrella remained. Whilst Nono's searing late compositions dominated the final five days, the first weekend paired James Dillon and Terry Riley. And whereas James's music was densely notated, the high-point of Terry Riley's visit was his mesmerising late-night improvisation. The festival began in the theatre with *The Black Spider* performed by young musicians and students. Two days later the Leeds-based Phoenix Dance appeared with jazz percussionist Orphy Robinson; and two days after that George Russell and his Living Time Orchestra. A uniquely magical centrepiece was the world premiere of Stephen Mottram's animated theatre, *The Nature of Things,* with hand-carved wooden puppets and an electroacoustic score commissioned by the festival from Glyn Perrin. It had to be scheduled late one evening in St Paul's, but was so remarkable that I revived it in 1997, now renamed *The Seed Carriers*, for four performances in more intimate surroundings.

and innovatory masterpiece, *Momente*. It was given by Angela Tunstall (soprano), costumed choruses from Birmingham university and conservatoire, instrumentalists from Birmingham Contemporary Music Group and BEAST sound diffusion, the whole directed by Vic Hoyland and conducted by Jonty Harrison. The production had premiered in London, and had been seen in Birmingham before arriving in Huddersfield, but this only accelerated interest and St Paul's was soon sold out. Atmospherically lit, resonating to the tones of two Hammond organs, specially made 'kidney' drums and a huge gong resplendent in the chancel, the setting enhanced the sense of ritual. Bringing the work to the festival fulfilled a personal ambition – one we had not been able to realise in 1988 when Stockhausen himself was in Huddersfield. But, agonisingly, I missed

RIGHT:
Terry Riley.
PHOTO: SELWYN GREEN

Ensemble concerts included the Moscow Art Trio and the UK premiere of Kagel's sleazy 'travelogue', *The Compass Rose,* given by musikFabrik after playing the world premiere in Berlin twenty-four hours earlier. Late one evening, two groups of festivalgoers took a *Sonic Walk* through the streets and arcades of Huddersfield, encountering performances and installations along the route (see page 195). On another evening they gathered in Byram Arcade to be entertained by Sophie Hannah and Huddersfield's Albert Poets, alternating with the virtuoso Canadian accordionist Joseph Petric, whilst hot baked potatoes were served to ward off the November chill.

'Forget Paris, try Huddersfield!'

National attention had unexpectedly focused on Huddersfield in the summer of 1994, when the new Conservative heritage secretary, Stephen Dorrell, in his first keynote speech, urged culture-seekers to take weekend breaks in Britain rather than Paris. When asked where, he replied that 'the modern music festival in Huddersfield has a lot to recommend it. You get better modern music in Huddersfield than in Paris,' adding that 'The festival is widely recognised in the world as being one of the leading festivals for that type of creative art to be found anywhere.' This astonishing comparison was a gift to headline writers. Huddersfield's tourist officers were delighted and the festival's standing soared. Less evident was the minister's underlying theme that heritage should be mainly self-supporting and that money generated from tourism was better for the health of the arts than funding from the taxpayer.

Dorrell had been told about the festival by Sir Ernest Hall during a function at which both were present. A talented pianist, cultural philanthropist, chancellor of the university and millionaire, Sir Ernest had earned world-wide admiration for his regeneration of the huge Dean Clough mill complex in Halifax, as a home for small and medium enterprises and the visual and performing arts. He rarely attended the festival but was unstinting in his praise. Although briefed by his civil servants, Dorrell had never set foot in the town. Kirklees Council promptly issued an invitation, and on 21 November the minister arrived to visit Huddersfield's Media Centre (then under construction), the newly opened theatre, and to attend a lunch-hour concert in St Paul's. It happened to be a recital by the twenty-four-year old Japanese violinist, Mieko Kanno, and consisted of unremittingly tough (mainly solo) pieces which would hardly have been my first choice for the secretary of state. Wondering how he would react, I collected him from the theatre and we walked to St Paul's. Our two reserved seats appeared to be the only ones still unoccupied. The hall was abuzz, not only in the tiered section but with parties of sixth-formers and FE students crammed along the full length of both aisles. It was clearly a very young audience. Far from being stooges bussed in to impress the minister, their teachers had chosen this from the festival's various access offers, because it included an open rehearsal in which Jonathan Harvey would explain the interface between live ensemble and electronics in *Bhakti,* a lecture by Sir Peter Maxwell Davies, and group admission to a performance of *The Lighthouse* in LBT that evening.

I had not heard Mieko play, but it was the first of many engagements. This one was co-promoted with the Park Lane Group, whose director John Woolf I had known from when he administered the SPNM, and whose recommendation was more than vindicated. Playing from memory, standing alone on a bare stage, Mieko was mesmerising: thrillingly in command of the complex virtuosity required by Dillon and Boulez, and in the long, dense and intense *Maps and Diagrams of our Pain* by Gordon McPherson – the only duo in the programme, in which she was partnered at the piano by Thomas Amstrong. It confirmed yet again that it is better to be fearless than to pull one's punches. The audience gave her thunderous applause and the minister, who had probably never heard anything like it before, seemed to be impressed.

The Creative Town

Among the council and its officers there had been a marked change of attitude. Like other towns which had prospered from textiles, by the 1980s Huddersfield was in economic decline. The metropolitan borough of Kirklees, formed in 1974 out of eleven smaller towns and districts, was too insular and divided to have a clear sense of purpose. But with the election of the shrewd and enlightened John Harman as leader of the Labour council in 1986,[11] and the appointment of Robert Hughes as chief executive, a new vision emerged, welcoming external partnerships. A consortium led by the council spearheaded the construction of the McAlpine Stadium (now the Galpharm Stadium) which opened in 1995, and the first phase of the Media Centre was also completed that year. Arts groups were quick to take up the invitation to collaborate, and collectively, as Cultural Industries in Kirklees (CIK), joined the council in a task force. Meanwhile, the borough had positioned itself to take advantage of the government's challenge funding schemes, and garnered millions of pounds for economic, environmental and community regeneration, whilst other boroughs languished.

Kirklees had been working with Charles Landry and Franco Bianchini, authors of *The Creative City*,[12] to reformulate cultural policy, which in 1995 was designated the 'Creative Town Initiative'. It coincided with an economic revitalisation competition launched by the European Union, offering £3 million to cities with the best and most innovative redevelopment proposals. Although only a town, Huddersfield was one of 500 to compete and one of only twenty-five throughout Europe to win.

The festival's role in creative regeneration, and the theatre project which it had helped to energise, had undoubtedly contributed – not least because it annually attracted a level of media coverage of which other towns and cities could only dream. 'Brave new Huddersfield' proclaimed an *Independent on Sunday* headline

Interviewing John Tavener in 1996.

in 1991. 'Who needs Vienna when you've got Huddersfield?' *The Observer* headed Fiona Maddocks's review in 1997. 'Huddersfield, centre of the musical universe' the *Independent on Sunday* splashed across five columns in 1998. Dorrell's speech had already prompted headlines ranging from 'Musicville W. Yorks' above a full-page review in *The Daily Telegraph* (which included six photographs), and 'Hurrah for Huddersfield' in *The Observer,* to the *Yorkshire Post's* excruciating pun: 'Say Non to Paris...get an Eiffel of Huddersfield.'

On 27 November, 1994 *The Sunday Times* ran two substantial articles: Paul Driver's regular review, warmly approving the new theatre; and an affectionate, often amusing, portrait of the town by A.A. Gill labelled 'Huddersfield honeymoon', with a sub-heading: 'Forget Paris. Stephen Dorrell was right about the romantic ambience of a Yorkshire town'. Having had his breath taken away by 'the sensationally beautiful doeskin-coloured edifice' of the station – 'quite the most remarkable in a town without a cathedral I've ever seen', Gill admits that 'Huddersfield isn't exactly beautiful. It's honest and attractive in a matronly sort of way [with its] chunky municipal Victorian buildings that seem to have their thumbs in their waistcoat pockets... It's all very dignified.' But then comes the heart-warming insight: 'It's the people that are Huddersfield's gold.'

But November can be an inhospitable month. In 1996, lured by the presence of Stockhausen, for the only time the *Daily Express* printed a review. Stephen Pettitt's approval of the festival was unstinting, but his description of the town could have been written by Dickens:

Huddersfield in November is a forbidding place. Dark, satanic and disused mills brood among the eddying mists on the undulating horizon. The wind sweeps through the streets with a ruthless chill, the shoppers grimly bracing themselves against its power. Everything is a dismal shade of grey or brown, including the air. Up at the railway station even the wheezing, smoke-belching diesel trains seem reluctant to approach the platform, where the old-style buffet serves bacon butties at bargain prices. The visitor, limbs already aching with the damp, checks into the Victorian hotel in the station courtyard. The service is well-meaning but quaintly erratic, the room as often as not dingy. Time might have stood still for a couple of decades...[13]

A week later, Denis Kilcommons devoted his diary column in the *Huddersfield Daily Examiner* to a firm rebuke.[14]

1996–2000

More interesting than the return of Stockhausen was the world premiere in 1996 of Tan Dun's *Orchestral Theatre III: Red Forecast,* which treats weather forecasts as a metaphor for history. The performance was given by the BBC Scottish Symphony Orchestra in a darkened town hall, with Tan and the soprano Susan Botti theatrically spotlit, and dominated by an enormous screen showing Mike Newman's video collage of 1960s newsreels, and scenes of China during the Cultural Revolution. A joint commission between the festival, Radio 3 and BBC television (which co-funded the video), it made a powerful impact. Costs were shared with the BBC and the Barbican in London, where the performance was repeated the next day. In Huddersfield I chose to precede *Red Forecast*, in a programme called 'Requiem and Revolution', with John Tavener's *Akhmatova: Requiem* – one of his finest compositions. Setting the chilling poetry of Anna Akhmatova, it was sung with great beauty and dignity by Patricia Rozario and Stephen Richardson.

This was the first of two Huddersfield visits by Tan Dun, whose reputation at the time was in the ascendant. It was high even in Germany, where his guitar concerto had just been performed at Donaueschingen, and an opera magazine had named Tan composer of the year, after the world premiere of his opera, *Marco Polo,* at the Munich Biennale.[15] As Tan was also associate composer-conductor of the BBCSSO, the success of *Red Forecast* prompted a further collaboration with the orchestra and the Barbican to present *Marco Polo* in a concert performance in 1998. The BBC and Tan chose soloists, the Royal Scottish Academy of Music and Drama provided a chamber chorus, and the UK premiere took place in Huddersfield on 22 November.

The opera owes its post modern character to the East-West axis at the fulcrum of which Tan, and before him Marco Polo, had found themselves. With a libretto by Paul Griffiths, it combines extended vocal and instrumental techniques, elements of Peking Opera (including Chinese instruments integrated into a Western orchestra)

With Tan Dun at the 1996 festival.
PHOTO: STEVE FORD

and a melodically rich operatic lyricism evolved from twentieth-century archetypes. It is a polystylism very different from Schnittke's, and embodies the heady ambiguities of a China opening up to the West following the Cultural Revolution. The *Orchestral Theatre* series and *Marco Polo* belong, in my view, to the most convincing years of Tan Dun's compositional career. In Huddersfield both works were received enthusiastically, even by those who had regarded his music with scepticism. The festivals from 1998 to 2000 were in many ways the most successful of my years as artistic director, and contained some of the performances I recall with most pleasure. Their expanded A5 brochures provided a daily double-page spread, which encouraged us to identify a predominant theme for each day, conveyed by a striking full-page photo, and with clearer, more enticing signposts for the public. Energetic marketing attracted numerous newcomers, and the festival achieved some of its largest audiences.

For the twenty-first festival 11,766 tickets were sold, which, with the addition of those attending free events, amounted to a total audience of around 15,000. Not remarkable for a mainstream festival perhaps, but gratifying for one devoted entirely to new music. There were four town hall concerts. The first, given by

Wajahat Khan and his Indian Chamber
Orchestra, was heard by 600, amongst whom a
third were Asian. For *Marco Polo* the audience
numbered 492; for the Estonian Philharmonic
Chamber Choir, Hilliard Ensemble and Tallinn
Chamber Orchestra 981; and at a concert of
Steve Reich's music overseen by the composer
1063. This concert included *Hindenburg,* with
split-screen video footage created by Reich's
wife Beryl Korot, that in shortened form would
become the first part of their video-opera *Three
Tales.* The last two concerts actually sold out,
the discrepancy between the number of tickets
sold being due to different amounts of extra
staging. More significantly, the £23,225 grossed
by these four concerts approached half that
year's total ticket income of £54,458 – the
highest the festival has achieved.

Financial dynamics were always a concern, and
attracting new audiences a constant motivation.
I had no misgivings about presenting four such
accessible concerts in the town hall. Critics
might take issue with Górecki, Pärt and Tan
Dun. No way could I regret introducing any
of this music to those who had never heard it.
Or providing the collective intensity of live
performance to those who had. A survey
conducted at the Reich concert revealed that
most of the audience had never been to a festival
event before, and knew very little about it.
It was an ideal induction.

There was plenty else in 1998 to interest the
cognoscenti. Ensemble concerts explored the
little-known music of Karel Goeyvaerts,
Luis de Pablo, and Stefan Wolpe. Others were
devoted to George Crumb, who had been

featured at the first festival and whom I had
now invited back. The Ardittis with Ursula
Oppens gave a ninetieth-birthday tribute to
Elliott Carter (also present). There was Faulty
Optic's Theatre of Animation, and Newband
playing Harry Partch's legendary sculpted
instruments in the Lawrence Batley Theatre
(see page 65). The festival began with four
performances of Holt's opera *The Nightingale's
to Blame*, and continued with the world
premiere of his *eco-pavan* and other Holt
performances. The Steve Martland Band gave a
characteristically high-octane concert in LBT,
their intoxicating bravura and virtuosity,
although not quite their precision, echoed by
Volharding some days later. Both concerts
attracted a high proportion of students.

Hindenburg had been a challenge to deliver, to
which Maria Bota, the festival manager, and the
technical director, Tim Garbutt, devoted
determined energy. The extended version had
not been performed when the festival's final
commitments had to be made, and its technical
requirements were known only in outline.
The artists' contracts were comparatively easy.
Obtaining a complete technical specification,
scouting for equipment, duplicating it for
London rehearsals, finding Steve and Beryl a
synagogue, hiring two linked high-powered
projectors able to match to a millimetre
simultaneous projections of the same video
(to double its brightness on screen) and
synchronise both with the music, were not
inconsiderable tasks. All came successfully
together, and the performance made an
immensely powerful impact.

Music by Chinese composers at the Almeida
Festival, and later meeting Tan Dun, had
increased my interest in that country's music
and culture. Coincidentally, in April 1999,
I received an invitation from the Visiting Arts

Unit to join a small group of theatre and festival directors on a tour of China, as guests of its Ministry of Culture. Our three weeks there were more fascinating than I could have imagined and, of international visits I made whilst artistic director, this was the one I felt most privileged and fortunate to enjoy. Some tedious hours in dance academies were offset by rewarding visits to the Central Conservatory of Music in Beijing, and an academy of traditional Chinese music in Guangzhou. Here a traditional instrument orchestra played especially for us. At the rear were a monumental set of tuned bells which, after the performance, Tim Joss and I were invited to strike with heavy wooden poles.

Over tea in a Shanghai park, Jude Kelly arranged a meeting of journalists, writers and poets, whilst in Guangzhou, some of us visited a school of puppetry engaged in the ten-year training of master puppeteers for China's sixty-two publicly funded puppet companies. There was a routine evening of Beijing Opera, a more genuine version I saw in Guangzhou, and an organised visit to a tired acrobatic show laid on for tourists. Departing through the adjoining shop, we all purchased battery-powered toy pandas (Ruth Mackenzie bought four) which the assembled theatre and festival directors set rocking from side to side and flashing their eyes on the foyer steps of our five-star hotel – incongruously towering over Beijing's ancient hutongs[16] – accompanied by much hilarity. Besuited and on our best behaviour, we made our way to a day of starchy formal meetings at the Ministry of Culture, culminating in an audience with the minister, whose exaggerated smile failed to disguise his rigid control of cultural policy and anachronistic perceptions of the UK.

The minister's underlying agenda was to secure a large-scale tour of Beijing opera. But none of us were able to receive it. My own visit resulted

With Brian Eno at the 1999 festival. Luke O'Shaughnessy and his future wife behind.
PHOTO: PAUL HERRMANN

in performances at the 1999 festival by some wonderfully accomplished traditional instrument players from the Central Conservatory in Beijing, and in the Lawrence Batley Theatre by the Guangdong Modern Dance Company from Guangzhou. The Guangdong's premises were shabby, but their technical prowess and choreography, influenced by Martha Graham, of a high standard. The minister had cited classical ballet as his ideal, and Dickens's descriptions of London as how he envisaged Britain. The modern dance of the Guangdong company he declared unsuitable to be seen in China, but he was willing to approve their appearances abroad. Making arrangements for the conservatory musicians and Guangdong dancers to perform in Huddersfield could not have been more straightforward, and their emails were characterised by exemplary efficiency and courtesy.

The 1999 festival had its formal concerts. There were four performances by members of the Arditti quartet, Avanti's portraits of Lindberg and Saariaho, Apartment House playing Richard Ayres (not so formal), Lontano introducing the music of Rebecca Saunders, Hodges playing Sciarrino, a rare recital on the St Paul's organ by Kevin Bowyer, and the 'uncompromising and shattering' severity of Ustvolskaya's music[17] performed by the Schoenberg Ensemble. A populist, if somewhat controversial, focus of the first weekend was a live performance by Bang on a Can All-Stars of Brian Eno's *Music for Airports* with a video by Frank Scheffer, preceded by an entertaining and

Listening to Nye Parry's Living Steam *in the Victoria Tower on Castle Hill.*
PHOTO: PAUL HERRMANN

Helmut Lachenmann and Wolfgang Rihm at the festival in 2000.
PHOTO: PAUL HERRMANN

to visit and experience all three. One was *Living Steam,* an electroacoustic installation by Nye Parry leading up the stairs of the Victoria Tower on Castle Hill (built for Queen Victoria's jubilee) to its open platform at the top. In the Hudawi Centre beyond the ring road Ray Lee had installed *Swing,* and in the University Dance Studio six performances were given of Beppie Blankert's haunting *Double Track,* in which two dancers on a long, bleak platform mysteriously materialised and disappeared. These absorbing productions are described on pages 190–91.

revealing interview with Eno. The magisterial climax of the second weekend was Andriessen's large-scale *Trilogy for the Last Day,* presented on the last day itself. Light-hearted late-nights included Philip Sheppard and friends improvising soundtracks to Buster Keaton movies, and the slapstick hilarity of Barry Russell's *Pub Operas* performed on four evenings in The Head of Steam, a real-ale pub adjoining Huddersfield station. Raucously entertaining, they had the performers and audience rubbing shoulders with unsuspecting drinkers – all hastily retreating as dollops of tomato ketchup daubed the two protagonists with simulated blood. My son Ben joined me after a brass band practice. We couldn't persuade his fellow percussionist, a good friend, to come, although he would have enjoyed the show and a drink. It might be in a pub, but it was 'contemporary music'. Off limits.

Three of the most memorable events were installation/performances, each presented more than once so that the public could choose when

My final festival as artistic director in 2000 gave me much satisfaction. The mix of genres seemed nearly ideal and there was little to cause misgivings. In the Lawrence Batley Theatre the London Sinfonietta Opera, Music Theatre Wales, Trestle Theatre with BCMG, and Autumn Leaf Performance staged their four operas, each to a large audience. The productions of Vivier's *Kopernikus* and Turnage's *Greek,* in particular, were as fine as any we had presented. Festivalgoers who travelled to Halifax in the final four days were rewarded with the unique experience of IOU's *Cure* in its extraordinary setting (see pages 201–3).

Works by Lachenmann and Rihm were given highly charged performances by the BBC Symphony Orchestra. The previous day St Paul's had been packed for Ensemble Modern's performance of Rihm's *Jagden und Formen,* its sustained energy and virtuosity constantly astonishing. There was the UK premiere of Ligeti's inventive *Síppal, dobbal, nádihegedűvel* performed by Amadinda percussion ensemble with the mezzo soprano Katolin Károly a dazzling and alluring soloist. A concert by the Composers Ensemble concluded with the world premiere of Deirdre Gribbin's *Celestial Pied Piper* – a Faber Music millennium commission. The University New Music Ensemble revived her *Tribe,* which had been given a striking performance by Athelas three years earlier, along with two works by my colleague, Margaret Lucy Wilkins, to mark her sixtieth birthday. Among smaller groups, the Trio Fibonacci from Canada were superlative in the UK premiere of Rihm's fecund and dramatic *Fremde Szenen I–III* – music of infectious energy, pulsatingly obsessed with Schumann. There were the rich, sonorous voices of the Latvian Radio Choir, a tribute to Boulez from the Nieuw Ensemble, more of Barry Russell's bawdy and hilarious *Pub Operas,* a

Ensemble Al-Kindi.
PHOTO: PAUL HERRMANN

Julian Jâlal Eddine Weiss with his microtonal qānūn (zither).
PHOTO: AL-KINDI

performance involving Derek Shiel's sound sculptures in the Art Gallery, and an improvised late-night concert played by Theo Leovendie (saxophones), Guus Jansen (piano) and Adama Dramé (djembé).

The largest audience was attracted to music neither notated nor contemporary; in fact of ancient origin, although interestingly microtonal. This was the Sufi liturgy from the great Ummayad Mosque in Damascus, performed by Al-Kindi – ten highly accomplished Arab musicians brought together by the Swiss qānūn (zither) player Julian Jâlal Eddine Weiss, then living in Aleppo. I had heard Al-Kindi in Helsinki and Bergen and had determined to invite them. An objection could have been – but wasn't voiced – that this ancient tradition was out of place in a showcase of contemporary music (it happened also to include whirling dervishes). I would have replied that its microtonal character was perennially relevant: as Julian Weiss fascinatingly demonstrated in an explanatory talk the following day.

My retirement

One day I received a letter beginning, 'Dear Mr OBE, I am an Italian composer and am including hereafter some materials...".

My inclusion in the Queen's Birthday Honours of 1995 had been an agreeable surprise. But a deeper pleasure was receiving the Performing Rights Society's Leslie Boosey Award for 'services to contemporary music' three years earlier, because it bestowed possession for two years of a handsome bronze eagle sculpted by Elisabeth Frink. I was permitted to house this noble raptor at home, where it perched on my desk as if about to launch itself into the garden, too proud to admonish the cats sprawling in the sun beside it and rendering writing impossible. When the time came for repatriation I felt its loss keenly, only slightly consoled that the next recipient was my friend Stephen Plaistow, whose contribution to the finest years of Radio 3 made him eminently deserving.

The first decade of the New Labour government saw significant new funding for the arts, although galleries, museums and regional theatre benefited more than music. But at the turn of the millennium, the financial prospects for the festival were worrying. In June 2000, I presented a pessimistic assessment to the Board, based on the fact that the project grants that had so valuably underpinned our recent achievements were running out. Had I been working entirely for the festival, I might have found other sources. But the climate was

Julian Jâlal Eddine Weiss with his microtonal qānūn (zither).
PHOTO: AL-KINDI

The Elisabeth Frink eagle.
PHOTO: RICHARD STEINITZ

After the final event of my last festival. From left to right: Sir Ernest Hall, Richard Steinitz, Denis Ripley, John Casken, Luke O'Shaughnessy.
PHOTO: PAUL HERRMANN

unsympathetic, and I was employed by the university to which I had a primary allegiance. I had meant to steer the festival until its twenty-fifth year. But in July 2000, I succumbed to severe bronchitis whilst struggling to get the programme to press; and, after a summer of slow and incomplete recovery, realised that I had insufficient energy to do so.

In early September I concluded that it was time to retire. At its next meeting I explained to board members a decision which had surprised myself, but which I knew was right. I would go at the end of March. On 5 April 2001, Ann Denham, mayor of Kirklees, generously held a reception to mark the occasion. A month later, what had been regarded merely as asthma was diagnosed as a leaking heart valve, and in February 2002 I went into hospital for open heart surgery to have it repaired. To read, walk and laze while I convalesced was a blissful change from writing financial applications, and I could concentrate on completing my book on Ligeti. Unusually for a former director, I have remained close to the festival and attended all its subsequent editions. But I knew I must take no further part in its management, nor breathe down the necks of my succesors. We remain on the friendliest of terms, and if something looks ill-advised I quietly bite my lip, continuing to be proud of its successes.

My decision had been made easier by knowing that festival's existing financial position was strong, its reserves healthy, and that it had an excellent executive team. They consisted, at the time, of Luke O'Shaughnessy, general manager; Alison Povey and Ruth Sidwell, administrator and assistant administrator; Stella Murrell, development director; Mirian Walton who had just succeeded Bill Vince as education director, and Tim Garbutt, technical manager. All the nuts and bolts that I had once handled, were now managed very efficiently by others. During the autumn, apart from teaching, I concentrated on the compilation and editing of the 2000 programme book, which became a significant component of the university's next submission to the higher education Research Assessment Exercise. Then I enjoyed the music. At the time of my retirement the following April, most of the next festival programme was in place.

During my twenty-three years as artistic director, the festival had notched up a history of success. From the early 1980s, the weaving of integrated thematic strands around the visits of major international composers had put it decisively on the map. It had striven to make new music accessible. Audiences had grown year after year, astonishing Londoners and an increasingly large number of visitors from overseas. Good design and high standards of comprehensibility distinguished the publicity and programme book (the latter specially commended in *The Guardian* Arts Review of 1988 for its clarity and breadth of information). The educational and outreach initiatives launched in 1984 had been hailed by David Cairns in *The Sunday Times* as 'filling him with optimism for the future'.[18] Since then, they had involved thousands of participants. The festival had branched out into opera, music theatre, dance, video and film, visual art, sculpture and installations, circus, puppetry, world music, crossover, new technologies and multimedia. There were areas it had not well represented, which my successors could rectify. But I was pleased to think that, for a great many people far and near, it was a highpoint of their year.

10 *Venues*

A cultural quarter

In 2010 a group of promoters and presenters from Scandinavia and Eastern Europe, invited to the festival by the British Council, asked a familiar question: 'Why in Huddersfield?' One answer might be because of the conjunction of interests and individuals who started it. Another could cite the rare symbiotic relationship between an academic music department and a public festival. Another could point to the millions of people who live in the North of England, and the map which shows Huddersfield more-or-less in the middle. What better place for an international festival! A socio-historical explanation would identify the strategic motivations present at a time when the English regions were forging new cultural identities – in Yorkshire with particular vigour.

What gives Huddersfield an edge over larger conurbations is the proximity of its venues. Huddersfield Town Hall, the Lawrence Batley Theatre, Huddersfield Art Gallery, St Paul's Hall, the Creative Arts Building and other university facilities are within a few hundred yards of each other; and Bates Mill is not much further. Their visual and acoustic qualities are complementary, their capacities appropriate. The relative intimacy and informality encourage friendliness. The town itself is compact. Festivalgoers can walk from its centre and from one venue to another in a matter of minutes, enjoying full and varied days – the most dedicated, it must be admitted, balancing cultural and bodily sustenance with a certain gaunt determination, as Gerald Larner wryly remarked in a *Guardian* review in 1986:

There is scarcely time to eat in Huddersfield. Lunchtime is claimed by one of the two major concerts of the day; the late afternoon tends to coincide with something irresistible, like a tour of the art gallery with a musical commentary from a solo cellist, and after the main evening concert there is always another event to fill in the time until everything is closed but the curry houses. Which is why the contemporary audience looks so lean... breathing exotic spices at each other in the morning seminars.[1]

During the 1990s, as part of its programme of urban regeneration, Kirklees Council approved the formal designation of a 'Cultural Quarter'. There was a plan for the Georgian Crown Court, next to the Methodist Mission (now the theatre) and built six years after it in 1825, to become a national poetry centre in recognition of Huddersfield's poetic credentials. For years local poets, including Simon Armitage, had been reading in the Albert Hotel and, only slightly tongue-in-cheek, Radio 4's *Kaleidoscope* had dubbed Huddersfield 'the poetry capital of Great Britain'. The Yorkshire poet Ian McMillan remarked that 'The Albert will, to future literary historians, be as important a site as those coffee houses that Dr Johnson messed about in; and those trenches that all those war poets crouched in, scribbling. It's in the middle of Huddersfield (of course) and it houses one of the liveliest series of readings in the known universe.'[2] To celebrate the Year of Literature in 1995,[3] the festival included readings from the award-winning *Black Spiders* by the Scottish poet Kathleen Jamie in the newly opened Media Centre, which neatly followed a performance of Judith Weir's opera *The Black Spider*. Late one evening in Byram Arcade, Sophie Hannah, Stephanie Bowgett and John Duffy offered poetic commentaries on music new and old, alternating with the virtuoso Canadian accordionist Joseph Petric in an event called 'Hot Potatoes' (they were, indeed, served).

The orchestra pit in the Lawrence Batley Theatre.
PHOTO: PAUL HERRMANN

169

A poem was commissioned from Sophie Hannah to print on a beermat (widely distributed but now a rare memento). This and another of her poems were reprinted in the programme book:

When a Poet Loves a Composer
The Beermat Poem

One look at him and I forgot
Embarrasingly soon.
That music ought to have, if not
Lyrics, at least a tune.

He's highbrow in a big, big way
But when he sees that I'm
The one, he'll think that it's okay
For poetry to rhyme.

Her Kind of Music

Her kind of music was a song
About a broken heart,
While his was complicated, long,
And labelled 'modern art',

With links to the chromatic scale.
The opera he wrote,
To her ears, was a tuneless wail
Upon a single note.

She struggled to acquire his taste
(As frequently occurs),
While, with enthusiastic haste,
He did away with hers.

Regrettably, the proposal to buy the Crown Court was outbid, and the building became one of an over-concentration of pubs and nightclubs in the lower part of the town. The poets countered with a lottery application to transform the third floor of Byram Arcade into a National Centre of Literature for the North. This too failed. More positively, the opening of the Media Centre was followed with further phases. By 2008 this pioneering concept had grown into a lively hub of four buildings, including the biggest 'double-skin' eco-friendly glass structure in the UK. Designed to accommodate up to 600 people, the Media Centre is now the largest cluster of its type in the North, and the third largest in Britain, housing creative, digital and media businesses. Most years it hosts festival events. Meanwhile, the university reaffirmed its cultural commitment with the opening of its lauded Creative Arts Building in 2008, a substantial new investment in research, and increased financial support for the festival, acknowledged in a new titular partnership.

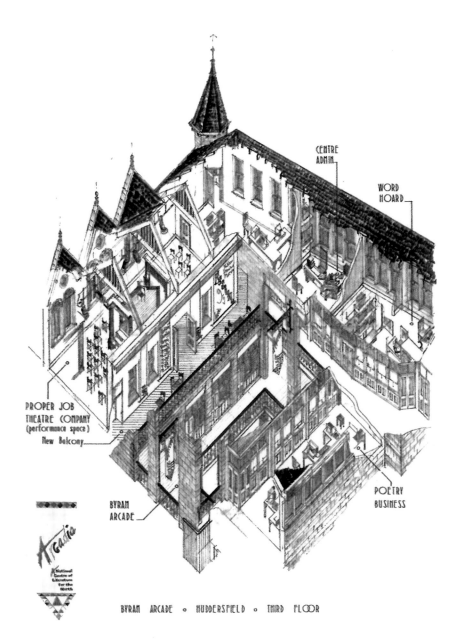

BYRAM ARCADE ○ HUDDERSFIELD ○ THIRD FLOOR

The plan for 'Arcadia': A National Centre of Literature for the North.

Great Hall and Recital Hall

Very little of this existed in 1978. The first festival used only three venues: Huddersfield Town Hall where the opening concert took place, the Polytechnic Great Hall and the music department's Recital Hall. The Great Hall stood where the new Creative Arts Building, housing Music, Art and Design, has now replaced it. 'Hall' it was but 'Great' it was not, except in so far that it had the largest capacity on the campus. An ugly, utilitarian building, with poor sightlines and a dry acoustic, its inadequate stage and technical facilities were a frustration. But in the second festival, by relocating lectures and temporarily acquiring the adjoining 'extension' as a reception and exhibition area, at least we had a focal point for visitors. Insulated by the surrounding rooms, the hall provided a noise-free, neutral space into which Denis Smalley could project electroacoustic pieces by François Bayle and Bernard Parmegiani. But for live musicians it was dispiriting. After St Paul's Hall opened in 1981, I avoided using the Great Hall, until an emphasis on music theatre in 1984, and on sound-sculpture installations a year later, made its return to the roster useful. It occasionally accommodated workshops, including a four-day CoMA residency in 1996. But years passed during which its tawdry appearance, increased use for examinations, and better options elsewhere kept the festival away. There had once been an intention for the whole complex to be made over to the music department, in which case refurbishment might have improved it. No tears were shed over its eventual demolition.

The Recital Hall still stands adjacent to the former music department building, now occupied by Estates. In the early years of the festival it could seat up to 170, depending on how it was used. A twelve-sided multi-purpose hall built for the department, it extraordinarily had no sound insulation, because further education building criteria at the time funded no such provision. Its position adjacent to the department foyer was advantageous, however, as passing students could not fail to notice festival events taking place and were more inclined to enter. They stewarded, sold programmes and provided refreshments, but a greater number purchased tickets. Other rooms in the department accommodated rehearsals and a music shop. We moved in extra display boards to festoon the foyer with posters (many designed by art students), with pictures, reviews and explanatory texts updated daily. By the 1990s, increasingly restrictive licensing regulations set lower capacities, but the absence of sound insulation was a greater nuisance. I wrote annually to the commanding officer of the adjacent Territorial Army barracks, asking him to suspend use of the firing range only a few yards from the hall, but other noise had to be tolerated.

Despite these limitations, the Recital Hall hosted a wide range of events. The 1993 festival opened there with a towering recital by the American pianist Anthony de Mare, twice first prize winner of the international Gaudeamus Competition. After UK premieres of pieces by Louis Andriessen, John Zorn and Christopher Fox, the concert concluded with a devastatingly powerful performance of Frederic Rzewski's *De Profundis,* with de Mare simultaneously playing and declaiming Oscar Wilde's bleak text. During the rest of the festival events took place in the Recital Hall every day:

The Guo brothers performing in the Recital Hall in 1988.
PHOTO: SELWYN GREEN

Friday 1pm
  Anthony de Mare: piano recital
Saturday 5pm
  Peter Sheppard & Aaron Shorr: violin
  & piano recital
Sunday 11am
  Rainer Bürck & Robert Rühle piano duo
  with Simon Emerson sound diffusion
Monday 11am
  'Downtown New York': a discussion between
  David Lang, Michael Gordon & Julia Wolfe
Monday 2.30pm
  Fine Arts Brass: Young Composers' Award
  workshop
Tuesday 10.30am
  Discussion between Louis Andriessen,
  Gerald Barry & Frederic Rzewski
Wednesday 10.30am
  Marimolin: Young Composers' Award workshop
Wednesday 5pm
  Frederic Rzewski: piano recital
Wednesday 6.15pm
  György Ligeti: pre-concert talk

Wednesday 9.45pm
    'Portrait of Galina Ustvolskaya':
    Peter Sheppard & Aaron Shorr
Thursday 10.30am
    Lawrence Cherney & Erica Goodman oboe
    & harp, YCA workshop
Thursday 5pm
    Marimolin concert
Friday 10.30am
    Marimba masterclass
Saturday 5pm
    Saschko Gawriloff: violin recital
Sunday 11am
    London Winds: concert
Sunday 5pm
    'Musical Formation and Fractals': illustrated
    lecture & discussion between Heinz-Otto Peitgen
    & György Ligeti

Venues needed to be fully used. But a purpose of this virtual mini-festival was to draw in students, and kindle interest in the wider programme. We took trouble to improve the hall's appearance, with drawn curtains, decorative floral bowls, stage lighting, and occasionally visual art hung on the walls behind the performers – one year a triptych by Colin Rose, another some of Barry Guy's graphic scores.

In the mid 1990s, Health and Safety ordered the construction of a partition to separate the foyer from the stair well, which was now identified as a potential fire conduit. The hall itself became less visible, and one could walk through the diminished foyer unaware that an event was taking place. Free-standing displays were now forbidden, leaving only wall-mounted notice boards behind glass. When the Lawrence Batley Theatre opened in 1994 with its additional Cellar Theatre, we used the Recital Hall much less. Meanwhile the number of music students continued to grow, as did the number of courses and pressure on teaching and rehearsal space. To maintain the Recital Hall in a presentable state was more difficult, whilst external noise remained a nuisance. Susanna Eastburn chose not to use it at all. But the reduced visibility of the festival was reflected in decreased student involvement, and the substitution of venues with lower capacity tended to reduce attendance in general.

St Paul's and St Thomas's

The reopening of St Paul's in 1981 as a medium-sized concert hall transformed the festival's

Stefan Niculescu rehearsing London Winds in 1993.
PHOTO: SELWYN GREEN

resources and international profile. Had I known the origin of this handsome Georgian church when Klangforum Wien arrived in 1994, I would have told them of their superior right to perform there. For the church had been built with Austrian money after the Napoleonic Wars, when Parliament used an unexpected repayment of a £2,000,000 war-loan to build churches in areas of expanding population. Constructed between 1828 and 1830, St Paul's was a major beneficiary and cost £5,700, the third highest expenditure among ninety new churches funded in Yorkshire. It was a curious reversal, for some six centuries earlier the inhabitants of London had raised funds to ransom King Richard I – money that was used by the Austrians to rebuild Vienna's defences, so saving the city and possibly the whole of Europe in 1683 from being overrun by the Turks.

Over time, commerce encroached, public buildings arose and the residential parish disappeared. In 1959 St Paul's became the chapel of the College of Technology, although it was more often used as an examination hall and for concerts by the School of Music. Stripped of pews, the interior looked neglected. But in the early 1970s the new polytechnic purchased the building from the Church Commissioners and agreed to finance a forty-one-stop tracker-action organ built by Wood of Huddersfield. It was inaugurated in 1977. The original plan had been to place the instrument in the Great Hall. But (against the wishes of the then-head of the music department, Patrick Forbes) I argued for it to be installed in the still dilapidated church.

*RIGHT:
The architects' drawings
for the conversion
of St Paul's church to
a concert hall.*

*FAR RIGHT:
The interior of St. Paul's.*

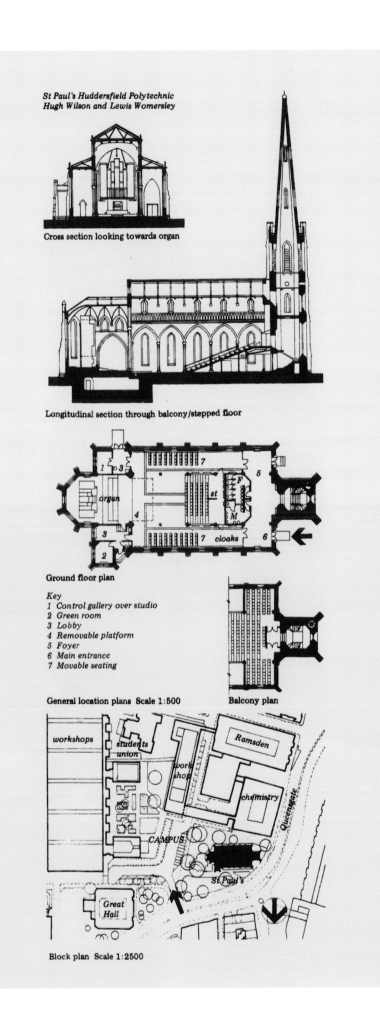

St Paul's Huddersfield Polytechnic
Hugh Wilson and Lewis Womersley

Cross section looking towards organ

Longitudinal section through balcony/stepped floor

Ground floor plan

Key
1 Control gallery over studio
2 Green room
3 Lobby
4 Removable platform
5 Foyer
6 Main entrance
7 Movable seating

General location plans Scale 1:500

Balcony plan

Block plan Scale 1:2500

The decision to do so was later described by the architects as 'a bold step and the key factor in securing the building's future'.[4] But the sequel was bizarre. Within a year the organ was ignominiously sealed off, and the nave requisitioned as an annexe for the polytechnic library. Soon after, a survey revealed structural defects, and the building closed for substantial repairs. Such was the cost that it might have been postponed for a decade – or indefinitely. But the recent investment in an expensive instrument required action. Plans for a concert hall were drawn up, with tiered seating to accommodate new toilets, which could not be housed within the budget in a built-on extension, because of the listed building status. The polytechnic – and festival – thus acquired an exceptionally handsome concert hall earlier than expected.[5]

The elegance of the auditorium compensates for the paucity of backstage facilities. As one looks down from the steeply raked central seats, spirits are lifted by the lofty proportions, the ribbed and bossed ceiling reconstructed from lightweight materials, and David Graebe's restrained and dignified organ case, its silver pipes in dark red frames springing from green-stained oak panels.[6] The acoustic can affect clarity, especially for pianists, but affords a thrilling brilliance and immediacy of contact with the audience. Extremely soft playing holds listeners spellbound. Performances by a few musicians – medieval or modern, vocal or instrumental – sound sensuously rich. The hall has proved ideal for the sinfonietta-size and smaller ensembles which, during the 1980s and '90s became a mainstay of the festival. Imaginatively lit, it can be a striking setting for music theatre – except that anyone seated towards the rear of the aisles has no view at all.

Theoretically the hall accommodates 400, but unless seating is added in the performance area or chancel, capacity is less. For the UK premiere of Pärt's *Canon of Repentance* by the Estonian Philharmonic Chamber Choir in 1998 the audience numbered 361. A more usual total was between 150 and 350. Fewer than 150 of the fixed seats have a perfect view; so, from the 1994 festival the seats were numbered, after repeated complaints from Friends that the limited time between events prevented those who attended everything from obtaining reasonable seats. Season ticket holders who happened not to be present now left gaps in

prime positions, and numbering was discontinued in 2006.

The festival has rarely used the Parish Church, partly because of the intrusion of traffic noise. But in 1993, Tim Slater, a former music student, then teaching at All Saints School, suggested that I should look at St Thomas's on Manchester Road, where he was responsible for the music. Its vicar was involved in re-planning church interiors throughout the diocese, and already St Thomas's, which had been designed by Sir George Gilbert Scott, with a lofty sanctuary, two aisles and a relatively short nave, had been handsomely refurbished. There was little noise intrusion and I thought we should try using it. That year two late-evening chamber concerts took place, whose spiritual nature was enhanced by the setting. One consisted of two pieces by Górecki, the other of music by Ustvolskaya: the first time any of it had been played at the festival. The following year the National Youth Chamber Choir sang there, and in 1995 the New London Chamber Choir in a programme of Birtwistle, Scelsi, Kagel and Alvarez. St Thomas's continues to be used

A late-night concert in
St Thomas's church in 1993.
PHOTO: SELWYN GREEN

during most festivals, and the trudge towards
the Colne Valley, sometimes in snow, to be
greeted by Tim and his helpers with hot drinks
and biscuits, bestows a welcoming warmth on
each occasion.

In 2009 St Thomas's hosted daily performances
of Jonathan Harvey's tape composition *Mortuos
Plango, Vivos Voco,* with an accompanying
video projected onto the floor, both
continuously replaying (see pages 134–35).
The ambience and acoustic of the church,
especially at dusk, provided a perfect setting.

Huddersfield Town Hall

Completed in 1881, Huddersfield Town Hall
is the most attractive and musically satisfying
of Yorkshire's Victorian concert halls. Designed
by the borough architect John Abbey, its
ornamental pilasters and plaster were reputedly
modelled on the Paris Opera. The auditorium
was conceived specifically to accommodate the
Father Willis organ, which had been bought one
year before from the Albert Hall in Newport.

From early on the acoustic was widely admired.
Barbirolli regarded it as one of the finest in
Britain. Andreas Seidel, who performed there as
leader of the Leipzig Gewandhaus and Leipzig
Chamber Orchestras, remarked that there were
other acoustics for chamber orchestra in the
world as good as Huddersfield Town Hall, 'but
none better'.[7]

The building impressed everybody I took into it.
I remember Stockhausen's gasp of admiration
when he first entered in 1988. Others likened it
to such foreign jewels as Basle's Stadtcasino
concert hall, built five years earlier, and – perhaps
too flatteringly – Vienna's famous Musikverein.
These too are 'shoe-box' halls of relatively
modest proportions with a bright, clear acoustic.
In Huddersfield, the tight curvature of the steep
choral 'risers' (almost a semi-circle) reflects
sound cohesively into the centre, although brass
and percussion placed high up can dominate too
easily. After the hall's redecoration in the second
year of the festival, its visual impact was
breathtaking, so that even non-orchestral events
most at odds with the aesthetic gained
something from their surroundings.

Despite its height and grandeur, the auditorium has a feeling of intimacy, almost like a large room. More capacious than London's Queen Elizabeth Hall but barely half the capacity of others – Manchester's Bridgewater Hall, for instance – it was, nevertheless, much too big for the festival's initial audience, although it could be made more intimate by drawing curtains round the area and closing the gallery.

The town hall's role in the festival increased in 1984, when the BBC Symphony Orchestra gave the first of a series of 'invitation concerts'. An agreement with Kirklees to use the hall free of charge for a week (and occasionally more) proved its value in 1988, when we were able to offer Stockhausen, his technical team and his performers, uninterrupted access for seven days. This could not be achieved by London's South Bank Centre, which resulted in Stockhausen coming only to Huddersfield. Three days of preparation were followed by three evening concerts, two of them semi-theatrical. The assessment carried out by Stockhausen's sound engineers had been thorough, and the hiring and positioning of speakers was done without compromise, to ensure effective diffusion over all three levels.

As the festival grew, the town hall proved to be an ideal size. The acoustic made the most delicate timbres magical, while the power of a *fortissimo* was visceral and thrilling. A memorable town hall concert raised the profile of the whole festival, and, if well attended, demonstrated that it was possible to reach an audience beyond the new music coterie. At two-thirds or three-quarters full it doubled the capacity of other venues. But I wanted to fill it, and so considered carefully the content and timetabling of concerts. Ideally they took place at weekends to coincide with the greatest number of visitors. The most successful were thematic, like the pairing of Tippett and Birtwistle in 1991, and Lachenmann and Rihm in 2001, which, if not exactly 'popular', attracted a substantial and dedicated audience.

Because its seats are removable, the area can be an open space in which to promenade: as it was for *Roaratorio* in 1989 and Rebecca Saunders's *Chroma* in 2010. Or a fairground: as it became for the performance of Berio's *Accordo* in 1985 (see pages 29–30). Or a folk club: as in 1990, when a Polish dance group led informal folk dancing to the playing of Troika, whilst members of the Polish community served traditional food. In 2001 a diagonal 'catwalk' was constructed for the 'nautical extravaganza', *Sea Tongue,* devised by Orlando Gough and Richard Chew and directed by Lucy Bailey. On this occasion, London's multi-ethnic choir The Shout led 250 amateur singers and dancers in a musical and visual pageant, whose inventive use of space, skilful co-ordination and theatrical exuberance provided a rewarding experience for the participants and audience.

In 2005 Tom Service commissioned Janek Schaefer to create 'a one-hour installation concert for town hall organ, vinyl, field recordings and light'. This resulted in one of the most unusual uses of the space, when festivalgoers, arriving for a late-evening event after a long day, were invited to lie prone on the area floor. Some of the most memorable festival events in the town hall had multimedia dimensions. But from 2007, the introduction of Bates Mill rendered the town hall less useful. My successors used it less frequently, unwilling, perhaps, to tolerate the cramped balcony seats – still configured for an age when people were of smaller stature – the limited circulation space, lack of facilities, and décor that can seem anachronistic in the digital age.

Venn Street Arts Centre

Around 1970, I was asked to attend a committee of the town council which was about to consider the conversion of Queen Street Methodist Mission into an arts centre and theatre. The meeting was chaired by the Tory leader, Alderman Graham, a gruff Churchillian figure before whom other councillors quailed – until he retired in a fit of coughing and they made nervous jokes about selling off the civic plate until he returned.[8] Back in the chair, after the briefest discussion, Graham dismissed any significant expenditure as unwarranted. The council allocated £20,000: just enough to paint the interior, build a basic stage and replace the downstairs pews with chairs. The balcony remained untouched and nothing was spent on the fabric. It was a stop-gap measure, but at least saved the Mission from demolition. Four years later the rear wall was declared unsafe and the building closed, to reopen in 1978 as a squash club. The leasing company repaired the wall and gutted and reconstructed the interior.

But business was poor, and the receivers were called in. Once more the doors were locked, leaving the restaurant tables still laid for dinner. It would be over a decade before the building was imaginatively transformed.

Seeking an alternative, Kirklees Leisure Services lighted on the parish rooms in Venn Street and acquired a lease to install raked seating and operate a small civic theatre. Accommodating just over a hundred, the Arts Centre, as it was called, had basic lighting, and presented small professional touring companies and local amateurs. Annual bookings by amateur organisations took precedence; but, when available, it was a useful venue for small-scale music theatre, recitals, jazz, workshops, and anything needing a small stage and blackout.

In 1979, three festival events took place there, but the following year only one, and then none until 1984. That year my theme of music theatre was served, amongst others, by Northern Music Theatre from York, which staged two pieces by Kagel, attended by the composer. The building's relative intimacy was ideal for viewing the 'scene machine' constructed for Kagel's ironic depiction of folk-art in *Kantrimiusik,* which showed a sequence of cartoon-like country landscapes and cut-out animals, whilst beside it three vocalists popped their heads through holes in a painted sheet, like singing postcards.

The Shobana Jeyasingh dance company in Venn Street Arts Centre.
PHOTO: SELWYN GREEN

In 1991, Stephen Mottram's first marionette show took place there. In 1993 there were four late-night events: Orphy Robinson's jazz

quartet, Shobana Jeyasingh's Indian dancers carefully avoiding collision (with music played by Roger Heaton and the Smith String Quartet), a concert for oboe, harp and tape, and a sequence of 'mini-operas' performed by six singers. One afternoon Ligeti joined the audience to watch the final staging of an educational project based on his surreal *Aventures* and *Nouvelles Aventures* (see pages 218–19). By then, work was well advanced on the future Lawrence Batley Theatre and, when its doors opened in September 1994, the Arts Centre closed for good.

Lawrence Batley Theatre

Like most children, I was taken to pantomimes and loved their seasonal delights. Later, in my teens, I was doing the rounds of the second-hand bookshops one day, and found the window of one of them full of 'penny plain, tuppence coloured' Victorian toy theatres. Fascinated, I went in and spent my pocket money on a small Pollock's theatre, cut it out and assembled it, so initiating a series of home performances with dialogue recorded by the family. The shop remained a magnet from which I couldn't stay away, until one day I found that the theatre fronts and sheets of scenery and characters had all disappeared – purchased, I was told, by a London museum. Not quite all, however. There remained a pile of partly cut out sheets and figures retained for the shopkeeper's children. There it sat undisturbed until, after persistent pestering, no doubt to get rid of me, I was allowed to purchase the lot.

Out of these I constructed a much larger theatre, with a recessed painted proscenium, apron stage, orchestra (which, with its musicians, had already been 'coloured') and a deep stage behind. I bought lighting battens and dimmers, made spotlights with coloured gels, built scenery, recorded longer plays with music, and immersed myself for many happy hours in its make-belief and magic. My theatre had a gauze, which could be lit from either side to effect transformations, and which I used in our most ambitious venture, *The Miller and His Men,* with Webb's hand-painted scenery based on its last London production at the Haymarket theatre in 1861. I was in good company; for, as a boy, Winston Churchill also had a juvenile theatre, and *The Miller and His Men* had been his favourite play.

Awareness of the more probing power of theatre came later, through performances of Pirandello, Becket, Ionescu, Marlowe and the like at the Arts Theatre and ADC in Cambridge, and being taken by my parents to the original, sensational *Beyond the Fringe,* then in 1961 to a wonderful production of *The Cherry Orchard,* starring Peggy Ashcroft, John Gielgud and Judi Dench – in which the long silences were as laden with meaning as the text.

Hence my acute disappointment when I arrived in the autumn of that year to take up my job in Huddersfield, and found its Theatre Royal empty and dejected, awaiting demolition, posters for Ballet Rambert peeling from the walls. What might the festival have staged there, had it survived! Built in 1881, the Theatre Royal had witnessed glamour and gloom (see the picture facing page 1). Plays by Ibsen, Shakespeare and Shaw rubbed shoulders; Anna Pavlova danced there, and in 1929 the premiere of Joseph Holbrooke's opera *Bronwen* was followed five months later, on 9 July 1929, by the first performance anywhere of Pirandello's *Lazzaro.* The General Strike and Depression depleted audiences, and in 1930 poor support for a production of *Back to Methuselah* led Shaw to remark that 'Huddersfield is plainly in a dark and pagan condition'. Opera productions remained popular, however, and, during the Second World War, tours by the D'Oyly Carte, Sadlers Wells and the Old Vic companies were warmly received. But the postwar period was difficult and the Theatre Royal, like many others, closed its doors.

These were bleak years for theatregoers, until, seemingly against the odds, a new generation of producing theatres began to appear. In the North they started with the Bolton Octagon in 1967, followed by The Crucible in Sheffield in 1971. New regional and touring companies emerged, and architectural jewels that had narrowly escaped demolition – notably the Bradford Alhambra and Lyceum in Sheffield – were beautifully restored, both with EU money. In Huddersfield what had looked like a lost cause became a movement with hope. After the abolition of the English metropolitan counties in 1986, West Yorkshire MCC made a dying bequest of £1 million to the nascent Kirklees Theatre Trust. Richard Voase, principal assistant arts officer, became planning co-ordinator and convened meetings to which I was invited. Theatre Projects Consultants were appointed to advise on feasibility, and their representative, Iain Mackintosh, infected everyone with his enthusiasm. Iain had a world-wide reputation in theatre design, which including courtyard theatres like the National's Cottesloe, and the Wilde Theatre in Bracknell. Concurrently with Huddersfield, he was designing Glyndebourne's new opera house, which would open in the same year. Iain and the council's architects and cultural officers had considered several existing buildings, as well as a new structure beside the civic centre. One was the large redbrick railway warehouse behind the station. Iain was keen, and an outline scheme was drawn up, but to be viable it needed a mixture of arts, commercial and residential usage which could not be brought together. In the summer of 1987 they turned their attention to the Methodist Mission.

When it opened in 1819, this was the largest Wesleyan chapel in existence. Built by the firm of Joseph Kaye, to whom Huddersfield owes some of its finest buildings (including the railway station and George Hotel), the chapel's dignified façade and well-proportioned courtyard reflected Methodism's new status. Its two substantial wings housed the minister's family and functionaries. One minister, remembered on a plaque inside the building, was George Browne MacDonald, appointed in 1847, whose wife had eleven children, seven of whom survived. A daughter married Edward Burne-Jones, a son-in-law became president of the Royal Academy, and their grandchildren included Rudyard Kipling and Stanley Baldwin.

In 1906 the building was renamed the Methodist Mission, but the facilities were unsuited to its new social purpose, whilst the congregation gradually declined. In 1970 the Methodists moved to premises in King Street. Conversion to a theatre was proposed, but, as we have seen, changes were minimal and the venture short-lived. Then Novosquash took out a lease on the main building, and the music department of the polytechnic rented the wings for instrumental teaching. Some years later, the department moved back to the polytechnic campus, Novosquash went into liquidation, and the building closed to await its fate. In 1987, when the Kirklees team and Iain unlocked the doors, it looked as if nobody had entered for several years. The restaurant tables were still laid for dinner, now with the addition of a few dead pigeons.

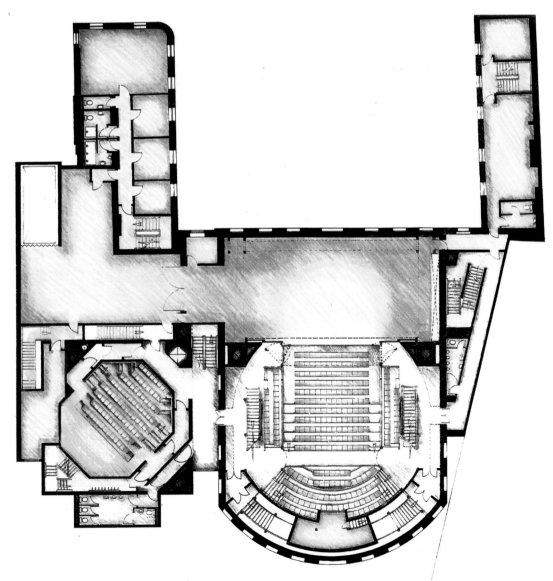

Iain Mackintosh's first plan for the theatre. Note the studio theatre (later deleted) and the reverse orientation of the main auditorium from its final configuration.

Iain's first proposal included a studio theatre built onto the south side of the building, with the main auditorium reversed from its eventual configuration, so that the curved end wall stood behind the semicircular rows of seats. To have the public enter through the stage area posed problems, however, and the scheme was also too expensive. In 1990 a revised plan was presented, cutting expenditure from £9 million to £5.1 million, eliminating the studio theatre, but including other ideas which had emerged during three years of planning. It also incorporated acoustic recommendations from Arup, world leaders in the field. This plan Kirklees Council approved. A local business entrepreneur was persuaded to plug the financial shortfall, thereafter recognised in the theatre's name. The following June, I joined the interviewing panel which appointed Ron McAllister as project manager and future artistic director. He came with an impressive record of running the Maltings Arts Centre in Berwick-on-Tweed, and was also a music graduate who knew his Babbitt from his Birtwistle. Ron brought vision both to the project and its artistic programme, and later proved to be a gifted composer and musical director of LBT's annual Christmas musicals, successfully selling them on to other theatres.

Ron arrived in time to have the stage dimensions increased to accommodate dance. Ahead of the opening, we collaborated on a

successful National Lottery bid to fund the festival's presentations on stage, and the theatre's extension of these in a year-round programme of professional dance, theatre and opera. The quality of touring companies engaged made a strong initial impact, but Ron was equally supportive of amateur work, and the mixture of local and professional input (which included poetry, and a week of puppetry and animated theatre) attracted audiences of all ages. During the first few seasons, there were performances by the National Theatre, Compass Theatre (a regular visitor), Complicite, the Reduced Shakespeare Company, Phoenix Dance and Birmingham Touring Opera with Graham

Viewing a model of the Lawrence Batley Theatre with (left to right) Councillor Denis Ripley, Ron McAllister and Lord Harewood.
PHOTO: SELWYN GREEN

The festival's youth production of Judith Weir's The Black Spider.
PHOTO: SELWYN GREEN

Vick's productions of Verdi's *Falstaff* and *Macbeth*. Given the main auditorium for a week in which to 'devise', Complicite premiered one of its most iconic creations, *Mnemonic,* at the Lawrence Batley Theatre in July 1999.

Interviewed on BBC Radio 3 during the 1995 festival, Ron spoke warmly of 'an exciting relationship', citing the theatre's contribution to the festival's youth production of Judith Weir's *The Black Spider* as a step towards originating its own work. 'The festival,' he said, 'brings to the theatre a younger audience, a more international audience, than we can attract normally; but it does give us the opportunity to reach that audience again in the rest of our programming; so that for music theatre, and particularly for dance, we can build on the audience we have here. Audiences that are coming to Huddersfield to see something in the festival are beginning to notice the venue, to trust the venue, and come back for things in the rest of the year.' In reality, it was a two-way process which benefited theatregoers and the festival. Those attending performances throughout the year were more easily encouraged to try the festival programme too.

The official opening took place on 11 September 1994, featuring Sellers Engineering Band, Huddersfield Choral Society, Thelma Barlow, Bill Owen and Patrick Stewart. Two days later, Opera North presented operatic excerpts hosted by Lord Harewood, president of the Theatre Trust and also of the festival. Others lending support included Alan Ayckbourn, Dame Judi Dench, Christopher Gable and Prunella Scales. Ahead of the opening the Contemporary Music Festival won an Arts Council/British Gas award 'for its outstanding contribution to urban regeneration' and we immediately decided that the prize of £5,000 would go towards commissioning Simon Holt to compose an opera to perform in 1997. In the event, £8,000 towards the Holt commission was contributed by Arts Council England, topped up by the festival. The British Gas award was used to commission the video accompanying Tan Dun's *Orchestral Theatre III: Red Forecast,* performed in the town hall in 1996.

What we staged

Iain Mackintosh insisted that he was designing an opera theatre for the festival, as if this was the purpose he had most in mind. So it was with a sense of fulfilment that the festival's first promotion, on 17 November 1994, was the world premiere of HK Gruber's *Gloria: a pigtale,* co-commissioned with, and performed by Opera North. After four days of preparation in the building, *Gloria* gamefully trotted the boards through three evening performances and a matinee. The festival and the theatre were viewed as joint ventures, cornerstones of a new cultural energy which had contributed to Huddersfield's designation as a 'creative town'. In line with its existing agreement regarding the use of council venues, Kirklees Cultural Services agreed that the festival should have use of LBT for a fortnight rent free. It was a verbal understanding which seems never to have been documented, and the lack of a written agreement caused problems for my successors, especially after its originators had all moved on. The financial problems confronting the theatre in the next decade would, in any case, have necessitated reconsideration.

Naturally I intended to use the festival's allocation of a fortnight to the full, and the remaining eight days of the 1994 festival saw seven performances in the main house given by six different companies. The schedule ran:

Thursday 7.30pm
  Opera North: *Gloria* (WP)
Friday 7.30pm
  Gloria (second performance)
Saturday 3pm
  Gloria (third performance)
Saturday 7.30pm
  Gloria (final performance)
Monday 7.30pm
  Music Theatre Wales: *The Lighthouse*
Tuesday 1pm
  Nouvel Ensemble Moderne: Harvey
  Mortuos Plango, Vivos Voco & *Bhakti*
Wednesday 7.30pm
  Goldberg Ensemble & Tom Yang (dancer):
  Maxwell Davies *Vesalii Icones*
Thursday 2.30pm
  Siobhan Davies Dance Co & SPNM composers:
  'Composers Choreographed'
Friday 7.30pm
  Vienna Art Orchestra: *Beauty and the Beast* (UKP)
Saturday 3pm
  Beauty and the Beast (second performance)
Sunday 3pm
  Laurie Booth Dance Co & Gavin
  Bryars Ensemble: *Wonderlawn*

During the same period, eleven different events took place in the Cellar Theatre, including seven concerts (four of them late-night) and a live broadcast of *In Tune* on Radio 3. The technical burden of rigging and turning round these twenty-two events, for staff still familiarising themselves with the venue, was extremely heavy. Vaughn Curtis, technical manager, brought his sleeping bag and spent most of the fortnight in the building, rarely going to bed until the early hours. Technical crews expect antisocial hours, but this was excessive, and I sought him out to apologise and thank him profusely. Reviewing what had undoubtedly been an exciting programme for the public, we agreed that in future the technical burden had to be less. As it happened, the next year's tribute to Nono meant less activity in the theatre, and in 1996 Stockhausen's occupancy was unexpectedly relaxed.

I was disappointed that we were unable to engage Rambert Dance. The company had expanded to present in much larger theatres, and declared the LBT stage too small. But performances by the Laurie Booth, Jonathan Burrows, Phoenix and Richard Alston dance companies, and the Guangdong Modern Dance Company from China were full of interest. Laurie Booth's company was accompanied by the Gavin Bryars Ensemble; the Guangdong by recorded music. Only Richard Alston, in my view, engaged with the serious core of contemporary music that characterised the festival, and his company's performance in 1997 included Birtwistle's *Nenia: The Death of Orpheus,* music by Jo Kondo, and two Xenakis percussion pieces, all played live.

The path to originating opera was strewn with pitfalls, as Chapter 9 will have made clear. It was much easier to show touring work, and the mix of music theatre, multimedia, film, dance, puppetry, animated theatre and concerts which LBT made possible was exciting. It little compromised the festival's distinctiveness if productions were also seen elsewhere, as the programme contained much else unique to Huddersfield. Tours generated interest and media coverage. Previous reviews helped validate what, for ticket-buyers, might otherwise be a plunge into the unknown.

Two of the most inventive and entertaining evenings were provided by the short-lived Gogmagogs. Brought together by the theatre director Lucy Bailey and violinist Nell Catchpole, they were seven highly skilled string

A scene from Greek *by Mark-Anthony Turnage, performed by London Sinfonietta Opera in 2000.*
PHOTO: PAUL HERRMANN

Lynne Plowman's House of the Gods *staged by Music Theatre Wales.*
PHOTO: BRIAN SLATER

players who had abandoned sheet music, stands and chairs to develop a novel language of inventive theatricality and physical bravado. They had also invited an interesting group of young composers – including Roger Eno, Jane Gardner, Luke Stoneham and Errollyn Wallen – to devise work in conjunction with them. After their inaugural show at the ICA, Gogmagogs were invited to the Purcell Room, and then the Traverse for the 1996 Edinburgh Festival. They appeared in Huddersfield that autumn during a whistle-stop UK and international tour, with nine pieces so seamlessly integrated, so polished, exhilarating, funny, serious or serene, that I had no hesitation in engaging their next show, 'Gogmagogs Gigagain', in 1997. Both were late-night performances: the second virtually selling out the theatre. The concept could not easily have been sustained; but, during its brief flowering, offered a joyful antidote to the predominantly serious demeanour of much contemporary music.

The most productive period of the festival and theatre's association was during its first ten years, when a wide range of work was presented. Since then it has been used as often for amplified concerts, for which a dry acoustic is desirable. There have been fewer touring productions on offer appropriate to the festival; and, for some that have been seen during the last few years (e.g. *Sandglasses* in 2010), because of its larger performing area, Bates Mill has been the only suitable venue. A list of the most memorable productions in the Lawrence Batley Theatre appears in Appendix B (page 286).

Trio Fibonacci perform music by Michael Finnissy to accompany a live film screening in the Lawrence Batley Theatre.
PHOTO: BRIAN SLATER

With Ron McAllister's departure in 2001 to the Wilde Theatre in Bracknell, the collaboration between festival and theatre became less close.

That year was still rich in staged work. The outstanding *Hashirigaki* and *Lohengrin* were joined by Saariaho's *From the Grammar of Dreams* (all three supported by the Réseau Varèse) and two other productions: Maxwell Davies and David Pountney's new *Mr Emmet Takes a Walk*, and five short collaborations between UK composers and librettists presented by Tête à Tête. Thereafter the amount and variety of staged work dwindled, apart from a few fine exceptions – notably Birtwistle's *Io Passion* performed by Almeida Opera after its premiere in Aldeburgh in June 2004. With the exception of *Mr Emmet*, these were all non-narrative, imbued with a richness and ambiguity more thought-provoking than contemporary storytelling operas often achieve.

Apart from the Agrava 'noise duo' with dancer, and two hard-hitting concerts with projection, the 2005 festival saw no staged work. In 2006 the theatre housed six concerts and two theatrical productions: Theatre Cryptic's collaboration with Gavin Bryars, and Lynne Plowman's *House of the Gods* performed by Music Theatre Wales, but less appropriate to the festival's current priorities than other productions by the company. Another concert was given by Trio Fibonacci of music by Finnissy to accompany the screening of three silent

films – a medium to which LBT particulary lends itself. In 2007 there were six concerts and two staged productions: Faulty Optic's *Dead Wedding* and an 'instrumental installation' by Aperghis involving the Helios Quartet.

By 2006–7 the quality of the theatre's own year-round programme had seriously declined and, as attendances flagged, its survival became precarious. The crisis precipitated a change of artistic director and the appointment of a new board of management. But the understanding that LBT would host the festival rent-free had disappeared. A condition of the local authority's current grant aid is that the theatre must levy a higher percentage of box office income from all organisations using it. And, as the festival also has to maximise income, and can do so more effectively in other venues, it uses the theatre less frequently. In 2008, only two festival events took place there. One was an interesting collaboration between the Scottish Flute Trio and Curve Foundation Dance Company; but, as it took place at noon and was omitted from the dance pages of the theatre's brochure, the general dance audience appeared to be unaware. The three theatre events in the 2010 festival were all concerts with minimal staging. Under its current director, Victoria Firth, the Lawrence Batley's programme has been revitalised, and its professional components are stronger. But as widespread cuts in public services affect both local government and the Arts Council's support for touring – the viability of small regional theatres may again be threatened.

Creative Arts Building

The opening of a £15 million state-of-the-art facility for Music, Art and Design in 2008 coincided with a redefined partnership between the festival and university. The music accommodation includes lecture, rehearsal and practice rooms, staff offices, and one of the largest musical technology studio systems of any university in Europe, with sixteen world-class, single-user computer composition and recording studios, four large teaching labs and the blue-clad 'cube': a cutting-edge experimental research studio for sound spatialisation. The glass atrium, framing a spectacular view of St Paul's, has proved an ideal space for receptions, the music shop and information desk: a place to meet over coffee, relax and keep warm, and an agreeable environment for less formal concerts,

TOP:
The Io Passion *by Sir Harrison Birtwistle, performed by Aldeburgh Almeida Opera in 2004.*
PHOTO: *BRIAN SLATER*

MIDDLE:
The Scottish Flute Trio and Curve Foundation Dance Company in 2007.
PHOTO: *BRIAN SLATER*

BOTTOM:
Faulty Optic's Dead Wedding *performed in 2007.*
PHOTO: *BRIAN SLATER*

such as the 'hcmf// shorts'. The reverberant acoustic favours solo performance and the voice, as exemplified in 2010 by Peyee Chen's sensitive interpretation of *Song 1* and *Song 16* by Finnissy and delicate deconstructions of Erin Gee's *mouthpiece I* and *II*.

The former Recital Hall has been replaced by the Phipps Hall, named after the donor of its two-manual organ, based on a late seventeenth-century north-German instrument and tuned in unequal temperament. The hall itself seats 120–140, is fully soundproof and equipped for professional recording. Its limited capacity and asymmetric design at first seemed unhelpful. But it has proved well suited to unconventional formats, as well as more intimate recitals.

The recorder player Genevieve Lacey gave a beautifully expressive solo recital there in 2009. Three days later Phipps Hall became an ideal space for the festival debut of Musica Elettronica Viva, where the playfully creative exchanges between Alvin Curran, Frederic Rzewski and Richard Teitelbaum could be appreciated close to.

In 2010, the festival and university co-produced two concerts in Phipps Hall to celebrate the twentieth anniversary of empreintes DIGITALes – a label which has championed the best acousmatic compositions. Projection facilities have been variously used, most entertainingly in some wittily surreal music theatre performed by Plus Minus in 2010. Phipps Hall also suited the violinist Monica Germino, whose previous festival appearance in 2007 had taken place in the much smaller Studio 1, causing some hopeful punters to be turned away. Her Phipps Hall recital included *Fugue* by Arnoud Noordegraaf, in which Germino played against her double in an intriguing intercutting of images projected onto a semi-transparent screen. Behind it the real Monica appeared and vanished; but, unlike the slow transitions in Beppie Blankert's *Dubbelspoor*, the changes had an electrifying abruptness.

Bates Mill

Bates and Co were traditional woollen yarn spinners. When the company needed new buildings, including a blending shed, they were erected over the disused Huddersfield Narrow Canal. Much later, when a project emerged to restore the canal, it had to be re-tunnelled under both Bates Mill and Sellers Engineering before

it could reopen in 2001. As the textile trade collapsed, Bates followed the example of other mills in renting out office and retail space and creating 'art studios'. The 5,000 square metre Blending Shed became an event space with the unusual advantage of vehicular access.

Audience facilities are basic, and foyer there is none. But as punters hurry in, wet and windswept from the November rain or snow, they find mulled wine brewing and can carry drinks to their seats. During the 2008 and 2009 festivals improvements were made to the lighting, the seats and the entrance, whilst the performance area was curtained. With a stage installed at one end, seating capacity is around 350. Air vents and water pipes contribute ambient sounds, and sightlines are not ideal. But nor are they in parts of St Paul's.

The adoption of Bates Mill – for financial, practical and aesthetic reasons – has given the festival a new focus. By 2007 it had become the leading venue after St Paul's, used almost every day. Its flexibility facilitates promenade performances and any seating configuration,

useful for the presentation of experimental work and mixed media. The yard provides parking and is big enough for bands to march up and down. In *Night of the Unexpected*, an umbrella programme which opened the 2007 festival, the public were invited to cross and re-cross the yard to hear simultaneous performances in an adjacent shed. For the British debut of the Vienna Vegetable Orchestra, the Blending Shed should have doubled as a soup kitchen. This being Britain, however, serving homemade soup was banned by Health and Safety.

The informality and industrial ambience of Bates Mill chimes with Graham McKenzie's artistic vision. Its flexibility and neutrality well suited Kyriakides's *Buffer Zone,* whose staging there is discussed on page 266. In 2009 the Blending Shed was used more often with end-on seating, and for performances of music involving installations – like Justė Janulytė's fine *Sandglasses* seen in 2010 – Bates Mill was the only venue with the ambience and space required. For anything involving amplification it is preferable to St Paul's, and for the gritty physicality of rock-influenced work the Blending

An event in Bates Mill.
PHOTO: JOHN BONNER

Kitchen Motors performing in Bates Mill in 2006.
PHOTO: JOHN BONNER

Shed is ideal. This was exemplified during a day of performances to mark Louis Andriessen's seventieth birthday. His celebrated *Hoketus* of 1975–77 made a huge impact: its 'impact-rebound' alternations as machine-like as an iron foundry, and as boldly revolutionary as thirty-five years before.

The addition of Bates Mill allows three or four ensembles to prepare and perform in different halls on the same day. This was demonstrated on several occasions in 2010. On the last Saturday, 27 November (a notably rewarding day), Ensemble Klang performed in Phipps Hall at noon, the Arditti Quartet in St Paul's at 3pm, musikFabrik in the town hall at 5pm and the London Sinfonietta in Bates Mill at 7.30pm – a feast indeed! Highlights of this festival are described in Chapter 16.

11 *Other spaces, other media*

The many faces of music theatre

Multimedia and interdisciplinary components enriched programmes, especially when they took place in spaces not normally used. Although the four described below were very different from each other, all were remarkable in concept and execution. Each was performed at least twice, some of them many times.

In the polytechnic annexe, St Peter's, during the 1980s the drama department ran a small performance venue. Situated two floors up in an ex-YMCA building, it had no pretensions to elegance, but was serviceable enough. There, in 1989, Georges Aperghis's Atelier Théâtre et Musique (ATEM) made its British debut in *Enumerations,* a wonderfully witty, small masterpiece of visual and acoustic music theatre. Emerging from a paper 'house', the six actor-musicians proceeded to transform small everyday events into an absurdist exploration of sounds, words, gestures and onomatopoeic lists: an invented language devoid of meaning, yet comic, touching, poetic, and undoubtedly musical. *Enumerations* was typical of Aperghis's early work. With its simple ideas and resources, it was arguably the most perfect of his theatrical creations seen in Huddersfield. Its fluctuating balance between word, gesture and sound encapsulated the very essence of music theatre. Two performances of *Enumerations* were preceded by an Aperghis portrait, in which the three soloists of the Strasbourg group, Accroche Note, performed five UK premieres. They included part of *Récitations,* a brilliantly inventive series of fourteen pieces (composed for the actress Martine Viard) built from accumulative patterns of phonemes, syllables, assonances, alliteration and fragments of singing. Sections of *Récitations* were performed

again by Nicola Walker-Smith in 1990 and 1992. On this first occasion, overshadowed by the presence of Cage, Boulez and Messiaen, Aperghis's work was too little noticed and there were no press reviews.

Some years later, the drama studio moved to the original YMCA hall at street level, which, with raked seating, could accommodate around ninety people and was more presentable. Here, in 1997, we installed *The Seed Carriers,* Stephen Mottram's powerful and disturbing 'animated theatre' based on Richard Dawkins's *The Selfish Gene,* with its eerie Bosch-like wooden puppets and evocative electroacoustic score commissioned from Glyn Perrin. Originally titled *The Nature of Things,* the collaboration had been premiered in St Paul's two years before, but merited revival in a more intimate setting. Four performances were given, three of which sold out. 'I wouldn't argue with anyone who wanted to call this a masterpiece,' wrote David Fanning in *The Daily Telegraph.*[1]

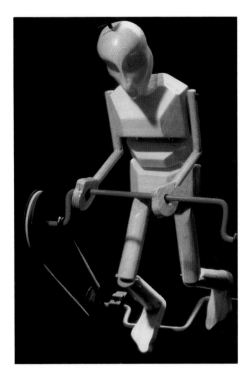

In the same venue, in 1999, the festival presented a highly original dance theatre creation by the Dutch choreographer Beppie Blankert. Her *Dubbelspoor (Double Track)* – 'a dance performance about waiting' – had been inspired by Samuel Beckett's 'Text for Nothing no. 7', and was accompanied by music specifically composed by Louis Andriessen. The version seen in Huddersfield was a remake of the original production from 1986, and it is indicative of Andriessen's regard for the collaboration that, when awarded the Johan Wagenaar prize in 2008 and asked what he would like it to facilitate, out of all his *oeuvre* he instantly named this piece.

In *Dubbelspoor* the audience watches a long narrow platform on which there is a single bench. Beyond and above it, twin videos show an abandoned station through which trains pass but never stop. A dancer sits on the bench. Another mysteriously appears and disappears. Whilst visible, they interact, melt into each other, dance and embrace, even as the second dancer fades from view. In reality the public sit in front of a nine-metre-wide mirror, in which they see, on a stage behind them, the principal dancer who also speaks the text. The second dancer exists only behind the mirror and, when revealed by the lighting, appears uncannily to partner the dancer on the stage, even to touch and hold each other. Andriessen's music uses the idea of mirroring in several ways. It is heard three times, first played by the harpsichord, second doubled by a piano, third with the addition of celesta and bells, but omitting notes from the chords so that there is 'the shadow of a mirrored melody which, while not played, is nonetheless heard'. The strange beauty of the choreography, dream-like nature of the experience, and uneasy urgency of the text proved an extraordinary conjunction. The technical requirements of the set limited audience capacity, but six performances enabled many to see the piece.[2] It was a stroke of good fortune that Beppie Blankert's revival allowed

Wooden puppets made by Stephen Mottram.

Swing *by Ray Lee, performed*
in the Hudawi Centre in 1999.
PHOTO: *PAUL HERRMANN*

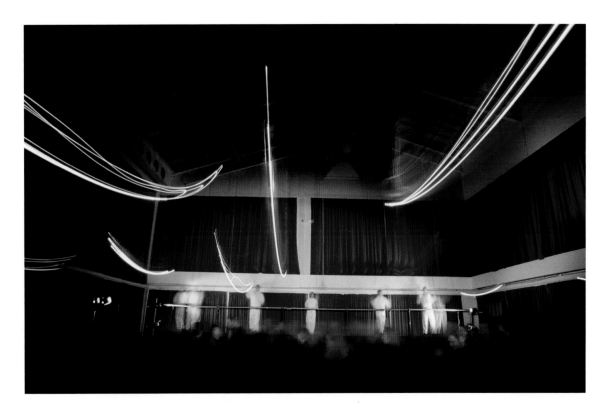

Dubbelspoor to be presented in the same festival
that climaxed in Andriessen's large-scale *Trilogy
of the Last Day.*

The performances of *Dubbelspoor* were backed
against others created by the performance artist
Ray Lee, so that those who wanted could attend
both. His *Swing: Change Ringing with
Loudspeakers,* installed in the Hudawi Centre,
consisted of twenty tiny loudspeaker cones
suspended in lines horizontally above the
audience, who could choose whether to sit
against the walls or wander underneath. Each
was separately wired to a tape recorder, and
emitted its own low-amplitude electronic sound.
Soldered to each cone, small filament light bulbs
traced the movement of the speakers through
the air. A team of ringers – or 'swingers' as they
were soon called – drawn from the university
and Huddersfield New College pulled them to
and fro. Performed in near darkness, the
miniscule Doppler effects made a delicate
tapestry of fluctuating sounds. Keith Potter
remarked that they 'activated the soulless
modern space of the Hudawi Centre with a
fascinating counterpoint of sound and light'.[3]

HOUSE

Created in 1998 by the theatrical partnership
of Louise Anne Wilson and Wils Wilson, with

poetry by Simon Armitage, music by Robert
Rimbaud (aka Scanner) and four actors,
HOUSE was another brilliantly original and
unusual complement to the concert programme.
Like IOU's *Cure* two years later, it was an
independent initiative which the Wilsons wanted
to present in association with the festival.
Their initial proposal contained a schedule of
community engagement, discussions, social
impact, psychology and philosophy, like a
checklist for the politically correct. Moreover, its
nineteen pages were entirely printed in capitals!
Whatever musical component there would be
had yet to be decided. Among the festival team
I detected a degree of scepticism. But I was
intrigued. Basically the Wilsons' idea was to find
a derelict house and transform it into an
installation-cum-performance, through which
visitors would pass, a few at a time, several
times a day. When it became clear that we
would not have to contribute funds, I gave the
proposal a cautious welcome. But where to find
a building?

Several weeks later Louise and Wils returned
to say that they had found a site, not on the
outskirts of town as we had expected, but
abutting the Lawrence Batley Theatre. While
the lower part of Huddersfield was awaiting
redevelopment, the developers would make
available two empty cottages in Goldthorpe's
Yard, one of the town's oldest cobbled enclaves

and due to be preserved. Inside were relics of their history. These became artefacts of the installation, and through meticulous research revealed a fascinating past. In 1812 Luddites had been imprisoned in the yard. In the 1860s members of Huddersfield Naturalist Society had met in No. 3 and discussed Darwin's new theory of evolution, whilst preachers in the adjacent Wesleyan chapel (now LBT) were doubtless refuting it. An advertisement in the local paper brought a reply from a Mrs Middleton, aged ninety-two, who had lived in one of the cottages in the 1920s, and gave an account of other inhabitants and their lives. We agreed that *HOUSE* should be associated with the festival, and in the next few months the Wilsons developed what would be a unique experience: part installation, part theatre, part archival research. The audience was limited to fifteen per performance. Journeying slowly from cellar to attic, they passed through rooms, peered into closets, encountered 'inhabitants' (played by the actors), fragments of stories, objects to examine, strange images and sounds, their rites of passage illuminated by the poetry of Simon Armitage and the discreet sound-score by Scanner. In a corner of a recreated 'laboratory' on the top floor, they could read 'An Expedition' – Armitage's cleverly imagined poem tracing the archaeological adventure back in time through the metaphor of an Antarctic exploration.[4]

Seventy-two performances were given during the festival and in December. Word spread and they quickly sold out. My own visit left me deeply moved and immensely proud that *HOUSE* had been part of the festival. That it was theatre more than music, and installation more than either, was immaterial. As an adjunct to *HOUSE* itself, enacted on four evenings on the cobbles outside the cottages, pupils from Honley and Shelley high schools performed *Yardies,* a piece they had created with Shelley's inspirational teacher Steven Downs. Later, under a full moon in the November cold, another devised piece, *Timelines,* was performed by students of Huddersfield New College under the guidance of Liz Heywood.

The theatre critics were ecstatic. In *The Guardian* Lyn Gardner remarked that *HOUSE*

Four scenes from HOUSE.
PHOTOS: FIVER
(WILSON + WILSON)

was 'not theatre as we know it, but more of an archaeological dig or geographical survey whose time-span is from Adam and Eve to the present day', and marvelled at how the company had made 'these collapsing walls breathe and speak, tell stories, weep tears, pulsate with anger, yield up secrets'.[5] 'I cannot recommend *HOUSE* too highly,' wrote Charles Spencer in *The Daily Telegraph*, adding that it was 'equally worthy of both theatrical awards and the Turner Prize'.[6] With one exception, none of the music critics reviewed either *HOUSE* or *Dubbelspoor*. Perhaps, despite daily performances, they could not obtain tickets. Perhaps their editors wanted only concert reviews. Yet some of the festival's most original and thought-provoking presentations were not in a conventional concert format. Only Andy Hamilton covered *HOUSE* in a comprehensive review of the festival in *The Wire*, finding 'its polyphony of events... hard to describe [but] absolutely beguiling'.[7]

Promenade events

Swing and *HOUSE* were not the only events at which the public could move through the environment. An early example was Frances-Marie Uitti's *Moveable Feast: Gallery tour with*

solo cello in 1986; another the UK premiere of Stockhausen's *Sternklang* in Huddersfield Sports Hall in 1988, already described (see pages 110–11). At the performance of Cage's *Roaratorio* in 1989 the public wandered freely in the 'area' of the town hall; as they had also done in 1985 – on that occasion mingling with unicyclists, stilt-walkers and other street entertainers – for the UK premiere of Berio's *Accordo* (see pages 29–30).

In 2010 another perambulating audience wandered around the town hall auditorium, breathing in the special magic of Rebecca Saunders's *Chroma*, in which the mobility of listening mirrors the fluidity of its material (see pages 271–74). The Blending Shed at Bates Mill can assume any configuration, and, being the only sizeable venue with no fixed seating, it was particularly apt for the UK premiere of James Tenney's *In a large, open space* performed by the Bozzini Quartet 'and friends' in 2008. Tenney's work is written for twelve or more instrumentalists sustaining single pitches within a given range, distributed around the space, and playing so softly that listeners had to approach and bend close to hear each clearly. As with *Chroma*, the freedom to move and sample sounds combined the quality of an installation with the variability of live performance.

Preparing for the lantern procession.
PHOTO: COURTESY OF THE HUDDERSFIELD DAILY EXAMINER

Things that go bang in the night

Scheduling outdoor events in November can be hazardous. When the weather was tolerable they could be fun, and on a dry, crisp evening quite magical. For several years I avoided the risk until, in December 1987, I was invited to an event called 'Ten Lamps of Fire' at Spring Grove Junior School, and was captivated by the mainly Asian children parading paper lanterns around its snowy playground.[8] These colourful creations had been made during workshops led by Adam Strickson, whom I asked to devise something similar for the festival in 1988. Ann Suggate, the festival's part-time administrative assistant, who had recently taken on educational liaison, organised the participation of Carlton Junior and Infant School and Royds Hall High School. The idea expanded to include The Satellites, well-known specialists in outdoor celebratory performances, and the Cragg Vale Gamelan, a 'community orchestra' formed in a Calderdale village by Mick Wilson. It already had around thirty-five members aged seven to seventy, who had built their own Balinese-style instruments to perform their own compositions.

For a setting we chose the canal basin on the polytechnic campus, and I wrote to British Waterways requesting permission to float lanterns on the canal. A 'jobsworth' refusal arrived. Insulted by the accusation that we would leave debris (the canal was full of it already), I decided to go ahead anyway, confident that no official would arrive to check. The performance took place after dusk on a fine starlit evening, its ethos – as Adam Strickson wrote in the programme – 'a celebration in light and music drawing together some of the different cultures which make West Yorkshire such a rich and inspiring place to be living'. Assisted by the lantern-makers and puppeteers, the children had assembled an 'oriental market': its produce hot spicy food which was served to the audience. Fruits and vegetables were represented by lanterns and shadow puppets, whilst a barge hung with lanterns floated silently past the spectators.

Judy Meewezen's review in *The Times Educational Supplement* nicely conveys the atmosphere:

Scarcely a word was spoken as a slow procession of young people made its way along the canal. With them they carried almost the only source of light:

an array of bright lanterns in the shapes of huge vegetables and fruits. The gentle but percussive tones of Indonesian-style music – played by a community gamelan orchestra – accompanied the marchers, drawing them towards the focal point of the celebration. The extraordinary dignity of this opening persisted throughout the evening. The stillness, the dusk and the water all worked in harmony with a pleasing series of surprises involving shadow puppets, a floating pineapple and finally a giant tree, which glided down the canal towards us like a vision from another world.

The children had been taught to use simple material, painted paper and candles, and to make maximum impact by cautious, well-timed movement. One banana burst into flames and a sad bag lady, inspired to sing her own woeful tune, was gently moved away. But neither of these momentary diversions nor the freezing temperatures detracted from a festival event which, for its optimism and devotion, surely deserves a crown of its own.[9]

Watching and listening was the Canadian composer R. Murray Schafer who, more than any other artist, had built a reputation from creating ambitious site-specific projects in remote wilderness areas as well as urban locations. Impressed by the event, Schafer answered my enquiry about devising something for Huddersfield with a vision of communities carrying torches and descending from the hills all round the town. Fearful of its cost, and Schafer's reputation for escalating complexities, I held the project at bay and never pursued it.

Earlier in the 1988 festival, late one evening, another gamelan performed: the celebrated Bow Gamelan from the East End of London, whose mixture of music, sculpture and performance art had led *City Limits* to call them the 'most stunning cross media project of the decade'. The three members spent the day assembling industrial junk instruments in a corner of the piazza, and at 10pm the show began: energetically physical, the performers wearing helmets sporting flares, and overalls to protect them from the welding flames and pyrotechnics, whilst thwacking everything in sight. The event became more theatrical as it gradually began to snow. I stood watching with George Benjamin, whose *At First Light* had just been performed by the London Sinfonietta, but who, with increasingly numb fingers, soon repaired to the Shabab for a curry.

From the 2007 festival brochure.

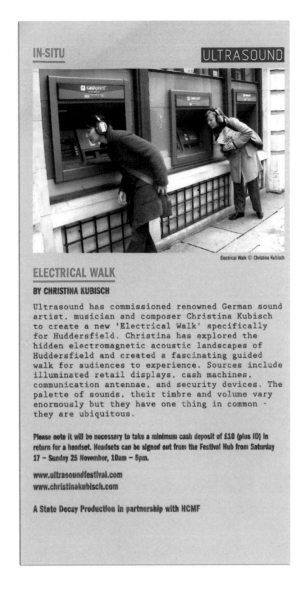

IN-SITU   ULTRASOUND

Electrical Walk © Christina Kubisch

ELECTRICAL WALK

BY CHRISTINA KUBISCH

Ultrasound has commissioned renowned German sound artist, musician and composer Christina Kubisch to create a new 'Electrical Walk' specifically for Huddersfield. Christina has explored the hidden electromagnetic acoustic landscapes of Huddersfield and created a fascinating guided walk for audiences to experience. Sources include illuminated retail displays, cash machines, communication antennae, and security devices. The palette of sounds, their timbre and volume vary enormously but they have one thing in common - they are ubiquitous.

Please note it will be necessary to take a minimum cash deposit of £10 (plus ID) in return for a headset. Headsets can be signed out from the Festival Hub from Saturday 17 – Sunday 25 November, 10am – 5pm.

www.ultrasoundfestival.com
www.christinakubisch.com

A State Decay Production in partnership with HCMF

On the Colne Valley Sculpture Trail in 2008.
PHOTO: BRIAN SLATER

Especially memorable was the *Sonic Walk,* devised by the festival's education officer, Bill Vince, in 1995. This was a creative music project whose participating groups worked independently and came from different constituencies. Like most of the festival's outreach projects with a performance outcome, it was publicised in the main programme and marketed like every other event – except that the public did not pay. On a quiet Sunday evening, after a concert by English Northern Philharmonia in Huddersfield Town Hall, some 200 or more curious festivalgoers assembled in the piazza and were despatched in timed processions on a musical mystery tour through the heart of Huddersfield. Entering the deserted Imperial Arcade, they were ambushed by the instrumentalists of Kirklees Youth Wind Orchestra emerging from darkened shops. In Byram Arcade, strangely disembodied electronic sounds floated down from the cast iron

balustrades. Outside the grand portico of Huddersfield's neoclassic station, students from Bretton Hall College, illuminated by flaming braziers, played industrial junk in the manner of Bow Gamelan. Arriving at the Parish Church, the walkers filed in and sat in the pews for another performance. Outside the Lawrence Batley Theatre they were met by exuberant wind players and drummers, tables of food and drink, and firecrackers; whilst inside, the celebrated North Stars Steel Orchestra performed on stage with their acclaimed panache.

The weather had been kind to these events; even the snowflakes falling on Bow Gamelan enhanced the industrial décor. In 1996 we were less lucky, when a carnival-style procession led by Eugene Skeef battled against wind and rain. Undeterred, in 1997 the indefatigable local animateur Barry Russell composed and directed a piece for multiple young instrumentalists during the interval of a Huddersfield Town football match in the McAlpine Stadium (described on page 223). The event drew attention to the festival, but, in so large a space was difficult to choreograph and hard to hear.

No further outdoor events took place for several years. Then in 2007, Graham McKenzie programmed an *Electrical Walk* on which members of the public could embark at a time of their choosing. It had been commissioned by Ultrasound, a programme of experimental sound and electronic music produced by the Digital Research Unit at Huddersfield Media Centre, and launched to coincide with the 2002 festival. But the notion that Ultrasound would attract and benefit attendees at the festival was flawed; for every festival programme was already packed with events. Ultrasound ceased to exist after 2007, and the *Electrical Walk* appears to have been its final project. Devised

by the German sound artist and composer, Christina Kubisch, it enabled 'walkers' to explore the hidden electromagnetic fields emanating from retail displays, buses, security devices, telephone boxes, neon lights etc. To do so, participants wore customised headphones and followed suggested routes around the town centre, where they could be seen listening intently to buildings, street furniture, ATMs and the cosmetic cabinets in Boots. It was a quirky but effective demonstration of the new festival slogan: 'Music lives in everything'!

Exhibitions, sound art and installations

In 2008 the festival collaborated with the River Colne Sculpture Trail to commission a permanent sound sculpture from sound artist Matthew Sansom. Consisting of two aluminium acoustic mirrors overlooking the river and canal in Slaithwaite, it was inaugurated on the first day of the 2008 festival (see the illustration on page 195). Prior to this, Sansom had worked with pupils from the local Nields School to make location recordings, using parabolic listening and recording devices. These were combined with sound archive descriptions to create the River Colne Soundwalk, focusing on the soundscape of the Colne Valley and experienced by using an MP3 player. The project was funded by an anonymous donation and the Arts Council, and co-ordinated by the festival's education and outreach officer, Heidi Johnson.

I had hoped to commission two sound sculptures in 1985, after a large-scale exhibition of international sound sculpture was shown in Huddersfield Art Gallery during that year's festival (see pages 31–32). Among the exhibits, which occupied all five galleries, were works by the British and German sculptors, Peter Appleton and Paul Fuchs, and, on a Sunday when the galleries were closed, these were transported to St Paul's and played in concert by their creators. Afterwards we explored ideas for two permanent commissions. Maquettes were made: by Fuchs for a sculpture on a pedestrian precinct in the town; by Appleton for one on the banks of the canal. I applied to the Henry Moore Foundation and elsewhere for funds, but was everywhere turned down, and the project was never realised.

But the exhibition led to further collaborations between the festival and art gallery. In 1986 an

Krachtever (Invigorator) in Huddersfield Art Gallery during the 2000 festival.
PHOTO: PAUL HERRMANN

Arts Council touring exhibition of graphic scores, called *Eye Music,* occupied one large gallery; paintings by Colin Rose another. In 1987 Xenakis's music-drawing UPIC computer was installed in the large gallery, and an exhibition showing the work of Xenakis in different disciplines hung on the walls. That same year, in one of the smaller galleries, a collection of Piranesi's original *Carceri d'Invenzione* etchings, lent from London, illuminated the UK premiere of Brian Ferneyhough's eponymous composition.

During the next twelve years, concerts and workshops took place in the Art Gallery: notably a 'Minimalist Marathon' in 1993. There were also exhibitions, including another of work by Colin Rose. In 1995 a display of photographs, facsimiles, working sketches and diagrams relating to Luigi Nono was lent by the Nono archive in Venice, but it was shown in the Cellar Theatre of the Lawrence Batley Theatre, where many festival events were now taking place. In the Art Gallery there was nothing major relating to the festival until 2000, when the gallery mounted two sound installations. One was *Krachtever (Invigorator)* by Peter Bosch and Simone Simons: a wall of wooden crates placed diagonally across the largest gallery, each containing different materials and mounted on steel springs. A computer programme activated their vibrations, producing a clunking, clattering acoustic tapestry of sounds. Another gallery contained a series of sound sculptures by Derek Shiel, which on one afternoon were 'played' in a concert with flute and percussion.

These two installations revived the association between festival and art gallery, and were followed, in 2002, by a nostalgic, slightly teacherly exhibition called *Groove,* exploring vinyl and turntables in art from Cage and Duchamp to contemporary DJs. For three days during the 2005 festival, the gallery hosted an interactive installation, *The Art of Walking on Water,* in which members of the public could construct instant 'compositions' by treading

Philip Thomas performing Cage's Electronic Music for Piano *(1964).*
PHOTO: BRIAN SLATER

selectively on sound pads covering the floor. But the gallery more fully regained its prominence when Graham McKenzie moved from Glasgow's Centre of Contemporary Arts – where he had curated numerous exhibitions and installations – to become artistic director of the festival in 2006. Since then he has programmed sound art every year, not only in the Art Gallery but also in other venues, particularly Bates Mill, reflecting its greater currency in contemporary arts worldwide.

For his second festival in 2007, Graham commissioned the sound artist Janek Schaefer to create *Extended Play (Triptych for the Children of War).* This was launched on the first day of the festival and continued until early January. A sensitive and beautiful installation involving multiple turntables, it drew its inspiration from Schaefer's Polish heritage and the World War II system of broadcasting pre-coded musical recordings, many of them Polish folk tunes, to transmit vital messages to the Polish underground (see the picutre and further description on pages 264–65). In one of the smaller galleries an installation called *Ha, Ha!*

Every Day is a Good Day *in
Huddersfield Art Gallery.*
PHOTO: BRIAN SLATER

Your Mushrooms Have Gone generated bio-electric sounds from live locally grown mushrooms. The following year saw another audio installation by the artist James Webb, and, in a second gallery, a documentary exhibition about the Dutch composer and theatre maker Dick Raaijmakers, one of the founders of electronic music.

Every Day is a Good Day

The arrival in 2010 of an exhibition of John Cage's visual art, twenty-one years after Cage himself had attended the festival, revived cherished memories. The Japanese Zen Buddhist 'Nichi, nichi kore ko niche' – meaning 'every day is a good day' (or 'every day is a beautiful day') – was one of Cage's favourite sayings, encapsulating that optimism and delight in the

world that was one of his most inspiring characteristics. The exhibition, taking *Every Day is a Good Day* as its title, had been conceived by the British artist Jeremy Millar, and organised by Hayward Touring in collaboration with the BALTIC Centre for Contemporary Art in Gateshead and the John Cage Trust in New York.

Cage was no mean artist. Leading New York artists were his close frends. The work he made after being invited to Crown Point Press in 1977, and to Mountain Lake in Virginia in the 1980s, is technically and conceptually assured, and unmistakeably distinctive. It has an unfettered innocence, yet a sense of spiritual harmony and – for work that is fundamentally abstract – a surprising philosophical and emotional depth. It also embodies a paradox. For, despite the use of chance to determine, for

*The artist Colin Rose
looking at one of the
Cage exhibits.*
PHOTO: BRIAN SLATER

instance, the position, size and number of circles and rectangles, or shades of colour and texture, the concept of each work involves personal choice. In 1987, for example, Cage made twelve similar plates, each printed with a unique mixture of colours: hues, however, that all exist in smoke, whilst real smoke was used as an acid 'resist' when the plates were etched. These were artistic decisions, and were followed by another when, two years later, Cage recalled the plates, which he thought looked too like wallpaper, and added black rectangles along the lower edge of each impression. The scattering of the rectangles was determined by chance; but adding them only to the lower part of each etching was a considered choice.[10]

The exhibition included quotations from Cage, and videos reflecting his work and attitudes as a composer. The works of art were hung according to chance procedures, and, in each gallery on the tour, were taken down and rehung several times. In Huddersfield after the final rehanging, many seemed to have migrated to the peripheries, leaving large areas of empty wall. I thought I had become familiar with the work, but the rehanging felt refreshingly like a first encounter.

Alongside the exhibition were discussions and live performances. Most memorably, on the day following the launch, Philip Thomas gave a twelve-hour performance of Cage's *Electronic Music for Piano* (1964) ending at midnight, which the public could drop in and out of whenever they pleased, moving around the galleries, sitting or lying on the floor. 'For the listener, or I should say the viewer,' Philip explained, 'I would hope that I am colouring their experience of the art. In some ways it will impact upon their perception of the visual art; and, likewise, the art itself will in some ways reflect upon their perception of the music. Like John Cage and Merce Cunningham's music and dance performances, the two things coexist: they go on at the same time, and seeing one without the other is a different experience from seeing the two together.'[11]

Since the early 1980s, all the co-promotions with Huddersfield Art Gallery had been in collaboration with its director Robert Hall. Robert retired in 2011 and, due to local government cuts, he is not be replaced.

Industrial environments

Talking with Annette Morreau in the early 1980s, she urged me to visit Musica, the most prestigious contemporary music festival in France, held each autumn in Strasbourg. It was good advice. In September 1986, my wife and I drove with our three children to Alsace, where we rented a *gîte*, explored the countryside by day and, without the children, drove into Strasbourg each evening for the festival. With a budget many times greater than any British equivalent, Musica did nothing by halves. That year Boulez was featured throughout its three-week duration. Bussotti's opera-ballet *Le Racine* was staged at the Théâtre Municipal, and Bernd Alois Zimmermann's *Requiem pour un jeune poète,* with its huge resources including choruses from Cologne, Hamburg and Vienna, performed in the Palais de Congrès. Of particular interest was Musica's use of non-standard venues. We heard Electric Phoenix perform *Stimmung* on a floating podium in the art nouveau swimming baths, and Edmund Meisel's score for Eisenstein's *Battleship Potemkin* played by the Junge Deutsche Philharmonie before an audience of a thousand in front of a huge screen in the Central Electricity Generating Station. A structure to support the orchestra and audience had been erected over one of the turbines, beside which ten or more turbines ranged the full extent of a hall at least as vast as that in Tate Modern. There were many French premieres, but Musica did not shoulder the full cost. The Zimmermann, for example, was produced and largely funded by Westdeutscher Rundfunk in Cologne. Similar partnerships with radio orchestras enrich the programmes of Ars Musica in Brussels and Ultima in Oslo. It was a model I cited in discussions with the BBC Philharmonic – but to no effect.

The second Musica in 1983 had been launched with *Train musica FNAC,* a trip around the region by special train accompanied by the Groupe Alsace Percussion. On another occasion the audience travelled by Wagons-Lits to Colmar for a concert in the Mulhouse-Dornach Railway Museum. Some events at Musica '87 took place in a special tent erected in the Parc de l'Orangerie, its buildings, sculptures and glades imaginatively lit by the light artist, Yann Kersalé. Ten years later the director of Musica, Jean-Dominique Marco, solved the problem of co-promoting a Swiss production of Kagel's opera *Aus Deutschland* by transporting the whole audience to Basle, again by special train. It would have cost much more to bring Herbert Wernicke's production to Strasbourg, with its indulgent stage set including numerous grand pianos.

Impressed, I wondered what industrial or other unusual indoor environments might exist in or around Huddersfield; but I could find none. In South Yorkshire there were disused steel works with cavernous empty sheds. Huddersfield's old woollen mills had multiple floors, low ceilings and forests of pillars to support long-departed looms. Few of these buildings remained, and those which did were either in use, too derelict, or about to be demolished. Graham McKenzie had better luck – or greater persistence – when he found the relatively modern Bates Mill Blending Shed, redesignated as an event space. To try it out he programmed a performance by the Reykjavik-based artists' collective Kitchen Motors, on tour in 2006 with the Contemporary Music Network, for whose enveloping wash of amplified sound, fuzzy film, clouds of dry ice, and roving beams of light accompanying drifting ambient harmonies, the Blending Shed was – in name and ambience – splendidly appropriate.

At the time of my retirement, a more sophisticated conversion was taking place at Brooke's Mill Armitage Bridge, where the former wool spinning sheds were being transformed into the North Light Gallery. Although spacious and attractive, the gallery was initially closed during the winter, but when this changed with adequate heating installed, Graham presented occasional events there.

Excursions

In 1991 Robert Saxton's opera *Caritas* had its world premiere in Wakefield's Grand Theatre and Opera House. This was the first co-commission between the festival and Opera North and, as in Strasbourg, special buses took the audience to the three performances. As a curtain-raiser to the 1993 festival, an excursion was organised in collaboration with Opera North to its production of Michael Berkeley's opera *Baa Baa Black Sheep* in Leeds. A few days later, a coach took festivalgoers to the Media Museum in Bradford, to see Godfrey Reggio's film, *Koyaanisqatsi,* where Philip Glass's music would benefit from the auditorium's superior sound system. In 1994 there was a morning expedition to Yorkshire Sculpture Park for a guided tour of the large Henry Moore sculptures, and another expedition took place to the park in 1998. In 2010 some intrepid festival supporters boarded

The audience at a performance of Cure *re-emerge into the street. (see pages 202–3)*
PHOTO: PAUL HERRMANN

an early bus for a dawn performance of Cage's *Score (40 Drawings by Thoreau) and 23 parts...* in the Sculpture Park's James Tyrell deer shelter.

Such excursions were relatively rare. The most unusual was to Dean Clough, Halifax, during the 2000 festival. This sprawling nineteenth-century mill colossus had housed the largest carpet manufacturer in the world. After the carpet factory closed, it was purchased by the pianist and entrepreneur Ernest Hall, and its regeneration as a powerhouse for the arts, design, education and small businesses had been widely acclaimed. I had long admired Sir Ernest's utopian vision and the refreshing inventiveness of the two theatre companies based there – Northern Broadsides and IOU, whose *The Sleep of Reason* had been created for the 1983 festival (see pages 22–23), long before the company relocated to Dean Clough. In 1987 the festival had presented a more conventional production with, unusually for IOU, an extensive text. Twelve years later I was approached about a new project being developed at other venues and festivals – and evidently ambitious. The complete piece, called *Cure,* would be ready in 2000, and the

suggestion was to launch it in association with the festival.

Three things commended the proposal: my admiration for IOU, that the festival would not have to finance the production, and that it would take place at Dean Clough. Nine storeys high, stretching for two-thirds of a mile, the mills of Dean Clough stand spectacularly at the bottom of a steep valley. In the cavernous cellars below the viaduct that once spanned the ravine is a unique auditorium – as much dungeon as theatre. Above it, art galleries, studios, shop and restaurant entice the visitor. We agreed that *Cure* would have its world premiere during the festival, which would include two performances, although IOU would give many further performances in the following weeks.

Special buses took the festival audience to Halifax. On arrival the public assembled in a shed to find a wedding reception in progress, although going bizarrely awry, until a grotesquely pulsating giant leech entered scarily from the street through the double doors. The audience was led away from this Kafkaesque apparition, and descended stone steps into the

Four scenes in Cure
PHOTOS: IOU

One of Barry Russell's Pub Operas performed in the Head of Steam real-ale pub.
PHOTO: PAUL HERRMANN

passages below. Here they followed signs through dimly lit cellars, and were confronted by 'a labyrinth of quack remedies and patent diseases, inhabited by mendicant patients and impatient medics', to quote *The Guardian's* Alfred Hickling. Elsewhere, they were lured by 'curative contraptions... from the patient-frying, bicycle-driven scanning device to a ward full of swinging, singing colostomy bags'. In the 'dungeon' theatre they witnessed an operation performed on a recalcitrant patient. Guided from the scene, they re-emerged in a cobbled street, beside which stood the hut depicted on the festival brochure, by night still engulfed in flames. Lou Glandfield's music added a 'delirious soundscape' part pre-recorded, part performed live – 'a thing of forlorn, fractured beauty' wrote Hickling.[12]

It was left to Graham McKenzie to schedule the festival's first train trip in 2010, with Apartment House and the Edges Ensemble performing on board. Curated by Alvin Curran, the idea stemmed from a musical train ride which Cage had devised between Bologna and Porretta in 1978, and which Curran himself revived thirty years later. In Huddersfield the weather was colder. Northern Trains are hardly Wagons-Lits. But the destination was consoling, for Stalybridge Station boasts one of the best real ale pubs in the country, cosy, friendly and full of railway memorabilia.

Clubs and pubs

In 1990 I was looking for an interesting venue (ideally with marine associations) in which to mount Gavin Bryars's *The Sinking of the Titanic*. Someone suggested the Flicks Nightclub in Northumberland Street, and I went to inspect it. Originally a woollen warehouse, the building had been converted into the Princess cinema in 1923, where I had occasionally seen films. The nightclub which succeeded retained the auditorium's three levels, but removed the seats and balustrades, replacing these with steel posts and wire hawsers surmounted by wooden rails. With companion-way-like steps connecting gallery, balcony and stalls, and walls and ceiling painted deep blue, one could imagine being on board a liner. Where the screen had been was a large video wall, and I immediately wondered how we could employ it. Colleagues in the drama department took up the challenge and, during the autumn term, their students created a compelling multi-screen video montage using archive film and recent underwater footage to accompany the performance.

Students from the music department gave a poised interpretation of the score, retaining their composure as the public squeezed past them. I had scheduled the event for an afternoon, and the almost mythical status of the music and its subject matter evidently crossed barriers. To my surprise, there were people who had travelled from as far away as South Wales specifically to hear it. David Fanning deemed the event 'a flop',[13] but it was a minority view. Gavin Bryars himself thought the video a 'superb visual creation'. The bar marketed a 'Titanic cocktail' (advisedly without ice) and, pleased with the success, Gavin set up a tab for the students who had been involved. 'It cost me!' he remarked later, 'It was the beginning of the slide…!' I would like to have used the venue for other events, but the nightclub soon closed, and for a decade the building was used for bingo. When this went out of fashion there were further years of inactivity, until the former cinema was reborn as a casino in October 2010, stylishly refurbished and with the dome in the centre of the ceiling and the sweeping balcony restored.

In 1999 The Head of Steam real-ale pub adjacent to Huddersfield Station was the setting for Barry Russell's effectively funny cabaret-style *Pub Operas*. The following year the hard-edged amplified ensemble [rout] played in Bar & Club Non nearby. My successor artistic directors were bolder in placing events in nightclubs and the occasional pub. In 2002, Bar & Club Non was used again by Susanna Eastburn for a late-night performance given by the Apollo Saxophone Quartet, with music composed and remixed by my former student, Matthew Wright.[14] From his arrival in 2006, Graham demonstrated his intention of broadening the festival's reach by scheduling two events in clubs, both during weekend afternoons. In a six-hour programme at Livingstones, opposite the university campus, sixteen works – all more-or-

less 'experimental' – were performed by members of [rout], both on the dance floor and in a room above, where *Walk* by Michael Parsons was shown on film. A week later, a four-hour 'Improvised Installation', featuring Rhodri Davies, David Toop and Lee Patterson, took place in Tokyo, the bar and club now occupying Huddersfield's early nineteenth-century Court House – the building which it was once hoped might become a national poetry centre. Ticket-holders could drop in and out of both events at any point between performances. But clubs are not easy environments in which to perform new music, and none have been used in recent years.

Fringe and Festival of Light

As early as 1982 a fringe was mooted, but nothing came of it until 1987, when Kirklees Leisure Services decided to organise a five-day programme of street entertainment and jazz, gospel and African music, in pubs, clubs and the Hudawi Centre. It made a limited impact and did not long survive, although a fringe of sorts intermittently resurfaced, activated by other parties. In 1997 there was a more vigorous attempt to launch a 'Huddersfield Contemporary Music Festival Fringe' with money raised from the local authority, sponsors and the National Lottery. We were concerned about the competition for funds and venues, an apparent hijacking of the festival's name, and the potential confusion of brands. A joint meeting was held and dividing lines were agreed. It resulted in a week-long programme at the Media Centre calling itself 'Huddersfield Fringe '97', and featuring band performances, DJ evenings, a theatre collaboration with the Huddersfield drug and alcohol agency, plus workshops covering the design of music journals, CDs and albums. This was its only manifestation. Because the main festival encompassed jazz, theatre, visual media, street entertainers, and had presented out of doors and in pubs and clubs, it was difficult for a fringe to establish a separate identity, and there was little public interest.

In 2006 Kirklees Council followed the example of other towns and cities by installing an ice-skating rink on the piazza for the Christmas season. Its inauguration coincided with the switching on of the seasonal street illuminations and an existing annual Festival of Light centred

The Festival Hub.
PHOTO: BRIAN SLATER

on St George's Square, also promoted by the council and timed to mark the opening of the Contemporary Music Festival. The first Festival of Light, on 18 November 2004, began with a musical set-piece devised by Barry Russell as a festival outreach project, with instrumentalists and a choir performing in front of the station, and 'operatic' singers leaning out of the upper windows of the George Hotel and Britannia Buildings. A large crowd watched this and the associated fireworks, but the sequence was over-long.

In subsequent years the Festival of Light has engaged increasingly impressive international street theatre professionals, some producing their own music. In 2005 the spectacle was created by the Spanish company, Xarxa Theatre, in the style of a Catalan *correfoc*. In 2006 the French aerial theatre, Transe Express, presented *Maudits Sonnants,* with choreographed trapeze artists and instrumentalists hanging from a giant mobile hundreds of feet above the spectators, in a performance of surprising poise and gracefulness. By now the Festival of Light had become the largest street theatre event in Yorkshire, seen by an audience of around 15,000. On this occasion the council used it as a platform for its promotion of Huddersfield as 'one of Britain's top twenty creative towns'; and, as the Contemporary Music Festival was regarded as a driver of the renaissance, Graham was asked to contribute an account of its activities and took the opportunity to stress the festival's regional and wider partnerships.

But the simultaneous scheduling of the 'Nights of Fire and Light', with an international music

festival at the leading edge of innovation became harder to reconcile. Anticipating an ever larger audience, the Festival of Light in 2008 spread over two evenings: the very Friday and Saturday on which the Contemporary Music Festival had annually launched its programme. Meanwhile, to mark a new partnership with the British Council, the Contemporary Music Festival was welcoming international guests, as well as hosting a meeting of Reséau Varèse, the consortium of European new music promoters to which Huddersfield belongs. Its priority was to present concerts of the highest standard, which the guests would attend.

Accepting that the coincidence of dates was insensitive, the Festival of Light moved into December, and in 2010 mounted its biggest programme yet, seen by 25,000 people. An expenditure of around £35,000 reflected the popularity of the outdoor spectacle, and of an art form with a pedigree going back centuries, via carnival processions, masks, mystery plays and religious rituals, to the 'triumphs' of the Caesars.

Festival Hub

Any festival needs a central meeting place, but it was not easy to find an ideal location. During the first fourteen years, for a nominal charge, visitors were given temporary membership of the polytechnic staff common room. But it did not solve the problem of where to find hot food on a cold, wet Sunday. When the common room was requisitioned for an extension to the library, the club moved to the George Hotel and, the following year, to the Union Bank pub in the centre of town. Two years later it moved again, to the first floor of the bistro bar at the Lawrence Batley Theatre. This was comfortable and convenient, but its limited kitchen capacity could not cope with the influx of people between events. Three years later, the idea of a club was abandoned, and the programme book merely listed available places to find food and refreshments, including the theatre.

In 2002 Susanna Eastburn had a covered performance platform erected on the piazza, where young players and ensembles contributed a daily series of free performances. The following year a much larger enclosed and heated marquee replaced it, becoming a Festival Hub in the heart of the town. The Hub was

The Natural Theatre Company building a steam sound sculpture in the piazza in 1989.
PHOTO: SELWYN GREEN

soon providing hot food, tastefully prepared by the university's hospitality management students, and served with commendable speed in the short period between performances. It was popular with festivalgoers, whether to chat over drinks, find information, buy CDs, books and scores from Forsyth's music shop, or listen to discussions. Here what Susanna christened Hub Shorts provided a platform for emerging and less established performers.

But the Hub failed in its aim of attracting the general public and improving awareness of the festival in the centre of town. Like any marquee – especially one with doors (necessarily closed in November) – it could not avoid the impression of hosting a private function. The marquee was expensive to provide, and when Graham McKenzie arrived, facing an inherited deficit and a very restricted budget, the functions of the hub returned to the Lawrence Batley Theatre. Here a tented annexe was erected in the courtyard, and caterers engaged. This too was a short-lived solution. After the university's Creative Arts Building opened, and its atrium was equipped with a coffee bar and comfortable chairs, this became an agreeable forum for informal gatherings and receptions, for the music shop and an information desk – a bright, warm environment for socialising and, indeed, for small-scale performances.

12 *Education and outreach*

I was engaged in education long before becoming a festival director, initially teaching gifted young instrumentalists and singers O and A-level music, then degree students and postgraduates, some of them talented composers. A primary focus was technique. But an equal concern was to fuel appetites for music across a broad spectrum, in a spirit of adventurous curiosity, openness and shared insights. When the contemporary music festival began, emerging as it did from the music department, it seemed self-evidently to be an educational resource. Yet it took a few years of uncertain progress and initially lukewarm response before that potential was realised. Operating on a shoestring budget with little to spend on marketing, I was more concerned to ensure that the organisation ran smoothly than to coerce students. Keith Potter noted their minimal presence in 1978, and, after attending four of the first six festivals, reported that student attendance was still 'not as strong as I feel it should be'.[1] There needed to be a more collaborative effort among the music department staff. There was also the issue of defusing the bogeyman perception of contemporary music.

In 1978, when the first festival took place, education posts existed in theatre, dance and the visual arts. There were none attached to music performing organisations. Perhaps they were considered unnecessary, given the strength of music teaching within schools, where full-time specialist staff were supported by networks of peripatetic instrumental teachers, youth orchestras, choirs and ensembles, enabling millions of young people to experience music through performing it. I have already cited Leicestershire as a model, whose extensive schools music provision was established in

the postwar years by its music advisor, Eric Pinkett, and whose top-of-the-pyramid symphony orchestra, under Pinkett's successor Peter Fletcher, regularly programmed such twentieth-century greats as Ives, Messiaen, Tippett, Carter and Xenakis. In the West Riding of Yorkshire between 1945 and 1974, educational policy stemmed from its far-sighted chief education officer, Alec Clegg (knighted in 1965). Clegg believed that creativity was latent in everybody, and inspired many to take up music and the arts, among whom was the Barnsley poet, Ian McMillan, who acknowledges Clegg's influence on his becoming a writer. Clegg's vision of the centrality of the arts in education led to the establishment of Bretton Hall College specifically to train teachers of music, art and drama.

It was in such a climate that, in 1961, I took up my post in Huddersfield. Around the same time (1959–62), Peter Maxwell Davies was the charismatic young director of music at Cirencester Grammar School. The music he wrote there, the composition and performance activities he encouraged, and the catalytic impact of such a magnetic personality working in a school, demonstrated that young people can discover a natural affinity with new music: a cause to which Davies has devoted much of his life. It is a belief predicated on the conviction that they can and should learn musical notation, and that doing so leads not only to musical, but to wider educational achievement.[2] Doubtless, music teaching in some schools was dull and regimented. But there were others refreshing its methodology and stimulating creativity, such as John Paynter (1931–2010), whose innovative approach sprung from his own years of experience teaching music in primary and secondary schools.

A harp student performing with others from the RNCM and University of Huddersfield at the debut concert of Rhodri Davies's harp ensemble 'Branches' in 2007.
PHOTO: BRIAN SLATER

Paynter published his influential book, *Sound and Silence: Classroom Projects in Creative Music,* co-written with Peter Aston, in 1970.[3] Four years later the younger Peter Wiegold founded one of the first ensembles – appropriately named Gemini – dedicated to the twin pursuits of performance and education. When Wiegold was appointed visiting composer at the Arnolfini Gallery in Bristol in 1976, he and Gemini pioneered exploratory workshops for school, college and adult groups, gradually formulating the philosophy that musical understanding is best achieved through a balance between active participation and formal concerts.

At the second Huddersfield festival in 1979 Gemini were, in effect, 'in residence': workshopping new compositions for the Young Composers' Competition, performing a concert that ended with *Pierrot Lunaire* sung in English, and holding an improvisation day for primary school children led by Wiegold. This took place in Banney Royd Teachers' Centre, a Grade 1 listed art nouveau former mill-owner's residence belonging to the local education authority, whose dignified oak-panelled interior had rooms ideal for the purpose. Three years later David Bedford led creative workshops there for young and older children, then attended rehearsals in St Paul's by the Polytechnic Symphonic Wind Band for its first performance of his *Sun Paints Rainbows on the Vast Waves.* This was the festival's first commission: an exhilarating, effective piece which band members evidently enjoyed, and which was frequently revived. Regrettably, the education authority sold Banney Royd during the financial cuts of the mid 1980s.

People and participation

Apart from these two days of creative workshops, the first six festivals contained no special provision for schools, although from 1981 each secondary school received a poster pack and offers of cheap group admission. Some of their staff had been music department students, and so were well equipped to introduce their pupils to twentieth-century music. Adult festivalgoers could extend their understanding through talks, seminars, masterclasses, films, a jazz workshop, introductions to concerts and discussions with composers. Efforts – by now more successful –

to enthuse music students and my own lack of time delayed the development of a wider outreach programme. But the example of Bedford, Davies, Paynter, Gordon Crosse and, of course, Benjamin Britten, allied to my own inclination, prompted something bolder. The board thought so too, notably Arthur Jacobs, head of the polytechnic music department. When I presented my plans for 1984, he expressed concern that it was 'more distanced from the layman than in previous years' and urged 'more emphasis on community-based events and on popular pieces'.[4] Other members of the board endorsed his view that the festival

'Uncle Jambo's Pendular Vibrations': an electronic music workshop in the Hudawi Centre in 1984.
PHOTOS: KEITH GLOSSOP

should be 'more accessible to the general public'. One event clearly would *not* be. It was the revival by the BBC Symphony Orchestra of Davies's *Worldes Blis* which (as described in Chapter 3) had, at its first performance, famously alienated most of the audience. But with many of his other compositions, designed for young performers, no one was a more gifted pied piper than Max himself.

As it happened, I was already planning a concert to involve Max and hundreds of school pupils, which would, I hoped, also engage their families. Around it I began to assemble a parallel festival, different from but overlapping the professional programme. Advertised on one side of an enlarged publicity leaflet, it was headed: *PEOPLE AND PARTICIPATION: Five days of participatory and educational events created within the community* (see the illustration on page 240). The reverse announced seven days of international concerts. Opening the folded leaflet, either side could appear first. Although they shared venues and both charged for admission, one was emphatically home grown. Like many other people, I was dismayed by the implications of Margaret Thatcher's landslide re-election in 1983 and her government's decimation of schools music services. So I was particularly pleased when David Cairns, in a long *Sunday Times* review, chose to write about the 'participatory and educational events', rather than the professional programme:

In spite of weather like the end of the world, Huddersfield this past week has been a cheering place for a musician to be. The annual Festival of Contemporary Music... is a model of bold planning and clever use of limited resources which in a few years has raised itself to international status while remaining rooted in the locality... Huddersfield is not a large or very wealthy town; but the Festival's response to a time of financial stringency and general uncertainty and depression in the arts has been actually to extend its activities, and strengthen its links with the community.

As elsewhere, this educational 'outreach' represents just a beginning. But it is, or rather it could be, a beginning pregnant with possibilities, and an act of faith with potential enriching and therapeutic consequences for our whole society. The effect of these few days in Huddersfield has been to fill me with optimism for the future, perhaps against reason. It is a fact that more and more composers and musicians are becoming aware of their responsibility to society, of what they can do to better it. Yet the irony of the present situation is that brutal and crassly shortsighted education cuts are threatening music at the moment when we are coming to understand the incalculable good it is capable of doing.[5]

What Cairns had witnessed included a series of free workshops in electronic music and video imaging, strategically sited in the Hudawi Community Centre at the heart of the Afro-Caribbean community. Devised by Edward Williams, they were marketed baring the curious title: 'Uncle Jambo's Pendular Vibrations (The Electron Ice Dream Pleasure Drome)'. On another day Cairns observed a course in warm-up games, improvisation and 'co-operative' composition for children and teachers led by Gemini. He also attended four home-grown concerts. The first, mainly performed by students, featured compositions by polytechnic undergraduates and a recent graduate, Nick Redfern (one of my own pupils), who had won the wind quintet category of the Young Composers' Competition in 1983. Among the undergraduates was David Williams, appropriately for the 1984 festival a composer of music theatre, to which he brought an endearingly quirky imagination. The following lunchtime, the polytechnic's 'formidable Brass Band' (as Cairns described it) performed Tippett's *Festal Brass with Blues,* Globokar's theatrically peripatetic *La Tromba è Mobile,* and a 'fine account' of Birtwistle's *Grimethorpe Aria* (see the photo on page 8). Later that afternoon the department orchestra played Nigel Osborne's *Sinfonia No 2,* following an open rehearsal with the composer. Both concerts were conducted by Barrie Webb, who had directed his professional Northern New Music Players (subsequently renamed Firebird) at previous festivals, and performed as solo trombonist. This was the first of many occasions when Barrie conducted departmental ensembles in a succession of impressive festival appearances.

Lectures were given by Nigel Osborne on music theatre, and by Maxwell Davies on 'The Composer and the Community' – who, as Cairns reported,

talked in fascinating detail of his experiences at Cirencester in the late 1950s and his discovery of the natural inventiveness innate in nine out of ten people, but often inhibited by rigid, unimaginative teaching attitudes and methods – a musicality which, once released and harnessed had improved, sometimes dramatically, the pupils' work in other subjects as well as providing a crucial liberating discipline from which the whole personality benefits.

No transcript exists, but Cairns's reference to musicality 'released and harnessed', and to the notion of a 'liberating discipline', are food for thought.

A Schools Concert of Music Theatre

The schools concert, attended by Maxwell Davies and David Cairns, attracted the first capacity audience at any event solely promoted by the festival in Huddersfield Town Hall. So many were the public and few the stewards, with more people than seats and over 300 young performers moving on and off stage and among the public, I watched with a mixture of delight and slight apprehension. But to see Max beaming down from the front row of the balcony was reassuring. His *Songs of Hoy* were sung and played by pupils from five junior schools and Honley High School, rehearsed and conducted by the Kirklees music adviser, Muriel Gill. To accompany them, students from Fartown High School provided an effective dance and mime, choreographed by their tutor Mary Oldroyd. After extensive re-arrangements, there followed Barry Russell's *Encounter,* composed while he was assistant at Holmfirth

High School, and performed by its school orchestra, two off-stage brass groups and a brass brand entering from the rear of the hall: in all some 110 players. Alan Simmons, who directed this Ivesian jamboree – a 'major civil engineering project' as he described rehearsals – later succeeded Muriel Gill as music advisor.

Albert in F, the slick and hilarious finale, was sung and acted by pupils of St. James's School, Almondbury. It had been composed and was conducted by the school's head of music, James Morgan, another department of music graduate, and the first to be awarded a first class degree. Jim had conceived *Albert in F* as 'a musical seaside portrait, drawing on music-hall tradition in both staging and scoring, with jokes both visual and musical: great fun to perform and, we hope, to watch'.[6] Racy and entertaining, the performance was also noteworthy for the professionalism and exuberance of its staging. Liz Heywood, who directed, later moved to Huddersfield New College, where she joined Roger Scaife in running a fine performing arts department with which the festival enjoyed many collaborations, some presented in its own Boilerhouse Arts Centre. Tim Garbutt, playing 'Pa' in *Albert in F,* would fourteen years later become the festival's technical and then production manager, an increasingly complex and crucial role which he still holds, now in partnership with Adam Long.

Peter Maxwell Davies at a rehearsal of his Songs of Hoy *in 1984.*
PHOTO: YORKSHIRE POST

There was no education officer to credit with overall management. The festival did not have one; indeed, it had only appointed its first part-time administrator one year before. Muriel Gill and staff in the schools organised rehearsals and transport. Edward Wilson himself arranged the workshops in electronic sound transformation, video imaging and computer graphics, in collaboration with the Huddersfield-based video artist Brian Johnson, and also devised a concert with live musicians involving both technologies.

'People and Participation' had made its point. In the years that followed, I preferred to integrate such events into the general programme. In 1985 performances by student ensembles from seven different institutions opened and closed the festival. But from 1988, when the festival first spread over two weekends, performances by young musicians and educational workshops took place throughout. Apart from a useful contribution to the main programme, they showcased good work and proclaimed its importance.

The 1985 festival opened with a further lunchtime concert of works composed and played by existing and recent students. That evening in St Paul's, string players from Bretton Hall College, Chetham's School of Music, the Huddersfield music department and local junior schools performed music by Bartók, Tippett, Berio (the UK premiere of his *Duetti*) and a composition of my own (see page 30). The final concert was given in the town hall also entirely by students: on this occasion four wind bands from Huddersfield Polytechnic, the Royal Northern College of Music, Huddersfield Technical College and Kirklees Schools Music Service. It concluded with the UK premiere of Berio's *Accordo* and Khachaturian's *Battle of Stalingrad,* in which all the bands united (see Robert Cockroft's description also on page 30).

The changing fortunes of music education

In 1983 the London Sinfonietta became the first music ensemble or orchestra to appoint a full-time education organiser. That it happened as the Conservative government's Education Act of 1981 became law, on 1 April 1983, appears to have been coincidental; although the government's measures were widely criticised for damaging schools music services. In practice the act reversed section 53 of the Education Act

1944, which had empowered schools to provide instrumental tuition, as well as lessons in music theory, without charging their pupils. Many initiatives sprang up to counter the effect of these developments, and in the wake of Margaret Thatcher's famous remark, 'There is no such thing as society'.[7] Whatever she meant by it, as projects began to be located in inner cities and prisons they had a social as well as a musical purpose. Some people's lives were changed. Others were introduced to new cultural experiences and discovered talents they hadn't known they possessed.

Gillian Moore, appointed to the Sinfonietta post, quickly made her mark, and in 1986 we got in touch to explore the possibility of an educational project in Huddersfield. As it turned out, the scheme mapped out continued for three autumns, each devoted to composition but with different outcomes. The first was instrumental involving 120 pupils in seven secondary schools; the second, vocal, involving Huddersfield Technical College and fourteen schools (some of them continuing from the first year); the third, theatrical, involving six schools. What was remarkable was not only the quality of the compositional models – in concerts by the Sinfonietta, Electric Phoenix and Opera Factory – and of the results, but that the animateurs were composers and performers of the highest professional standing.

The quality of pupils' compositions was evident from year one, when the 120 participants came together in St Paul's to perform their own pieces both individually and in groups. The composer Nigel Osborne, with Antony Pay (clarinet) and David Hockings (percussion), all of whom had visited the schools, were present to comment, encourage, and take part in the performances. It was a rich harvest, remarkable for the variety and freshness of the ideas, their enterprise and accomplishment. For the music critic of the *Yorkshire Post,* this was 'among the most exciting, encouraging and moving festival events one can recall'.[8] In the second year Terry Edwards and Trevor Wishart introduced vocal composition with electronics, linked to the concert by Electric Phoenix. The third focused on music theatre, guided by the producer Stephen Langridge, Mary King and other members of London Sinfonietta Opera Factory whose performances of Berio, Beckett, Berberian, Weir and Saariaho alternated with the students' own creations.

Following the precedent of the previous two years, the 1986 festival contained another concert performed entirely by young musicians, apart from its two conductors and the pianist Keith Swallow, soloist in Lutosławski's *Paganini Variations* with Kirklees Youth Orchestra. I had asked Lutosławski if he would unearth some of the unpublished children's songs with small orchestra that he had written in Poland in the early 1950s, after the communists banned his first symphony and composing functional music for the radio was his only source of income. With the help of a Polish friend I made English translations, and these charming miniatures were given their first ever concert performance by children from four Kirklees junior schools, accompanied by the Polytechnic Twentieth Century Ensemble.

A philosophy of engagement

The third stage of the Sinfonietta scheme took place alongside three other mind-stretching experiences, all described in earlier chapters. Uniquely inspiring for those who took part was the performance of Stockhausen's *Sternklang* prepared by Peter Britten, and mentored during the final rehearsals by Stockhausen himself. Its privileged participants came from the Guildhall

School of Music and Drama, City University, Cambridgeshire College of Arts and Technology and Huddersfield Polytechnic (see pages 110–11). In a similar spirit, but actually under the stars, was the Oriental Lantern Procession beside Huddersfield Narrow Canal, created by primary school children with the help of the Satellites, and accompanied by the Cragg Vale Gamelan (see pages 193–94). The most testing, technically and in terms of ensemble, was a concert containing UK premieres of Andriessen's *Symphonies of the Netherlands* played by Kirklees Youth Wind Orchestra, his *De Stijl* performed by the Polytechnic Twentieth Century Ensemble with the dancer/narrator Beppie Blankert, and Murray Schafer's *Threnody,* in which the Polytechnic Orchestra and Technical College Choir were joined by narrators from Wooldale Junior School and Huddersfield New College (see pages 41–42).

Neither *De Stijl* nor *Threnody* had been composed for students, but Andriessen and Schafer oversaw the final rehearsals, and their presence and attention to detail both challenged and inspired. This concert took place on a Saturday evening in the town hall; for, as I have already indicated, I believed that the achievements of young musicians in such important work deserved to be heard at prime time by a paying audience. Educationalists,

Terry Edwards leads participants in a composition workshop involving voices and electronics.
PHOTO: YORKSHIRE POST

Poster designed by a student in the School of Art.

more concerned with nurturing individual creativity, may regard such disciplined music-making as too authoritarian. I would argue that to immerse oneself in another person's artistic vision can also be liberating, when it extends intellectual and emotional experience. There are the triple achievements of being able to read musical notation, of being able to master unfamiliar situations and techniques, and of contributing confidently to a complex collective whole. To strive together towards a shared goal can be spiritually elevating and awaken deeper currents. High-flying professionals spend their lives realising ideas conceived by other people, sometimes in dauntingly prescriptive detail. The Arditti String Quartet have made a point of working closely with composers in order to realise faithfully the creator's vision. If this is the lifestyle of professional musicians, why should it not also be an aspiration for the less advanced?

This was the philosophy pursued by CoMA (Contemporary Music-Making for Amateurs), founded five years later in 1993 by Chris Shurety, with the aim of creating a specific new repertoire for adults, to be worked at intensively in a non-competitive context. Residencies and performances organised by CoMA took place during the 1995 and 1996 festivals, and again in 2004. Rehearsing with the composer helps to illuminate the ideas and mechanics of a piece. It may involve learning something relatively straightforward like Maxwell Davies's *Songs of Hoy*. It may be through performing work as challenging as *De Stijl* and *Sterklang*. It could be through playing alongside professionals in *Le Jongleur de Notre Dame*, or (as we shall encounter shortly) profoundly deaf students performing with a symphony orchestra. It could be the musicians of CoMA working with Michael Finnissy.

For young participants who had worked so assiduously, the performances delivered something profound and durable. I regarded such achievements more highly than the loosely constructed improvisation-based performances which occasionally happened in the new millennium, their game-playing approach not noticeably different from routines used in non-contemporary contexts. True, the former involved more advanced students, the latter mostly younger children who might not be learning a musical instrument. But I thought that all the festival's outreach activities should in some way address its more challenging

attributes, however tailored to age and experience. Some, of course, were not age-related. Those working with Xenakis's UPIC drawing computer in 1987 were of all ages and levels of experience, including students with learning difficulties. The performers in *Piano Phasing* in 2009 (see pages 227–28) were pianists aged from twelve upwards, including at least one in her seventies. If the more ambitious projects mostly involved secondary school, college level and older participants, it was because they were at an appropriate age to embrace the technical and aesthetic concepts specific to contemporary music.

Younger children lack prejudice and are naturally receptive. They enjoy making and building things, exploring sound, communicating, drawing and inventing their own notation. All these open the mind and develop aptitudes useful later. But I believe that nothing is so enabling and rewarding as learning to play an instrument and doing so in an ensemble. And these, unhappily, are no longer such widespread and classless activities as they were before the demise of free tuition.

At any age notation can be a barrier. But projects can be equally mind-stretching without a prescriptive score and the ability to play it. As Cage demonstrated, music can be made with anything – which does not mean, however, that 'anything goes'. In 1989 the composer's presence at the festival inspired a rewarding project at Huddersfield Technical College, in which students from HTC and New College were challenged to re-examine accepted norms and reach out conceptually within simple but clear parameters. Its subject was *Roaratorio,* Cage's great sonic portrait of *Finnegans Wake,* a centrepiece of that year's festival, performed in the town hall with Irish folk musicians, a sixteen-channel tape (a collage of sounds mentioned in the *Wake*) and Cage himself reading his mesostics derived from Joyce's text.

Roaratorio is a particular realisation of a template that can be used to produce a sound portrait of any literary text. Guided by Julia Winterson, a lecturer at the college, and by the composer and EMAS technologist Robert Worby, the students created their own version, informed by studying and discussing Cage's ideas, and by culling texts from the *Huddersfield Daily Examiner*. Their recorded soundscore amalgamated reggae, brass bands, the hum of textile mills and other sounds typical of the locality. The final rehearsal and performance were attended by Cage himself, 'a charismatic presence with a Zen-like stillness', looking on approvingly. His replies to subsequent questions, as Julia relates, were 'always economic – a mixture of wit, honesty and erudition – and were frequently interspersed with great burst of laughter. He was unpresumptuous yet iconic…, quietly private yet always open and accessible'. Julia's engaging account of this encounter appears in full in Appendix A (page 279). For Robert, as he later recalled, the opportunity to work with Cage 'changed my life … [and] abruptly halted a temporary career in pop music. I never regretted it. He was one of the most wonderful humans I have ever met.'[9]

The festival's first education co-ordinator

To pull these projects together I was now assisted by Anne Suggate. In the mid 1980s Anne had joined the volunteer front-of-house staff. In 1987 she was appointed the festival's first part-time administrative assistant, and a year later added to her brief the new role of educational co-ordinator. Having taught in a Kirklees school, she had useful contacts. When, in 1989, the administrator Kate Wright needed to reduce her hours, Anne took on fundraising as well as education. An early success was the sponsorship of Waterman Pens, which had a dedicated Huddersfield retailer and whose personnel were impressed to find that Anne already wrote with one of their pens. The following year the company was swallowed up by Gillette, and the sponsorship unfortunately ceased.

In 1989 Anne's main educational focus was to co-ordinate an electroacoustic composition project in eight secondary schools run by EMAS (the Electroacoustic Music Association of Great Britain). The project began with a training day for teachers, followed by school visits from Ian Dearden, Stephen Montague, Trevor Wishart and Robert Worby, and the finished compositions were diffused through a professional system in the town hall by the students themselves, under the guidance of Jonty Harrison and Roger Smalley. For several schools, this was their introduction to electroacoustic composition and resulted in

some schools purchasing their own equipment. So successful was the project that it led EMAS to found its own education division. Meanwhile, for the duration of the festival, the polytechnic's recently extended electroacoustic studios held open house, displaying three visiting systems: new IRCAM software, Durham University's Transputer Project and the latest equipment from the commercial company Roland. Visitors were invited to book personal demonstrations and gain hands-on experience. Interspersed were explanatory lectures and discussions, culminating in the remarkable interview between George Benjamin and Pierre Boulez, described earlier in the book and due to be published separately (see page 88).

In 1991 the Festival won a Sainsbury's Award for Arts Education for an imaginative performing arts proposal – one of only five chosen from around 300 applicants. To deliver it, Anne began working with six Kirklees secondary schools and colleges on a bold plan to integrate drama, dance, design, instrumental and electroacoustic music in a single production. In the early autumn, no less than seven animateurs arrived and fanned out into the schools to steer the project forward. They were from the MacLennan Dance Company, Major Road Theatre, and what had been EMAS (now renamed Sonic Arts Network), and faced the unusual challenge of integrating, and mediating between, three different disciplines. The final rehearsals and performance took place during the festival in the town hall.

Part of a performing arts project led by the MacLennan Dance Company, Major Road Theatre and Sonic Arts.
PHOTO: SELWYN GREEN

Hearing-impaired young people performing Stories from the Dreamtime *with English Northern Philharmonia in 1992.*
PHOTO: SELWYN GREEN

Working with deaf children

Another pioneering project derived in 1992 from a proposal made by Paul Whittaker. Despite being profoundly deaf from birth, Paul had become an accomplished pianist and organist, and had gained a music degree from Oxford. Early on he had decided to devote his energies to bringing music to hearing-impaired people. Founder of the national charity, Music and the Deaf, he also happened to live in Huddersfield. The charity had commissioned a work from David Bedford for deaf children to perform with a professional symphony orchestra. Its planned premiere in London had fallen through, and we gladly accepted Paul's suggestion that the festival should adopt it. Anne organised the participation of specialist schools in Birmingham, London, Derby, Boston Spa and Yorkshire, whose pupils commenced rehearsals months in advance, guided and inspired by Whittaker and Bedford. All of them came together at the start of the festival for a residential weekend in Huddersfield. At the start of the project, few could read music or had ever played an instrument. That they learnt to do so with such sustained concentration owed much to the dedication of their teachers.

Stories from the Dreamtime, based on aboriginal myths, was performed in a concert given by English Northern Philharmonia (the orchestra of Opera North) with Richard Stilgoe narrating, and signed by Peter Llewellyn-Jones. The participants' eight percussion groups were positioned behind and above the orchestra, each consisting of five players led by a professional percussionist, who guided their co-ordination

with the orchestra. On either side of the balcony, two larger groups of non-music-readers played pebbles, wind glasses and wind machines. Apart from the work's effectiveness in performance, and the thrill for the pupils of playing with an orchestra, *Stories from the Dreamtime* was an impressive realisation of Whittaker's mission to introduce deaf youngsters to an art form from which they probably expected to be excluded.

Differently heart-warming was 'Constructions', a project based on Cage's *Constructions,* in which children from six Kirklees junior schools built, composed for, and played their own instruments. Making instruments is a familiar school activity, but the input of the two leaders, Simon Limbrick and Kevin Renton – and his unusual collection of instruments – lifted it onto a high level. After the final workshop before a joint concert, the children sat on the floor in St Paul's, and the four percussionists of the Helios Quartet donned colourful costumes, moustaches and bulbous noses to play for them. The theatricality of their performance, and the delight of the children, can be seen in the photographs overleaf.

Bill Vince's projects

Both projects had been partly funded by the Prudential Award for Music, which the festival won in 1992. The following year Anne moved to Northumberland to work on a broad-based community song project, and Bill Vince became education officer, bringing with him the experience of having run schemes in South Yorkshire and his acquaintance with some gifted animateurs. During the next six years, Bill delivered more than twenty strongly differentiated and original projects. We worked closely in their planning, both of us believing that educational and outreach performances, whether by adults, young people, music students or amateurs, should, as far as possible, be accorded the same status in the schedule as those given by professionals. A general (although not rigid) premise was that they would stem from music programmed in the festival, one consequence being that we hoped participants would be better equipped to appreciate the professional work to which their own related.

Students privileged to perform for a distinguished composer might receive a personal endorsement. The Technical College and New College students had done so for Cage. We did not know whether Ligeti would come to the final performances of a project based on his

surrealist mini-operas *Aventures* and *Nouvelles Aventures* – but when he arrived one could sense the *frisson*. The participants were performing arts students from Dewsbury College, Huddersfield New College and the Technical College. The leaders were the stand-up comedian and storyteller John Mowat, the Huddersfield-born soprano Linda Hirst, about to perform in *Aventues* and *Nouvelles Aventures* that evening, and Malcolm Singer, one of Ligeti's former composition pupils. Between them they had led twenty-seven sessions.

For the afternoon performance in Venn Street Arts Centre, in which a paying audience were treated to a richly varied compendium of acting, gesture and movement, with voiced and unvoiced sounds devoid, as in the Ligeti models, of any recognisable words. The occasion was filmed for a promotional video, and asked on camera what he had thought of it, Ligeti replied:

BELOW AND RIGHT: Children watching the Helios percussion quartet performing Giorgio Battistelli's Heliopolis Primo in 1992. PHOTOS: SELWYN GREEN.

I like it very much… Such a lot of humour, understanding, and deeper levels. It had something to do with what I did in *Aventures* and *Nouvelles Aventures*, but there were different things. For me it was a bit long… but a lot of wonderful ideas. And personally I enjoyed the idea (which I never had) of the chords using bottles. Some of them have real acting talent. I wonder whether I could say thank you through the camera: 'Mm…hm mm hmm. Mm, and Györg..mm hm hmm. Mm not for hmm, but Ihm see it and mm like it hmm… somehow hhmmm…!'

And his impression of the festival?

What Richard Steinitz did is really wonderful: always bringing together a lot of such different good musicians. And [he] has dared to do things which are not sure. Most festivals only want big names, and things which they already know… I like the pluralism, and taking risks. Most of the people who organise festivals want to be sure that the public will like it. I like people who take things you don't know beforehand whether they will succeed.

Punching pianola roles

In 1994 Bill Vince proposed a project from which arose a professional concert, rather than vice versa. The idea was to involve children with learning difficulties aged between seven and sixteen, and have them draw or paint original compositions on graph paper that could be punched onto pianola rolls and performed by a mechanical piano or street organ. The search for an enabler led to Rex Lawson, one of the world's leading pianolists, living in southeast London with five cats, eleven Apple computers, some 10,000 piano rolls and a beard reaching half-way down his chest. Employing Rex solved technical issues, as he could bring his own mechanical piano and have the drawings transferred by computer onto piano roll masters, then perforated on eighty-year old machines in Sussex. He was also a sensitive and charismatic workshop leader.

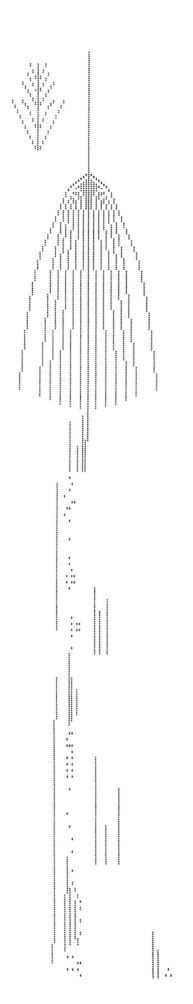

Bill Vince.
PHOTO: PAUL HERRMANN

We decided to alternate the newly composed pieces with music by Grainger, Hindemith, Nancarrow and Stravinsky presented by Rex Lawson in a morning pianola recital in the Cellar Theatre of LBT. Among the thirty-six children, a few were chosen to 'perform' their school's pieces by operating the controls, whilst the remainder, and the public, looked on and listened. Appearing in front of an audience, standing up and bowing, listening to the other pieces, and visiting the Lawrence Batley Theatre with its plush décor – all these were experiences entirely new to nearly all of them. As one of the teachers remarked: 'To do it in front of total strangers in a proper theatre was magic.' The downside of the project was that, although enjoyable and stimulating, it could not easily be taken further. It had used an instrument and a methodology the teachers could not emulate.

The following year saw a young people's production on the main stage of LBT of Judith Weir's opera *The Black Spider*. The singers were mainly members of a community theatre group and Kirklees Chorale (an ensemble run by the schools music service), whilst the orchestra was supplied by the university. It was a creditable production directed by Steven Downs, head of drama at Shelley High School, with whom the festival subsequently engaged in several collaborations (see the photo on page 180).

I have already described the *Sonic Walk* (see page 195). Although an outreach project, it was

Part of a pianola roll designed by pupils in one of Kirklees's special schools.

also a sequence of site-specific performances, whose surprising locations, variety and spectacle, made a unique addition to the 1995 festival. I doubt if anything quite like it has ever happened elsewhere. Outdoor installations are common enough, and also performances. But a conducted tour, both indoors and out, in which an orchestra jumps out at you from a parade of shops; a scrap metal assembly, lit by flaming braziers, thunders to the beat of drumsticks outside a station; mysterious electronic sounds fill an empty arcade, and at the end of their excursion the walkers are greeted by an outdoor fiesta of hot food and fireworks, and an indoor finale from an orchestra of steel pans! This was street theatre with a difference, yet with serious musical intent, performed against the silent backdrop of a town strangely deserted on a Sunday evening, like a Chiroco painting.

Tan Dun's *Orchestral Theatre III: Red Forecast,* given its world premiere in 1996, and his opera *Marco Polo* given its UK concert premiere in 1998, were ideal subjects for educational work. On the morning after the opera performance, Tan himself gave a talk about 'Peking Opera', illustrated by a pipa player and a Chinese and a Western singer. The earlier project was much bolder, although triggered less by *Red Forecast,* which had yet to be performed, than by ideas from Chinese philosophy, including quotations from the *I Ching*. It resulted in a remarkable theatrical creation devised by students of Huddersfield New College with the help of Jan Hendrickse, and, although not specifically instrumental, bore the title 'Orchestral Touring Theatre'. Partly to spark interest in Tan's music, but more to extend their experience and share good practice, the New College students performed their work in several other schools,

Open Ears carnival procession in 1996.
PHOTO: LIZZIE COOMBES

leading younger children in associated workshops. On the morning of the BBCSSO concert, the New College piece was presented in the Lawrence Batley Theatre, watched with evident pleasure by Tan, who afterwards joined in one of the most illuminating of discussions between a distinguished composer and young performers. That he gave generously of himself on a day when he had also to rehearse and perform, was entirely in character. Anyone who encountered him in person could not but be charmed by his gift for inspiring people. Better prepared than most of the public, as was usual for the participants in educational projects, the New College students were given tickets for the premiere that evening of his new composition.

Open Ears and Common Currency

A free-standing project, unrelated to any music in the festival, arose from our desire to bring together participants of different ages and ethnicities. Christened 'Open Ears', it was led by the Zulu-born animateur Eugene Skeef, and vocalist, sitar and tabla player Baldip Panesar. At the preliminary open workshops in the Recital Hall, Eugene inspired everyone present, so much so that two third-year music students (one of whom, Jim Pywell, assisted with the workshops) subsequently moved to Africa to teach. But those taking part were nearly all white. The intention was to build a multiethnic project, and Bill Vince worked energetically to engage Asian, Afro-Caribbean and other ethnic communities across Kirklees. In Huddersfield it was relatively easy; in east Kirklees, around Dewsbury and Batley, whose large Asian communities are more inward-looking, very much harder. A stricter religious practice precluded involvement in public performance, and families were reluctant for their children to take part. The concept of 'contemporary music' was so removed from their culture that they could see no reason to become involved. Bill felt disadvantaged to be a white male, and realised, in retrospect, that it might have helped to enlist an intermediary from among the Asian community leaders.

Eventually he established groups across West Yorkshire: the Carriacou Cultural Big Drum Dancers, Huddersfield Caribbean Community Choir, students from several schools and colleges including Leeds College of Music, as well as individual musicians. The arrival of

Eugene raised confidence; although, as he had to travel from south London before visiting any of the groups, keeping to an agreed timetable was difficult. When the various participants and helpers came together on the day of the performance, they were so assailed by wild weather that the carnival-like procession through the rain-soaked streets caused few bystanders to linger. Arriving at Huddersfield's Sikh Leisure Centre the main performances proceeded smoothly. It was an effective celebration of different cultures, but in a venue the festival had not previously used and, disappointingly, relatively few people came to listen.

The attempt to involve different ethnicities had encountered the inherent separateness within diversity. In 1997, a project designed to bring together two European communities, which we had assumed would be straightforward, exposed unforeseen tensions. Although optimistically named 'Common Currency', the British approach to creative education, unfamiliar on the continent, turned out not to be common at all. The participants were again students from Huddersfield New College, now in an exchange collaboration with a class from Die Arbeitsgemeinschaft Neue Musik Leininger Gymnasium Grünstadt in Germany. In what was intended to be its first stage, all the participants assembled in Huddersfield to create a joint music theatre performance based on concepts in the music of Mathias Spahlinger. His work was being performed at the festival by Ensemble Recherche, and Spahlinger would be present. But the deconstructive theories of an extremely esoteric language were not easy to take on board. Furthermore, the structural orderliness of the German students' approach, and the improvisational intuition of the English, proved almost impossible to reconcile: the one seemingly too rigid, the other disconcertingly open – or so it seemed from the opposite points of view. Whether this was due to different educational systems, or national temperament, one could only surmise. A joint performance did take place before a large audience in the Boilerhouse Arts Centre at New College. But it was difficult to raise funds for a reciprocal visit to Grünstadt, and, as doubts about its viability had already emerged, the second stage of the project did not take place.

More conventionally, in 1999, Bill launched the 'Junior Composer's Scheme' to support pupils composing in schools. Composition had been the basis of the London Sinfonietta scheme, and a return to the issues of notated composition at GCSE level was timely – indeed, it was now a course requirement. The project directors were Colin Riley and our former student Fraser Trainer, with the Kaleidoscope Ensemble from the music department engaged to play the pieces. Like the Yorkshire Arts Young Composers' Award, the opportunity to hear one's work in professional (or semi-professional) performance was central to the scheme. And, as the ensemble consisted of third year and postgraduate students, it was practical and economic to run sessions on three successive days. The beneficiaries were pupils from six high schools plus Mirfield Free Grammar School. The following year the scheme transferred to four other schools, and focused on composing for marimba and violin, played by Damien Harron and Helen Brackley-Jones, with selected pieces performed in their festival concert. The leaders were now Colin Riley and John Cooney, who returned in 2001 for a third stage with A-level students at Greenhead College. On this occasion the goal was to compose a song-cycle for soprano and three instrumentalists.

I have mentioned the semi-staged production of Pascal Dusapin's *Roméo et Juliette* in 1997, and my regret that it had not been more successful (see page 132). It did, however, stimulate an educational project based on the ideas of Dusapin and his librettist, the poet Olivier Cadiot, which resulted in one of the best collaborative performances the festival has seen. This was the first time the festival's education energies had joined forces with those of Opera North, and the involvement of Dominic Gray as director, the composer and animateur Hugh Nankivell and photographer and designer Lizzie Coombes, fifty singers and instrumentalists (A-level and BTEC students from Greenhead College and the Technical College), three Opera North instrumentalists and one professional singer, ensured that the project would, at the least, aspire high. Initially, it focused on pairings: two groups of students, Dusapin/Cadiot versus Shakespeare, language and music, the professional clarinettist and the student, the representative and the abstract, Romeo and Juliet. But the final piece emerged from the dynamics of working collectively in one large rehearsal space. As Hugh Nankivell explained in a stylishly printed programme:

The music, the visuals and the drama were nearly always created in the same space, so we were thinking of each other always, able to fashion and operate as a group whilst spanning different disciplines. Perhaps most importantly of all, the project allowed a group of people who had never previously worked together to learn how to relate as an ensemble, how to collaborate, how to understand give-and-take, how to support each other and how to play together.

Particularly arresting were the images relating to love and relationships assembled by the students: of cafes, bars, meeting places, hands touching, a telephone unanswered, couples moving apart. Projected onto large screens and imaginatively melded by Lizzie Coombes, they flowed from one to another, creating ambience, narrative and mood, helping, in their turn, to determine the structure. Neither the professional production, nor the educational, had much time to rehearse in their respective venues, and I knew that, in the latter, there had been occasional tensions. But the performance, with its disparate ingredients, achieved a remarkable cohesion. More than that: it was sophisticated and touching, musically and visually arresting. I was proud to have presented it in St Paul's, the festival's principal concert venue, in the middle of a full weekend.[10]

On the Saturday afternoon one week earlier, 12,617 Huddersfield Town and Reading

football supporters in the McAlpine Stadium watched and listened to the curious spectacle of *Football Special*. The idea came from Barry Russell, whose Bretton Hall students had contributed impressively to the *Sonic Walk*. Barry was liberal with proposals and, among several *outré* ideas, this was one of the wackiest: a massed musical performance on the pitch at half-time during a first division match. Around 700 junior and intermediate instrumentalists took part, drawn from the seven centres of Kirklees Music School embracing all its outlying areas, whilst students from Shelley High School and Newsome Youth Club performed as gymnasts and majorettes. There was surprisingly little time to get everyone onto the pitch, perform the piece, and withdraw. But instruments were assembled, marshals marshalled, the electronic scoreboard flashed up 'Huddersfield Contemporary Music Festival' and the name of the piece, *Arcade Games*. The scoreboard was then used to trigger events, with the public address system playing a pre-recorded tape. If the result was neither refined nor subtle, *Football Special* did, at least, raise awareness.

That the names of Huddersfield New College and Shelley High School appear frequently in these pages, is due to their outstanding drama departments. Shelley had distinguished itself at the annual National Student Drama Festival,

Instrument maker Kevin Renton and a pupil from Newsome Junior School.
PHOTO: ASADOUR GUZELIAN
(WWW.GUZELIAN.CO.UK)

and its head of drama, Steven Downs, inspired several of his pupils – now accomplished professional actors – to pursue careers in drama. In 1998 he and his students created a beautifully conceived piece for outdoor performance in the cobbled Goldthorpe's Yard, as an adjunct to Louise and Wils Wilson's remarkable installation-cum-performance piece *HOUSE,* already described (see pages 191–93). Presented on four frosty evenings in the relative intimacy of the yard, the Shelley pupils probed its history: the imprisonment of two Luddites; the soldier sentenced to 300 lashes for refusing to fire on his fellow man; the meetings of Huddersfield Naturalist Society, and the ordinary lives of those who had lived in the 'House'.

In 1999, led by Steven Downs and his colleague Julie Root, two dozen Shelley pupils devised an 'experimental piece of musical drama', involving 'ambient theatre with self-generating images' and based on some of the ideas of Brian Eno. Its particular focus was his theory of 'Edge-culture' and 'Africanising' (ie. freeing up our culture rather than compartmentalising it), exemplified in the hundred-or-so cards called *Oblique Strategies* which Eno and Peter Schmidt published in 1975.[11] Each card is printed with a brief suggestion or a thought for consideration, with the intention that an artist in any medium encountering a 'block' can pick a card at random and, by adopting its 'strategy', find a positive direction forward. Following the precedent of 'Orchestral Touring Theatre', Shelley's thoughtful and intelligent *Oblique Strategies – Concrete Results* toured to other schools in Kirklees, where each performance was accompanied by a workshop with the musical director Sophy Smith. For the festival audience it was performed in the Lawrence Batley Theatre, and it was subsequently entered for the forty-fifth National Student Drama Festival.

Sea Tongue

Whether due to inclement weather or scale, outdoor projects could be difficult to manage. An exciting and well-choreographed indoor project was realised in Huddersfield Town Hall in 2001. The participants were local school and youth groups, a gospel choir, the Choral Society Youth Choir, individual singers, ballroom dancers, pianists from the university, and Orlando Gough and Richard Chew's London

community choir The Shout. The production took up all levels of the tiered stage and the whole of the area floor, across which had been built a diagonal catwalk. *Sea Tongue* was about marine phenomena: whaling, diving, voyages, scurvy, storms, shipwrecks, panic and fear. In that the idea and its realisation were devised by Gough and Crew, and the participants who sang and acted had little scope to explore their individual creativity, it could have been criticised for being too manipulative. I doubt whether any of those involved would have made this complaint. In groups, as soloists and together, they had the satisfaction of performing in an extended musical and staged drama, integrated by Gough into a composed, purposeful structure lasting forty minutes, and culminating in a final section for massed voices, instruments and 'movement' of unexpectedly grand and thrilling effect. Performers flooded the stage and area, and the audience packed the balcony and gallery. It seemed that even the youngest performers were moved to find themselves contributing to an event with such a broad and powerful sweep.

By now Bill Vince had left to work for the Buxton Festival and then full-time for Yorkshire Youth and Music. In Huddersfield he had never been employed full-time, partly because of the festival's prioritisation of funds for the artistic programme (although that also included the cost of outreach projects and their culminating performances). In 2001 Mirian Walton became education director, and took over the complex detailed management of *Sea Tongue.* In 2002 she organised a new collaboration with the education division of Sonic Arts Network, this time to provide hardware and expertise enabling pupils from Honley High School to create a 'walk through' music and video installation in the crypt of Huddersfield Parish Church. Another project, *Making Tracks,* was designed to help young women in their teens, with otherwise little or no access to music technology and musical training, create original songs with the help of a team of community musicians. It extended over six months, supported by the National Foundation for Youth Music in partnership with Kirklees Young Peoples' Service, and took place in youth clubs. The most ambitious project involved a team of artists led by Barry Russell working with some 200 school children, students and amateur musicians. Called *Foundscapes, Soundscapes and Wor(l)dplays,* the final performance took place

in Huddersfield Town Hall and involved live and recorded music, singing, drumming, dance and design. During the next three years the education programme was run by Liz Muge, mainly on established lines, although with renewed emphasis on access schemes to encourage attendance at festival performances.

New directions

Heidi Johnson's succession to the post in 2006 coincided with the arrival of Graham McKenzie as artistic director and chief executive, and

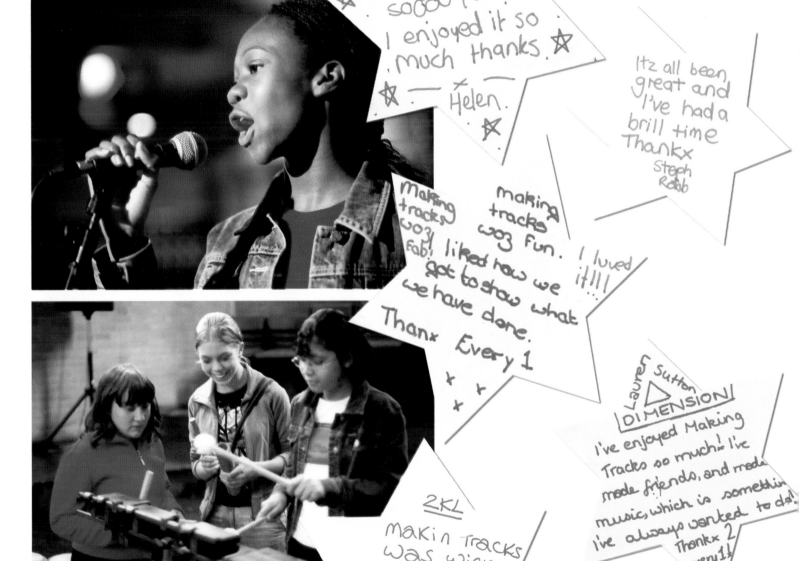

Making Tracks.

225

Nikki Cassidy as festival manager – so installing an entirely new team at the heart of the operation. A major commitment of Graham's strategy was to extend participation. Thanks to the award of an Arts Council 'Thrive' organisational development grant, for three years between 2008 and 2010 the education post became full-time, allowing an expansion of activity throughout the year. As he remarked in an interview for *Classical Music,* 'Participation really does sit at the core of every thing we do; in 2009 we invested approximately £96,000 in directly engaging with local communities and schools and so on through our programme of events.'[12] This important development received welcome support from the Esmée Fairbairn Foundation in 2011, ensuring that the post would continue to be full-time for at least another three years.

Appropriately for the new century, projects increasingly explored music technology and digital media – although with some colourful exceptions – and more have catered for adults and families. Wanting to reflect this wider range, including adult learning, and aware that for

some the word 'education' implied only working in schools, in 2009 the education and outreach programme was rebranded as 'Learning and Participation'.

Sonic Arts Network was the instigator of a 2006 project called 'Sonic Postcards', in which local environmental sounds were gathered as source material, mixed together, converted into MP3 files and emailed between the schools involved. A creative composition project called 'Take Note' used Barry Guy's graphic scores as a model, and the results produced by the children

Hugh Nankivell leading a schools composition project performance in the Hub.
PHOTO: BRIAN SLATER

LEFT:
A participant in the 2005 education programme
PHOTO: BRIAN SLATER

FAR LEFT:
Foundscapes, Soundscapes and Wor(l)dplays *performed in Huddersfield Town Hall.*
PHOTO: BRIAN SLATER

Playing vegetable instruments at Huddersfield Open Market in 2007.
PHOTO: BRIAN SLATER

were exhibited in Huddersfield Art Gallery alongside work by Barry Guy, who led 'performances' of them in a concert.

The penultimate day of the 2007 festival was dominated by the only visit to the UK of the Vienna Vegetable Orchestra, whose evening performance on carrot flutes, pumpkin basses, leek violins and cucumberphones was preceded by hands-on vegetable instrument-making for Saturday shoppers in Huddersfield's open market. Their stall attracted enthusiastic crowds, with families especially having fun as their wide-eyed children discovered the musical potential of the domestic kitchen. In a related project called 'Audio Munch', Duncan Chapman led workshops for A-level music students at Greenhead College, bent on investigating the sound and nutritional aspects of school dinners and packed lunches, using a special software programme.

Among other projects was a partnership with Live Music Now and the *Huddersfield Examiner* to take performances into residential homes, hospitals, and training centres for adults with learning disabilities. In 2008, again in partnership with Live Music Now, a young vocal trio called Juice delivered participatory performances for people who have difficulty accessing live music (e.g. community day centres, and Huddersfield Down's Syndrome Support Group), and led a residency for young people with disabilities at the Technical College. The partnership continued in the early part of 2009, when the festival and Live Music Now delivered two eight-week residencies by the Fell Clarinet Quartet in two schools for children

'Sonic Postcards': an educational project in association with Sonic Arts in 2006.
PHOTO: BRIAN SLATER

with a range of physical and learning problems. Throughout the year, a new vocal ensemble in North Kirklees funded by Youth Music met in weekly workshops to develop singing techniques and create new works.

The latter project concluded with a performance in Huddersfield Town Hall during the 2009 festival of Alvin Curran's *Oh Man Oh Mankind Oh Yeah,* in which the singers were joined by a choir from the university and members of Huddersfield Choral Society. The piece featured unusual vocal techniques and improvisations, thirty harmonicas, plastic tubes, four bass drums and a horn called a shofer. There were settings of words by John Cage and James Joyce and an arrangement of the spiritual *Shall we gather by the river.* For the young singers it was 'crazy but fun', one remarking that he had most enjoyed 'mumbling like gorillas'. But some Choral Society members – who had sung the UK premiere of Schnittke's *Faust Cantata* at the 1990 festival, Górecki in 1993, and in 2011 would present the UK premiere of Jonathan Harvey's intricate but immensely impressive *Messages* (so far performed only by the Berlin Philharmonic and Berlin Radio Choir) in their own subscription series – found Alvin Curran's improvisatory miscellany less rewarding.

Developing skills

Indisputably successful was the performance of Kristoffer Zegers's *Piano Phasing* and its related project. With money from the government's Transformation Fund (set up to support innovative informal adult learning projects), the festival launched a range of piano-related activities for adults wanting to learn to play keyboards or hone existing skills. A comprehensive programme of weekly workshops for 'first-time learners', monthly

surgeries for lapsed players, music-making and online resources was created to tie in with the performance of *Piano Phasing,* in which fifty pianists, ranging from college students to retired people, played simultaneously on twenty-five pianos. Sessions were free, with transport costs covered for people of limited means. The online element, extending the festival's increasingly active web profile, included multimedia demonstrations, podcast interviews with composers and pianists, exercises and games. One could also download the parts required to take part in *Piano Phasing* as well as information about new music for the piano. In February 2010 the scheme concluded with 'Piano Dances', a week-long music and dance project for adults and children.

120 brass band players kick off Night of the Unexpected *in 2007.*
PHOTO: BRIAN SLATER

LEFT:
The performance of Piano Phasing *in Huddersfield Town Hall – part of an extended learning project involving fifty pianists, organised by Heidi Johnson.*
PHOTOS: BRIAN SLATER

Dutch creativity was behind three futuristic sound-making sculptures from the Muziekgebouw aan 't IJ concert hall in Amsterdam. Installed in a disused shop in Dewsbury during July 2010, this interactive 'Sound Playground' included spheres and columns which could be rotated, lifted and moved to produce and modify sounds, a musical pie whose 'slices' activated abstract sounds, and a multi-coloured toadstool whose 108 enamel segments triggered different sounds when touched, and could be loaded with samples ranging from world music and techno to classical recordings. The festival offered weekday schools sessions (quickly booked up) and weekend fun workshops for families with children aged between seven and twelve. Funds were provided by the Clore Duffield Foundation and Kirklees Council.

In 2008 the festival announced a three-year scheme to provide professional development for student composers from northern universities. Those chosen would work with the Nieuw Ensemble in the Netherlands, culminating in performances of their compositions at the 2009 and 2010 festivals (see page 57).

The project was a successor to the earlier Young Composers' Awards, from which Susanna Eastburn had already removed the competitive element, retaining the workshops and professional performances, and adding commissions for young composers. In 2010 the Nieuw Ensemble initiative was enlarged to become the European Composers' Professional Development Programme, involving the Nieuw and two other ensembles: Icarus in Italy, and Ensemble 10/10 in the UK. Funded by the European Commission Culture Programme, the Musicians Benevolent Fund and each of the three ensembles, it is intended to enable twenty-four 'talented composers at the start of their careers' – representing the three partner countries – each to compose for one of the ensembles. The composers also take part in workshops, either in Amsterdam, Reggio Emilia or Liverpool, where they can try out ideas, receive guidance from tutors and established composers, and attend business advice seminars. This broad-based learning trajectory culminates in high-profile performances of the completed compositions in 2011 and 2012, plus CD recordings; whilst scores by the UK participants will be published by the University of York Press.

13 *The University and Music Department*

The 'Cube': a research studio for sound spatialisation in the new Creative Arts Building.
PHOTO: MARK BOKOWIEC

From College of Technology to University

When I joined Huddersfield College of Technology in 1961, no one could have forseen the transformations that would take place during the following five decades. To imagine that the ugly concrete towers housing engineering and technology completed only two years before – along with the Great Hall and other utilitarian postwar buildings – would so soon be demolished would have seemed like fantasy. That the former primary school in which I worked would be replaced with a purpose built music department was a not unreasonable hope, and happened in 1966. But that this would be succeeded forty years later by an iconic Creative Arts Building attests to a rapidity of change I had not thought possible. That the college of technology would become a polytechnic, and the polytechnic a university catering for five times as many students, would have seemed even less credible, although there must already have been arguments for wider participation in higher education. The scale of the transformation is evident in the expansion of the campus, with its award-winning mill conversions. But to me it is most visible in the library: a single large room when I arrived; a state-of-the-art learning centre on four floors, comfortable, superbly resourced, and stretching in every direction, in 2011. The once dingy campus has become spacious, bright and vibrant; some of it architecturally distinguished.

The symbiotic relationship between the festival and its host was crucial from the beginning. An important asset was the free use of venues owned by both Kirklees and the polytechnic, and office space in the latter. The benefits were mutual, but not always so recognised.

To colleagues in the music department they were obvious. The festival was a unique educational and performing resource which, as it grew bigger, increasingly attracted music students and staff to Huddersfield, in preference to other institutions. To the rector and some senior staff they were questionable. Press reports were glowing but rarely trumpeted the institution. When polytechnics acquired corporate status in the late 1980s, accounting methods changed, and spending on the festival was challenged. Not unreasonably we were required to itemise all expenditure (relatively straightforward) and quantify the benefits (not easily evaluated financially).

It was difficult to ensure that the institution received media credit. One could hardly dictate copy, but music critics did what they could, and journals like *The Times Educational Supplement* did more. Nevertheless, when in 1989 Waterman Pens became the festival's first 'title sponsor', the polytechnic complained that its profile had been downgraded. A difficult meeting ensued between representatives of Yorkshire Arts and the head of the department of music (plus myself) on one side, and pro-rector Tom Gaskell and the suitably named Mr Smelt, head of finance, on the other. We reached what seemed an equitable agreement, but the relationship remained strained.

George Pratt, head of the music department from 1984, and Arthur Jacobs who preceded him, were committed advocates, shaping attitudes within the department and influential outside it. George's enthusiasm was heart-warming and empowering, urging integration of aspects of the festival into the music modules – including, of course, his own musical awareness course. It was naturally a part of twentieth-century musicology, composition and contemporary musical language.

The students were undergraduates, mostly in their late teens or early twenties. In 1978 there were no postgraduate courses, few, if any, research students, and the polytechnic itself had little structured research. Lecturers were employed to teach, and as contact hours were generous, composition staff in particular had ample opportunity to motivate their charges. It took time to build up a pattern of attendance, but, by the early 1980s, students were becoming a significant section of the festival audience. There began to be a core of committed enthusiasts who influenced others by osmosis. There being no computers, no MP3 players, no mobile phones, few clubs and – mercifully – no reality television, there was less need than now to compete for attention. First year music students lived on campus,[1] and most grants were sufficient to spare them from taking part-time jobs, at least during term. In the evenings they practised in the department, played in ensembles or worked in the music library, then housed in the building. To attend festival concerts relieved the routine. The experience could be discomforting; but, at the same time, composers like Messiaen, Stockhausen, Cage, Berio and Ligeti were at the peak of their careers, and receiving extensive media attention. None had the celebrity of a Frank Zappa, Pink Floyd, Bob Dylan or the Sex Pistols, but neither were they marginalised by an overarching pop culture. It was acceptable to be involved in art music. 'Cool' still meant the opposite of 'warm', and had nothing to do with comportment, behaviour and social acceptability.

Students specialising in performance were encouraged (or required) to attend solo recitals. I gave each cohort of first years an illustrated introduction to the festival, and we made strenuous efforts to ensure that they attended a portfolio of concerts. I did likewise for groups of second and third-year students, although by then they were less pressurised, and could choose for themselves. Some, who had taken little notice in their first and second years, were suddenly motivated in their third, realising what an opportunity they would soon be without. A number of the most interested continued to attend festivals after their graduation (as did others from Huddersfield Technical College). But it was not all positive. When regular teaching was suspended to allow

attendance at the festival, there were those who regarded it as a holiday; and, as the financial burden of higher education increased, others used it as a window in which to earn money.

Students also attended from other departments: art students in the days when they designed posters and handbills; drama students throughout, especially after the opening of the Lawrence Batley Theatre; and a few (evident from their dress) from the Middle East and Asia. George Pratt was a vocal ambassador amongst fellow academics in Huddersfield and further afield. By the early 1990s most staff in other departments appreciated the festival's contribution to the institution's profile.

In 1992 the polytechnic became a university, and with the arrival in 1995 of John Tarrant

Professor George Pratt, head of the music department, with Karlheinz Stockhausen.
PHOTO: SELWYN GREEN

Damien Harron, then a third-year undergraduate, playing Xenakis's Rebonds *in a masterclass with Roland Auzet in 1992.*
PHOTO: SELWYN GREEN

as vice-chancellor, attitudes at senior level changed dramatically. At an early meeting we explored details of the relationship and he assured me of the university's support. John and his wife attended events and became personal friends. But the university's profile remained a concern. Title sponsorship by the Halifax between 1994 and 1998 and alliances between the festival and other partners tended to upstage this core association. In the late 1990s, the Higher Education Funding Council for England (HEFCE) commissioned a report on the role of higher education institutions in the provision of cultural and sports facilities of benefit to a wider public. Published in April 1999, and called *Partners and providers*, it examined two festivals associated with universities. A very positive account of the relationship in Huddersfield was compared favourably with the looser connection between the Belfast Festival and Queen's University.[2] But the publication went unnoticed by the media.

Bob Cryan, John Tarrant's successor, happened to have been born in Huddersfield, attending schools in the town, and had graduated from the polytechnic in 1986 with first class honours. During a distinguished university career in Manchester, Swansea and Northumbria, he observed the development of his home institution with local pride. Following Cryan's appointment as vice-chancellor in 2007, he declared an ambition to develop international collaborations, postgraduate student recruitment and the university's research profile, in which the festival was identified as an influential contributor.

CeReNeM

These were also priorities within the music department, to which Michael Russ was appointed as head in 2002, becoming Dean of the School of Music, Humanities and Media in 2008. In both capacities he has followed his predecessors' strong support for the festival. He also oversaw the expansion of the curriculum in areas of music technology and popular music, the move into the Creative Arts Building, and the appointment of three international composers to the staff – Aaron Cassidy from the USA, Pierre Alexandre Tremblay from Montreal, Liza Lim from Australia (taking up a new research professorship) – as well as the pianist

Philip Thomas, a specialist in the performance of new and experimental music. With existing composers on the staff such as Monty Adkins, Mary Bellamy, Michael Clarke and Bryn Harrison, the department has reinvigorated and redefined its commitment to new music and become a magnetic environment for international postgraduates. These energies are embodied in the Centre for Research in New Music (CeReNeM), a launch pad for contemporary composition and performance, for interdisciplinary work in new sonic media, sound spatialisation, improvisation and new notations, as well as research into acoustics, musical perception and cross cultural aesthetics.

Under the banner of CeReNeM, the staff's composing, recording and performance activities are both documented and coordinated. In the first half of 2011, for instance, they included the premiere of Lim's most recent composition, *Tongue of the Invisible,* at the Holland Festival; a performance by the London Sinfonietta of Harrison's *Six Symmetries* at the Queen Elizabeth Hall, and performances of Cassidy's String Quartet and Second String Quartet by the JACK Quartet across the USA. The quartets were played again at the Ultraschall Festival in Berlin, where a multichannel electroacoustic composition by Tremblay, commissioned by the TU Berlin studio, also received its premiere. New CDs were released by Thomas, Adkins and Tremblay, and Cassidy was commissioned to write a new work for EXAUDI – one of twenty works (each lasting twelve minutes) commissioned for the London 2012 Cultural Olympiad. Interdisciplinary work was represented by Mark Bokowiec's *V'Oct(Ritual),* involving a vocalist, the Bodycoder System and live Max/MSP, presented at NIME in Oslo, a sound and video composition by Maria Castro as part of an exhibition involving UK and Chinese artists in Beijing, and a portrait DVD of the work of composer and film maker Geoffrey Cox made in collaboration with Philip Thomas (piano) and Keith Marley (film). The latter was issued under the CeReNeM's own label, Huddersfield Contemporary Records. Rupert Till's collaborative 3D animated sound-field model and composition, *Stonehenge Ritual Sound,* was performed in the George Square Theatre in Edinburgh as part of a new initiative called Palaeophonics, in which composers, film-makers and archeologists aim to make innovative work accessible to a wide public. The link between the department's research activities and the festival is demonstrably close and was reinforced in 2008 by the appointment of the festival's artistic director as an honorary research fellow of the university.

In this twin role, Graham McKenzie has re-built relationships, restoring the department's participation in planning and performances, recognising that web-based communication and social change has lessened young peoples' attendance at live performances, but that a differently accessed audience is there to be engaged. In 2008 a new funding partnership was agreed. The University of Huddersfield became headline sponsor for the next three years and, for the first time, its role was prominently displayed on all publicity and print. As this reached its third year in November 2010, despite the severity of the cuts facing higher education, at a reception to welcome delegates invited by the British Council, the vice-chancellor announced the university's continued commitment. An outcome of the partnership between festival and university has been the establishment of a fully-funded three-year PhD scholarship for a composer. From many international applicants, the first award in 2009 went to the Greek composer, performer and Gaudeamus prize winner, Lefteris Papadimitriou, who, as part of the scheme, receives a world premiere performance from the London Sinfonietta at the 2011 festival. In consideration of their international standing

and a significant involvement in the festival, the university has, at different times, awarded honorary degrees to James Dillon, Fred Frith, Jonathan Harvey, Denis Smalley, Paul Whittaker and Christian Woolf.

Music department ensembles

Despite the crucial role of external partnerships, it was particularly within the music department that the festival prospered. From the beginning, colleagues were involved as performers, as composers, and in providing technical support. Presiding over sound diffusion and electroacoustic events were Phil Ellis, first director of the electronic music studio, followed by Michael Clarke – both composers. The studio manager Mark Bromwich (who later adopted his family name of Bokowiec) ensured that equipment matched the expectations of a leader in the field like Xenakis. And, as a composer, Mark became increasingly recognised as a pioneer in the development of interactive technology. As already noted, throughout three decades Barrie Webb took part in numerous festivals as trombonist and conductor, directing department ensembles in some exceptionally demanding scores, meticulously prepared and performed to an impressively high standard. In its initial form, the honours degree established in 1970 focused in equal parts on performance, musicology and composition,

James Saunders
performing his #211106
at the 2006 festival.
PHOTO: BRIAN SLATER

234

with a strong bias towards twentieth century
music. The festival was a logical extension of
this emphasis, and the composers on the staff its
natural advocates. Over the years, besides those
already mentioned, they have included Arthur
Butterworth, Geoffrey Cox, Duncan Druce,
Christopher Fox, Stephen Oliver, James
Saunders, Patric Standford, Rupert Till, Harold
Truscott, Nick Williams and Margaret Lucy
Wilkins, as well as myself, and for one year
John Casken when he held a fellowship.

I have already described the world premiere
by the symphonic wind orchestra of David
Bedford's *Sun Paints Rainbows on the Vast
Waves* in 1982, and concerts by the department
symphony orchestra and brass band in 1984.
Besides the UK premiere of Berio's *Accordo* in
1985, given by ensembles from the polytechnic
and three other institutions, that year three
canonic ensemble works by Aldo Clementi were
given UK premieres, performed mainly by
instrumentalists from the music department.
In 1986, after intensive rehearsal, a fine
performance was achieved by the orchestra
of Heinz Holliger's technically very difficult
Atembogen, directed by Barrie Webb, for whom
the language was as familiar as, for the students,
it was decidedly strange.

In the 1987 festival, both the Polytechnic
Twentieth Century Ensemble and Symphony
Orchestra gave concerts, including the European
premiere (indeed only the third performance) of
Henry Cowell's piano concerto of 1930, with
Stephen Montague as soloist, plus music by
Henry Brant, and Varèse's monumental *Arcana*.
This established annual performances by the
orchestra, which increasingly worked with
major composers. I have cited rehearsing with
Andriessen and Schafer in 1988, and for some
fortunate third year students, the unforgettable
experience of working with Stockhausen.
Andriessen was again present in 1993 when the

Twentieth Century Ensemble, with the soprano
Valdine Anderson, gave the UK concert
premiere of *Hadewijc*. Both *Hadewijc* and
De Stijl (given its UK premiere by the ensemble
in 1988), are parts of *De Materie (Matter)*,
composed for the opening of Amsterdam's
new Muziektheater in a production by
Robert Wilson in 1989, and a summation of
Andriessen's work up to that time. Although
conceived for the theatre, all its four component
parts work well in concert form.

Being mentored by creative personalities of such
standing did much to increase students' wider
interest in the festival. Similar instances were a
performance of James MacMillan's percussion
concerto, *Veni, Veni, Emmanuel* in 1995, with
our recent graduate Julian Warburton an
accomplished and moving soloist, and the UK
premiere of Tan Dun's *Concerto for pizzicato
piano and ten instruments,* as well as his
Orchestral Theatre I: Xun, with Tan himself
as xun and vocal soloist. The xun is an
ancient Chinese ceramic wind instrument,
somewhat like an ocarina. Ten of the orchestral
woodwinds had also to double on xuns, and
Tan's virtuoso example, and his encouragement
and engagement with the students, made
another inspirational encounter.[3]

These performances, too, were conducted
by Barrie Webb, whose work in Romania as
trombonist and conductor led to the polytechnic

orchestra's performance of Câlin Ioachimescu's *Oratio 2* in 1990, plus the UK premieres mentioned earlier of Doina Rotaru's Flute Concerto and Symphony no. 2. In the mid 1990s, with what were by then university ensembles, he made a commercial CD of both pieces, plus Rotaru's Saxophone Concerto with Pierre-Yves Artaud and Emil Stein as soloists.[4] Barrie himself gave a lecture-recital in the 1982 festival, at the start of what became an international career. On this occasion he discussed and played *Sequenza V,* along with Globokar's *Res/As/Ex/Ins-pirer* and *Recirculation* by a recent winner of the Young Composers' Competition, Christopher Fox.

In 1991 the music department contributed to the festival's opening weekend by pairing Birtwistle's bravura *Verses for Ensembles* with Tippett's great humanitarian oratorio *A Child of Our Time.* The performances in Huddersfield Town Hall were given by the Polytechnic Twentieth Century Ensemble, Symphony Orchestra, four professional soloists, and the Polytechnic Choir augmented by the Technical College Chamber Choir. Barrie Webb conducted the Birtwistle and I conducted the Tippett – one of only three occasions when I directed a performance in the festival. Both works were a challenge, and their rehearsals time-consuming, especially whilst attending to other festival preparations. But the performances were rewarding: the confrontational exchanges between woodwind, brass and percussion in the Birtwistle brilliant and exciting, the Tippett less urgent than it should have been, perhaps, but deeply moving nonetheless.

In 1998, the University Symphony Orchestra gave the world premiere of *Awakenings* by Joe Cutler, who had been a student in the music department between 1988–90. He had conceived the work on one of many journeys by coach between London and Warsaw, where he had been awarded a three-year Polish scholarship to study at the Chopin Academy of Music. Looking up from reading Sebastian Faulks's *Birdsong,* Joe realised that the neat, sleepy villages and well-tended fields through which he was passing, were the very area in which the carnage of the First World War, described by Faulks, had taken place. In 2000, *Awakenings* won second prize at the prestigious T ru Takemitsu Composition Award in Japan.

By the late 1990s, the department included talented postgraduate performers, and in 1999 a postgraduate ensemble, named Kaleidoscope, gave workshops and a concert. That year, the University Symphony Orchestra gave the world premiere of David Lang's *Grind to a Halt* and the UK premiere of Joji Yuasa's Violin Concerto with Helen Brackley-Jones, also a postgraduate, as soloist. Barrie's rehearsal schedule for these performances was invariably intensive, and I soon learnt to programme department ensembles, when possible, near the beginning of any festival, so that rehearsals would not prevent students from attending other concerts. In 2001 the orchestra gave the UK premiere of Hans Abrahamsen's Symphony no. 1, along with works by Diana Burrell and Arne Nordheim. The next two contributions focused on the experimental tradition. In 2002 a concert featured the world premiere of *Spring Symphony: The Joy of Life* by Michael Wolters (a former Huddersfield student), *Like Wool* by James Saunders (another former student, by then a member of staff) and the UK premiere of Christian Wolff's *Ordinary Matter.* In 2003 Gavin Bryars's *Jesus' Blood Never Failed Me Yet* was performed by the New Music Ensemble. A further concert was shared between the University of Huddersfield Orchestra and New Music Ensemble in 2005, pairing works by Scelsi and Takemitsu with two conductors, Nicholas Ponsillo and Webb, who was also the trombone soloist in Takemitsu's concerto: *Fantasma/Cantos II.*

There were other formats in which students contributed. The experimental tradition was never more engrossing than in an inspired realisation of Kagel's *Acustica* by an Experimental Music Group directed by James Saunders in 2003. It is a piece without any specified order or synchronisation, but scored for an outlandish range of 'sound-producers', including balloon, blowtorch, vinyl records and loudspeaker membranes played with nails and matches. Closest to any conventional instrument is the 'nail violin' (i.e. nails of varying 'pitch' which have been hammered into a piece of wood so that they can be bowed). The performance was an hour-long sequence of delicate delights, baring out Björn Heile's description, in his book on Kagel, as 'a catalogue of sounds and ways of exploring them artistically, as exciting and anarchic as it is nuanced and sophisticated.'[5] That, surely, is a formula for the best experimental music.

Gamelan Sekar Petak from York University performing in St. Paul's.
PHOTO: SELWYN GREEN

In 2006, directed by Philip Thomas, the New Music Ensemble played Cage, Feldman, Wolff and the world premiere of a festival commission from Nick Williams. The concert had the distinction of being broadcast on Radio 3. It was the first time any of the university's ensemble contributions to the festival had been broadcast by the BBC, although earlier performances certainly merited it. In 2007 Barrie Webb conducted Joe Cutler's *Sal's Sax* and Andriessen's *De Stijl,* nearly twenty years after giving the Andriessen's UK premiere. Also in 2007, a new university group called the Edges Ensemble performed with Fred Frith. By three years later, with a significant complement of postgraduate students, the Edges Ensemble had become the ensemble of choice, mostly directed by Philip Thomas and similarly focusing on experimental and improvised music. At noon on the opening day of the 2010 festival, the players took part in Alvin Curran's 'unstructured' *Ear Training* on Huddersfield Railway Station, and later that afternoon performed Cage's *Variations II* in Huddersfield Art Gallery, to celebrate the opening of the exhibition, 'Every Day is a Good Day'.

The brass band participated in *Night of the Unexpected* in 2007, and the University Percussion Ensemble in the 2008 festival. But neither the symphony orchestra nor wind orchestra have performed in recent years, removing a direct involvement in the festival experienced earlier by the majority of undergraduates. Barrie Webb has retired, but it is also more difficult in the present educational climate to field an orchestra containing players of a consistently high standard.

It would be an oversight not to acknowledge the contributions made by individuals and ensembles from other institutions, beginning with the Manson Ensemble Wind Quintet from the Royal Academy of Music in 1982. Continuing throughout the 1980s and '90s, they have included ensembles from the Royal College of Music, Royal Northern College of Music and York University, and contributions from the Chamber Choir of the Royal Scottish Academy of Music and Drama. The relationship with York University has been close, including a seventieth birthday tribute to the French composer Betsy Jolas performed by the York New Music Group in 1996 and two visits by its Gamelan Sekar Petak. Three staged performances, mounted by 'collectives' of staff, students, graduates and professional musicians, have already been noted: Birmingham's performance of Stockhausen's *Momente* in 1994, and the two productions by Northern Music Theatre from York University in 1983 and 1984. For the second of these, the company numbered three dozen staff, students and professional musicians, many of whom have continued in prominent professional careers. But, being drawn from a largely transient academic population, Northern Music Theatre's existence was short-lived.

14 *Marketing and audiences*

Early impact

Marketing during the first three years was low-key. The leaflets produced by the civic public relations department contained only basic listings, with minimal design, no descriptions and no pictures. The first festival was attended by a small number of enthusiasts, professionals and critics – and a sprinkling of students, until the final concert by the Warsaw Music Workshop when the Recital Hall filled up with undergraduates and colleagues from the music department. In Venn Street Arts Centre one concert plugged into an existing series. Reviewing the second festival,[1] Hilary Bracefield described 'a ready-made audience of retired people, ladies in hats and shoppers with carrier bags... not, alas, because of the reputation of the performers, but because this cheap (10p!) Tuesday programme was also one of a series which has become a staple part of Huddersfield's concert going'. A Contemporary Music Network concert featuring Cage's *Sonatas and Interludes* and electroacoustic music in the Polytechnic Great Hall drew disappointingly few. A year later, Robert Cockroft reported that another Great Hall concert by the barely known Garbarino Ensemble from Milan, 'pulled in no more than sixty, of which fifty were students and three were critics – not the healthiest state of affairs'.[2]

The opening of St Paul's Hall gave the festival a huge boost. But it was clear that publicity and marketing needed to be more upbeat and visually compelling. In 1981 a freelance designer reformatted the leaflet and I contributed descriptive copy and press plaudits. A year later photographs were added. To market the expanded programme that coincided with the opening of St Paul's, I thought that every evening concert needed its own handbill or poster, and asked Reginald Napier, head of the Polytechnic School of Art, whether his students could design them. Napier agreed, and each autumn I briefed a cohort of art students, suggested themes and images, and returned a few weeks later to view the results, delighted with their variety. Finished artwork was printed professionally, usually in one colour on A4 stock, but exceptionally a design would merit more. A striking example was the silk-screen poster created for the BBCSO's portrait concert of Maxwell Davies, which depicted an Orkney stone circle etched in black and white against a low horizon of blues, greens, yellows and orange, each copy having its own unique colouration (see page 26). The dozen or more posters displayed in the polytechnic, town hall, public library, information office and shops and schools increased interest and helped build a local audience. After the School of Art closed in the mid 1980s, I negotiated a similar arrangement with Huddersfield Technical College Art Department, until 1991 when most of the festival's print was entrusted to professional designers using computer graphics.[3]

Design

The leaflet changed dramatically in 1984 following a persuasive 'pitch' from the Manchester printers Revell and George. I assembled visual material, and their first effort was such a riotous collage of images, cartoons, graphics and avant-garde notation that crucial information was almost obliterated. But it conveyed the festival's exuberance and variety. The images prioritised people – playing, dancing, doing things – dominated by a beaming, tousle-headed Maxwell Davies.

This human vitality was intended to counteract the abstraction with which contemporary music was too easily associated. On the cover, a figure with head thrown back and mouth wide open stood as if transfixed. In agony or ecstasy? In fact, it was the dancer Tom Yang poised at the climax of Davies's *Vesalii Icones*. Beneath him a small drawing (taken from CMN publicity) showed the head of a man waggishly blowing a horn, notes flying, two semiquavers for an ear. The leaflet had doubled in size and sported the festival's first logo – retained for five years. The number and range of events had also grown, and the combination of enticing copy, visual variety and press accolades amounted to an appetising invitation. A sentence from *The Musical Times* summed it up: 'Huddersfield

has now become synonymous with all that is most imaginative in British music-making, not to say an essential rendezvous for adventure-seekers of every persuasion.'[4]

If this first collage was somewhat cluttered, it set the style of future print. There were similarities with the Almeida Festival, but I also looked at other examples including some from abroad. The association of text, image and design was key, and I maintained a keen interest in its tone and appearance. I wrote all the text, believing that it had to be done from a direct knowledge of, and enthusiasm for the music. Media endorsements helped dispel suspicions that everything would be incomprehensible and dry.

One side of the 1984 festival publicity leaflet.

The leaflets that followed were somewhat home-spun but never bland, and so crammed with information and visual content that there was little, if any, unused space. The design lacked the finesse of the French, whose EIC/IRCAM brochures downplayed the pictorial in favour of blocks of colour floating on a sea of white: stylishly 'contemporary', and with content that was invariably compelling. But the tone of the French establishment was vaguely elitist, and Huddersfield had to be inclusive.

Audience surveys

With the appointment of Tim Sledge as administrator in 1990, publicity became a team operation. Good design and energetic distribution increased audiences, but how much was due to marketing, artistic content, or the festival's growing reputation it is hard to say. A limited audience survey was organised in 1988, which revealed that, whilst the leaflet was indeed effective, press advertising was not, and that, besides a large proportion of first-time attenders, there was a growing core of regular supporters, some of whom had been coming since 1978. In 1991, another modest survey was conducted professionally. Six hundred questionnaires were distributed among a total audience of around 10,000, of which 334 were returned. They showed that nearly 30% of the sample were aged nineteen or below, and 46% aged twenty-four or below. Countering the high proportion of students – with which the festival was now, perhaps, too readily identified – 54% of respondents were aged twenty-five and over, including 30% who could be termed middle-aged. Ten out of the 334 had attended all fourteen festivals since 1978. The strategies adopted as a result focused on marketing packages, and increasing the adult audience through mailing and other means.

The most remarkable statistic of the 1991 survey was that, even at the fourteenth festival, nearly a third of the audience were aged nineteen or below. But the number of regular festivalgoers was increasing so that, during the next two decades, the transient teenage audience gradually became a broad-based adult constituency, many returning annually. A survey conducted in 2004 revealed a high level of loyalty, including 28% who had already attended seven or more festivals. Now 26% of the sample were aged 17–25, 13% aged 26–44, 20% aged 45–54 and 21% aged 55 or above. Nearly a third of respondents (31%) were first-time attenders, but the audience as a whole was more adult, many with an established interest in new music, whilst the teenage community that we had sought to 'convert' in the 1980s and '90s was less in evidence. The 2004 survey also revealed that 55% of respondents lived in West Yorkshire, another 24% within one hour's driving time (not including West Yorkshire) and 21% from the rest of the UK and beyond.

Already in the 1980s the festival attracted the knowledgeable, like Fred Booth of Holmfirth, who subsequently bequeathed his library of books and twentieth-century scores to the music department library. A cherished visitor was John Warnaby. Blind from birth, he had pursued a career with British Steel until the opportunity of studying for an Open University degree stimulated an intense passion for contemporary music. John became an authoritative musicologist, writer and critic, attending all the major new music festivals in the UK and Germany and recording German radio broadcasts. I valued his suggestions, and appreciated being introduced to music I did not know. After he died in 2007, in a touching obituary for the Friends newsletter, Philip Clark recalled that 'the sight of John, with his partner Elfriede, shuffling towards their seats in St Paul's was as important an ingredient to the Huddersfield I remember as all those composers and their pieces'. Another affectionately remembered Friend was Lady Elisabeth Melville, whose husband had been first chair of the Britten-Pears Trust. In the mid 1990s, feeling that Aldeburgh had become 'stuffy', she decided to try Huddersfield and became one of the festival's most enthusiastic supporters.

In 2004 almost a quarter of those surveyed worked in the arts or media and 19% in education. Other commonly recurring professions included health, technical/IT and local authority employment. But there were others one might not have expected. Paul Herrmann, a professional photographer whose work appears in this book, told me that, on an occasion when he was photographing a rehearsal in St Paul's, he observed a grey-haired man sitting alone in the audience seats. 'Are you the composer?' asked Paul. 'No, I'm a sort of writer.' 'Oh, really. What do you write about?' 'Wild swimming.' It was Roger Deakin.

Images

The main design appeared on the leaflet, programme book and a festival poster. For twenty years we could afford no more than two-colour printing, to counter which in 1986 the printers suggested feeding different inks into the separate jets across a plate, producing a rainbow of tints from a single impression. The montage designed by Ron McSweeney in 1987 was particularly strong, juxtaposing a graphic study by Xenakis for the Montreal Polytope, a child 'drawing' on the UPIC computer and a phrase of music from *Time and Motion Study 1* by Brian Ferneyhough, with his bespectacled face gazing out from behind. Arriving to be featured for the first time in a European festival, John Adams was alarmed by the 'terrifying notation and composers leering at me' (illustrated on page 99), but, if it also frightened potential festivalgoers, more were probably gained than lost. For the 1989 encounter between Boulez and Cage after their thirty-six-year rift, Ron tore grainy images of the two composers from photos I had degraded through repeated photocopying, and juxtaposed their frayed edges.

It was still normal practice for artwork and text to be cut up and pasted onto board. The move to computer design was initiated by Tim, who, like his successor Andrea Smart, shared my enthusiasm for distinctive print. None of us were trained in marketing or design, but that we knew the product and what to communicate mattered more. The first computer-designed leaflet in 1991 (now a sixteen-page brochure with one day to a page) achieved a new professionalism. An initial meeting with the designer had been tense. But the image that emerged from the ragbag of ideas, of a monkey with hands over its ears ('hear no evil') clutching a metronome, realised exactly our aim of gaining attention through an enigmatic juxtaposition. Tim had the design and new logo printed on sweatshirts and T-shirts, a first venture into merchandise which enabled stewards and stagehands to wear matching tops – afterwards much coveted. In 1999, the Performing Right Society marked its sponsorship by providing a stash of swanky red and white umbrellas. These too became collectors' items, particularly when, after the festival, the surplus mysteriously disappeared. When Andrea became administrator in 1992, she obtained Arts Council support to produce

Design for the 1991 festival.

the brochure on audio tape, in large print and in Braille, achieving for Huddersfield the distinction of being the first festival to make its publicity available in four formats.

The monkey and metronome led to other quizzical juxtapositions: a crocodile flying through clouds on a dismembered keyboard in 1993 (the connection with Ligeti was a little obscure), and a dark trilby-clad stranger (shades of *The Third Man*) with a precocious piglet in 1994, to mark the premiere of *Gloria – a pig tale* by the Viennese composer HK Gruber. The designers depended on being fed striking photographs, and it was important to be proactive in obtaining them. After engaging Naked Design in 1994, Andrea or I would spend hours in their office in Leeds sitting beside the graphic designer at his computer. The shared input triggered impromptu inspiration and also increased accuracy, although not always clarity. Superimposed colours that looked vibrant on screen, like the blue and red in 1995, could be barely legible when printed. But, in general, the print was clear and stylish, and, to improve the layout, I readily rewrote copy on the spot. It was a fascinating process: creatively rewarding, physically draining and often uncomfortably close to deadlines.

Distribution

The first festival leaflets were mailed nationally by the London-based Contemporary Concerts Co-ordination (CCC). But there were no regional networks and, if you wanted material seen, it was best to place it yourself. During the weeks before each festival I drove around Bradford, Halifax, Huddersfield, Leeds, Sheffield and Manchester, delivering leaflets to music shops, universities, concert halls, theatres, galleries and art house cinemas, placing them prominently wherever I could. These time-consuming excursions gave way to more professional marketing only around 1990, with the growth of regional distribution networks.

Lamp-post banners for the 1989 festival.
PHOTO: SELWYN GREEN

I particularly focused on secondary schools in Kirklees and the regional further education colleges, in some of which (both schools and colleges) our former students were teaching. The dozen or so different posters, including Bob Linney's brilliantly quirky designs for the Contemporary Music Network, were sorted into packets for the Education Authority to deliver to individual schools. Others were mailed to university music departments and FE colleges countrywide. The music staff were glad to display them, as they helped stimulate the interest of the pupils they planned to bring. Many came for half a day or longer, contributing to the 'wall-to-wall' predominantly young audiences approvingly noted by the critics. Later, volunteers and trainees helped with these tasks, mounting displays in the public library, tourist-cum-ticket office and anywhere suitable to raise local awareness. In the late 1980s lamp-post banners were introduced to increase the festival's impact in the town.

By 1982 the audience had grown. On the opening day, Malcolm Cruise, critic of the *Huddersfield Examiner*, reported little evidence of the improved ticket sales I had confidently claimed, but, after the final concert, concluded that I must be 'well pleased'. In the *Financial Times* Dominic Gill wrote:

In Huddersfield 'festival' does not mean a prestigious, elitist showcase – cultural *parachutisme* from the capital to the provinces, of most evident benefit to a handful of journalists and Arts Council representatives. It means a serious forum, a lively meeting place, at which new music is performed and discussed by composers, performers and audiences in a local milieu. It was one of Huddersfield's most remarkable achievements this year to include so many events which alone would have justified a trip to Yorkshire. The halls were crowded, however – sometimes to near-capacity – not just with visitors but with local (and local student) faces.[5]

Ticket prices

From the beginning, it was agreed with Yorkshire Arts Association that admission charges would be little more than nominal so that young people could afford them. At £1.20 for an evening concert and 60p during the day (half price for students and senior citizens), they were incredibly low, even for the late 1970s. A decade later, in 1988, prices had risen to £4.50 (£2.50 concession) for evening concerts

in St Paul's, and £2.50 (£1.50) at lunchtime.
A Festival Saver cost £55 (£35) for thirty-one
ticketed events, including four major
Stockhausen concerts overseen by the composer.

Another ten years later, venues included the
Lawrence Batley Theatre, and in St Paul's all
seats were numbered, with two price ranges to
accommodate the larger audiences. Now tickets
for the majority of evening concerts in St Paul's
cost £12.50 (£7.50) or £7.50 (£5). In the theatre
the top price was £10 (£7.50). The highest cost
was for attending the final town hall concert
featuring Steve Reich, at which you could
choose between the balcony at £18 (£15), area
at £15 (£10) and gallery at £10 (£7.50). That
year (1998) a Festival Saver cost £204.50
(£135.50) – nearly four times the rate ten years
earlier, although it covered 20% more ticketed
events. In fact, all ticket prices had increased by
more than inflation. In the early years we had
targeted impecunious students; now prices were
aimed at the relatively well-off and generated
significant income. In 1978 total ticket sales
raised only £563. In 1988 this had increased to
£11,960, and in 1998 to £54,458.

One might have expected the student proportion
of the audience in 1998 to have decreased,
but due to various access schemes, particularly
charismatic programmes and persuasive
marketing, this was not the case. Nevertheless,
by the start of the new millennium, the
composition of the audience at many concerts
had noticeably changed.

By the festival's thirtieth anniversary in 2008
ticket prices had risen further, but only by a
small amount – indeed, some remained at a
similar level to 1998. The majority ranged from
£10 (£8) for a solo recital to £18 (£16) for an
evening ensemble concert. Although the
percentage discount was now less, it increased
to as much as a third for booking online –
unlike many concert halls and theatres which
load online bookings with handling charges,
many think unreasonably.

Access schemes

Higher ticket prices have been offset in recent
years by an advantageous scheme for seventeen
to twenty-five year olds. Sponsored by the Royal
Philharmonic Society, it makes 1,200 tickets
available for all events at only £6 for evening

> HUDDERSFIELD
> CONTEMPORARY MUSIC FESTIVAL
> 1988
>
> 69
>
> **WEEKEND BARGAIN 2**
>
> **This ticket gains admission to the Festival Club and to all concerts from
> 7.30 pm on Friday 25 November to the end of Sunday 27 November.**
>
> **Student/Claimant £13 50**

*A concession ticket
admitting the holder to nine
ticketed concerts during
the final weekend of the
1988 festival.*

concerts and £4 for others. That these are
comparable, or even lower than the rates in
1998, suggests that other reasons than price
explain why fewer teenagers now attend. In
2009 the number of seventeen to twenty-five
year olds still constituted more than a quarter
of the total audience – although we should
note that in 1991 it had been nearly half.

Throughout the life of the festival, bursaries
have been offered to help young people of
limited means to attend, especially those living
further away. Initially supported by the Ralph
Vaughan Williams Trust, since 1990 they have
been funded by the Holst Foundation. In 1986
twenty-three bursaries were awarded, mostly to
young composers; in 1987 thirty-six, including
visitors from abroad.

During the 1980s, full-time music students
of the polytechnic and other educational
institutions in West Yorkshire were admitted to
weekday lunchtime concerts free of charge, and,
to make the series more rewarding, I tried to
devise five or six complementary programmes.
At the 1990 festival, 644 tickets were given free
to students, approximately 450 of them to
members of the music department, although
thirty-seven bought Festival or Weekend Savers.
Apart from the benefit to the students, and to
the festival of their enthusiasm, this meant that
an average of 110 young people boosted the
audience at every lunchtime concert – most of
them in St Paul's – and visitors, such as Dominic
Gill (quoted above), were impressed by the
lively and vibrant atmosphere. In 1991 a charge
of 50p was introduced which, by 1995, had

risen to 80p. Lunchtime concerts were still packed with students, however, as when Stephen Dorrell, Minister of State for National Heritage, attended in 1994.

Nevertheless, I wanted these youngsters – two-thirds of them our own students – to experience the most remarkable evening events, both in the theatre and the town hall (which in any case we wanted to fill). Accordingly, we devised packages, each containing a variety of genres and scale. In 1998, for example, music department students were offered ten concerts and a programme book for a total of £17.50. Incredibly cheap in relation to the normal concession prices, this continued the practice of charging students so little that cost could not deter them. To spread their presence across the whole festival, each purchaser chose one of three different packages. Package C, for instance, consisted of:

Town Hall	Tan Dun's opera *Marco Polo* UKP.
St Paul's	Estonian Philharmonic Chamber Choir: 'Casting Spells'.
LBT	Jonathan Burrows Dance Group.
Town Hall	Hilliard Ensemble, Estonian Philharmonic Chamber Choir & Tallinn Chamber Orchestra.
St Paul's	Orchestra 2001 in music by George Crumb.
St Paul's	Northern Sinfonia in music by Simon Holt and Diana Burrell.
St Paul's	Arditti Quartet & Ursula Oppens: Tribute to Elliott Carter.
St Paul's	Apollo Saxophone Quartet, Psappha & Michael Torke (piano).
LBT	Newband playing Harry Partch's instrument-sculptures.
Town Hall	Ensemble Bash, Smith Quartet, Synergy, Steve Reich & Beryl Korot in an all-Reich programme, including the UK premiere of *Hindenburg*.

This was not only a bargain, but a stimulating and charismatic series of ten fantastic concerts. No wonder the halls were packed.

Audience building

I believed that a major purpose of the festival was to build audiences for the future. Capturing the imagination of teenagers was part of the strategy, winning over potential enthusiasts among the general public another. A new leaflet design, introduced in 1991, employed larger print, with each event well separated from its neighbours. Panels drew attention to concerts in venues of greater capacity. There were now regional distribution networks and an expanding mailing list. National awareness increased when Andrea Smart introduced a widely distributed return-mail card, inviting recipients to request the brochure (see the illustration on page 152). But, to increase local audiences at events in the town hall and theatre we needed flyers. These were now designed professionally, an early example (funded by a sponsor) being for the Kronos Quartet, on which – apart from the festival logo – the words 'Huddersfield Contemporary Music Festival' did not appear, deliberately to avoid negative preconceptions. Widely distributed, it helped achieve a gratifyingly large audience.

There were many times during the 1980s and early '90s when the festival's choice of title seemed unfortunate. 'Festival' was apt but unoriginal, 'music' too narrow for its varied activities, 'Huddersfield' perceived by potential sponsors as unprepossessingly provincial. As for 'contemporary', it sent shudders of alarm through the conventionally minded. Too late, I envied Strasbourg and Oslo their pithy but all-embracing 'Musica' and 'Ultima', and the oldest and most famous of new music festivals its 'Warsaw Autumn', indicating the location and time of year, but nothing else. How carelessly we had adopted our alienating name. Occasionally the Board debated its replacement, but could find no better alternative; although, as Graham McKenzie lamented in 2007, 'You've kind of lost the will to live by the time you've got to the end of the title.'[6] By then, however, the fashion for acronyms and email-style lower case had spawned 'hcmf', and the uninitiated might wonder where and what it was – except that by typing www.hcmf.co.uk, or merely 'hcmf' a single Google click would reveal all.

The more expansive A5 publicity brochures, introduced in 1998, were influenced by theatre and dance marketing, although there were also musical models – notably 'Secret Theatres: The Harrison Birtwistle Retrospective' on the South Bank in 1996 and 'American Pioneers' at the Barbican in 1998. Both adopted A5 brochures strikingly designed, and attracted huge audiences (despite Birtwistle's perceived 'difficulty'), which the more esoteric manner of some trendy contemporary arts venues might not have done. This was not the way in Europe,

where modernity of style is more evident –
addressed, perhaps, to a populace more
receptive to the new. In Paris the annual Festival
d'Automne, as well as other metropolitan
foreign festivals, used a tabloid magazine
format, in the manner of *Le Figaro,* an effective
means of reaching the newsprint readers of a
café-based society. I floated a similar idea with
the *Huddersfield Daily Examiner* (which already
gave the festival good coverage), but the cost
was too high, and distribution problematic.

We aimed to court a broad public, but not to
conceal the festival's bold and exploratory
purpose. I favoured imagery that played upon
the familiar but was enigmatic. I have already
mentioned the main image used in 2000
(adapted from IOU theatre, whose
extraordinary *Cure* in the bowls of Dean
Clough Mill in Halifax was part of the
programme), which showed a violinist in
Wellington boots and anorak on a desolate
beach, about to enter a blazing hut. Nothing
explained what this meant. But anyone who
later progressed through the dark dungeons of
Dean Clough, and out into the street,
encountered the hut itself set above them with,
at night, flames still billowing from its roof.
Such publicity was intended to appeal to a wide
interest-base, in the belief that most of what the
festival contained would be rewarding for
people generally culturally aware. The concern
for inclusiveness, and to avoid any suggestion of
a new music 'ghetto', probably influenced my
programme choices, which, towards the end
of the 1990s, contained less that was
uncompromisingly radical. The variety of high
quality concerts, theatrical genres, installations
and non-conventional locations continued.
But there was less, perhaps, newly probing the
frontiers of electronic media, crossover formats,
experimental and improvised music, for
instance, or challenging the nature of the art
form itself.

Redoubling our efforts to achieve capacity
audiences in the larger venues, in 1998 Maria
Bota produced an additional small booklet
featuring eight of the most engaging events:
three in the town hall, five in LBT. This was
the festival's first print in full colour,[7] and
undoubtedly effective. On the outside it bore
the one word 'Festival' and the dates, above
the bright, laughing eyes of a child. It could be
slipped into a pocket and opened to reveal a
feast. Maria's copy was glowing and the

*Publicity brochures for the
2000 and 2009 festivals.*

presentation enticing. A year later the main
brochure itself became full colour, but still with
the addition of a smaller leaflet highlighting a
selection. We maintained this two-pronged
strategy for three years, until economies dictated
a retrenchment, and were rewarded between
1997 and 1999 with a 28% further increase in
audiences.

Surveys taken among the town hall audiences
when the Kronos Quartet returned in 1993, and
at Reich's *Hindenburg* in 1999, showed that the
majority of respondents had never attended the
festival before, and knew little about it. Their
information came less from the brochure than
from our saturation leafleting, or from the
media, listings and word of mouth. In the new
millennium, of course, the non-print network of
web links, email and social networking would
become increasingly significant.

Multicultural audiences

A town hall concert in 1998, featuring the sarod
player Wajahat Khan and nine other Indian
musicians, posed a marketing challenge. The
idea of a larger than usual number of Indian
classical instrumentalists playing together had
originated in Khan's *A Garland of Tributes,*
performed in London for the fiftieth anniversary
of Indian independence in 1997. I had not been
present, but the notion of members of a

Members of the audience in St Paul's in 2005.
PHOTO: BRIAN SLATER

arts venues and organisations both sides of the Pennines.

Some 600 people attended the concert, and, from the front row of the balcony, I could see that over a third were Asian. This success was applauded by community leaders, and we should have built on it, but it was a one-off, not easily replicated and its marketing labour-intensive. The concert took place near the beginning of that year's festival; but, although enthusiastically received, there was no evidence that the Asians in the audience came to anything else. Having made such contacts, I regret that we did not progress them, perhaps by flagging up Tan Dun's *Marco Polo,* or programming something of Indian (as well as Chinese) origin the following year. One has to recognise, however, that the festival's contemporary agenda and traditional cultures are, historically and geographically, poles apart. Attracting an Afro-Caribbean audience to a formal Victorian concert hall would have been more difficult, and to a former church on the University campus harder still. At other concerts of non-Western music – even when performed, as in the Arts Council's 'Dunya' tour, by musicians from Mali and Rajasthan – audiences were predominantly white; which explains, perhaps, the motivation behind *Speakers Corner,* with its rapper and beatboxer, toured by the Contemporary Music Network in 2007 (see page 54). Educational projects are different. Reflecting the composition of the schools they serve, they can be unselfconsciously multiracial.

The decline of student attendees

As we have noted, a third or more of audiences during the 1980s usually consisted of students, most of them under the age of twenty. During

traditionally soloistic genre addressing issues of ensemble playing seemed justification enough to invite Khan and his colleagues to the festival. Could we attract the Asian communities of West Yorkshire and Lancashire, despite the concert appearing under the banner of a contemporary music festival? Provided with contact lists by Kirklees Council and the Asian Music Circuit, Maria and Alison Povey (then assistant administrator) worked out a strategy. Its impressive extent I fully appreciated only when, while researching aspects of this book, I consulted their file documenting the task. A press release was sent to Asian promoters, journalists and newspapers (in which the concert was also advertised). 12,500 flyers were delivered door-to-door with copies of the *Huddersfield Weekly News,* which ran a related editorial and a competition. Another 12,500 flyers were mailed, with introductory letters, to previous attenders at Asian arts events further afield, to the families of participants in workshops, and (in batches) to Asian stores,

Wajahat Kahn and his Indian Chamber Orchestra.
PHOTO: STEVE FORD

the 1990s the balance changed and, in the first decade of the new millennium, undergraduates and sixth-formers who had been such a vibrant and visible core during the '80s and '90s, were much less evident – if present at all. The festival still attracted good audiences, but of discerning adults, former students, music professionals and international visitors. Young attenders were not absent, but were more likely to be aged over twenty than below. There were a variety of reasons, some specific to Huddersfield, some more general. The music department's first-year undergraduates were now accommodated at Storthes Hall, five miles from the main campus, instead of the Central Services building, and disinclined to catch evening buses back into the town. The Recital Hall had been phased out as a venue and there were fewer charismatic town hall events. Furthermore, changes in the department's course structures, and in the musical experience in schools, coincided with an explosion of clubbing and pub culture and the increasing dominance of popular music. Once prominent figures – like Berio, Cage, Schnittke, Górecki, Messiaen, Pärt, Reich and Stockhausen – had lost their magnetism, and no one of similar stature appeared to exist to succeed them.

During the 1980s and '90s the festival capitalised on the 'wow' factor. But it was easier then than now, when 'wow' has been hijacked by media celebrities and reality TV. In the twenty-first century virtually every student has a computer and smartphone, with access to broadband, numerous applications, television channels, film and music downloads. But if the internet has changed the dynamic, its influence is far from negative, providing a Borgesian infinity of information and a conduit for persuasive marketing, profile building, communicating activity and for feeding expectations. Competition for attention is enormous, however, and websites tend to be visited by those already interested. Marketing on the internet is much cheaper than on paper. But it is questionable whether its ability to gain the attention of the uncommitted is as effective as well-aimed print.

Access schemes in the new century continued to provide substantially discounted tickets for individuals aged between seventeen and twenty-five, and to help school groups to attend (although still charging four-fifths of the full price). By the end of the decade, the less formal

daily Hub Shorts, introduced by Susanna Eastburn as a platform for up-and-coming musicians, had become strongly established and participation an aspiration for newly constituted contemporary groups around the country. In 2008 Graham McKenzie decided to concentrate them on a single afternoon of intensive activity, and the following year introduced the concept of 'free Mondays', including what had now been renamed hcmf// shorts, without admission charges.

Observing that some festivalgoers did not buy the full programme book, because the free brochure provided sufficient information, the new executive team in 2003 removed detailed listings from what now reverted to a folded leaflet, reduced in size and low-key in design. I thought it a very unwise economy and a reason for declining attendances. Music department students reported that nothing seized their attention. Ironically, the appointment of professional marketing specialists coincided with audiences significantly smaller than the festival had drawn in the 1990s. Meanwhile the programme book adopted full colour and, entrusted to Impromptu Publishing in Manchester, assumed the glossy design style of its *Muso* and other house publications, although some of its content, such as composer biographies, became cursory.

Concerned that the festival was underselling itself, in 2007 Graham and Nikki Cassidy – who, as a former music department student, had experienced the festival in the 1990s – restored the stapled brochure, distinctive design, detailed descriptions and full listings. More art-house in

Philip Thomas and Graham McKenzie with the festival brochure for 2008.
PHOTO: BRIAN SLATER

style, it proclaimed a new direction and helped rebuild attendance. The value of listings was demonstrated when I sat next to a couple at Genevieve Lacey's recorder recital in 2009. They had chosen to attend only this concert in the festival, because the brochure listed four pieces by John Rodgers, of particular interest to them as each depicted an Australian bird. Further print was unnecessary because, on this occasion, Lacey introduced each piece verbally. But that is unusual. All festivals providing only a comprehensive programme book confront the attender at a single event with a quandary: whether to buy the full programme book or not. A generous compromise is to make basic notes available online.

In 2008, the brochure became a pocket-book with up to eighty-eight pages, in which most events occupied a full page. Full colour was used only for advertisements. Elsewhere monochrome photographs in denim blue lent an archival tone to the programme, reflecting the focus on early electronic music, the 'recreation' of Cage's historic 1958 concert in New York Town Hall, and tributes to other dead composers: Cardew, Stockhausen, Sun Ra, James Tenney and Zappa.

Not that the new had been abandoned, for the brochure also announced thirty UK and twenty-seven world premieres – although many of the latter by relatively little-known composers. The programme book contained more substantial content, particularly in the contributory essays and more informative composer biographies. With a restrained but stylish use of colour in their brochures, the 2009 and 2010 festivals emphatically celebrated the living, although not without tributes to Cage again, and to Kagel who had died in 2008.

By 2010, the web and social networking sites were being effectively employed, as were plasma screens in the venues and external projections onto the Creative Arts Building and the wall opposite the Lawrence Batley Theatre. The role of internet marketing had hugely increased, with promotional emails sent to recipients known to be interested. With a degree of realism, perhaps, the festival appeared to be targeting a more specialist audience – aware, knowledgeable and committed. To people out and about in Huddersfield there was less evidence of a festival taking place: no lamp-post banners, no large banner hung from St Paul's, and no saturation leafleting.

15 *Partnerships and management*

Partners and funders

On the first inside page of the 2008 festival programme book is a large panel containing the names and logos of over forty 'Event Partners'. Few of them are commercial sponsors. Rather, they are a collection of British and foreign government cultural and educational organisations, as well as trusts, empathising with and motivated to support the festival through collaboration and/or funds. After Graham McKenzie's introduction and a diary of events, two pages headed 'Festival Support' contain essays by the directors of four partner institutions extolling the benefits of working together. None of them – BBC Radio 3, the British Council, Music Centre the Netherlands, and the Society for the Promotion of New Music – could be regarded as occasional associates, having in one guise or another supported the festival throughout most of its history.[1] Nevertheless, the prominence given to these partnerships, and to the University of Huddersfield as 'Headline Sponsor', indicated the increasing importance of co-production, collaboration and international links.

For the BBC, Andrew Kurowski explained the advantages of co-commissioning, and the relationship between the festival and Radio 3's 'Cut and Splice' and 'Hear and Now' programmes. Shoël Stadlen highlighted the spnm's 'Shortlist' in nurturing the next generation of composers. For the British Council, Cathy Graham stressed the interest in the festival amongst producers worldwide, and the role of the British Council in bringing people together, brokering co-production and exchanges, with the intention of inspiring 'yet more work across borders'. Henk Heuvelmans wrote about strengthening new music in Great Britain and the Netherlands through co-productions and exchanges, and the value to Dutch new music of promoting work in Huddersfield, because 'the eyes of not only British but especially international new music life are on HCMF'. The Netherlands he saw as a 'flourishing garden in which McKenzie happily wanders and chooses what to present to his audience'. In 2010 the essays by festival partners extended to three pages, adding to existing partners the PRS for Music Foundation, University of Huddersfield and Music Information Centre Norway.

International collaborations have been an important component of the Huddersfield festival since the middle of the 1980s. They underpinned the UK debut of Ensemble Modern, the UK premiere of Ferneyhough's *Carceri d'Invenzion,* performances by Australian, Canadian, Austrian and Scandinavian ensembles, and the appearance of many Dutch musicians. Some were negotiated directly with ensembles, such as Asko and BIT-20; some with foreign government cultural agencies, such as the Goethe-Institut, Association française d'action artistique and Rikskonserter in Sweden. Most have been a combination of both – or, in Holland, of a web of associated musical organisations including the publisher Donemus. Undoubtedly, the festival's standing in Britain, the international content of its programme and consistent high standards of performance increasingly motivated foreign government cultural agencies to welcome it as a platform.

At the turn of the century, the newly created Réseau Varèse delivered some immensely impressive productions, and has supported further co-productions throughout the decade.

Graham McKenzie welcoming guests to a reception during the 2010 festival.
PHOTO: BRIAN SLATER

One of the most interesting was *Sandglasses* by the Lithuanian composer Justė Janulytė seen at the 2010 festival (illustrated on the cover of this book). This was a co-production with the Galda Festival, MaerzMusik and the Holland Festival, as well as the Lithuanian Cultural Foundation and Ministry of Culture – in co-ordinating which Graham McKenzie had played a leading part. In most instances, the products of all these collaborations have, in the UK, been experienced only in Huddersfield.

Since being appointed artistic director in 2006, Graham has worked tirelessly to position international partnerships at the heart of artistic strategy. A priority has been to establish longer collaborations, ideally lasting three years, as agreed with the Dutch in 2008 and with the Norwegian Ministry of Foreign Affairs through the Music Information Centre Norway in 2010. Another goal is to broker co-productions with a wider range of partners, and sell them on to the benefit of both the originators and an increasing number of recipients. The performance of Bernhard Lang's *TablesAre Turned* by turntable sound artist Philip Jeck with six musicians of the Italian ensemble Alter Ego at the 2011 festival could be regarded as a generic model. The proposal came from the ensemble, which already had one producer on board. Graham liked the project and agreed to be a partner, arguing, however, that if he could enrol others the cost to each should come down. By the autumn of 2011, *TablesAre Turned* had five co-producers – hcmf//, MaerzMusik, Wien Modern, November Music and the Wundergrund Festival – with the possibility of others. Those without the premiere get a well-honed performance, and all co-producers benefit from their names being 'on the road' throughout the year.

Broadcasting

Three concerts were due to be recorded by BBC Radio 3 from the Polytechnic Great Hall in 1978. But fog prevented the Gaudeamus Quartet flying from Holland and only the Aulos Ensemble was broadcast. After this inauspicious beginning, nothing was transmitted from the 1979 and '80 festivals, as neither the department of music Recital Hall, where most concerts took place, nor Venn Street Arts Centre were adequately soundproofed. Concerts from the town hall had been broadcast for many years, notably those given by Huddersfield

Choral Society, and performances by any of the BBC orchestras were routinely broadcast, so that the BBC Northern Symphony Orchestra concert which ended the 1981 festival followed the pattern.

That year also saw the opening of St Paul's, and in 1982 four programmes from it were broadcast on 'Music in our Time' – predecessor of 'Hear and Now' – for which the festival received a modest facility fee. Its suitability for broadcasting raised the possibility of a more balanced sharing of performance costs. In 1985, soon after proposing Berio's *Coro*, whose performance (in the town hall) would be substantially funded by the BBC, Stephen Plaistow asked whether we would like to receive the premiere of *White Winter, Black Spring*, a cantata with tenor and bass soloists by John Hopkins, which Radio 3 had commissioned for performance by Lontano. For this the BBC would pay all the fees, the festival would cover expenses, and the programme could be made up with a winning work in the Young Composers' Award and my proposal of *Canti del Sole* by Bernard Rands. Bernard had moved from York University to the USA in 1975, and this would be the UK premiere of a piece stylistically very different from his Berio-influenced early work, but which, in its orchestral version, had won a Pullitzer Prize one year before.

The next year saw an even stronger partnership with Radio 3, with eight concerts recorded for future transmission, culminating in a co-promoted invitation concert given by the BBC Symphony Orchestra. Amongst them were three concerts featuring the UK debut of Ensemble Modern with Heinz Holliger, for which Radio 3 agreed to contribute to the fees. With financial support from the Goethe-Institut, and the recently formed Ensemble Modern charging much less than ten years later, the cost to the festival was little more than £5,000. Without such collaboration, however, either the visit would not have happened or the rest of the festival would have been constrained.

In 1987 Radio 3 again recorded eight concerts, plus my interview with Iannis Xenakis and a lecture by Brian Ferneyhough (although this was never broadcast). The BBC also agreed to share the cost of the three Stockhausen concerts in 1988. Each was advertised in *Radio Times* as 'A Radio 3 co-promotion with the Huddersfield Contemporary Music Festival', so raising the

Lucia Ronchetti's comic 'madrigal' about cooking, Anatra al sal *(Duck with salt), performed by Neue Vocalsolisten Stuttgart in 2005 and recorded for a subsequent broadcast by Radio 3.*
PHOTO: BRIAN SLATER

festival's profile amongst its readers, including any who did not tune in. One could not expect such a formula to continue annually. But it happened again in 1995 when the BBC co-produced the festival's Nono retrospective, on this occasion making a rare live broadcast from the town hall of a late-night programme timed to coincide with 'Hear and Now'. The concert included UK premieres of *A Pierre. Dell'azzuro silenzio, inquietum* and the beautiful *Das atmende Klarsein,* the live sounds of both pieces transformed and dispersed electronically, floating through space to touch the hall's furthest recesses with soft, mysterious tones. So nearly silent, Nono's late work was a challenge to the BBC engineers – but even more to radio listeners, who needed to give this delicate, fleeting music their undivided attention.

I have already mentioned the live broadcast of Simon Holt's open, *The Nightingale's to Blame* in 1998. A further live broadcast took place in 2011, when the world premiere of Barrett's *CONSTRUCTION* was transmitted from the town hall in an extended 'Hear and Now' on Radio 3. Neither the town hall nor St Paul's Hall are insulated from the most penetrating noises. So, when in 1986 Stephen offered a chamber music invitation concert as part of Radio 3's 'Russian Season', we agreed that it should take place during the relative peace of a Sunday morning. The concert had just begun

when I became aware of a persistent rumble, and saw through the window an orange flashing light. Hurrying outside, I found a procession of monster machines occupying the nearest carriageway of the ring road, enveloped in the smoke and aroma of molten asphalt. It had never occurred to me that the highways authority might think Sunday morning an optimum time for resurfacing. Finding the foreman, I asked if they could stop until the end of the concert. A forlorn hope, I thought, but, surprisingly, he agreed. After that I wrote annually to the highways department requesting that no work should be undertaken for the duration of the festival.

Reading this story, Graham McKenzie was reminded that, during the 2010 festival, 'it was reported that I left a concert by ELISION at the interval, and that this was taken as some kind of comment on the music! In fact I had just been told that workmen had arrived to dig up the road outside St Thomas's where Clemens Merkel was due to give a solo violin recital later that afternoon. I left to try and retrieve the situation and ask that they suspend activities for the duration of the concert. Some things never change...!'

Under Graham the partnership with Radio 3 was strongly reaffirmed in terms of joint commissions and broadcasts. After each of the

2008, 2009 and 2010 festivals, five broadcasts took place on 'Hear and Now', relaying performances from fifteen concerts in 2008, ten in 2009 and twelve in 2010. Those in 2009 included a live broadcast from Bates Mill of Harvey's *Bhakti* and Barrett's *Mesopotamia* performed by the London Sinfonietta with Sound Intermedia. In 2007 Simon Fell's *Positions & Descriptions* was also broadcast on 'Jazz on 3'.

Conveying the flavour

As the number of broadcast concerts increased, so, too, did arts reviews and previews on both Radio 3 and Radio 4. The earliest was a flattering portrait presented by Michael Oliver and produced by Graham Sheffield for *Music Weekly* in 1986. That year reviews of the festival were broadcast on radio programmes in Germany, Hungary and Russia. In 1987 the BBC recorded the Lontano concert containing *Into Eclipse* by Stephen Albert, which had caused controversy and provoked audible protest. Andrew Kurowski decided to follow the broadcast with a discussion between David Bedford, James Dillon, Christopher Fox and Stephen Montague – composers of very different stylistic allegiances – and invited me to chair it. Being no Stephen Albert, I'm afraid that I failed to trigger the confrontational disputation Andrew had hoped for, and the discussion was (disappointingly?) harmonious.

The variety, international buzz and sheer excitement of the festival were conveyed to a wider public when Radio 4 broadcast its prime-time *Kaleidoscope* arts programme direct from Huddersfield in November 1990. The presenter was Natalie Wheen, who mixed pre-recorded interviews with Schnittke, Rozdestvensky and Gerard McBurney, clips from the concerts, animated comments from members of the audience and Huddersfield Choral Society, live discussion between Gerald Larner, Natalie and myself, and folk music played in the Cellar Theatre, temporarily enrolled as a 'studio', by the New Music Ensemble of Vilnius. Natalie's enthusiasm, and her skilfully compiled broadcast, painted an engaging impression of the festival at the beginning of its second decade. The focus on post-*glasnost* activity in Russia and Eastern Europe was topical and gave the programme extra immediacy. There had been an earlier *Kaleidoscope Extra* presented by

Luke O'Shaughnessy, general manager from 1999 to 2001.
PHOTO: PAUL HERRMANN

Michael Berkeley in 1986, which concentrated on interviews with Lutosławski, Nigel Osborne and myself. When Michael presented another survey in 1992, and Lynne Walker a live programme in 1996, they were for Radio 3's *In Tune,* which, at the time, was broadcast on location as often as from Broadcasting House.

Augmenting these national broadcasts were interviews on local and regional radio, and for arts programmes in other countries. One of the best, in my view, was a half-hour programme with well-chosen musical illustrations presented by Ian McMillan on BBC Radio Leeds in 1994. In 2006 the festival was featured on Radio 4's 'PM' programme. The following year a four-minute profile, filmed in Huddersfield, was broadcast on Japanese television. But the peak of prime time attention was achieved in 2010, when the 'Cage Train' and other events were featured on the BBC's 'Today' programme.

Management

At first the festival had no formal structure. The accounts were managed by Kirklees Leisure

Services which, had there been a deficit, would have underwritten it; but I didn't intend to overspend. When Yorkshire Arts and the local authority insisted that the festival should have a constitution and steering committee, I briefly resisted – until overruled. If there had to be such a body, I wanted people who understood the artistic brief as well as new music. In fact, they were easier to recruit than representatives of business and management. The first steering group met in 1982, and by the end of the year consisted of the composers David Blake and Patric Standford; Arthur Jacobs, head of the music department and Phil Ellis, director of its electronic music studio; David Patmore, music officer of Yorkshire Arts Association; Brian Pearson and Ron Morton representing Kirklees Leisure Services; representatives of Kirklees council and West Yorkshire MCC; Helen Hale, the festival's first (part-time) administrator, and myself. The chair for many years was Councillor Denis Ripley, a keen advocate of the arts who also served as chair of the education and cultural committees for the local authority. A constitution was drawn up, modelled almost exactly on that of the York Early Music Festival. Philip Wood was appointed company secretary, and produced minutes in admirable detail.

At a meeting of the steering group in 1983, Patric Standford observed that 'the artistic director's allowance was a derisory figure'. I was inclined to agree, but stressed the greater desirability of employing an administrative assistant, pointing out, however, that 'the budget could not possibly sustain this'.[2]

Subsequent members included the composers John Casken and Nicola Lefanu; Anthony Sargent, then director of arts in Birmingham; Alistair Graham, director of the Training and Enterprise Council in Kirklees and Calderdale, and afterwards in Leeds (until he was appointed chair of the Parades Commission in Northern Ireland, and then of the Committee of Standards in Public Life); Ken Baird, former director of music at the Arts Council; and my university colleagues Michael Clarke and George Pratt, head of the music department between 1986 and 1992. Of the Yorkshire Arts music officers who followed David Patmore, David Whelton (who subsequently moved to the Arts Council in London before becoming managing director of the Philharmonia Orchestra) and Jim Beirne made key contributions. Joining the board around the turn of the century were Jonathan Drake, Brian's successor as director of Kirklees Cultural Services and Sarah Derbyshire and Rosemary Johnson, both working for organisations with whom the festival had a long relationship. In 2003 Dr Mick Peake, cancer clinician, Friend, benefactor, CoMA member

The festival's four artistic directors during its first thirty-three years. From left to right: Graham McKenzie, Richard Steinitz, Susanna Eastburn and Tom Service.
PHOTO: BRIAN SLATER

and very knowledgeable supporter of the festival virtually from its inception, succeeded Denis Ripley as chair.

It was an agreeably homogenous group, little given to objection or criticism, but insightful and imaginative in exploring and contributing ideas. Only Arthur Jacobs was disposed to be combative, having a propensity for acerbic argument. But he could be equally positive and supportive. The board operated by consensus and rarely voted. Issues were raised, and advocacies voiced, that I might not otherwise have considered. I particularly valued the artistic input of the composers. At February meetings we reviewed the last festival and tabled plans for the next. The officers and I would present what we proposed, explain the budget and its challenges, and invite comments. By June, the programme was virtually complete, although supported by a budget that might still be speculative and, perhaps, not balance. Since firm commitments had to be made before the board reconvened, we were trusted to make responsible decisions. Throughout my time as artistic director there was no significant deficit, except in 1992, when a serious accident to the festival's technical director followed the devaluation of Black Wednesday – two events we could not have forseen. But, as technical specifications became increasingly elaborate, breaking even was harder to ensure. With turn-over approaching half a million, there was greater scope for miscalculation or misfortune. The Board was relatively laissez-faire in its reluctance to scrutinise in detail, and probably over-reliant on the artistic director and general manager to keep the festival solvent. But board members were busy people. One was grateful for their time (Huddersfield not being the easiest destination for meetings), especially when some gave two or three days to shortlist and interview new appointees.

In 1990 Yorkshire Arts commissioned development consultants to examine the festival's operation. Being employed to make proposals as well as analyse, the consultants recommended strengthening board membership, and the establishment of three sub-committees to focus respectively on Finance and Management, Artistic Content, and Development. An F&M sub-committee might have scrutinised the finances more rigorously, but the board rejected it. They probably felt, as I did, that the administrator/general manager presented both budget and cash flow with admirable clarity, and that the festival had a history of accuracy and precision. A development sub-committee was instituted, but lacking business representatives with sufficient clout, it did not long survive. As for the artistic committee, although keen to pool ideas, I thought it unlikely that we could

The UK debut of Ensemble Resonanz during the first weekend of he 2010 festival, co-funded by the British Council.
PHOTO: BRIAN SLATER

St Paul's seen from the atrium of the university's Creative Arts Building.

persuade busy arts practitioners to convene regularly in Huddersfield. So, for a few years, I invited selected guests to the last day of the festival (including some taking part in it), followed by a brainstorming meeting the morning after. The first, held on 2 December 1991, was attended by Val Bourne, founder-director of Dance Umbrella; David Jones of Serious Productions; the composer James MacMillan; Janis Susskind, promotion manager of Boosey & Hawkes; Andrew Kurowski of Radio 3 and Dr Mick Peake.

My retirement presented the board with inevitable changes. But the festival's future direction was of more concern after Susanna Eastburn's sabbatical move to the Clore Leadership Programme in 2004, and her resignation as artistic director one year later. The appointment of Tom Service as guest artistic director resulted in a strong artistic programme, although of narrower remit. But, as he was resident in London and on a one-year contract, financial security and forward planning suffered, and local relationships

weakened at a time when personnel were changing and the infrastructure was at its most vulnerable. The financial situation was also unhealthy, and the board faced worrying strategic decisions affecting the festival's future viability.

That the institution has returned to a position of strength does credit to the board as well as its executive. The festival has travelled a long way since being organised by a part-time artistic director with no other employees and no constitution. Thirty years later it has an artistic director who is also chief executive, a festival manager, a learning and participation officer (both full-time posts), a programme assistant, marketing director, two production managers and four other part-time posts. Their energies have led to a revival in audience numbers, increased international profile enhanced by a productive web of partnerships, pioneering initiatives in marketing, special needs and IT, impressively smooth-running events and a substantial increase in income.

16 *The new millennium*

The decline of art music?

Entering the new millennium, it was disturbing to observe the virtual elimination of new music from many concert series in Britain. Even the Contemporary Music Network had embraced the prevailing pop culture of folk, rock and techno, and, in doing so, all but abandoned its original *raison d'être*: contemporary 'classical' and jazz. Before long, the Network, too, had disappeared. Anyone looking further afield might conclude this to be a peculiarly British (or English-speaking) malaise, observing that in continental Europe, including Scandinavia, new music continues to flourish, ensembles to tour and audiences to come and listen.

London remains a unique vortex of cultural energy and enterprise. With its five symphony orchestras, two opera houses, the South Bank Centre, Barbican arts complex, Wigmore Hall, King's Place concert halls, numerous other performing organisations and several festivals, there is probably no other city in the world so richly endowed with live art music performed to such a high standard. The spectacular success of the BBC Proms suggests that not only is classical music popular, it is socially democratic. Wide-ranging programmes encourage open-minded listening, so that one finds audiences of several thousand applauding work that is both unfamiliar and intellectually elevated; whilst the broadening of the Proms to include 'World Routes' and film music, including John Wilson's brilliant reconstructions of the finely crafted scores of Hollywood musicals – even comedy and 'Horrible Histories' (a free family Prom) – has revitalised the concept.

To a limited extent the vibrancy is replicated in Birmingham, Manchester and some other cities.

But elsewhere a diminishing and ageing audience, the narrowing of programmes into repetitive cycles of core repertoire, a distaste for aural and stylistic adventure, and the marginalisation of classical music in the media is eroding vitality. Orchestras appoint composers-in-association, providing valuable opportunities for those early in their careers. But, except for the BBC orchestras, they rarely promote the music of living composers unattached to them, nor do they venture into the vast riches of twentieth-century repertoire beyond the relatively familiar. We should not, however, measure musical health only in terms of

LEFT:
The UK premiere of
NONcerto for horn *by*
Richard Ayres performed
by Wim Timmermans and
Asko in 2004.
PHOTO: BRIAN SLATER

RIGHT:
The soloist Wim
Timmermans speeding
across the stage
(see page 56).
PHOTO: BRIAN SLATER

orchestras, whose socio-historic origins and sheer scale remove them from the evolving landscape of other genres.

The investment in infrastructure, in new and refurbished buildings funded from the National Lottery, is to be applauded, as are the crowds who flock to art galleries and the lively young audiences one sees in the most vibrant regional theatres. More negative have been the contraction of instrumental teaching in schools and downgrading of cultural education in general: of history, languages, philosophy, ethics – the essential ingredients of intellectual maturity and, one might argue, of personal development and social cohesion.

Whether we live in an age of cultural enrichment or decline is endlessly debatable. Cultural engagement has become a wider issue, inextricably bound up with the fissures that divide society. What is indisputable is that the make-up of society has changed. British cultural vitality in the postwar years owed much to the influx of refugees from the Nazi-dominated continent of Europe; before that from the Russian revolution, and later from the Soviet stranglehold of Eastern Europe. To name a handful of the most influential refugees – Sir Isaiah Berlin, Lucian Freud, Ernst Gombrich, Nikolaus Pevsner, Tom Stoppard, Victor Hochhauser, Walter and Alexander Goehr, three-quarters of the Amadeus Quartet, Martin Esslin (head of drama at the BBC) and Hans Keller (in its music department) – is to identify only the tip of an iceberg. The flood of European intellectuals, followed by immigrants from a wider world has contributed to a nation of extraordinarily diverse cultural energies, although, some might argue, also to its segmentation. According to data published by the Office of National Statistics in August 2007, more than a quarter of babies currently born in Britain have at least one foreign-born parent. In London in 2005, 51% of births were to a mother born overseas. Rick Muir, of the Institute of Public Policy Research, points out that we can no longer regard Britain as an old, long-established, relatively static place. Global mobility has made the UK 'mutable, energetic and changeable, like young Australia or frontier America... a society of multiple cultures and identities'.[1]

The experimental tradition.

It was in an apparently stable and optimistic climate that Huddersfield Contemporary Music Festival was born, and in a world of rapidly changing allegiances that it has grown up. A festival of the new must surely reflect the present. Or should it equally proclaim the artistic achievements of the last fifty years? In its fourth decade, any festival of innovation risks the ultimate irony: predictability. Experimental music has become history. In his definitive 1974 book, *Experimental Music: Cage and Beyond*, Michael Nyman describes experimental music as a 'musical tradition that grew essentially from the music and ideas of John Cage in the period after the Second World War'.[2] But if experiment becomes tradition does that not raise the question of what happens when the unorthodox becomes orthodox? Does the adrenalin drain from what was once breath-catchingly unpredictable? Cage defined 'experimental' as descriptive 'of an act the outcome of which is unknown'.[3] In the work of present-day experimentalists, the minutiae may surprise; but the package can seem tediously conventional compared with the unsettling iconoclasm of Cage and his predecessors – or of the Portsmouth Sinfonia murdering the classics in the Albert Hall to an audience many of whom thought they were about to hear a professional orchestra.

Even the term 'contemporary' has become retrospective, seeming less appropriate to the music created now than it was to the seismic upheavals of half a century ago. In a discussion between Christopher Fox, Graham McKenzie and two other festival directors in 2007,[4] Graham drew on his previous experience as director of the Centre for Contemporary Arts in Glasgow to make a comparison between the currency of 'contemporary' in the visual arts:

...whereas in contemporary music, I found that last year I was endlessly dealing with seventieth birthdays, eightieth birthdays, 100th birthdays, and I found myself asking: 'is this contemporary?'. The term 'contemporary' to denote composers who are alive or who were recently alive can really get in the way of emerging composers and practitioners who are trying to break through. Of course you need to keep a balance, and in visual arts I think things have gone too far in rejecting artists at too early an age, but I feel that in contemporary music things are too far weighted towards the older and established.

The dance critic Judith Mackrell takes a slightly different view. 'Modern dance', she wrote after the deaths of Pina Bausch and Merce Cunningham in 2009, 'is now 100 years old, and while its focus, rightly, is on the creation and encouragement of new work, it has to look at conservation too.'[5]

Outside the contemporary music market place, the label 'contemporary' is now little used for concerts of new art music. The calendar for London's Kings Place Festival in September 2011 lists events as either 'Classical', 'Folk', 'Jazz', 'Interact', 'Spoken Word', 'Contemporary', 'Comedy' or 'Food & Drink'. Under 'Contemporary' we find *Chiptunes* – three concerts 'with live visuals, mixing glitched video and images with circuit-bent hardware, retro games consoles and creative common hardware' which have been 'revolutionising the

contemporary music industry all over the world'[6]. The London Sinfonietta's portrait concerts of Carter, Pärt and Julian Anderson are labelled 'Classical', along with the music of Haydn, Mozart, Mendelssohn, Janáček and Shostakovich. 'Contemporary' has been appropriated by a burgeoning popular culture, whilst it would seem that classical music, in all its various guises, is regarded with opprobrium by many of the young.

Conservation or change

After two defining decades, my successor artistic directors had to consider how far to carry the festival forward in a similar vein, how much to change. Creativity and conservation are not such clear opposites, however. New work in the same mold can seem routine. Whilst the festival's increasingly frequent focus on dead composers – Cage, Cardew, Feldman, Stockhausen – depends on the premise that their work, more than most, remains perennially experimental.

Susanna Eastburn's festivals between 2002 and 2004 maintained the emphasis on new notated music, but with a variety of adjuncts to the core concert programme following the pattern of the previous decades. Taking over in April 2001, she inherited much of that year's choices, adding, however, to my planned Nordic thread, and continuing it through the next three years. In 2001 this led to visits by Hans Abrahamsen, Arne Nordheim, Bent Sørensen and Rolf Wallin. In 2002 the focus was on Per Nørgård, with other portrait concerts devoted to Simon Bainbridge, Aldo Clementi, Stephen Mackey, and Gerald Barry, whose opera *The Bitter Tears of Petra von Kant* received a partial UK concert premiere. In 2003 there was the UK premiere of Harrison Birtwistle's *Theseus Game,* preceded by a fascinating discussion between Birtwistle and Jonathan Cross – so much more engaged and revealing than the edgy encounter between Birtwistle and Tippett in 1991.

A performance of Birtwistle's *The Io Passion* by Aldeburgh Almeida Opera was a high point of the 2004 festival. Similarly 'mainstream' were Nigel Osborne's opera *The Electrification of the Soviet Union* in 2002, and in 2003 a chain of *Sequenzas* in memory of Berio, who had died in May 2003, culminating in an entertainingly droll performance of *A-Ronne* by Neue

Vocalsolisten Stuttgart. The following year focused on Kevin Volans, Howard Skempton and the Dutch composer Richard Rijnvos, plus a seventieth birthday tribute to Sir Peter Maxwell Davies and – most interestingly, perhaps – substantial works by Richard Ayres and Rebecca Saunders. Their performances were entrusted to musikFabrik, Recherche and Asko, with *choler*, a festival commission from Saunders, given its world premiere by Rolf Hind and Nicolas Hodges. Susanna also focused on the 'experimental tradition' with a tribute to Cardew in 2001 (the twentieth anniversary of his death), a portrait of Christian Wolff in 2002, another of Helmut Oehring in 2003, and a group of pieces by composers such as Joanna Baillie, Lawrence Crane and Christopher Fox under the title 'Harmonic Fields Forever' in 2004. All these were performed by Apartment House, now (with the exception only of 2005) an annual visitor to the festival. That Apartment House, with its avowed focus on experimental music, has become the only ensemble in thirty-three years to perform so regularly, would seem to indicate a change in the festival's emphasis.

As guest director in 2005, Tom Service devised a festival on familiar lines, most impressively in

Ensemble Modern's performance of Lachenmann's large-scale new ensemble composition *Concertini*, described by Lynne Walker in *The Independent* as a 'scaling of extraordinary musical heights'.[7] There were other fine ensembles, including the debut of Ensemble Nomad from Tokyo performing music by Japanese composers, notably Jo Kondo who was being featured at Huddersfield for the first time. To mark the hundredth anniversary of the birth of Giacinto Scelsi, the New London Chamber Choir performed eight of his works. There was a memorable CMN concert given by the accordionist Evelyna Petrova and the Pokrovsky Ensemble Choir, drawing on the manner and rituals of Russian village music and including an extraordinarily earthy interpretation of Stravinsky's *Les Noces*. A handful of solo and duo recitals included Noriko Kawai's complete performance of Dillon's *Book of Elements*.

But there were some unfortunate misjudgements, particularly opening the festival with an esoteric programme of music by obscure or little-known composers, played by the Freiburg Baroque Orchestra in Huddersfield Town Hall. It attracted an audience of barely

Jo Kondo interviewd by Tom Service in 2005.
PHOTO: BRIAN SLATER

100, and to make matters worse, the first two pieces by Benjamin Schweitzer and Nadir Vassena, as Ivan Hewett reported in *The Daily Telegraph*, 'seemed little more than desultory doodles, tricked out with irritatingly pretentious programme notes'.[8] With the public thinly scattered across ten times as many seats, the atmosphere was dismal; and the reviews and their headlines made uncomfortable reading.[9] At the opposite extreme, the use of the new Studio 2 in Milton Hall, with an audience capacity of barely eighty, for weekend concerts usually attracting twice that number, resulted in some potential visitors (unable to purchase weekend savers) deciding not to come at all.

Ivan Hewett's view was that Tom 'has kept faith with the Huddersfield Festival's guiding principle, which is to have no truck with neo-Romantic pap, sub-minimalist film music, or indeed anything remotely easy-going'.[10] Was that really what I had been doing? I thought it much too narrow a perception. Ligeti, after all, had praised the festival for its non-ideological breadth and willingness to programme what might turn out to be 'bad music'. The stylistic range of earlier festivals had been wide, embracing ambient music, minimalism of all kinds (including Philip Glass's film scores), even unabashed neo-romanticism. Indeed, I had developed an increasingly populist streak – keen to build an audience far wider than the new music coterie – as this book should make clear. In November 2010, Clare Stevens headed an article in *Classical Music* with: 'Huddersfield Festival used to be a byword for the more arid regions of the contemporary classical world, where only the most devoted disciples of the Darmstadt school could be guaranteed a good time.'[11] Anyone who attended the festival in the 1980s and '90s knows how patently untrue is that assessment. Had she ever visited it, I wondered?

Whether or not Hewett and Stevens were right, Graham McKenzie's appointment signalled a more decisive change of direction. From his previous role as artistic director of the Centre for Contemporary Arts in Glasgow, Graham brought an enthusiasm for visual and experimental work and multidisciplinary practice across genres. This chimed with a resurgence of experimentalism among younger composers, and an increasing engagement with mixed media, digital technology, installations and performance art. Graham's use of non-traditional performance spaces avoided the alienating associations of the concert hall, and his managerial experience, collaborative disposition and concern to reinvigorate a strong and supportive infrastructure were particularly timely. Only after he arrived did it become clear that the festival's finances were dangerously insecure. He had inherited an unprecedented deficit which might have deterred any other appointee from taking up the reins. Instead, he quietly proceeded to address it. But it is hardly surprising that the festival has engaged no full-size symphony orchestra since 2002.

Graham McKenzie's festivals

With only six months to assemble his first festival in 2006, Graham found nothing already planned. To create a central thread, he engaged John Tilbury and the Smith Quartet to play ten concerts devoted to Morton Feldman's music for strings and piano and, around these, devised a series of relatively hardcore events, many involving advanced electronic technology, crossover genres and improvisation. Among them were ensembles new to the festival such as zeitkratzer, Alter Ego and Pan Sonic, as well as second appearances by Poing and [rout]. Barry Guy presided over performances of his music by the City of London Sinfonia and his own New Orchestra, made up of leading European and American improvisers. John Butcher made a first festival appearance and other improvising musicians included the Christian Wallumrød Ensemble from Norway. A series of performances lasting several hours took place in the Tokyo and Livingstone's nightclubs, where members of the audience could come and go at will. In the newly discovered Bates Mill Blending Shed, the final Contemporary Music Network concert to take place at the festival was given by the Reykjavik collective, Kitchen Motors, featuring Icelandic musicians and the hypnotically slow-moving ambient soundscapes of Jóhann Jóhannson, accompanied by atmospheric lighting (see page 187).

If some festival regulars were disconcerted by the change of emphasis, Graham's second festival in 2007 asserted his agenda more emphatically. In the neutral ambience of Bates Mill – in which a new younger clientele could feel comfortable – he programmed experimental and installation-based work not easily categorised. *Night of the Unexpected,* which

*John Butcher performing
with Elision in 2006.*
PHOTO: BRIAN SLATER

kicked off the festival, was calculated to make a splash and draw the public to an evening full of surprises – appetising 'trailers' for events taking place during the following nine days. The low-key opening of some previous years was roundly banished. Audience numbers were higher than in 2006, and there was much discussion about the direction of the festival and its greater accord with twenty-first century mores. Many concerts featured only younger composers and artists embracing new technology. There was more emphasis on visual spectacle and the unusual. Assisted by members of the curiously named Vienna Vegetable Orchestra, shoppers at Huddersfield's open market were invited to make their own 'vegetable' instruments (see page 227). In a concert later that day, despite moments of Pythonesque absurdity, the ingenuity of their approach revealed, through close miking, an extensive menu of intriguing sounds.

It was nicely apposite that the Vienna Vegetable Orchestra should perform in the Blending Shed, in a concert co-produced with Cut & Splice, an annual festival of live and broadcast activity produced by the Sonic Arts Network and BBC Radio 3. Sky News arrived to film the fun, and Japanese television to shoot footage for its weekly Culture Show. The British media gave extensive coverage, especially of the festival's more *outré* aspects. For *The Guardian* Alfred

Hickling followed an 'Electrical Walk' through the town centre with amused approval (see the illustration on page 195). In a more conventional review, Andrew Clements was grudging, lamenting a lack of 'satisfying content'.

Jazz and improvisation played a major part. The fine interpretation of pages from Cardew's *Treatise* by musikFabrik has already been noted. But the extent of non-notated music seemed at times unfocused and sparked divergent reactions – most controversially, perhaps, when the members of Mimeo in a late-night concert, quietly contemplating their laptops like eleven trappist monks, ventured the sparest interjections to punctuate the silence. After an hour in the dark, some tired festivalgoers tiptoed away. The positive view was that the pioneering purpose of the festival was alive and well; that it had renewed energy and vision to stay ahead.

Among installations, Janek Schaefer's bittersweet *Extended Play (Triptych for the Children of War)*, commissioned for the 2007 festival, with its nine retro record players and individually recorded 12" vinyl records, was particularly affecting, its very restraint giving it a compelling veracity (see also page 197). *Extended Play* deservedly received wider recognition when it won the 2008 British Composer of The Year Award for Sonic Art as well as a Paul Hamlyn Award. It continues to tour and will be in Glasgow in 2012. Electronic sound processing or amplification were involved in almost every event in 2007, at some of which Mac laptops flooded the stage like dinghies at a sailing regatta. Presiding at their laptops – the current must-have accessories – composers, who would not previously have considered themselves executants, joined performers to stimulate further layers of activity. But the prevalence of live MAX processing was also levelling. Like the integral serialism of the 1950s, its ubiquitous timbral and textural characteristics seemed to swamp individuality.

Sarah Nicolls's performance of five world premieres for piano and interactive electronics was, nevertheless, a *tour de force*. In Jonathan Green's *Into Movement,* wrist sensors worn by the pianist initiated audible pitch-bending, emitted through invisible speakers inside the instrument, as if the live sounds themselves were being mysteriously slid up and down. In Larry Goves's *My name is Peter Stillman. That is not my real name,* the simultaneous playing of an additional MIDI-keyboard triggered samples, injecting them into an already dramatic discourse. Their constantly surprising properties, and Sarah Nicolls's subtle timing, made the performances both aurally and visually compelling. The five premieres, however, were only half the programme.

During the interval members of the audience were invited to board buses waiting outside St Paul's to be driven to a 'secret destination'. This turned out to be the North Light Galleries at Armitage Bridge, where Nicolls was joined by Mira Calix and David Sheppard for an improvised second half, surrounded by an art exhibition.

In 'Plugged and Unplugged' the Amsterdam-based violinist Monica Germino employed sound effects, lighting and projection to complement virtuoso playing of acoustic and electric violins, in some pieces simultaneously singing or speaking asides to the audience. Particularly effective was Nick Williams's *Hell,* in which pages of proverbs by William Blake were projected as a backdrop to an 'unstoppable' toccata. The multimedia nature of the event was well suited to Studio 2 – except that it was too small for all who wished to attend. Three years later when Germino returned to the festival, the more capacious Phipps Hall in the Creative Arts Building had become the small venue of choice, and Studio 2 was used no more.

Elsewhere visual theatricality prevailed, as in Tomoko Mukaiyama's piano recital-cum-fashion show – commissioned by the festival in association with other organisations, during which pianist and piano gradually emerged from

Extended Play by Janek Schaefer, commissioned by the festival in 2007.
PHOTO: BRIAN SLATER

billowing clouds of white fabric (see the photo on page 140). It might advantageously have been presented in the Lawrence Batley Theatre, but was certainly effective in Bates Mill. The technical demands of the current festival present challenges beyond anything previously undertaken, and it is more logical, perhaps, to contain them in a single venue. The technical budget alone in 2007 amounted to some ten times the *total* budget of the first festival thirty years before. But, thanks to an impressively skilled technical team, there were few, if any, glitches. Its key members – Tim Garbutt and Adam Long, production managers, and Ian Gibson and Matthew Padden of Warehouse Sound Services in Scotland – had worked together at every festival since the mid 1990s. Synchronising two huge projectors with each other as well as with the precise musical rhythms Reich and Korot's *Hindenburg,* which had seemed such a challenge in 1998, would now have been routine.

Kyriakides

An advantage of Bates Mill is that it allows any number of formats and usages, and has none of the middle-class connotations of conventional halls. In this respect it is more like Amsterdam's Paradiso, although a lack of raked seating may impair the view of those sitting at the rear. This was the case for some of the many who attended Apartment House's performance of works by Maciunas and Mazulis in 2007, attracted no doubt by Maciunas's notorious leadership of the Fluxus movement (see pages 72–73). For Yannis Kyriakides's haunting and disquieting *The Buffer Zone* Bates Mill was ideal. Born in Cyprus, Kyriakides had been influenced, whilst studying in York, by hearing the music of Louis Andriessen at the 1993 festival. It had prompted a move to Amsterdam and led to the nurturing of his career by the Dutch. In 2007 Kyriakides was the festival's first composer-in-residence, his work notable for a combination of technological and visual media with socio-political subject-matter. For *The Buffer Zone,* the audience sat on opposite sides facing inwards, divided by screens on which were projected a montage of images viewable from either side. In one zone a pianist played, in the other a cellist, while an actor/vocalist sat like a UN 'peacekeeper' on a stepladder surveying the scene, or descended to patrol one corridor or the other. Reflecting the absence of anything eventful – and the more

poignant absence, perhaps, of 'disappeared' persons – the live playing, electronics, video, and Beckett-like text made a moving, indeed, profound impression. The Brechtian alienation was eventually broken when the screens unexpectedly rose, and the two 'sectors' of the audience found themselves gazing at each other.

The Buffer Zone by Yannis Kyriakides.
PHOTOS: BRIAN SLATER

Improvised music

Looking back before his second festival in 2007, Graham McKenzie observed that for thirty years the festival had 'very well told the story of written, notated contemporary music', remarking that his mission now was 'to broaden out that definition and include other forms of experimental and non-mainstream music', and that the forthcoming festival was 'really concerned with the de-categorisation of music'.[12] Amongst other things, this embraced his interest in non-notated music and the concept of improvisation as a creative laboratory.

Improvisation had never been wholly absent from the festival, although some would say that I gave it too little attention. Apart from CMN tours by Anthony Braxton, Cecil Parker and Steve Lacy, on its own account the festival had programmed Howard Riley, Barry Guy, Evan Parker and Terry Riley. In 1990, I brought artists from the dissident Russian 'underground': the pianist Slava Ganelin, singer Valentina Ponomareva, and trio Orkestrion, followed in 1995 by the Moscow Art Trio. If Ganelin proved, on this occasion, to sound conventional, Ponomareva's mixture of gypsy, scat and avant-garde singing was a sort of heightened kitsch, whilst the Moscow Art Trio injected into a jazz-folk synthesis interesting echoes of their classical training.

Prior to 1994, the festival had lacked a suitable venue for amplified ensembles. The opening of the Lawrence Batley Theatre removed this constraint, and the festival's first programme there included two performances by the Vienna Art Orchestra of *Beauty and the Beast,* its jazz-theatre homage to Jean Cocteau. The following year there was a CMN concert by George Russell's Living Time Orchestra, followed by a morning seminar exploring his 'Lydian Chromatic Concept'. Both were ensembles at the top of their game. But I was sceptical about the work of some lesser groups, and had been disappointed when a mixture of 'composed

Tom Service with Evan Parker and Barry Guy.
PHOTO: BRIAN SLATER

music, improvisation, sound-text and computer inter-active performance' by the Australian group AustraLYSIS in 1996 seemed embarrassingly unfocused. My own programming, and that of Susanna Eastburn and Tom Service, tended to prioritise the written score, for which our backgrounds had given us a high regard, although not exclusively. In the new millennium, for instance, Evan Parker and his ensemble rank amongst the most frequent performers at the festival. I, too, recognised that the collaborative nature of ensemble improvisation could produce a democratic and exciting creative musicianship; also that it could be intricately structured without needing to be notated – or more than partially notated. The best ensemble improvisations could be thrilling, but at other times the density of multiple activity appeared too little controlled, and the playing itself routine.

Apart from Sam Hayden's *dB* written for Steamboat Switzerland – an hour-long modular work partly predetermined and partly improvised – the central thrust of Tom Service's festival had been its series of ensembles performing notated music. Thus Graham McKenzie arrived with the not unreasonable perception that the festival had 'operated within quite a narrow definition of contemporary music in its written and notated forms', and, to remain relevant and vital, it needed to 'embrace other forms of experimental and marginal music'.[13]

His enthusiasm for, and detailed knowledge of the genre brought a flood of improvising musicians and others working in less rigid domains. Besides those already mentioned, in 2006 there was the impressive duo of Marilyn Crispell (piano) and Michelle Makarski (violin); Rhodri Davies, David Toop and Lee Patterson's 'Improvised Installation'; John Butcher, Axel Dörner and Xavier Charles's 'The Contest of Pleasure', and Frances-Marie Uitti's *Mesognie della Notte*. The 2007 programme featured Insomino, the Dutch keyboard player and composer Guus Jansen, plus Martin Archer and the Simon Fell Ensemble. Evan Parker's Electroacoustic Ensemble also performed, having already played at both the 2002 and 2004 festivals. The 2008 festival included the Fuse(d) Ensemble, cranc's twelve-hour concert in the Media Centre, and John Butcher's *Composition for Eight Musicians*. There was also intricately notated music, including a substantial festival commission from Bryn Harrison called *Repetitions in Extended Time,* the Neue Vocalsolisten Stuttgart singing Sciarrino, and an Arditti Quartet concert ending with Birtwistle's recent *The Tree of Strings.*

Important was an emphasis on concept. It underpinned Dick Raaijmakers's *The Graphic Method: Bicycle,* in which a nude man on a bicycle was pulled forward very slowly, and Willem Boogman's *Sternenrest* depicting the life cycle of the star HD 129929, in which music for electric guitar, glass-percussion, the Spectra Ensemble and electronics was spatialised through nearly 200 loudspeakers. Two very different examples were James Tenney's soft and slowly unfolding illumination of a single gestalt in *In a large, open space,* and Dror Feiler's relentlessly high volume *Music is Castrated Noise.* Both Tenney and Feiler were featured in other performances. The three concerts devoted to Tenney given by the Bozzini Quartet and the pianist Eve Egoyan offered a rare opportunity to hear music by this exemplar of the experimental tradition. Tenney had been the focus of a highly-amplified concert by zeitkratzer in 2006, the year of his death. But the (mainly) acoustic strings and piano of the Bozzini's programmes – which featured UK premieres of eight works by Tenney and three transcriptions – enabled listeners to appreciate the extent of his investigations, in music more concerned with the nature of perception than with rhetoric or emotion.

2009 and 2010

The impression that Graham McKenzie was interested primarily in improvised and experimental music received a jolt with the publication of his programme for 2009, bristling with premieres of works by Andriessen, Barrett, Dillon, Harvey, Nunes, Rihm and others. Here were many of the leading ensembles associated with notated music: ELISION, Exposé, Ictus, musikFabrik, Remix, the Nieuw Ensemble, the Arditti and Diotima quartets, Hilliard Ensemble and the New London Chamber Choir. Improvised music had not been abandoned, and was most interestingly represented by Musica Elettronica Viva, a group with a long and venerable reputation across the avant-garde. Frederic Rzewski, one of MEV's founders, had performed in Huddersfield on several occasions. Alvin Curran – a composer-cum-musical activist, some of whose work at recent festivals

has already been described – I had thought to invite, but had never done so. Reunited with Richard Teitelbaum, forty-three years after MEV was formed in Rome, the three gave a spellbinding concert in Phipps Hall, testifying to the aesthetic breadth and range of electronic and acoustic sound sources that had given MEV its distinctive character and playful unpredictability. The performance was followed by a witty and revealing discussion between the three composers, prompted by questions from Robert Worby.[14]

As Andrew Clements remarked in a review of the opening weekend of the 2009 festival, 'After a couple of years when Britain's leading new-music festival seemed to be losing its way in a welter of improvisation, installations and electroacoustic environments, it's more like business as usual.'[15] An impressive succession of international ensembles had been made possible by substantial improvements in funding. But the centrality of notated music remained the following year – 'which happily returned to composers who have loomed large and luminous here in previous Novembers'[16] – and continued in 2011, with the music of Bent Sørensen and Xenakis particularly featured.

Following the 2009 festival, for the second time in its history, Huddersfield won the Royal Philharmonic Society award for Concert Series and Festivals. The citation read:

HCMF 2009 featured a wide range of major international composers not often heard in the UK,

Michael Finnissy at the 2006 festival.
PHOTO: BRIAN SLATER

Frederic Rzewski, Richard Teitelbaum and Alvin Curran, performing together in Phipps Hall.
PHOTOS: *BRIAN SLATER*

and reasserted itself as an important international and national event in the world of contemporary music – one all aspiring composers should experience. The programme, which did not shy away from the difficult, drew on major international links and attracted large, young, enthusiastic audiences. It puts Huddersfield firmly on the cultural map and is a shining example of global ambition that justifies the support the festival receives locally and nationally.

Programme content had been boosted by the Arts Council's Sustain fund, introduced to combat the effects of the recession, using money released by the council through reducing its

Lottery cash balances. In 2009 the festival was one of twenty-one organisations given extra support, receiving £117,000 spread over two years to assist 'in maintaining the quality and scale of the artistic programme in 2009 and 2010'. The festival budget, which had declined in the early years of the new millennium, now climbed to around £600,000, the highest in its history.

At the thirty-third festival in 2010, the benefits of this increase were even more evident, with twenty-seven ensembles taking part (including

Chroma *by Rebecca Saunders performed in Huddersfield Town Hall in 2010.*
PHOTO: PAUL GREENWOOD

two trios, two string quartets and two vocal groups) – more than at any previous festival, and encompassing numerous UK, world and European premieres. A few involved improvisation or open scores (notably those by Cage). But most concentrated on notated music, with works by Abrahamsen, Finnissy, Fitkin, Holt, Kagel, Manoury, Neuwirth, Nordheim, Nørgård, Nyman, Poppe, Rzewski, Skempton, Sørensen, Stockhausen, Wallin, Peter Ablinger, Dai Fujikura (winner of the Young Composers' Award in 1998), Ole-Henrik Moe, Rebecca Saunders, Julia Wolfe and others. Again, however, there was no conventional orchestra.

The two weekends of the 2010 festival were among the strongest in its history. The final event was an installation piece by Justė Janulytė, an already widely performed twenty-eight-year old Lithuanian composer living in Milan, working with the Italian video artist Luca Scarzella. In their collaborative *Sandglasses,* four cellists play inside four six-metre high gauze tubes, slowly emerging and fading from view, while onto the gauzes are projected fluctuating spirals of light particles. Separately

and intermittently they coalesce and pause in denser patterns of blue and white, wine-red and sepia, streaked with drips and gradually rotating (see the photos on page 277 and on the cover of this book). With live electronics and a richly fluctuating timbral soundscape, this was one of the most effective mixed-media performances of recent years and one of the most sophisticated uses of video. Were it to receive a series of performances in London's Tate Modern, hundreds of people would surely attend daily. Co-produced with several Dutch and Lithuanian organisations, the Huddersfield production of *Sandglasses* (and also of *Chroma,* which *had* begun life in Tate Modern) benefitted from financial support from the Réseau Varèse.

Emerging talent and composers-in-residence

The German composer and conductor Enno Poppe had made an impressive debut in 2008 with his three-piece cycle *Knochen – Salz – Öl (Bone – Salt – Oil)* performed by Klangforum Wien. In 2009 audiences heard a collaborative composition by Poppe and the Swiss electronic composer and percussionist Wolfgang Heiniger, this time performed by musikFabrik (see the picture on pages 62–63). Continuing his interest in Poppe, Graham McKenzie opened the 2010 festival with *Interzone*, the forty-year-old composer's most ambitious project to date. Played by the young Berlin ensemble mosaik, with a collage of texts from William S Burroughs's *Naked Lunch* sung by Neue Vocalsolisten Stuttgart and 'compound-eye' projections on four screens created by the Belgian video artist Anne Quirynen, *Interzone* attempted to explore 'the transitory, ambivalent nature of urban environments'. It was difficult to grasp what was actually being sung, but as sound and multidimensional experience *Interzone* was remarkable (see the photo overleaf). For Richard Morrison, writing in *The Times*,

There's nothing enigmatic about Poppe's extraordinarily dense yet mesmerising music. Blasts of high-octane jazz; fantastical, cartwheeling solos for instruments and voices; dark, thudding industrial ostinatos; screeching discords; eerie periods of nervous calm – all this masterfully mustered to create an ebb and flow like the rhythm of a turbulent city. The message? Live life on the edge, seek out the dark side, spurn security, die violently. Remember the name: Enno Poppe, a startlingly red-haired German, outrageously visionary, and just turned forty.[17]

Different but no less striking was Poppe's *Wald (Forest)* for four string quartets, given its UK premiere by the excellent Ensemble Resonanz – a new string chamber orchestra from Hamburg, formed to bridge the gap between seventeenth and eighteenth-century music and that of the present, and making its UK debut directed by Peter Rundel. In *Wald* Poppe weaves individual lines within a multi-linear texture, which grows from a predominantly low register through a 'trade-mark' ascent of increasing volume and intensity, to a powerfully dramatic climax.

Jonathan Harvey's long involvement in the festival has been documented in Chapter 7 (pages 134–36). More frequently performed here than any other composer with the exception of Cage, Berio, Ligeti and Stockhausen, it was fitting to mark his seventieth birthday in 2009 by designating him composer-in-residence, and the award by the University of Huddersfield of an honorary degree. His predecessor as composer-in-residence had been Kyriakides. His successor in 2010 was Rebecca Saunders, whose music had also been played frequently since the 1999 festival (see also Chapter 7, page 136). Prominent in 2010 were the UK premiere of her *murmurs* – already played many times by Recherche – and the larger *Chroma* performed by musikFabrik: two collage compositions tailored to the spaces in which they are to be played. With its ten players positioned around St Paul's, *murmurs* sounded delicately elusive, its subtle changes of coloration perfectly attuned to the acoustic of the building. *Chroma*, Rebecca's only ensemble composition commissioned in the UK, had been premiered in Tate Britain in June 2003, but with only seven instrumental modules in the vastness of the Turbine Hall. By May 2011, sixteen versions of *Chroma* had been performed, that in Huddersfield Town Hall being the fourteenth. Described by Rebecca as 'a spatial collage for several chamber groups and sound objects', and now with some twenty instrumental groups distributed on every level of a darkened auditorium, lit only by music stands, *Chroma* sounded often ethereal, at times sumptuous, with an abiding nostalgia, even melancholy, reminiscent of the unsynchronised modules in Birtwistle's *Fields of Sorrow*. Towards the end, multiple small musical boxes are set in motion, as in other works by Saunders. A central idea is that listeners determine their own aural perspective by choosing one or more positions

Members of the Nieuw Ensemble.
PHOTO: *BRIAN SLATER*

UK premiere of Interzone *in Bates Mill in 2010 (described on page 271).*
PHOTO: *BRIAN SLATER*

from which to listen, or by moving freely around the space. In Huddersfield *Chroma* was performed twice, allowing the audience, to experience the work from different perspectives. For some listeners *murmurs* and *Chroma* were the most beautiful and subtle pieces heard in the 2010 festival.

Interspersed between two other Saunders performances, musikFabrik's principal horn and trumpeter performed the seventeenth and twenty-first hours of Stockhausen's *KLANG*, the final project on which Stockhausen had been working at the time of his death. In these two concerts, the superlative quality of the musikFabrik players proved again to be beyond compare. No less welcome was the return of Recherche (after five years), whose performance of *murmurs* was accompanied by another intriguing UK premiere: the fifty-seven-minute *Schnee* by Hans Abrahamsen. It was proof that the composer's creative 'block' during the 1990s had been dazzlingly dispelled.

Not shy of its successes, plasma screens at the 2010 festival proclaimed:

80+ world, UK and European premieres; 50+ concerts, installations, talks, exhibitions and drop-in events; 50 creative partnerships in 2009 and 2010 with organisations in the Netherlands, Denmark, Norway, Sweden, Iceland, Germany, Italy, Belgium and North America; £96,000 invested in the local community in 2009; audiences up 8% for 2009; 67% from beyond the local area; 20% from further than 200 miles; 25% first-time attenders and 20% under twenty-five.

The looped presentation emphasised the priorities of 'programming, presenting, commissioning and collaborating'. Partnership with the University of Huddersfield received the most prominent acknowledgement on a vertical banner in the atrium of the Creative Arts Building.

The 2010 festival saw the start of a three-year relationship with Norway, intended to explore the work of its composers as well as its ensembles, whose high standards have been admired by Huddersfield festivalgoers for two decades. There was a tribute to Arne Nordheim, who had died in June, and a large-scale ensemble piece by Rolf Wallin given its UK premiere by the London Sinfonietta. Three Norwegian ensembles are billed to appear in 2011, including a first visit by the Trondheim

Soloists. Their programmes contain pieces by little-known Norwegians. But central to the 2011 festival are new and recent works by Barrett, Birtwistle, Dillon, Ferneyhough, Harvey, Romitelli and Rebecca Saunders, plus a tribute to Xenakis on the tenth anniversary of his death. The allegiance to composers frequently performed in the previous decade suggests that, while extending the range of genres and creative practice, in terms of notated music the festival has adopted narrower stylistic preferences than in earlier years. At the same time, it has introduced, and continued to promote, a range of international composers in their thirties and early forties, who, like Rebecca Saunders, are developing distinctive careers. Among the most prominent – besides Saunders – are Richard Ayres, Michel van der Aa, Dai Fujikura, Justė Janulytė, Olga Neuwirth, Lefteris Papadimitriou and Enno Poppe, all of whom have been mentioned in this book. There are others, of course, of equal or greater stature who have been rarely performed – such as Tom Adès, only just turned forty in 2011, who has demonstrated the ability to command a much larger public, yet still write music of probing intelligence and originality.[18]

It was a shrewd decision to choose the Danish composer Bent Sørensen to be the 2011 composer-in-residence. At fifty-three, Sørensen is barely ten years older than those just mentioned, although his music has been heard in Huddersfield since 1992 when *The Masque of the Red Death* for piano was performed by Rolf Hind. In 1997 four works were programmed, including his exquisitely imagined *The Deserted Churchyards* played by the Athelas Sinfonietta. In 2001 Susanna Eastburn engaged Cikada to perform seven more pieces. But a change to the published order made the interesting decision to play them in a continuous sequence, without any breaks for applause, slightly confusing. Apart from *Six Songs for voice and violin* and two cello solos, no other works of Sørensen have been heard at the festival during the last decade. Meanwhile, admiration for the composer's fastidious precision and unique aural imagination has continued to grow. The 2011 festival promises the UK premiere of *It is pain flowing down slowly on a white wall* performed by Trondheim Soloists and Frode Haltli, a composer portrait presented by Ensemble Scenatet including a silent film documentary, a collaborative improvisation based on fragments and ideas from *Funeral Processions* and the UK premiere of *Saudades Inocentes* by Sørensen and Anna Berit Asp Christensen for voices, guitar and accordion. There is also the UK premiere of *Shadowplay*, consisting of three independent trios differently constituted, each containing five movements, stitched together in a single tapestry in which the fifteen movements become 'part of the same story'.

Most interesting could be the first appearance in Britain of an out-of-doors sound installation devised by Sørensen. 'In recent years', he explains, 'I have worked increasingly in collaboration with other art forms. Through

Janek Schaefer at the controls and the audience lying on the floor for In the Last Hour, *commissioned for the 2005 festival, an 'installation concert for organ, vinyl, field recordings and light.*
PHOTOS: BRIAN SLATER

this, all the hidden stories and pictures – which have always been in my music – have become clearer, and the visual and narrative dimension suddenly became an important counterpoint.' Sørensen developed the notion of Concert Installations, rather than conventional concert programmes, during the five years he was engaged in composing his opera *Under the Sky*, 'and the step from these to a fully-fledged sound installation is very short and natural.'[19]

Positioned in the courtyard outside Bates Mill, the installation is produced by the festival with support from four Danish arts institutions.

The future

Two weeks after Britain's first coalition government since the Second World War emerged from the indecisive general election of 6 May 2010, the Department of Culture, Media and Sport announced a £19 million cut in the budget of Arts Council England. This, combined with a £4 million cut imposed one year earlier, amounted to a reduction of £23 million in the council's income for 2010–11. At that point the financial year was already underway and, mindful of the fact that 'in-year cuts are always the most difficult to manage, because plans have already been made against an expected level of income',[20] the Arts Council decided to minimise their effect by drawing on its historic reserves, access to which had previously been blocked by government. All the council's revenue clients sustained a blanket cut of only half a percent. It was much less than had been feared.

This, however, was only the beginning. Facing an unprecedented inherited deficit, the full impact of the government's austerity measures became evident after its autumn spending review, which (as we noted in Chapter 1) indicated that by 2014 the budget of Arts Council England would be reduced by nearly 30%, and funds available to its revenue clients would fall by approximately 15%. As a first step, grants to all revenue clients for the year 2011-2012 were cut by 6.9%. Meanwhile, the council began a process of re-evaluating the work of all its clients. Whereas future grant aid was withdrawn from some organisations and reduced for others, there were increases for those considered a high priority. The festival was amongst the latter, and the projected cash increase of 25% between 2010–11 and 2014–15 was an impressive endorsement of its current aspirations and achievements. For the largest and most enterprising arts organisations, global financial instability is likely to reduce what they previously raised from donors and other partners. Nevertheless, the majority remain optimistic.

Publicly funded arts organisations have to address the many, not the few, and the relatively small audience for contemporary art music is concerning. Modernist and avant-garde composers are often accused of being responsible for alienating the public, usually by those who themselves feel alienated. So it was surprising to find the festival's former artistic director, Tom Service, castigating the new music establishment in a strongly argued lecture delivered at north-east Scotland's Sound festival in October 2010.[21] The vigour of his criticism bore the authority of an almost unrivalled knowledge of the contemporary music scene and the irritation of the critic who has endured too many of its more pretentious products. The core of Tom's argument focused on a self-serving 'sub-culture… labouring under the misapprehension that what they're doing is the only single true path', which is 'the creation of a music that at once resists one side of society – the commercial, the populist, the meretricious, the false', and aims 'to reveal their vacuity by offering an uncompromising, ethically superior musical vision.' All very laudable, except that he added: 'Which, by the way, most people don't want to hear.'

There are schools of composition, whose dominant mode, Tom maintained, is 'a continuation of a high modernist stylistic language that, whilst it was once new, now threatens to become a parody of itself. Far from being 'new', the ideas that this music expounds, its practices, the institutions it's indebted to, are old-fashioned in the extreme'. There are many examples 'of a general shift… towards mannerism: the point at which a music, a language becomes affectation instead of style, a point of aesthetic redundancy and expressive emptiness.' At their centre is 'a school of heightened notational possibility', whose 'baroque complexity' is tied up with 'an ideology of elite musical practice that excludes all but the most fiendishly gifted practitioners,' and can be traced to the 'intellectual and critical approach [of] the postwar avant-garde, and the necessity of connecting social, political and musical renewal.' The irony is that their work

will 'probably only ever be accessed by a tiny minority of new music nerds.' State funding and institutional support – particularly 'universities in giving jobs' – enable composers to be 'sequestered in the state-sponsored ghetto… to write music that nobody really cares about, because they never have to try and really communicate with a wider audience for their livelihoods.'

'That's too cynical a view,' Tom admitted, adding, however, that it 'is a good way of ensuring that the niche remains a niche.' If the ideologies adopted are 'counter-productive, the music unappreciated and unknown by the vast majority of the listening public, and you can't make your living at it… the prognosis isn't good.' The basis of Tom's disaffection I found all too recognisable. Much of it I could endorse. But its focus on the limited if influential milieu of academic ideologues, Radio 3's 'Hear and Now' for example (which Tom periodically presents), and concerts in the Queen Elizabeth Hall, is only part of the story. Less convincing was his advocacy of composer-led collectives and the composer-performer ensembles that pioneered minimalism as a better way forward. For the first are hardly visible enough, the second already history.

Indeed, there appear to be no younger composers able to replicate their attention-grabbing forbears of the 1960s and '70s – whether a Cage, Stockhausen or a Reich – nor any to match the prominence of British visual artists and their uncanny ability to shock the public and simultaneously to engage it. The title of Tom's lecture (*So long, and thanks for all the noise: 2010 and the end of musical history*) would seem to cast unacknowledged nods in the direction of two celebrated books: Alex Ross's *The rest is noise*[22] and Francis Fukuyama's *The End of History and the Last Man*.[23] Writing in 1992 after the collapse of the Soviet Union and the implosion of communism, Fukuyama identified the culmination of mankind's ideological evolution in a universal acceptance of liberal democracy as the ultimate, ideal form of government. It was a claim soon proved false. But has the evolution of classical music reached a culmination? Has everything been done before? Are there no sounds to discover that have not already been heard? The answer to all these questions is 'no', because the creative contexts in which sounds are used are themselves constantly evolving. Composition is

*UK premiere of
Sandglasses by Justè
Janulytè and Luca Scarzella
which concluded the
2010 festival.*
PHOTO: PAUL GREENWOOD

a broad church, and the international spread of each Huddersfield programme contains much that is fresh and different. The festival has to be wary of growing too close to its host, the university, and to academic musics in general. But the danger is obviated by an increasing emphasis on multidimensional practice and in work that redefines convention.

To equate artistic value with marketing viability is to confuse the creative spirit with the commercial mechanics of concert promotion. Composers thrive on appreciative listeners. But the genuinely original compose because of an

inner compulsion that no more depends on the presence of an audience than does the lark singing aloft or the blackbird at sunset. Mankind is instinctively driven to musical utterance. Carl Nielsen argued, in relation to his Fourth Symphony, that music alone of all the arts expresses the elemental will to live, embodying birth, struggle, decay and perennial renewal. Music *is* life, said Nielsen, and like life it is indomitable and inextinguishable.

As long as there is life there will be composers. As long as there is society, there will be contexts in which composers can be heard.

Endnotes

1. *Background*

1. They had been combined in a single administrative authority by the Local Government Act of 1972.

2. The term 'musicology' was not yet widely current.

3. 11 November 1984.

4. Most of the critics were also scathing, except for Keith Potter in *Classical Music* (5 January 1985, p. 20), who called it 'a splendidly-played concert' and *Dressur* 'a tour-de-force of circus-like inanities turned, improbably, into curiously fascinating listening...'. Paul Robinson, writing in *Arts Yorkshire* (December 1984/ January 1985, p. 5), thought Trio Le Cercle 'deserved a better press than they received'.

2. *The first festivals*

1. *Dillug-Kefitsah* is the earliest work still in Dillon's catalogue.

2. In 2001, in conjunction with the Contemporary Music Network and to mark its thirtieth birthday, I asked the Warsaw Music Workshop to reconvene and perform the same programme. Twenty-three years later it sounded curiously bland and inoffensive.

3. 11 January 1986, p. 19.

4. 4 November 1979.

5. Hilary Bracefield in *Contact* 21 (Autumn 1980), p. 33.

6. The term 'sinfonietta' had been used in the nineteenth and early twentieth centuries for orchestral works of no fixed size – e.g. by Rimsky-Korsakov and Janáek. But a more direct model was Schoenberg's *Chamber Symphony, Op. 9* for fifteen solo players, premiered in 1909 by the Rosé Quartet with wind players from the Vienna court opera, but during the following half century rarely performed. Reviving the Schoenberg was a motivation for the London Sinfonietta's creation.

7. A lunchtime concert should have contained the first performance of John Casken's *Ligatura* for organ, but its dedicatee, Graham Cummings, had been unable to prepare it to his satisfaction.

8. February 1982, p. 118.

9. 25 November 1981.

10. 5 December 1982.

11. For some years before being identified as 'the Board', the initial steering group became the 'Management Committee'. It's first members are listed on p. 255.

12. 8 December 1992.

13. In 2000 as London Sinfonietta Opera.

14. 22 November 1983.

15. April 1984, pp. 31–33.

16. It is now at Dean Clough in Halifax.

3. *Expansion*

1. 15 November 1984.

2. 12 November 1984.

3. vol. 126, no. 1703 (January 1985), p. 40.

4. Composer's introduction: http://www.universaledition.com/Luciano-Berio/composers-and-works/composer/54/work/1619/work introduction.

5. 28 November 1985.

6. 26 November 1985.

7. 26 November 1985.

8. In 2006 the festival showed a new Cardew film by Luke Fowler, *Pilgrimage From Scattered Points,* devoted to the Scratch Orchestra.

4. *Orchestras*

1. *Yorkshire Post,* 27 November 1986.

2. *The Guardian,* 28 November 1986.

3. BBC MM288, vol. 16, no. 5 – issued with *BBC Music Magazine* (January 2008).

4. Box office statistics record an audience of 981 (94% capacity), but I recall that prospective ticket purchasers were turned away.

5. *Beatus Vir* had been composed at the request of Karol Wojtyla, whilst still Cardinal of Krakow, to celebrate the 900th anniversary of the martyrdom of St. Stanislaw. It was premiered in his presence in 1979, during his first pilgrimage to Poland as Pope John Paul II.

6. £19,553 in 1982, £355,521 in 1997.

5. *Ensembles and soloists*

1. 26 November 1989.

2. 21 November 1989.

3. *Changing Platforms: 30 years of the Contemporary Music Network,* Chris Heaton (London, Unknown Public 2001), p. 74.

4. 18 November 2000.

5. http://www.guardian.co.uk/culture/culture-cuts-blog/2011/mar/30/arts-council-funding-decision-day-cuts.

6. The world premiere was given by the SWR orchestra, with many of the same soloists, in Donaueschingen on 17 October 1986.

7. Asko was founded as a student orchestra (Amsterdams Student Kamer Orkest) in 1965; the Schoenberg Ensemble by Reinbert de Leeuw at the Hague Conservatory in 1974.

8. Asko recorded *Orchester-Finalisten* for the Stockhausen-Verlag in 1996. Its performance of the work in London in 2008, following the composer's death, was more favourably received.

9. 28 November 2001.

10. Adrian Smith in the *Huddersfield Daily Examiner,* 26 November 1999.

11. *Veni, Veni, Emmanuel* has received several hundred performances worldwide since its completion in 1992, confounding the view that new music has a small audience.

12. The originals are now at Montclair State University.

13. *The Sunday Times,* 28 November 1982.

14. 29 November 1982.

15. Carter later composed his fifth quartet for the Ardittis, which they performed in Huddersfield in 1999.

16. 28 November 1982.

17. Turnage's piano piece *Entranced* is now deleted from his catalogue (although listed in *The New Grove,* second edition, Macmillan 2001).

18. Not, however, *Sequenzas XII, XIII* and *XIV.* Since his death in 2003, Berio's music has disappeared from Huddersfield programmes – unlike other composers longer dead like Cardew, Feldman, Cage and Xenakis. I regret this neglect, but recognise that most of Berio's music needs large forces.

19. 'Contemporary Performance' vol 26ii, (Abingdon, Routledge 2007).

20. 2 December 1990.

21. 25 November 2005.

22. 9 December 2003.

23. 2009 hcmf publicity booklet, p. 41.

24. Johann Philipp Kirnberger (1721–83) was a German theorist who spent two years studying composition and performance with Bach, and wrote a valuable account of his 'method'.

25. *The Observer,* 7 December, 1997.

26. *The Times,* 2 December, 1997.

27. *The Daily Telegraph,* 23 November 2000.

6. *The shock of the new*

1. Regretfully, the policy was dropped in the mid-1980s, as the financial climate became tougher, and performing organisations tended to specialise in narrow areas of repertoire.

2. Iannis Xenakis, *Formalized Music: Thought and Mathematics in Composition* (Bloomington, Indiana University Press 1971).

3. Philip Glass, liner notes, *Music in Twelve Parts, parts 1 and 2* (Virgin Records CA2010, 1977).

4. Compare Paeder Mercier's experience of playing in *Roaratorio* (p. 119).

5. It had been created for *Cure* by the theatre group IOU, who gave the festival permission to use it.

6. The publication will contain interviews with John Adams (1987), Iannis Xenakis (1987), John Cage (1989), George Benjamin and Pierre Boulez (1989), Gérard Grisey (1992), Brian Eno (1999), Helmut Lachenmann and Wolfgang Rihm (2000) and James Dillon (2009).

7. Paul Driver in *The Sunday Times,* 1 December 1985.

8. Recorded by the BBC, this is one of the interviews to be published.

9. Gerald Larner, *The Guardian,* 22 November 1988.

10. Robert Cockroft, *Yorkshire Post,* 22 November 1988.

7. *Composers*

1. Berlin, Springer-Verlag 1986.

2. see endnote Chapter 6, no. 6.

3. Xenakis's obituary in *The Times,* on 5 February 2001, misleadingly stated that his music was only 'occasionally heard in this country' and that it was 1997 'before he enjoyed serious recognition through the medium of the BBC Proms and

the Bath International Music Festival, adding: 'that year he was also heard at Huddersfield'. The compilers curiously overlooked the performances given by Lina Lalandi's English Bach Festival every year except one between 1972 and 1977 (including the orchestral concert I had attended at the RFH), others by the London Music Digest, London Sinfonietta, Arditti Quartet and New London Chamber Choir, a Xenakis festival in Glasgow in May 1987, plus regular performances at the Almeida, Bath, Edinburgh and Huddersfield festivals, and the BBC Proms – all long before 1997. Eleven of Xenakis's compositions were commissioned and/or premiered in Britain.

4. When the festival gave the UK premiere of *Sieben Worte* in 1980, the programme note sent from Moscow was headed *Sonata*.

5. see endnote Chapter 6, no. 6.

6. ed. Richard Kostelanetz, *John Cage* (London, Allen Lane The Penguin Press 1971), p. 31.

7. Robert Schumann, tr. Paul Rosenfeld, *On Music and Musicians* (London, Dobson 1947), p. 32. There were occasions when I rued neglecting this advice!

8. 30 November 1987.

9. 6 December 1987.

10. 6 December 1987.

11. 24 November 1987.

12. 1 December 1987.

13. By the time Ferneyhough's *Shadowtime* was staged at the Munich Biennale in 2002, I had become deeply sceptical about the dramatic premise of the sections I had already heard in concerts. I did not attend the single semi-staged performance in London; but the reviews all criticised its lack of theatricality.

14. There was also Stephen Montague, a British resident for over a decade and, on this occasion, appearing as a pianist.

15. Recorded by a member of the public on a hand-held Walkman, the discussion survives and is to be published (see endnote Chapter 6, no. 6).

16. *The Independent* 1 December 1987.

17. John Adams's website: www.earbox.com.

18. 6 December 1987.

19. In conversation with Kevin Jackson in *Viewing the Century,* BBC Radio 3, December 1999.

20. Paul Driver, *The Sunday Times,* 29 November 1987.

21. *György Ligeti: Music of the Imagination* (Faber & Faber, 2003).

22. The event is described by Elliott Schwartz in *Contact 29* (Spring 1985), pp. 40–41.

23. 27 November 1987.

24. 1 December 1987.

25. 1 December 1987.

26. 29 November 1987.

27. Andrew Rosner interviewed by Malcolm Hayes in 'Still having a whale of a time 30 years on', *The Independent,* 24 January 1998 (http://www.independent.co.uk/life-style/still-having-a-whale-of-a-time-30-years-on-1140526.html).

28. Management Committee minutes, 26 February 1987, p. 2.

29. Stockhausen-Verlag, 18 A–B, 1992.

30. *Contact 34* (Autumn 1989), pp. 36–38.

31. 22 November 1988.

32. ECM 4006.

33. i.e. not all from Cambridge, as incorrectly stated in the CD liner notes.

34. Sony S2K 53346 (originally a Columbia LP).

35. To misquote La Monte Young's text-composition *Piano piece no. 3 for David Tudor,* 'Some of them were very old grasshoppers'. Young's influence on Stockhausen (e.g. *Mikrophonie I, Stimmung* etc) is rarely acknowledged.

36. 30 November 1996.

37. Reprinted in a book of collected interviews called *Dazed and Confused* (Phaidon 2000).

38. Thomas Moore, *Memoirs of the Life of Sheridan* (London, 1825) vol. 2, ch. 20.

39. A mesostic is a variant, invented by Cage, of an acrostic. In a mesostic a word is highlighted vertically in capitals down the middle of horizontal lines of text.

40. From his programme note (1989 festival programme book, p. 46).

41. From her programme note (1989 festival programme book, p. 40).

42. In a letter to *The New York Times,* 28 September 2000, Joan Peyser states that, in the 1970s, whilst writing her biography of Boulez, she interviewed Cage, who asked if she would arrange a meeting between the two men. She invited both to lunch at her house. Boulez arrived uncharacteristically late and 'the conversation covered little of substance'.

43. Letter to the Mayor, Councillor Ann Denham, on the occasion of my retirement reception on 5 April 2001.

44. This remarkable conversation was recorded, and will be published with others (see endnote Chapter 6, no. 6.).

45. Calvin Tomkins, *The Bride and the Bachelors* (London, Weidenfeld & Nicolson 1965), p. 120, republished as *Ahead of the Game* (London, Penguin 1968), p. 116.

46. Peter McCallum, 'An Interview with Pierre Boulez', *The Musical Times* vol. 130, no. 1751, January 1989, p. 8.

47. Jean-Jacques Nattiez, tr. Jonathan Dunsby, *The Battle of Chronos and Orpheus* (Oxford 2004), p. 181.

48. *Orientations* (London, Faber & Faber 1986), pp. 23–24.

49. No. 84, February 1991.

50. *ibid*

51. 24 November 1990.

52. 2 December 1990.

53. 2 December 1990.

54. 26 November 1990.

55. 2 December 1990.

56. Elmer Schoenberger, *De vrouw met de hamer & andere componisten (The lady with the hammer & other composers* (De Bezige Bij, 1992).

57. A piano sonata had been performed at the Almeida Festival as early as 1989, but somewhat overshadowed by other Soviet music.

58. Quoted in the Ustvolskaya catalogue (Musikverlag Hans Sikorski, Hamburg 1990), p. 4.

59. An acoustic engineer, engaged in the rebuilding of La Fenice after the fire of January 1996, found that the ambient nocturnal sound level in Venice is 32db, compared with around 45db in cities with road traffic (John Berendt, *City of Falling Angels* [London, Hodder & Stoughton 2005] p. 353).

60. 28 November 1995.

61. This was the first of four works by Dillon to win the Royal Philharmonic Award for chamber-scale composition.

62. *Musical Opinion* 1405, vol 118, Spring 1996, pp. 47–49.

63. Liner notes for the CD recording (Accord 201162).

64. *The Daily Telegraph,* 2 December 2009.

65. No 256, December 1973, pp. 42–50.

66. Teldec 8573 88261-2 & 8573 88263-2.

67. Recordings of these events are in the Festival Archive.

68. *op.cit.*

69. There had been an article by Susan Bradshaw on Arvo Pärt's music in *Contact* 26 (Spring 1983), pp. 23–28. It was a journal to which I subscribed, but I had not taken much notice.

70. 29 November 1998.

8. *Premieres and commissions*

1. Or so we thought. In 2007 Rihm made further changes and the latest version dates from 2008.

9. *The festival in the 1990s*

1. Tim Sledge, administrator from 1990–91, worked approximately four-fifths of full-time, taking several weeks out each summer to assist the Early Music Festival.

2. The Foundation for Sport and the Arts was established in 1991 using money donated from football pools companies. It ceased to take applications in 2009 and is due to close in 2012.

3. 29 November 1992.

4. 20 November 1994.

5. 21 November 1994.

6. 27 November 1994.

7. The application gave as an alternative to the Casken, *From Morning to Midnight* by David Sawer. Both were then in their early planning stages.

8. 22 November 1998.

9. In 2001 CBTO dropped 'touring' from its title. In the last decade it has dedicated itself to bringing opera to a wider public in Birmingham, by involving hundreds of ordinary people in productions in spaces not normally associated with opera. The first was Berg's *Votzek* performed in a warehouse on the edge of the Ladywood housing estate.

10. *The Independent,* 25 November 1993.

11. John Harman was knighted in 1997 for services to local government. From 2000 to 2008 he was chairman of the Environment Agency.

12. London, Demos 1995.

13. 24 November 1996.

14. 2 December 1996.

15. Although commissioned by the Edinburgh Festival, the opera has never been staged in Britain.

16. Particularly characteristic of old Beijing, hutongs are neighbourhoods of narrow alleys and traditional single-storey residencies grouped round inner courtyards.

17. Tom Service in *The Guardian,* 25 November 1999.

18. 11 November 1984 (see also p. 211).

10. *Venues*

1. 21 November 1986.

2. www.poetrysociety.org.uk. (click Poetry Landmarks and links).

3. Kirklees had been shortlisted along with Nottingham and Swansea to host the Year of Literature. Swansea won.

4. *Building* 12 June 1981, p. 41.

5. These days, it is questionable whether the construction of an organ would be allowed to obscure the fine triptych of stained glass in the apse of St Paul's.

6. This was the first organ case designed by David Graebe, whose has since designed casework for churches and cathedrals throughout the world. He also designed the Phipps organ case in the Creative Arts Building.

7. Said to Chris Robbins, whose historical survey of the local authority's involvement in orchestral concerts, in *Music Making in the West Riding of Yorkshire* (Cleckheaton, Amadeus Press 2000), pp. 187–196, contains much interesting detail.

8. Alderman Graham's grandfather had been chief contractor in the construction of Huddersfield Town Hall.

11. *Other spaces, other media*

1. 29 November 1997.

2. An idea of *Dubbelspoor* in performance can be gleaned from a YouTube video: http://www.youtube.com/watch?v=wJNNg7J0Kyo

3. *The Independent,* 7 December 1999. The building replaced the earlier Hudawi Centre which had burned down in 1985.

4. 'An Expedition' is published in Armitage's book, *The Universal Home Doctor;* and revised versions of 'Money Spider', 'Adam and Eve' and 'Growing Up' in his *Travelling Songs* (both Faber & Faber, 2002).

5. 16 November 1998.

6. 17 November 1998.

7. January 1999, pp. 72–73.

8. Spring Grove School was built in 1879 to an innovative design. In 1963 it became the first school in Britain in which West Indian and Asian children exceeded white children. (See *Spring Grove: the education of immigrant children* by Trevor Burgin and Patricia Edson, OUP 1967).

9. 2 December 1988.

10. *Every Day is a Good Day: The Visual Art of John Cage* catalogue (Hayward Publishing 2010), p. 130.

11. Interviewed for 'Hear and Now', BBC Radio 3, broadcast on 29 January 2011.

12. *The Guardian,* 25 November 2000.

13. *The Independent,* 1 December 1990.

14. The Camel Club had been advertised for this event, but the venue had to be changed.

12. Education and outreach

1. 'Huddersfield: a retrospective', *Contact* 28 (Autumn 1984), pp. 41–46.

2. See his keynote speech to the annual conference of the Incorporated Society of Musicians in April 2007: http://www.guardian.co.uk/music/2007/apr/10/classicalmusicandopera.comment.

3. Cambridge University Press.

4. Minutes of the Management Committee, 16 February 1984, p. 2–3.

5. 11 November 1984.

6. Composer's note in the 1984 festival programme book, p. 12.

7. Interviewed for *Woman's Own,* 31 October 1987, pp. 8–10.

8. Robert Cockroft, 22 November 1986.

9. Interviewed by Helen Wallace in *BBC Music Magazine,* 1 December 2009, p. 113.

10. The collaboration with Opera North was followed by another, called 'Lorca Unmasked', in 1998.

11. Opal OBLIQUECARDS Misc (www.rtqe.net/ObliqueStrategies).

12. 6 December 2010.

13. The University and Music Department

1. In what is now the Central Services Building.

2. *Partners and providers. The role of HEIs in the provision of cultural and sports facilities to the wider public* (Higher Education Funding Council for England, ISBN 1 902369 30 0), pp. 88–94.

3. Tan Dun has since withdrawn *Orchestral Theatre I: Xun.*

4. MPSCD007 (1998).

5. Björn Heile, *The Music of Mauricio Kagel* (London: Ashgate, 2006), p. 84.

14. Marketing and audiences

1. *Contact* 21 (Autumn 1980), pp.31–33.

2. 29 October 1980.

3. Examples of all the festival's print are in the archive held by the University of Huddersfield Library.

4. Martin Dreyer, *Musical Times* (February 1984), p. 104.

5. 8 December 1982.

6. *New Notes,* November 2007 p. 4.

7. Apart from one handbill in 1988.

15. Partnerships and management

1. Earlier British Council support was effected through Visiting Arts which, until 2001, was a department of the British Council. Likewise, the agent for Dutch support was the Gaudeamus Foundation until it became the new music department of Music Centre the Netherlands.

2. Minutes of the steering group meeting on 13 January 1983, p. 3

16. The new millennium

1. http://hotnewsandarticles.blogspot.com/2007_08_01_archive.html. See also Rick Muir, *The New Identity Politics* (Institute for Public Policy Research, February 2007).

2. 2nd ed. (Cambridge, 1999), fly-leaf.

3. John Cage, *Silence* (Wesleyan University Press, 1961), p. 13.

4. Matt Lewis, director of Foldback (a festival of experimental sound based in London) and Martel Ollerenshaw of the London Jazz Festival. Printed in *New Notes,* December 2007, pp. 4–7.

5. 'And the troupe danced on', *The Guardian,* 6 August 2009.

6. Kings Place Festival 2011, programme book, pp. 32–33.

7. 30 November 2005, p.53.

8. 25 November 2005, p.30.

9. see also Richard Morrison in *The Times,* 22 November 2005, p.25, and Lynne Walker in *The Independent,* 24 November 2005, p.51.

10. *The Daily Telegraph,* 25 November 2005, p. 30.

11. 6 November 2010, p. 31.

12. *New Notes,* November 2007, p.5.

13. *New Notes* (October 2006), p. 2.

14. To be published with other festival interviews (see endnote Chapter 6, no. 6).

15. *The Guardian,* 23 November 2009.

16. Paul Driver in *The Sunday Times,* 5 December 2010.

17. 22 November 2010.

18. Tom Adès's piano piece *Traced Overhead* was performed by Richard Uttley in a hcmf// shorts concert in 2009. *Living Toys* had been performed in 1994 and *Arcadiana* in 1999. But the fact that it was virtually impossible to secure an Adès premiere militated against more extensive programming of his music.

19. From the 2011 festival brochure, p. 9.

20. Statement by Dame Liz Forgan, chair of the Arts Council, on 18 June 2010.

21. http://www.sound-scotland.co.uk/site/2010/diary/10_23@1400_transcript.htm.

22. Fourth Estate, London, 2008.

23. Free Press, New York, 1992.

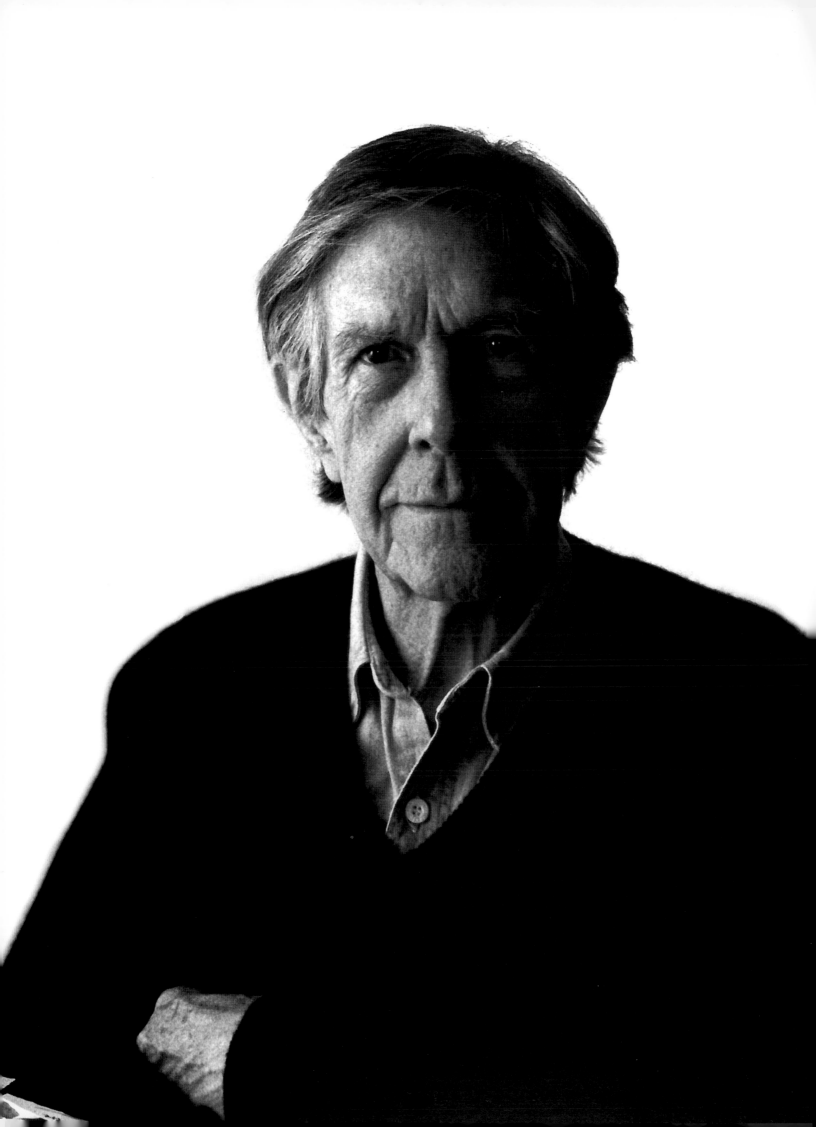

Appendices

A *On Meeting John Cage*

by Julia Winterson

In November 1989 John Cage came to Huddersfield where, as part of the Contemporary Music Festival, a retrospective of fifty years of his music was performed. His reputation came before him. John Cage: experimental composer, inventor of the prepared piano, champion of chance music and pioneer of the happening, the man who claimed that anything and everything was music. Cage's music and ideas can be baffling and uncompromising, but anyone interested in the culture of the twentieth century needs to know about him. Critics are still divided – some accuse Cage of being eccentric, or worse, a charlatan, others are thrilled by his boundless, creative invention. He is adored and ridiculed in equal measure.

The keynote concert for the year's festival was Cage's *Roaratorio: An Irish Circus on Finnegans Wake*, a massive rendering in sound featuring recordings of Irish folk music and sounds from the local Irish countryside diffused over thirty-two loudspeakers. The Chieftains played live and Cage read passages from an enjoyably elusive text. *Roaratorio* is the most famous realisation of a generic score by John Cage entitled _____, __ _____ *Circus on* _____, essentially four pages of instructions that are used to produce a realisation in sound of any literary work. For six weeks my Technical College music students had worked on their own version. While Cage made use of *Finnegans Wake* as the basis for his realisation, we opted for the local newspaper, the *Huddersfield Daily Examiner*. Tapes of mill sounds, brass bands and reggae came together to create an aural representation of the West Riding locality.

The students were well-prepared for their performance, having listened to Cage's music, talked about it, and created their own pieces based on his ideas. The first session had opened with a

John Cage in Huddersfield.
PHOTO: SELWYN GREEN

performance of *4'33"* (or 'My silent piece,' as Cage called it). It is an empty structure, the most empty piece and therefore the most full of possibilities, perhaps the most talked about piece of music ever written (or not written). We listened to it and discussed it. *4'33"* was the first startling Cage event to be presented. Over the succeeding six weeks together we unleashed more events and non-events – radio collages, multimedia happenings, pieces determined by star charts. The initial modicum of scepticism over Cage's radical ideas evolved over the course of the project into fascination and a fuller understanding.

The final rehearsal and performance were about to take place. We gathered together on that cold November morning in the old West Riding Methodist Hall that formed the hub of the Technical College Music Department. The door was suddenly flung open.

'He's coming, he's coming, John Cage, he's walking up the road now, he'll be here any minute!' The head of Music Technology could barely contain himself. We had been told that Cage might drop in to see some of our rehearsal, but we hadn't really dared to expect it. But now that colossus of twentieth century music was here and about to walk through the door.

Seconds later, John Cage shambled in clutching an old shopping bag and looking more like *Coronation Street*'s Roy Cropper than the most radical American composer of all time. A tall thin man, he walked hesitantly, slightly hunched over with a gaunt, weathered face. I found him a seat and asked him for the first time that day if he would like a cup of coffee. He looked at me enigmatically, and at first didn't respond. Perhaps he couldn't hear me, I thought, or perhaps he couldn't understand my Yorkshire accent. So I asked again. 'Mr Cage, would you like a cup of coffee?'

There was a long pause. Then came a well-considered reply, spoken very quietly and very gently with a reedy New York twang. 'No, thank you. I will wait as long as I possibly can – and then I will have one. It will be wonderful.' 'Call me John,' he added.

Cage had taken a temporary flat for his week-long stay at 53 New North Road. It should have a blue plaque on it now. The main reason for his reluctance to stay in a hotel was that he wished to be able to cook his own food and thus adhere to his macrobiotic diet. He had been introduced to this dietary regime by his New York neighbours John Lennon and Yoko Ono in an effort to alleviate some of his physical ills. It seemed to work, as Cage once said, since 'It seems to me that when I die I will be in perfect condition.' The basis of the diet is a combination of brown rice and beans. It is all to do with yin and yang and finding a balance between them. Coffee and alcohol are extreme yin and generally not recommended. The one cup of coffee was considered a huge treat.

The rehearsal began. We were a mixed bunch of brass banders and popsters, of different ages and instruments. The order of events was indeterminate, and in typical Cage fashion, every event hung on chance. Layers of sound were brought in and out according to the dice – mill shuttles, cornet solos, arias from Handel's *Messiah*, tuba basslines. Morgan, a thirty-seven year-old green-haired punk, was the dice thrower. He took on this role enthusiastically, declaring the numbers with a resonant punk-like sneer as simultaneous images of him flickered on old television sets around the room. Cage looked on approvingly, enjoying the exaggerated theatricality.

Martin Massey took centre stage, a commanding figure, 6'7" dressed in a tail suit with a top hat balancing aloft his waist-length ringlets. His role was to read out the mesostics – esoteric poems cleverly constructed from the everyday events reported in the *Huddersfield Examiner*. The Lovely Jamie was on bass guitar, peacock-like with his luxuriant dreadlocks, strutting his stuff, a fine bass player and a big noise on the local reggae scene. Mostly he didn't turn up to rehearsals, and we were lucky to have him there. He would just deliver on the day and get away with it. No one would notice. Cage stepped forward and walked into the middle of the hall, moving to Jamie's side.

'Why did you play that A minor riff three times; it should have been four? Do you know what's going on?'

Jamie looked abashed, rumbled even.

As word of Cage's whereabouts got around the festivalgoers, the hall slowly filled with onlookers. But Cage only had eyes for the students. He pointed out to them what worked well, what could be improved, what should be left out: comments that were incisive, encouraging and critical in equal measure and all with a huge musicality and eye for detail.

The performance went well. Cage sat there, straight-backed, legs neatly crossed, a charismatic presence with a Zen-like stillness. In the Q & A session that followed, the questions flowed – off the wall, not well rehearsed. First up was Marc, a long-haired drummer of the indie school.

'Do you like pop music?'

'No. I don't have a playing machine so it is awkward to find out, but I once listened to some of Brian Eno's music. What I liked about it were the silences in it. What I didn't like about it was the fact that after each silence the same kind of thing happened that had happened before the first silence.'

'Do you ever get bored?' asked Justin, who practised boredom to the level of a fine art.

'No. Do you? If something is boring after two minutes, try it for four. If still boring, then eight. Then sixteen. Then thirty-two. Eventually you'll discover that it's not boring at all.'

'Have you ever eaten a poisonous mushroom?' This question was not as bizarre as it seems. As well as being a major composer and graphic artist of note, Cage was an expert on edible mushrooms and a co-founder of the New York Mycological Society. Alongside lectures on Erik Satie and Virgil Thomson, he taught a class on mushroom identification at the New School for Social Research. Mushrooms fired Cage's imagination; he heard music in them. One lecture he gave dealt with the 'sexuality' of mushrooms. In 1959 he even won a quiz programme on the topic when he appeared as a mushroom expert on an Italian quiz show, *Lascia o Raddoppia*, winning about £4,000.

'Have I eaten poisonous mushrooms? Sure, many times. I've been hospitalised through eating wild plants more than once.' Then in a deadpan voice he described how he had gathered what he thought was wild skunk cabbage and cooked it for a dinner party.

He was the first to feel ill, his throat burned and he could hardly breathe. He had his stomach pumped and spent the night in hospital. Sometime later he read about the need to distinguish between skunk cabbage and the poisonous hellebore.

'Hellebore has pleated leaves. Skunk cabbage does not.'

'Who is your hero, John?' Martin asked.

'Marcel Duchamp. He is the artist who has most profoundly influenced my own work. If he had not lived, it would have been necessary for someone exactly like him to live, to bring about the world as we begin to know and experience it.'

Morgan was on the edge of his seat. 'Did you ever meet him?'

'Oh yes, many times, he taught me to play chess.'

'John, could you tell us more about Marcel Duchamp please?'

'Sure, Morgan. What would you like to know?'
Morgan could barely hold his enthusiasm back.

'Everything! Everything!' he shouted.
Cage grinned broadly, thrilled to talk about the anti-art pioneer, his own hero. The last time I saw Morgan he was standing outside Woolworths, swigging a bottle of methadone, and he said what he always says to me. 'I just want to thank you again for the Cage day. It was the best day of my life.'

The questions poured in and the conversations flowed, with topics ranging from contemporary dance, his partner Merce Cunningham, and the I Ching to drinking Guinness, the plants in his New York apartment, and Huddersfield night life. His use of words was always economic – a mixture of wit, honesty and erudition – and were frequently interspersed with great bursts of laughter. He was unpresumptuous yet iconic, humble yet hugely charismatic, quietly private but always open and accessible. That afternoon he stayed and stayed and stayed. As he moved to leave the room there was a great chorus of students shouting.

'John, John, will you come for a pint with us tonight?' A long pause, then, 'Yes, I would love to join you.'

And he did.

B Selected performances in the Lawrence Batley Theatre: 1994 to 2010

OPERA: Opera North: Gruber *Gloria: a pigtale* (world premiere, 1994) and Holt *The Nightingale's to Blame* (world premiere, 1998); Music Theatre Wales: Davies *The Lighthouse* (1994), Woolrich *In the House of Crossed Desires* (1996), Birtwistle *Punch and Judy* (1998), Berkeley *Jane Eyre* (2000), Osborne *The Electrification of the Soviet Union* (2002) and *The Piano Tuner* (2004), Plowman *House of the Gods* (2006); Kirklees young musicians: Weir *The Black Spider* (1995); Southwark Playhouse: Adams *I Was Looking at the Ceiling and then I Saw the Sky* (1999); Autumn Leaf Productions, Toronto: Vivier *Kopernikus* (2000); London Sinfonietta Opera: Turnage *Greek* (2000); Psappha: Davies *Mr Emmet Takes a Walk* (2001); Almeida Opera: Battistelli *The Embalmer* (2002); Aldeburgh Almeida Opera: Birtwistle *The Io Passion* (2004).

DANCE: Phoenix Dance & Orphy Robinson (1995); Richard Alston Dance Company (1997); Jonathan Burrows (1998 and 2004); Guangdong Modern Dance Company (UK debut, 1999); Psappha: Davies *Vesalii Icones* (1999); Willi Dorner/Wien Modern: Aperghis *[…]* (2003); Scottish Flute Trio & Curve Foundation Dance Company (2008).

ANIMATED THEATRE: ShadowLight Theatre: 'Lou Harrison tribute' (1997); Faulty Optic: *Tunnel Vision* (1998) and *Dead Wedding* (2007); Trestle Theatre &

Hashirigaki *by Heiner Goebbels, given its UK premiere in the Lawrence Batley Theatre in 2001.*
PHOTO: MARIO DEL CURTO (THÉÂTRE VIDY-LAUSANNE E.T.E.)

Birmingham Contemporary Music Group: *Bitter Fruit*
(2000); Animata: *Organillo* (2000).

MUSIC THEATRE: Stockhausen instrumental theatre
(1996); Recherche: Schnebel *Glossolalie* and Feldman
Samuel Beckett: Words and Music (1996); Huddersfield
New College: *Orchestral Touring Theatre* (1996);
Gogmagogs (1996) and 'Gogmagogs Gigagain'
(1997); Trestle Theatre & Britten Sinfonia: Horne
Beyond the Blue Horizon (1997); Trestle Theatre and
BCMG: Woolrich *Bitter Fruit* (2000); Théâtre Vidy-
Lausanne: Goebbels *Hashirigaki* (2001); Hebbel-Theater
Berlin: Sciarrino *Lohengrin* (2001); Kagel *Mare
Nostrum* (2003); Theatre Cryptic & Paragon
Ensemble: Bryars *The Paper Nautilus* (2006).

JAZZ & IMPROVISED MUSIC: George Russell &
Living Time Orchestra (1995); Moscow Art Trio
(1995); Mike Westbrook *Bar Utopia* (1996); Vienna
Art Orchestra (1997); Philip Sheppard Band
improvising soundtracks to two Buster Keaton films
(1999); Michael Riessler *Momentum Mobile*
(2001); Dhafer Youssef (2004); Evan Parker &
Friends/ElectroAcoustic Ensemble (2002, 2004 and
2007); Barry Guy New Orchestra (2006); Simon Fell
Ensemble: *composition no. 74* (2007); Apartment
House & Frank Gratkowski/ELISION & John Butcher:
including *For Braxton* (world premiere, 2009).

OTHER CONCERTS: Steve Martland Band (1998);
Volharding (1998); Newband playing Harry Partch's
sculpted microtonal instruments (1998); Recherche:
'The new In Nomine Consort Book' (1999); Saariaho
From the Grammar of Dreams (2001); Psappha:
Steve Mackey Portrait (2002); 'The GRM Experience'
(2003); Ictus: *An Index of Metals* multimedia project
(2004); Pokrovsky Folk Ensemble (2005); zeitkratzer
(2006); Ensemble MAE (2007); musikFabrik:
Poppe/Heiniger *Tiere sitzen nicht* (2009); Neue
Vocalsolisten Stuttgart (2010); Joëlle Léandre:
'A Tribute to John Cage' (2010).

FILMS: Stockhausen's *Helicopter String Quartet*
(1996); films about Adams, Partch, Xenakis (1999)
and Harvey (2009); Trio Fibonacci with silent films
(2006); [Buster Keaton *see Jazz & Improvised Music
(above)*].

c *Winners of the Young Composers' Award 1976–1999*

The award originated in 1976 as a Young Composers' Competition organised by Yorkshire Arts Association and restricted to composers resident in Yorkshire.

In 1978 the competition was adopted by the festival and opened to all British subjects and UK residents. Entries were usually invited in more than one category and workshopped by artists performing at the festival. Besides a modest financial prize, winning works were performed in the public concerts.

From 2001 the Young Composers' Award (as it had become called) was replaced with young composers' workshops, after which one or more of the participants were offered commissions for the following year.

1976   Robin Walker
1977   Anthony Powers
        (String Quartet)
1978   piano: James Dillon *Dillug-Kefitsah*
        ensemble: Michael Parkin *Aware*
1979   ensemble: Julian Dale *Comme s'en vont
        les écrevisses*
        percussion: John Weeks *Alas I shall not
        see my dear father again, unless...*
1980   chamber ensemble: David Cooper *Mes
        instantanes*
        tuba: Nicholas Williams *Pandora's Box*
        voice and guitar: David Bray *Returning we
        hear the larks*
1981   organ: Christopher Fox *Frames and
        Fragments*
        ensemble: Nicholas Gotch *Dance, monster,
        to my soft song*
        (commended: David Sawer and
        Christopher Woodley)
1982   piano (joint winners): Andrew Ford
        Portraits
        and Mark-Anthony Turnage *Entranced*

1983   wind quintet: Nicholas Redfern *The Dreams
        of Fallen Gods, Sad Vales and Streams*
        cello: John Kefala, *Abstract (No. 3)*
1984   music theatre ensemble (joint winners):
        David Lancaster *Fantasia*
        and James Harley *A Theatre on Mars*
        (second prize: Michael Clarke *First Rain*)
1985   guitar (joint winners): David Harvey *and I
        will sing of the sun*
        and Andrew Toovey *Veiled Wave III –
        Scarred Landscapes*
        ensemble: Stephen Kings *Snapshots*
1986   string quartet: Ian Willcock *In Praise of
        Action*
        clarinet and piano (joint winners):
        Colin Riley *Swan Song*
        and Michael (Zev) Gordon *High Sea-light*
        (commended for 'talent and promise':
        David Horne, aged fifteen)
1987   string sextet: Gordon McPherson *Prosen*
1988   clarinet, violin, cello and piano:
        David Horne *Splintered Unisons*
        (second prize: Richard Ayres *Quartet with
        Eb clarinet*)
1989   piano trio: Sohrab Uduman *Movements*
1990   string quartet: Arun Bharali *Funes*
        (commended: David Charlwoood, Paul
        Williams and Yannis Kyriakides)
1991   piano: Deirdre Gribbin *Per Speculum In
        Aenigmate* (overall winner)
        ensemble: Hugh Collins Rice *Small Music*
1992   string ensemble: John Stringer *Life in the
        light first image*
        (commended: William Needham)
1993   oboe, harp and tape: Daniel Goeritz *Gyve*
        (overall winner)
        brass ensemble: William Attwood *Giving
        Things Up To The Sky*
        marimba and violin: Bryn Harrison *As One
        Listens To The Rain*
        (commended: Christopher Hussey)

1994   five-piece ensemble: Camden Reeves
CASMA
clarinet trio (joint winners): David Murphy
Trio and
Paul de Aragon *Mahayana*
(commended: Joe Cutler and John Stringer)

1995   chamber ensemble: Jonathan Powell
Necronomic Fragments
violin duo (joint winners): Bryn Harrison
Frozen Earth
and Peter Rosser *A Book of Mirrors*

1996   chamber ensemble: Alan Stones *Twine*
saxophone quartet: Graham Hadfield
Trajectories II – Spectromorph

1997   electric guitar (overall winner): Michael
Keeney *Resilient Hope*
three flutes and percussion: Greg Boardman
Ensemble 3
(commended: Martin Parker)

1998   Orkest de Volharding: Dai Fujikura
Frozen Heat

1999   string quartet: Paul Usher *String Quartet*
percussion duo: Dai Fujikura *Grayed
Rainbow*

2000   ensemble: Daniel Giorgetti *Les Extrêmes
se touchant*

D *Selected world premieres and commissions*

1979	Lyell Cresswell *Hocket* Elizabeth Maconchy *Contemplation* Michael Parkin *Reflections from a Slow Country*
1980	Anthony Gilbert *Long White Moonlight* Edward Harper *the song of mehitabel* Geofrey Poole *Hexagram* Margaret Lucy Wilkins *A Dance to the Music of Time*
1981	Harrison Birtwistle *Clarinet Quintet* Harrison Birtwistle *Pulse Sampler* Richard Steinitz *Quartet in memoriam*
1982	David Bedford *Sun Paints Rainbows on the Vast Waves* (hcmf commission)
1983	James Dillon *String Quartet* (hcmf commission) Philip Grange *The Kingdom of Bones* Hans Werner Henze *Labyrinth* (first staged performance) Roberto Sierra *Cantos Populares*
1984	Michael Finnissy *Mysteries IV – The Prophecy of Daniel* Judith Weir *Sketches from a Bagpiper's Album*
1985	Michael Finnissy *String Quartet* (hcmf commission) Michael Finnissy '*... above earth's shadow*' John Hopkins *White Winter, Black Spring* (BBC commission) John Tavener *Trisagion*
1986	John Casken *Salamandra* (hcmf commission) Witold Lutosławski *Spring; Autumn; Four Children's Songs* (first concert performances)
1987	Milton Babbitt *Time Series* (world premiere complete) Henry Cowell *Piano Concerto* (European premiere) Michael Torke *Adjustable Wrench* (hcmf commission) Trevor Wishart *Vox IV*

1988	Colin Matthews *Fuga* Kaija Saariaho *From the Grammar of Dreams* (hcmf commission)
1989	Benedict Mason *Six Studies* John Cage *One* [2] John Cage *Four* Vic Hoyland *Piano Trio* (hcmf commission) Michael Torke *Rust*
1990	Gavin Bryars *String Quartet no. 2* (hcmf commission) Liviu Danceanu *Palimpsest I* Simon Holt *Lilith* Hanna Kulenty *String Quartet no. 2* Bronius Kutavičius *Magic Circle of Sanskrit* Roger Marsh *Love on the Rocks*
1991	Michael Berkeley *Clarinet Concerto* Duncan Druce *String Quintet* Duncan Druce *We were like them that dream* David Lumsdaine *A tree telling of Orpheus* James MacMillan *Intercession* Robert Saxton *Caritas* (Opera North and hcmf co-commission)
1992	David Bedford *Stories from the Dreamtime* (Music and the Deaf commission) Gavin Bryars *The Old Tower of Löbenicht* Colin Matthews *Contraflow*
1993	György Ligeti *Nonsense Madrigals no. 6* Benedict Mason *Caprices* Stefan Niculescu *Psalmus* (hcmf commission) Julia Wolfe *my lips from speaking*
1994	Gavin Bryars *On Photography* HK Gruber *Gloria – a pigtale* (Opera North and hcmf co-commission) Roger Marsh *Espace* Gordon McPherson *Maps and Diagrams of Our Pain*

1995　James Dillon *Redemption*
James Dillon *Traumwerk I*
(concert premiere)
Stephen Mottram and Glyn Perrin
Seed Carriers (puppet theatre)
(co-commissioned by hcmf)

1996　Sofia Gubaidulina *Galgenlieder*
(hcmf commission)
Howard Skempton *Winter Sunrise*
Karlheinz Stockhausen *Bijou* (hcmf
commission)
Tan Dun *Orchestral
Theatre III: Red Forecast*
(BBCTV, Radio 3 and hcmf co-commission)

1997　David Lang *Eight
Memory Pieces*
Karin Rehnqvist *Anrop (movement 1)*
Steffen Schleiermacher *Zeit Verschiebung*
Rolf Wallin *Three Poems of Rainer Maria
Rilke*
Iannis Xenakis *O-Mega* (London Sinfonietta
and hcmf co-commission)

1998　John Adams *Hallelujah Junction* (European
premiere)
Simon Holt *The Nightingale's to Blame*
(Opera North, Munich Biennale and hcmf
co-commission)
Simon Holt *eco-pavan*
Douglas Young *The Eternal Water*

1999　Tansy Davies *Oscillating Mirrors*
Simon Emmerson *Five Spaces*
David Lang *Grind to a Halt*
Roger Marsh *Canto I*
Geoffrey Poole *ch'i kun*
Rebecca Saunders *duo 3*
Salvatore Sciarrino *Four Nocturnes*
(first complete performance)
Errollyn Wallen *Hudson, Mississippi,
Thames*
Guo Wenjing *String Quartet no. 3 with
bamboo flute* (hcmf commission)

2000　Joe Cutler *Five Mobiles after Alexander
Calder*
Deirdre Gribbin *Celestial Pied Piper*
(Faber Music Millennium commission)
IOU Theatre *Cure*
David Horne *Blunt Instruments*

2001　Diana Burrell *Gold* (hcmf commission)
Philip Cashian *The Masque of the Red
Death* (hcmf commission)
Luca Francesconi *Let me Bleed*
Bent Sørensen *The Hill of the Heartless
Giant*
James Wood *Autumn Voices* (BBC
commission)

2002　Joe Cutler *Szymborska Settings**
Jonathan Powell *Crépuscule**
James Saunders *#241102**
Arlene Elizabeth Sierra *Hand mit Ringen**
Ian Vine *oro y sombre**
Jennifer Walshe *theme from**
(*Twenty-fifth Birthday Festiva
Commissions)
Dai Fujikura *Reach Out* (Apollo Saxophone
Quartet and hcmf co-commission)
Bryn Harrison *low time patterns*
Per Nørgård *Stadia*

2003　Peter Ablinger *Voices and Piano*
James Clarke *String Quartet*
(hcmf commission)
Simon Holt *feet of clay*
Jonathan Powell *Lighea*

2004　Joanna Bailie *Splice* (hcmf commission)
James Saunders *#241104*
Rebecca Saunders *choler* (BBC commission
for hcmf)
Howard Skempton *Tendrils* (BBC and hcmf
commission)
Kevin Volans *String Quartet no. 9:
'Shiva Dances'* (BBC commission)

2005 Aaron Cassidy *The Crutch of Memory*
Lawrence Crane *Solo for Claire Edwardes*
(hcmf commission)
Joe Cutler *Sikorski*
Chris Dench *e(i)ther* (hcmf commission)
David Flynn *String Quartet no. 2: 'The
Cranning'* (hcmf commission)
Christopher Fox *A slice through
translucence*
Sam Hayden *impetus*
Richard Rijnvos *'cross Broadway*
Janek Schaefer *In The Last Hour*
(hcmf commission)

2006 Richard Barrett *Island*
John Casken *Farness*
Michael Finnissy *Whitman*
(BBC and hcmf commission)
Christopher Fox *1–2–3* (hcmf commission)
Dominik Karski *RiverBed*
Anna Meredith *Music for Ravens*
Timothy O'Dwyer/Lilla Watson
Soft Night Falling

2007 Simon Fell *Composition no. 74: Positions
and Descriptions* (hcmf commission)
Evan Parker *Piece for Fourteen*
(hcmf commission)
Janek Schaefer *Extended Play*
(hcmf commission)
Rebecca Saunders *Stirrings still*
Tomoko Mukaiyama *Show me your
second face*
Walter Zimmermann *AIMIDE* and *Voces
Abandonadas* (rev. version)

2008 Elvin Buene *Into the Void*
John Butcher *Composition for eight
musicians* (hcmf commission)
Dror Feiler *Music is Castrated Noise*
Christopher Fox *comme ses paroles*
(BBC and hcmf co-commission)

2009 Michel van der Aa *Transit*
Paul Archbald *Fluxions*
Richard Barrett *Mesopotamia*
James Clarke *String Quartet no. 2*
(hcmf commission)
James Dillon *String Quartet no. 5*
Richard Glover *Gradual Music*
(hcmf commission)
Bryn Harrison *surface forms (repeating)*
Liza Lim *Invisibility*
Roger Redgate *Concerto for improvising
soloist and two ensembles* (hcmf commission)

2010 Richard Barrett *Wound (parts I & II)*
Graham Fitkin *Twenty-six Days* (RLPO and
hcmf co-commission)
Dai Fujikura *Recorder Concerto*
Naomi Pinnock *Oscillare* (hcmf commission)
Frederic Rzewski *Flowers*
Rebecca Saunders *Solo bass clarinet*
Howard Skempton *Sirens*
Jennifer Walshe *Marlowe S.*

Index